Marlene Koch's Sensational Splenda Recipes

Also by Marlene Koch

50 Splenda Recipes: Favorites from Fantastic Food with Splenda and Unbelievable Desserts with Splenda

Fantastic Foods with Splenda: 160 Great Recipes for Meals Low in Sugar, Carbohydrates, Fat, and Calories

Low-Carb Cocktails: All the Fun and Taste without the Carbs (with Chuck Koch)

Unbelievable Desserts with Splenda: Sweet Treats Low in Sugar, Fat, and Calories

Marlene Koch's Sensational Splenda Recipes

Over 375 Recipes Low in Sugar, Fat, and Calories

MARLENE KOCH

Illustrations by Christopher Dollbaum

M. EVANS

Lanham · New York · Boulder · Toronto · Oxford

Published by M. Evans
An imprint of The Rowman & Littlefield Publishing Group, Inc.
4501 Forbes Boulevard, Suite 200, Lanham, Maryland 20706

Distributed by NATIONAL BOOK NETWORK

The paper used in this publication meets the minimum requirements of American National Standard for Information Sciences—Permanence of Paper for Printed Library Materials, ANSI/NISO Z39.48-1992.

Manufactured in the United States of America.

Designed and Typeset by Chrissy Kwasnik

Library of Congress Cataloging-in-Publication Data

Koch, Marlene.
  Marlene Koch's sensational splenda recipes : over 375 recipes low in sugar, fat, and calories / Marlene Koch ; illustrations by Christopher Dollbaum.
    p. cm.
  "A portion of this book includes recipes previously published in Fantastic foods with splenda, Unbelievable desserts with splenda, and Low-carb cocktails by Marlene Koch."
  1. Cookery. 2. Sucralose. 3. Sugar-free diet--Recipes. 4. Low-carbohydrate diet--Recipes. I. Title: Sensational splenda recipes. II. Koch, Marlene. Fantastic foods with splenda. III. Koch, Marlene. Unbelievable desserts with splenda. IV. Koch, Marlene. Low-carb cocktails. V. Title.
  TX714.K636 2006
  641.5--dc22
                        2005020397

Life is sensational—enjoy!

Contents

Acknowledgments   *9*

Introduction   *11*

Basic Nutrition Information   *13*

All About Splenda   13
The Scoop on Sugar   15
The Skinny on Fat   16
Diabetes   18
Nutritional Analysis of the Recipes   19

Cooking and Baking for Healthy Living   *21*

Sweet Ways to Cut the Sugar   21
Fantastic Ways to Lower the Fat   23
Ingredients A—Z   25

The Sensational Recipes   *33*

Ice Cold Drinks, Shakes, and Smoothies   35
Tempting Hot Beverages and Homemade Dry Mixes   57
Good Mornings—Breakfast and Brunch   75
Marvelous Muffins and Scrumptious Scones   93
Easy Quick Breads and Coffee Cakes   115
Sensational Side and Entrée Salads   135
Dressings and Marinades   161
Versatile Vegetables   177
Winning Condiments   197
Protein-Packed Entrees   219
Puddings and Custards   243
Mousses and Other Creamy Delights   261
Frozen Desserts   279
Everyone's Favorite Cookies   299
Classic Pies   323
Crisps, Cobbler, Strudels, and Tarts   349
Cakes for All Occasions   363
Cheesecake, Cheesecake, and More Cheesecake   391
Sweet Embellishments   419
Celebration Cocktails   443

Acknowledgments

To create a big book of sensational recipes you need sensational help—and I am very grateful to those who stepped forward. First and foremost, as always, I want to thank my boys, Stephen and James, for the love they give me every day. They have definitely learned (despite misgivings) how to share Mom with the grocery store, the kitchen, and the computer. Likewise to my husband, Chuck, who found himself once again living with a night-owl typist—I thank you for your support and encouragement.

Big thanks also go to two dedicated personal kitchen assistants, Lynn Kennedy and Stephanie Kay, who spent hours and hours in my kitchen and theirs, testing and developing recipes. Their help was truly invaluable. Gratitude is also in order for several additional talented recipe developers, including pastry chef Gena Bell, for keeping your sweet recipes coming with lots of laughs, and pastry chef Lynn Stiles, for your fantastic research skills on all your recipes. Also to chef Susan Chessor, for your great sense of flavor, and chef Karletta Moniz, for your terrific professional style, and last, but not least, to Fran Lavolta, my web friend at www.lavoltapress.com, for generously sharing your great Splenda recipes.

Once again, I am indebted to my ever-so-supportive editor PJ Dempsey for her time, friendship, and expertise. Without her ideas and encouragement, this book would not exist—thanks, PJ. On the publishing front, I also extend thanks to the rest of the team at M. Evans for constant assistance, and most especially to Diane Stafford, for your terrific copyediting and organization skills but more importantly for your positive, enthusiastic, and dedicated backing on this project.

Additionally, my personal appreciation goes to Nichole Gessell for holding my life together (and that of my kids) while I toiled on the book. You were everything I had hoped for, and then some—your hard work is sure to take you far. To my good friend Chris Sardo—thanks for taking the time (again) to climb on board despite your crazy, busy schedule and to Janice Robinson—thanks for your support and friendship. And as always, to my closest friend Nancie Crosby—thanks for being a part of my world.

Last, I would like to thank my family—in particular, my parents—for always aiding and supporting me, and, above all, my talented brother Christopher Dollbaum for enhancing my book with his remarkable illustrations.

Introduction

Four years ago I wrote the first cookbook to feature a then virtually unknown product called Splenda. Since that time, sales of the sugar substitute sucralose, sold as Splenda, has soared. In fact, it is now the preferred sugar substitute by most and can be found everywhere—in restaurants and coffee shops, sitting next to sugar at the market, and in literally thousands of food products. Moreover, in the search for better taste, Splenda has landed itself into the "giants" of the soft-drink world—Coca Cola and Pepsi.

But I am not surprised. The very first line on the introduction page in my first book, *Unbelievable Desserts with Splenda—Sweet Treats Low in Sugar, Fat, and Calories* stated, "Splenda is an amazing substitute for sugar," and it is. The truth is, four years and three Splenda books later, I am still amazed at the amazingly sweet, healthy, yet low-sugar foods, I can produce with the help of Splenda brand sweeteners.

In this book of sensational recipes, you will find the recipes from my bestselling dessert book as well as the recipes from my second book, *Fantastic Food with Splenda—160 Great Recipes for Meals Low in Sugar, Carbohydrates, Fat, and Calories.* However, even if you own those books, you are still in for a real treat. For this book, not only have I added an additional 125 delectable new recipes, I have re-edited all of the recipes, making loads of updates and revisions along the way. I have simplified and improved many recipes, added new ingredients and introductions, and tucked in plenty of new tips. Additionally, all of the Weight Watchers' point comparisons have been recalculated (to meet the most current guidelines) and can be found on all recipes.

But I am proud to say that this book tastefully offers even more. With more than 375 sensational recipes, you will find delicious recipes reduced in sugar, fat, and calories for everything you can imagine. From Decadent Hot Chocolate to wholesome breakfast treats like Oatmeal Cookie Pancakes and mouthwatering Blueberry-Topped Cheese Blintzes, your taste buds will have much to savor. Beyond beverages and breakfast, you will find more than two dozen sensational salads, tons of winning complements, and plenty of family-favorite entrees, like my own Pasta Marinara Dinner.

But, of course, the *piece de resistance* is always the dessert, and there are more, *way more*, to enjoy than ever. From creamy flans and Chocolate Custard to Two-Bite Cupcakes and Heavenly Cheesecake, you are sure to find lots of sweet treats to love. Another "first"—this book features recipes developed exclusively for Splenda Sugar Blend for Baking (a mix of ½ sugar and ½ sucralose). This product gave me just the edge I needed to finally produce some all-American classics that had previously eluded me, like Lemon Meringue Pie and real Chocolate Brownies. And last, but not least, I have chosen to end this book on a festive note by sharing recipes that take the sugar out of cocktail favorites. From the classic Margarita to the popular Mojito and even your very own Coffee Liqueur (yep, without sugar), you now have even more reason to raise your glass and cheer.

On a more serious note, I sincerely hope this book becomes a resource in your quest for good food and good health. I truly believe that whether you are watching the sugar, fat, or calories in your diet (or all three), you will be delighted with these guilt-free versions of the foods you love. I say this with confidence as I thank all my readers who have shared their wonderful stories of better health, weight loss, blood sugar control, and reduced cholesterol while enjoying my recipes. I especially thank those of you who have shared my food (and my books) with your friends and loved ones—there is no better compliment.

All About Splenda

I, like you, am not only interested in food that tastes good—I want it to be good for me. So, the first thing I did when I heard about Splenda was to research it, like any good clinician. That said, I use Splenda because I find it to be the best-tasting, most versatile, and safest sugar substitute on the market today. I do not speak for the company nor profit from Splenda sales. However, because of my nutrition background and my cookbooks, I have become a "sucralose resource" for many people. In this section, I share answers to the nutrition questions I receive most often about Splenda.

What is Splenda and how is it made?

Splenda is the brand name for the nonnutritive (no-calorie) sweetener that derives its sweetness from sucralose. Sucralose is made from sugar (sucrose) through a multi-step process that selectively replaces three hydrogen oxygen groups on the sugar molecule with three chlorine atoms. The result is an exceptionally heat-stable, intense sweetener that tastes like sugar (with no aftertaste). But sucralose cannot be metabolized for energy so it lacks sugar's calories. To create the yellow packets of Splenda No-Calorie sweetener, a bit of a natural bulking agent (maltodextrin) is added to sucralose. To create boxes or bags of Splenda Granular, which measures and pours like sugar, additional maltodextrin is added to give it the 1:1 sweetness of sugar.

What is Splenda Sugar Blend for Baking?

Splenda Sugar Blend for Baking is a 50/50 sweetening blend of real granulated sugar and sucralose. With Splenda Sugar Blend for Baking, you use only half as much as you would normally use sugar, because ½ cup of the "blend" has the sweetening power of 1 cup of sugar. Thus, with Splenda Sugar for Baking, you reduce the carbohydrates and calories of the sugar in a recipe by 50 percent. This blend was developed specifically for baking because real sugar has many positive baking qualities (browning, melting, adding bulk) that are not naturally present in Splenda Granular, which, in comparison however, reduces the calories and carbohydrates of sugar in a recipe by 90 percent.

How many calories (and carbs) are in Splenda?

It depends on which product you buy. Each packet has 0 calories as does a single teaspoon of Splenda Granular (as rounded down on the box—2 calories, to be exact). Once you start measuring in cups, the bulking agent, maltodextrin contributes a few calories to Splenda Granular, and the sugar component of Splenda Sugar Blend for Baking contributes a few more. See page 23 for a comparison chart.

Will Splenda affect blood sugar or raise insulin levels?

Again, it depends. Splenda No-Calorie Sweetener (in packets or granular form) is not metabolized by the body because it does not recognize sucralose. Therefore, unlike the other sugar "oses" (such as sucrose, lactose, or even fructose), sucralose alone does not raise blood sugar or insulin levels (an added bonus is that it doesn't raise triglycerides, either). On the other hand, because Splenda Sugar Blend for Baking is one-half real sugar (sucrose), it will affect blood sugar and insulin levels (although less than if you use all sugar). Remember, many factors, including the total amount of all carbohydrates you consume, will determine just how much.

Will Splenda help me lose weight?

It certainly can. Studies show that sugar substitutes, when used as part of a reduced-calorie diet, can help maintain dietary compliance, thus allowing people to lose more weight. In this book, you will find that all of the recipes are not only reduced in sugar, but also in fat and calories—the perfect combination to help you either lose weight or maintain a healthy weight—without ever feeling deprived!

Is Splenda safe?

Yes. More than one hundred safety studies over the last twenty years confirm its safety. **Splenda has no side effects (like GI distress)**, and, in fact, it is the only nonnutritive sweetener that has been approved by the FDA for use by everyone— including pregnant women and children— with no warning labels. Many health authorities, such as the American Dietetic Association, the American Diabetes Association, physicians, and even holistic health practitioners recognize Splenda as a safe alternative to sugar. Splenda has also been approved for use through the regulatory boards of more than 50 countries to date.

The Scoop on Sugar

Americans love sugar—I mean we *really* love sugar. But it's not our fault, because we're born with a natural sweet tooth. It's Mother Nature's way of ensuring we will get the nutrition we need to fuel our bodies. The problem is, Mother Nature intended us to get our sugar from Mother Nature's fruits and vegetables—not the sugar bowl. But what's the difference—is it truly a problem to add a little sugar to the diet?

Sugar, Sugar Everywhere

The truth is, a little bit of added sugar is not a problem. According to the USDA and the World Health Organization, a diet of 2,000 calories can handle about 10 teaspoons a day of added sugar. Even most diabetes associations concur. So why do we need to cut our intake of sugar (and why have I written this book)? Because most people in all of North America now consume at least double the recommended amount of sugar for good health—that's more than 20 teaspoons a day. Some reports list this figure as high as 30 teaspoons a day. What's more disturbing is that even preschoolers are consuming 14-17 teaspoons a day, and many teenagers get as much as 25 percent of their daily calories from sugar. In fact, we, as a nation, make up 5 percent of the world's population, but we consume 33 percent of the sugar. Wow. So where is all this sugar? Everywhere. Manufacturers know we have a proclivity toward sweets and put sugar into just about everything we buy—and lots of it. So, if you are looking at keeping your sugar consumption to a healthy 10 teaspoons—watch out. A simple glass of lemonade can set you back 8 teaspoons; a big muffin, 12 teaspoons; a serving of sweet and sour chicken, 10 teaspoons; a piece of lemon meringue pie, 15 teaspoons; and a single piece of carrot cake with cream cheese icing, as much as 16 teaspoons of added sugar!

Sugar and Your Health

Unfortunately, consuming wonderful, sweet-tasting foods can have adverse health consequences. First, sugar causes tooth decay. Second, sugar clearly raises triglycerides (the circulating fat in your bloodstream), which increases your risk for heart disease. Third, sugar is full of calories—empty calories, to be exact. In fact, those 20 teaspoons of sugar we eat each day add up to 110,000 calories a year, and that's 30 pounds worth! And those extra pounds create more problems—like increasing your risk for diabetes and creating insulin resistance. Last, if you already have insulin resistance (sometimes called pre-diabetes) or diabetes, excessive sugar can wreak havoc by raising your blood sugar too high, which has many additional negative consequences.

Sweetness Without Consequences

As you will read in the diabetes section of this book, my stepdaughter has diabetes. For her and all of the wonderful people with diabetes I've met, I was inspired to create the sensational, traditional, sweet foods they loved, without the negative consequences. With the help of Splenda—I have. The foods in this book are full of flavor and sweetness but low in sugar (as well as fat and calories). So, whether you are monitoring your weight, your heart, your blood sugar, or your family's health, you can indulge in all of the foods you enjoy—guilt-free.

Ice Cold Lemonade now has no added sugar, a healthy Oatmeal Muffin averages no added sugar, Sweet and Sour Chicken has only 1 teaspoon, tasty Lemon Meringue Pie has been reduced to 2 ½ teaspoons, and a moist piece of Carrot Cake with Cream Cheese Frosting has less than ½ teaspoon of added sugar per piece! Now that's what I call sweet.

The Skinny on Fat

Good Fat, Bad Fat, High Fat, Low Fat—oh, and let's not forget No Fat. There are also unsaturated fats, saturated fats, and now trans-fat. Is is any wonder we get so confused?

The Simple Fat Facts

One simple fact is that we eat too much fat (and too much unhealthy fat). Even though we need fat in our diet to help absorb fat-soluble vitamins and give us our essential fatty acids, the truth is that we don't need much (just a couple tablespoons a day). The Dietary Guidelines for Americans, Canada's Healthy Food Guidelines, the American Heart Association, and the Canadian and American Diabetes Associations all recommend a diet with fewer than 30 percent of calories coming from fat and fewer than 10 percent of the calories coming from saturated and/or trans-fatty acids. That's as low as 50 grams a day for a woman consuming 1,600 calories, and up to 75 grams a day for someone on a 2,000-calorie diet. Unfortunately, the average we now consume is far more than the recommended 30 percent of the diet from fat (34 percent in the U.S., 38 percent in Canada).

Again, it's no wonder we're confused when you look at the foods we love to eat. A large muffin at the coffee shop can have 25 grams of fat; a "healthy" serving of three-bean salad, 20 grams; a single serving of barbecued pork ribs, 35 grams (most of it saturated); chocolate mousse, 40 grams; and a single piece of cheesecake, perhaps an entire day's worth of fat.

Simple fact number two is that a high-fat diet can make you fat. Fat is dense in calories, and excess calories turn to fat—always has and always will. A recent long-term study of more than 3,000 people who had not only lost a significant amount of weight (more than 60 pounds each) but managed to keep it off, found a low-fat (calorie-controlled) diet was overwhelmingly used by most participants.

Fat and Your Health

My third simple fact is that saturated fats aren't good for your health. So, lean meats are in, and large amounts of butter are still out. Saturated fats (found in full-fat dairy and fatty meats) not only raise your risk for heart disease, but may also heighten your risk for several types of cancer and add to insulin resistance. What's new is that trans-fats—found in varying amounts in stick margarines, snack crackers, and packaged foods made with hydrogenated fats—may be just as harmful, so I have carefully selected the margarine I use (refer to the ingredients section for details). The most healthful fats are polyunsaturated fats, found in liquid oils such as corn and safflower oil, and heart-healthy monounsaturated fats. Foods high in monounsaturated fats include olive oil, canola oil, avocadoes, and nuts—ingredients you will find in many recipes throughout this book.

Full of Flavor without the Fat

All of the recipes in this book are low in fat—but high in flavor. Although a few simply required no fat, which is great, eliminating fat wasn't my goal for most of the recipes. My aim was to create terrific-tasting recipes with fat levels that easily fit into any healthy diet—and I believe I succeeded.

In this book, you will find more than a dozen moist and marvelous muffins to choose from (5 grams of fat or fewer), a truly healthy Three-Bean Salad (6.5 grams), Asian Barbecued Pork Tenderloin (7 grams, and only 2 saturated), rich Dark Chocolate Mousse (5.5 grams), and my very sweet and creamy Heavenly Cheesecake, with only 8 grams of fat. The skinny on fat—it's no problem here.

Diabetes

I often receive thank-yous from persons with diabetes who enjoy my recipes. This is very rewarding because it was diabetes that inspired me to create sweet yet low-sugar recipes. My stepdaughter has diabetes, as does an aunt of mine, and several colleagues. In fact, as I discuss my work with people, *everyone* seems to know someone with diabetes.

Given the alarming growth of diabetes, it's really no surprise. In North America, more than 20 million people have diabetes (18 million in the U.S. and another 2 million in Canada). Of those 20 million, 6 million don't even know they have it.

More alarming, it is estimated that another 45 million people have pre-diabetes, a condition in which blood glucose is above normal but not high enough to require medication.

Diabetes, Sugar, and Carbohydrates

Eating too much sugar does not give you diabetes—but when you have diabetes, it's not healthy to eat too much sugar. Diabetes is a serious health condition in which the body fails to properly use or make enough insulin—the hormone responsible for moving the sugar (from the carbohydrates you eat) out of your blood and into your cells (where the sugar is converted to energy). Without the proper amount of insulin, sugar (in the form of glucose) accumulates in the blood, raising blood sugar levels above normal levels. In turn, high blood sugar is harmful to the body in many ways.

If you have diabetes then, should you just avoid eating sugar and/or carbohydrates?

It's not that simple (nor is it that enjoyable). You need carbohydrates and, in fact, sugar, to fuel not only your body but your brain. The key to good diabetes management is to determine how many carbohydrates you need (your budget) and where they should come from (your expenditures). How much carbohydrate is right for you can be determined with the help of a registered dietitian or diabetes educator. According to most diabetes professionals, you may spend your carbohydrate budget on both complex carbohydrates, like those found in vegetables and whole grains that raise blood sugar slowly *and* simple carbohydrates like those found in fruit and yes, even sugar, which raises blood sugar quickly.

Living Well with Diabetes

Yes, I did say that if you have diabetes, you may have some sugar—but (and this is a big but), it needs to fit within your carbohydrate budget, *and* it should it not displace a healthy diet. The best way to live well with diabetes is to take care of yourself (that means exercise)—and to make sure you eat a healthy diet—one that is full of fruits and vegetables for vitamins and minerals, whole grains for added fiber, low-fat dairy for calcium, and lean meats for protein. Also, your diet should help you maintain or achieve a healthy body weight, and you should watch fats to protect your heart.

So where's the room for sugar, with its dense carbs and empty calories? Clearly, there's not much room at all. However, there is room for sweet foods of all kinds when you make them healthfully with Splenda. By using this book you can enjoy the foods you love because every recipe is reduced in sugar, fat, *and* calories, which makes them easy to fit into any dietary budget. I call that living well, as does a kind reader:

"I just had to take a moment to let you know how very much I appreciate all of the recipes you developed so I can enjoy the things I used to give up. I am a diabetic and was having lots of problems staying in the blood sugar range recommended until I found your book. Boy! Have I been having fun ever since! Every recipe I have tried has turned out to be fabulous. Even my husband who is not diabetic loves the food. Many, many, thank-yous!"

Nutritional Analysis of the Recipes

The nutritional information is provided for each recipe to help you make wise (and educated) dietary choices that suit your own needs and health goals. The information was calculated with the use of ESHA Nutrition Food Processor software along with manufacturer food labels. Here is some more information that may be helpful.

Portion Sizes

My goal is to give "real" portion sizes—not bigger-is-better restaurant size, but not "diet cookbook" miniscule size, either. These are the same portions you will find in any good cookbook. A pie serves eight; a 9-inch cheesecake, 12; and an 8 or 9-inch square pan is cut in either 3 x 3 or 4 x 4-inch squares to yield 9 or 16 servings (not 6 x 6-inch squares for 36 "bites," as suggested in a very popular healthy cooking magazine). Oh, yes, some of the desserts are very tempting, but you have to be sure to double the nutritional content when you eat double.

Diabetic Exchanges

As always, I have included both total carbohydrates and exchanges for diabetes meal plans. I used the most current guidelines of the American and Canadian Diabetes Associations. I hope you will note the substantial savings in carbohydrate and fat when compared to traditionsal recipes. And remember, this becomes multiplied when you combine several foods to make a meal. If you have any questions about what your daily allowances are, consult with a registered dietitian or diabetes educator (and please feel free to share the book—I'm sure they will be delighted).

WW Point Comparison

Weight Watchers and Winning Points are registered trademarks of Weight Watchers International, Inc., but for all my WW friends I have made "comparisons" based on the most current published guidelines (i.e., fiber cap at 4 grams). I also have "re-compared" every single recipe from my previous books to ensure their accuracy—as I know every "point" counts. Last, if you recalculate the point comparisons, using the rounded-off nutrition information provided (i.e., 1.3 grams of fiber would appear as 1 gram), you may occasionally need to choose between two values. I used the precise nutrition information to determine the "point" comparisons.

Fat

Fat grams are provided, but the fat percentage of the total calories is not (as is sometimes showcased in "healthy" cookbooks.) You will find the fat is healthfully low in all of the recipes, but it will not always be under 30 percent if you calculate it. Sometimes—in a salad, for example—there are so few total calories that the oil (or other fat source) simply makes up most of the calories even where there are only a few grams. More importantly, subtracting all of the sugar calories skews the fat percentage from comparative foods. For example, if a serving of a food in this book has 180 calories and 6 grams of fat, it would be 33 percent fat (9 calories for each gram of fat = 63 and 63 out of 180 = 33 percent). But if you added back the 60 calories you "saved" by using Splenda for sugar, the food would now be only 25 percent fat (63 calories from fat out of the new 240-calorie total = 25 percent). You would be getting the same amount of fat and more calories, but the percentage of calories from fat would look lower. Also, remember, the amount of fat in your diet need not be perfect for every food; it's better to think about fat in terms of your entire meal or even your entire day.

Other Tidbits

» If you want "net" carbs, subtract the grams of fiber from the carbohydrate.

» Items listed as optional or "if desired" are not included in calculations, with the exception of the powdered-sugar garnishes that add less than 1 gram carb per serving but really enhance the food's appearance.

» When a choice is given (¼ cup orange juice or reduced-calorie orange juice), the ingredient that appears first is the one used in the nutrition calculation.

Cooking and Baking for Healthy Living

Sweet Ways to Cut the Sugar

When teaching healthy cooking classes, I tell my students they must consider all of the qualities a particular ingredient brings to a recipe before making a substitution or eliminating it. This is especially true when it comes to sugar because sugar (as the Sugar Association touts) brings a lot more to cooking and baking than just sweetness. Sugar, and other natural sweeteners like honey, molasses, syrups, and even fruit juices to varying degrees, can add texture, structure, volume, color, moistness, and tenderness, in addition to a sweet flavor. The place where sucralose, the sweetening component of Splenda products, excels is in adding the wonderful sweet flavor of sugar to recipes. It also makes a great substitute for sugar because, just like sugar, it is heat-stable and aftertaste-free. In contrast, Splenda Granular (used in most of the recipes) doesn't have the physical and chemical properties of sugar for many of sugar's other functions.

In cooking with Splenda, in everything from beverages to breakfast foods, salads, side dishes, and entrees, the substitution is fairly straightforward. And, in many foods and beverages, the ability for Splenda Granular (or packets) to dissolve so readily is a bonus.

In baking, however, where many of sugar's other properties can be fundamental to the recipe, you may need to make adjustments and/or use small amounts of real sugar for a great outcome (especially when you're also lowering the fat). Although each recipe is different, over the years I have found there are some routine modifications and tips—a little bit of kitchen chemistry, if you will—that will help you understand my recipes and give you the ability to create your own.

Of important note: Splenda Sugar Blend for Baking is ½ granulated sugar and thus requires far fewer, if any, modifications. Conversely, you pay for this additional benefit by adding more carbohydrate and calories to the recipe. Thus, I have reserved its use only for recipes in which using sugar makes a significant quality difference. The Splenda Granular Versus Splenda Sugar Blend Versus Sugar chart highlights the nutritional differences so you can make your own choices. (You may substitute Splenda Sugar for Baking for Splenda Granular in any recipe in this book, but remember to use only half as much and adjust the nutritional content accordingly.)

Splenda Granular Versus Splenda Sugar Blend Versus Sugar

	SPLENDA GRANULAR	SPLENDA SUGAR BLEND	SUGAR
SERVING SIZE	1 cup = 16 tablespoons	½ cup = 1 cup sugar sweetness	1 cup = 48 teaspoons
CARBOHYDRATES	24 grams	96 grams	192 grams
CALORIES	96	384	768

Sugar-Reduction Tips for Splenda Packets or Granular

» In non-baking recipes in which smaller amounts (teaspoons or tablespoons) of Splenda were required, I have offered the option of using packets. Each packet has the equivalent sweetness of 2 teaspoons of sugar (or Splenda Granular). Also helpful for conversions is to remember that 1 tablespoon = 3 teaspoons.

» To thicken cooked sauces, dressings, and syrups, add a bit of cornstarch. You also can use xantham gum (see ingredients) or ThickenThin no/starch.

» Jams and jellies require no-sugar-needed pectins. You may also find that adding just a touch of granulated sugar will help with the clarity.

» For baked treats in which sugar is used primarily to sweeten (like in cheesecakes), no added sugar may be required or the natural sugars in the recipe may be all it takes to get great results with Splenda Granular. However, for many other recipes, most notably cookies and cakes or recipes that include bitter flavors, adding a small amount of real sugar (usually just a few tablespoons) can make a big quality difference. Remember—what sabotages your diet aren't the *tablespoons* of sugar, which might add a teaspoon or less to each serving, but the *cups* of sugar.

» Adding a touch of any real sugar will help drop cookies spread (or flatten). White sugar also adds a bit more crunch, and brown or liquid sugars (like corn syrup), extra moistness. To give cookies their traditional look, use a glass or spatula to flatten them before baking.

» Using a small amount of brown sugar or molasses adds color and aids in browning. Nonetheless, your baked goods may be slightly lighter in color than usual.

» Just a teaspoon or two of powdered sugar dusted onto muffins or cakes works wonders for their appearance and adds a miniscule amount of carbs and calories. A touch of granulated sugar placed on top will add sparkle.

» Additional leavening is often required to help low-sugar cakes and muffins rise. The producers of Splenda recommend an additional ½ teaspoon of baking soda per cup of flour, but this also adds extra sodium (saltiness). Another option is to use an extra teaspoon or so of baking powder (recipes vary as to how much leavening they need).

» Because Splenda Granular dissolves, it does not add the "bulk" of sugar. Therefore, the weight, volume, and yield will be less than if sugar was used. Consequently, you may increase other ingredients to make up the difference or use a smaller pan size (for example, your traditional recipe that used a 9-inch square pan may now need only an 8-inch square pan). For cookies and muffins, you can also simply adjust the yield.

» Baked goods will cook faster with Splenda. Cakes can easily be done a full 10 minutes sooner, muffins 5-8 minutes, and cookies 3-5 minutes sooner. Moreover, checking baked goods early, always just makes good baking sense.

» Be sure to wrap cooled baked goods tightly to keep them from drying out because both sugar and fat are elements that keep baked goods moist longer. You may also freeze cookies, muffins, quick breads, and most cakes. Simply thaw and or microwave to bring back the just-baked goodness.

Fantastic Ways to Lower the Fat

Years before I found ways to create sweet yet low-sugar foods, I was mastering the techniques of luscious low-fat cooking. (In fact, many of my already developed low-fat dessert recipes were the first to get Splenda makeovers.) As I went on to teach healthy cooking to culinary students, professional chefs, and the public through cooking schools—one thing became clear, and that was that the trick wasn't in cutting the fat, but in doing so without compromising the quality of the food.

It's no secret that fat adds flavor to food, but when lowering the fat, you must also consider how much moistness, texture, and mouth-feel it adds to the recipe. Fortunately, with all the wonderful better-tasting-than-ever reduced-fat products available today, and more years honing my healthy-cooking skills than I care to admit, I have found lots of fantastic ways to lower the fat in my sensational recipes. Here are some of my favorite tips.

Fat-Reducing Tips for Sensational Food

» While some foods (like many in the condiments section) simply don't require fat, most recipes do not fare well when you force all of the fat out of them. A reasonable goal is to reduce the fat to a healthy level (see the Skinny on Fat on page 16).

» Selecting the right fat for the job allows you to use less. For example, when only the flavor of butter will do, do use butter, but either use less or opt for light butter (if the recipe can handle its water content) for a significant savings in fat. Additionally, less shortening makes a flakier pie crust and is lower in calories than using lots of oil, and in baking, a healthy reduced-fat stick margarine (see Ingredients A-Z, for more information) can get the job done when a solid fat is required. Last, splashes (not splurges) of a good-quality oil is often more effective for taste than lots of a poor one.

» It's no wonder how fast the fat content climbs when ½ cup of "healthy" oil has 960 calories and 112 grams of fat (that's 120 calories and 14 grams per itty, bitty tablespoon), and a stick of butter or ½ cup of regular mayonnaise has 800 calories and 88 grams of fat.

» Reduced-fat mayonnaise and margarines make quick and easy substitutes (especially when you layer them with additional flavors) as do broths, or vegetable and fruit juices, for some of the oil in recipes.

» Nonstick cooking spray is a fat-saving wonder, whether you fill your own spray can or buy a commercial brand. But you only need a two- to three-second spray. You may not realize that the 0 calories listed on the can is only for a flash of a spray—each 5-second spray yields the equivalent of a teaspoon of oil and 4 grams of fat.

» When choosing protein, think lean. Key words to look for when selecting red meats are the words "loin" or "round"—as in round steak or pork tenderloin. Lean meats taste great when marinated for tenderness and served with flavorful condiments.

» Invest in good nonstick sauté pans and preheat them before adding food. A good hot pan will help evenly disperse small amounts of oil and keep meats from sticking.

» Reduced and low-fat dairy products make a big difference. Full of flavor (unlike many nonfat varieties) and yet significantly reduced in fat, they offer a wonderful, healthful alternative for cooking and baking. Don't get discouraged just because you tried a particular product once and didn't like it. The many different brands differ greatly in quality; simply try another product until you find one that suits you.

» A big exception to my limited use of nonfat products is nonfat half-and-half. It is not only a great replacement for regular (rich) half-and-half, but it's wonderful when used in combination with 1% milk to boost it to the richness of whole milk. The result is the creamy body of whole milk for cooking and baking with only a fraction of the fat.

» To reduce the fat (saturated fat and cholesterol) of whole eggs, you can use additional egg whites (2 egg whites = 1 whole egg) for some of the whole eggs in recipes that do not rely on the egg yolk for color or richness. I prefer extra whites over egg substitutes in baking because they usually yield a better texture in the finished product. (See Ingredients A–Z for more information on eggs.)

» Fruit purees are incredible as fat replacements, generating both moistness and flavor in baking. You will find that I use everything from prunes (great with chocolate) to apricots and applesauce. I don't, however, advise replacing *all* of the traditional fat with fruit purees—this can create gummy or spongy baked goods. Replacing half the original fat is a better rule of thumb.

» Last, don't be afraid to add bold flavor. Fat carries flavor and sugar enhances it, so foods low in sugar and fat need more flavor to wow your palate. That means using additional spice in both cooking and baking. It also helps to be sure that they are fresh and of good quality (like real vanilla).

Ingredients A-Z

When it comes to creating foods that are low in sugar and fat and that taste terrific, the exact combination of ingredients is essential. That said, you can substitute some ingredients (like herbs and spices) in many of the recipes, while you can't substitute others (like the type of fat) without having a major impact on quality or nutritional content. This section is designed to help you better understand the ingredients I have used and act not only as a guide to making appropriate substitutions, but as inspiration for creating your very own sensational recipes.

Applesauce

Always use unsweetened applesauce. The sweetened varieties are high in sugar, and the recipes are not calibrated for those that are sweetened with Splenda.

Buttermilk

Buttermilk is a terrific low-fat ingredient that adds great flavor to recipes and tenderizes baked goods. Buttermilk is made by fermenting skim or low-fat milk with a bacterial culture that gives it thick texture. A reasonable substitute is soured milk. Place 1 tablespoon of vinegar or lemon juice in a 1-cup measuring cup; add 1% milk to fill the cup and let set 3 minutes before using.

Cocoa Powder

My strong preference is to use Dutch-process cocoa powder. Dutch-processing reduces cocoa's natural acidity and bitterness, mellowing the cocoa and imparting a richer, darker color. I use Hershey's European Style, which can also be labeled "Special Dark." You can find it in some grocery stores, or you can find it and several other brands of Dutch-process cocoas reasonably priced in the gourmet food section at www.amazon.com.

Cottage Cheese

Cottage cheese is a wonder food when it comes to cutting calories and fat and adding healthful protein to recipes—especially when creamed. The simple trick to creaming it is to use the food processor (my choice) or blender and puree it until there are no curds left (so it looks like a thick sour cream). Low-fat or 2% is my choice for the best outcome.

Cream Cheese

I use Philadelphia-brand cream cheeses. You may select another brand— but they do vary greatly in taste (especially reduced-fat varieties.) When I specifiy the use of tub-style light cream cheese, you may use Neufchatel cheese with good results, but do note that it's slightly higher in calories and fat. I also use nonfat cream cheese only in combination with low-fat—a technique that significantly reduces fat while maintaining creaminess and flavor. I do not recommend using nonfat cream cheese when not specified, nor do I recommend full-fat cream cheese if you are concerned about calories and/or fat content.

Eggs

Whole eggs are no longer the bad guys we once believed they were. Today, researchers believe that eating excess saturated and trans-fat raises your cholesterol more than eating dietary cholesterol. Thus, even the American Heart Association says each of us can enjoy an egg every day.

But to keep the total fat (and cholesterol) in my recipes at a healthy level, I opt for more egg whites than yolks when feasible (2 egg whites = 1 whole egg). I prefer them to egg substitutes (especially in baking), but you may use an egg substitute if you like (¼ cup = 1 egg).

The other concern with eggs (when consumed raw) food-borne illness. The actual risk is very low; however, because effects on small children, the elderly, and the immunosuppressed can be severe, I recommend using pasteurized egg whites when you're cooking for these folks. Great solutions are dried egg whites found in the baking aisle, pasteurized egg whites sold next to egg substitutes in cartons (they must state "for whipping"), and pasteurized whole eggs that have been separated (whipping the whites will take a bit longer.)

Flavorings

Using good-quality spices and flavorings makes a big difference in the quality of the recipes. Vanilla extract should be "real," and dried spices should still be fragrant when you open the jars. (Even dried spices don't last forever.)

Filo Dough

Filo (or phyllo) dough is most commonly known for its use in baklava. You can find packages of the paper-thin pastry dough in the freezer cases of most grocery stores. This is a great, crispy, low-fat, and lower-carb alternative for both strudels and pie crusts. You can keep it from tearing by thawing slowly in the refrigerator, covering the sheets with a damp cloth or paper towels, and using cooking spray between the sheets.

Flours

You will find that I use many types of flour in my recipes, and any substitutions will affect outcomes. All-purpose flour is best for general baking because it has the right amount of protein for the proper rise and texture of baked goods. Cake flour has less protein and produces a lighter, more tender crumb and should be used when specified. Whole-wheat flour is prized for its higher fiber content but is also higher in gluten and flavor and produces denser, heavier baked goods. When you want to substitute whole-wheat flour for white in my recipes, I suggest you follow these three tips: Use whole-wheat pasty flour, for more fiber with less heaviness, select heartier muffin and full-bodied cake like Fresh Banana Cake for best results, and substitute out no more than half of the all-purpose flour. An additional trick is to use unprocessed bran flakes, with twice the fiber of whole-wheat flour, for the substitution (substituting out no more than one-third of the flour).

Margarine and Butter

You may substitute any brand of stick margarine or butter that you prefer, but cannot substitute equally tub margarines or light butter because solid fat (more than 65 percent by weight) is required for proper baking. I tested the recipes with several stick margarines that contained 10 grams of total fat, with a total of only 4 grams of saturated and trans-fat when combined, per tablespoon.

At this time, all stick margarines do indeed have some trans-fat, but they vary greatly (from 1.5 to 5 grams). So, look for one that is on the lower end. As for butter, it does impart great flavor—and it contains no trans-fat but it also averages 8 grams of unhealthy saturated fat in each tablespoon.

Milk

I specify low-fat (1%) milk, as it contains only 20 percent of its calories as fat but tastes far richer than skim milk. Comparatively, low-fat milk contains 35 percent fat and whole milk is 50 percent fat.

Nonstick Cooking Sprays

These are invaluable weapons in your low-fat arsenal. For baking, be sure to use only flavorless vegetable or canola oil sprays. For cooking, olive oil sprays are fine. Also, keep the trigger finger light—2 to 3 seconds is all it should take.

Nonfat Half-and-Half

Nonfat or fat-free half-and-half can work wonders because it has the creamy richness of half-and-half with none of the fat. The only quality substitute is real half-and-half, but this will add both fat and calories. Do not substitute nonfat milk for it.

Oatmeal

Lots of recipes use oats, which are hearty, high-fiber, and not likely to raise blood sugar as fast as refined cereals and flours. When I specify old-fashioned oats, you can use the regular variety (sold also as rolled oats) or the quick-cooking varieties. My personal preference is the larger-cut regular variety, especially for toppings. Never substitute instant oatmeal for old-fashioned oats.

Oils

All liquid oils contain the same amount of fat, so it's the flavor (or lack of) that primarily determines the type selected for each recipe. For a flavorless oil, I use canola, which is high in monounsaturated fat—but any flavorless vegetable oil is acceptable. When olive oil is specified, you don't have to use virgin or extra-virgin oils, so when I do specify extra-virgin olive oil (as in dressing), it is because I feel it's worth the quality and increased cost in that particular recipe. Sesame oil (made from sesame seeds) has a strong nutty taste and is only used in small amounts—but don't let that make you think you can skip it. It has a big flavor impact, and there is no equivalent substitute.

Orange Juice

New to my low-sugar pantry is reduced-calorie orange juice. Although natural, regular orange juice is a concentrated source of sugar. In recipes where using a low-sugar brand instead of regular reduced the carbohydrates by less than one gram, I opted for regular. However, in recipes with a greater difference, I chose reduced-calorie orange juice (with half the calories and sugar). Both Tropicana Light 'n Healthy and Minute Maid Light Orange Juice are sold in cartons next to the milk in most groceries.

Prune Puree

For convenience, baby-food prunes are specified in most of the recipes. You can use strained prunes in jars or the new Gerber "plums and apples" sold in plastic containers. I no longer can find Sunsweet Lighter Bake, but it is still on the market and I highly recommend it as a prune puree. To make prune puree, combine 1¼ cups unpacked pitted prunes and 6–8 tablespoons very hot water in a food processor and blend until smooth. You can store it in a covered container in the refrigerator for one to two months.

Protein Powder

Protein powder adds an extra boost of protein to foods, without unwanted fat or sugar. You can buy two very distinct varieties—canned designer brands (made from soy or whey), which are best for beverages—and soy protein in bags, which looks more like yellowed flour and is better for baking. The brand you choose isn't important, but just make sure it doesn't contain added fillers or sugar. (It should contain about 25 grams of protein and less than 1 gram of carbohydrate per 2 tablespoons.)

Rice Wine Vinegar

Rice wine vinegar, used extensively in Asian recipes, has less acid and a milder taste than regular white vinegar. When you're shopping, look for "natural" on the label rather than the seasoned or regular varieties, which have up to a teaspoon of sugar in every tablespoon.

Sour Cream

I use light sour cream because this is a good-quality, creamy replacement for full-fat sour cream. I have yet to find a nonfat version I care for as much, nor do I like the lack of creaminess in nonfat sour creams (or dishes made with them). Still, you may substitute a nonfat type if you have one you prefer.

Splenda

You will find several types of Splenda brand sweeteners next to the sugar in most markets. Splenda No Calorie Sweetener (Granular), as used in most recipes, is sold in a yellow box or a large "baker's" bag. You may confirm that you have the granular version by looking just above the weight on the front of the packaging. Splenda Granular measures 1:1 for sugar.

You will also find Splenda Packets sold in boxes. For conversion purposes, each packet equals 2 teaspoons of sugar (or Splenda Granular.)

Last, you will find Splenda Sugar Blend for Baking in an orange bag (it will be heavier than the granular box). The sugar blend is a 50/50 combination of regular granulated sugar and sucralose (Splenda). It is important to note you use only ½ the measure of Splenda Sugar for Baking when substituting it either for sugar or Splenda Granular. (See All About Splenda, page 13 and Sweet Ways to Cut the Sugar, page 22 for more information on the differences between Splenda sweeteners.)

Whipped Topping

Light whipped topping has only a fraction of the fat of real whipped cream and adds a great deal to recipes. You can find it in tubs in the freezer section of your grocery store. Be sure to thaw before using, by the way. My favorite is Cool Whip Lite, but I don't recommend the nonfat version, which is higher in sugar and not as creamy.

Yogurt

You can use plain nonfat yogurt and plain low-fat yogurt interchangeably (caloric and fat differences notwithstanding). Otherwise, use only the type of yogurt specified for the best results—specifically, do not substitute "light" or artificially sweetened yogurts for brands with sugar if that is what the recipe calls for. The quality will be diminished.

Zests

Many recipes call for the "zest," or grated peel, of lemons, limes, or oranges. I can't say enough about the terrific difference zests can make, and all are interchangeable, based on your taste. To zest a piece of fresh fruit, just wash it and then simply grate off the brightly colored outer layer of the whole fruit (not going deeply into the bitter white pith). Zest is best when finely grated, so use a small whole grater or finish it off by mincing it on a cutting board with a chef's knife before adding it to the recipe.

The Sensational Recipes

Ice Cold Drinks, Shakes, and Smoothies

Ice Cold Lemonade

Strawberry Lemonade

Sparkling Limeade

Hawaiian Fruit Punch

Watermelon Agua Fresca

Citrus Splash

Green Tea with Ginger and Honey

Creamy Iced Coffee

Frosty Mocha

Chocolate Frosty

Orange Sunshine Smoothie

Orange Creamsicle Frappe

Berry Blast Smoothie

Peachy Vanilla Slender Shake

Strawberry Banana Smoothie

Strawberry Almond Soy Smoothie

Triple Vanilla Breakfast Drink

Double Chocolate Breakfast Drink

Chocolate Banana Peanut Butter
          High-Protein Shake

Cold beverages, no longer simply on the sideline, have turned into a complete food industry unto themselves. Beyond traditional soft drinks and juice, there's a whole new world of choices. From fancy sweetened teas and creamy rich coffees to flavorful fruit-filled smoothies, you can find something cold and sweet for absolutely any time—any taste.

Great taste aside, though, the problem is that sweet beverages taste so good that it's easy to overlook what's in them—lots of sugar—and this can be a weighty mistake.

Scientific studies tell us that, in addition to raising blood sugar, the "sweet calories" from liquid beverages really add up yet they don't fill you up, like solid food. This means that when you drink a refreshing 175-calorie bottle of iced tea, a 300-calorie coffeehouse favorite, or a 500-calorie "health" smoothie, you can easily walk away with "extras" where you least want them—on your scale.

That's why I am happy to start this book with new ways to indulge your sweet tooth with beverages that don't deliver unwanted sugar or calories. In this chapter, you'll find refreshing drinks like Strawberry Lemonade and Green Tea with Ginger and Honey to deliciously satisfy your thirst without the added calories. Creamy Iced Coffee, for example, can help you kick your trip to the coffee shop, and smoothies that truly are healthful (like a tantalizing Orange Creamsicle) and creamy breakfast drinks like my Peachy Vanilla Slender Shake will fill you up—but not out. How's about a nice cold drink?

Ice Cold Lemonade

Serves One

Nothing beats the heat like cold lemonade. Unfortunately, the amount of sugar it takes to sweeten those lemons is enough to make you pucker. So, enjoy this sweet version without the added sugar or calories.

INGREDIENTS:

⅓ cup fresh lemon juice (1 large lemon) or ⅓ cup lemon juice concentrate

2 tablespoons Splenda Granular (or 3 Splenda packets)

Crushed ice

STEPS:

1. Pour the lemon juice into a tall (12-ounce) glass. Add the Splenda and stir until dissolved.
2. Fill with crushed ice cold water. Stir.

Sweetened beverages are the number-one source of added sugars in the American diet. By simply switching over from regular lemonade, you save 25 grams of sugar and 100 calories for each glass.

PER SERVING

Calories 30   Fat 0 grams
Carbohydrate 9 grams   Fiber 0 grams
Protein 0 grams   Sodium 0 grams

Diabetic exchange = ½ Fruit
WW point comparison = 1 point

Strawberry Lemonade

Serves Four

Pretty in pink! Here, strawberries turn ordinary lemonade into delicious "pink lemonade." I like the extra fresh taste of the strawberry puree in the lemonade, but you may strain out the pulp if you prefer a clear, crisp pink lemonade. Either way, it's delicious.

INGREDIENTS:

1 ½ cups strawberries, freshly halved (or frozen, slightly thawed)

1 cup lemon juice (about 4 medium lemons)

⅔ cup Splenda Granular

3 cups cold water

2 teaspoons lemon zest

STEPS:

1. Place strawberries in a food processor or blender; process until smooth and pour into a large pitcher.
2. Add lemon juice to pitcher. Stir in Splenda and water.
3. Strain out strawberry pulp if desired. Add lemon zest.
4. Serve in tall 12-ounce glasses filled with ice.

A very kind reader told me how much she was enjoying my recipes while keeping her blood sugar under control. She also passed on a great suggestion for this recipe—strain the juice and pour it into ice cube trays to make Strawberry Lemonade Ice Cubes. Drop into iced tea, and as she says, "Wow!"

PER SERVING

Calories 50	Fat 0 grams (0 saturated)
Carbohydrate 12 grams	Fiber 2 grams
Protein 1 gram	Sodium 0 milligrams

Diabetic exchange = 1 Fruit
WW point comparison = 1 point

Sparkling Limeade

Serves Six

Looking for something beyond the usual lemonade? Freshly squeezed lime juice and sparkling water give this new thirst quencher a refreshing zing. For a nice touch when you place the pitcher out for company, throw in a few thin slices of lime along with a sprig or two of fresh mint.

INGREDIENTS:

1 cup lime juice (about 6 limes)

¾ cup Splenda Granular

1 teaspoon lime zest

42-ounce bottle sparkling water

STEPS:

1. Combine lime juice, Splenda, and lime zest in a large pitcher. Stir.

2. Add sparkling water. Stir briefly.

3. Serve immediately over ice in tall 12-ounce glasses.

Remember to grate no deeper than the colorful green rind of the lime. The inner white flesh or pith tends to be bitter.

PER SERVING

Calories 25

Carbohydrate 7 grams

Protein 0 grams

Fat 0 grams

Fiber 0 grams

Sodium 0 milligrams

Diabetic exchange = ½ Fruit

WW point comparison = 1 point

Hawaiian Fruit Punch

Serves Six

This recipe is kid-tested and mother-approved. My boys love that it tastes just like the high-sugar stuff, and I love that it's made without any added sugars. Better yet, a glass delivers almost a day's worth of vitamin C.

INGREDIENTS:

2 cups light cranberry juice (like Ocean Spray Lightstyle)

1 cup light orange juice

½ cup pineapple juice

2 tablespoons Splenda Granular (or 3 Splenda packets)

1 cup water

STEPS:

1. Mix all ingredients in a large pitcher. Stir.
2. Serve in 8-ounce glasses filled with ice.

Fortified light and reduced-calorie orange juices like Minute Maid Light and Tropicana Light 'n Healthy are excellent sources of calcium and vitamin C, with ½ the sugar of regular orange juice.

PER SERVING

Calories 35	Fat 0 grams (0 saturated)
Carbohydrate 9 grams	Fiber 0 grams
Protein 0 grams	Sodium 0 milligrams

Diabetic exchange = ½ Fruit

WW point comparison = 1 point

Watermelon Agua Fresca

Serves Four

Agua fresca means "fruit water," and in Mexico, you will find jars of refreshing agua frescas at street stands in huge glass jars. Super healthy and oh-so-simple to make, these drinks require only a few essential ingredients. One tip: Because the main flavor of this beverage comes from the watermelon, choose the sweetest, ripest melon you can find.

INGREDIENTS:

2 cups watermelon cubed and seeded

2 cups water

Juice of 1 lime

¼ cup Splenda Granular

STEPS:

1. Combine all ingredients in a blender and puree until smooth. Strain juice.
2. Serve over ice in 8-ounce glasses.

Substitute melon for the watermelon to make Agua de Melon, strawberries to make Agua de Fresa, or even cucumber to make Agua de Pepino. Adjust Splenda Granular to taste.

PER SERVING

Calories 35

Carbohydrate 8 grams

Protein 1 gram

Fat 0 grams

Fiber 0 grams

Sodium 5 milligrams

Diabetic exchange = ½ Fruit

WW point comparison = 1 point

Citrus Splash

Serves Four

This refreshing drink is a great breakfast or afternoon sipper, especially if you make it with fresh juices. Lighter and a bit more tart than lemonade, this is the perfect beverage for a hot summer's day. Try it with a twist of lime.

INGREDIENTS:

⅔ **cup light orange juice**

½ **cup lime juice (about 3 limes)**

½ **cup lemon juice (about 2 lemons)**

6 tablespoons Splenda Granular (or 9 Splenda packets)

2 ⅓ cups club soda or seltzer water (lime or lemon sparkling water is also nice)

STEPS:

1. Combine juices, Splenda, and club soda in a large pitcher. Stir.
2. Serve immediately over ice in tall 12-ounce glasses.

For a party, measure juices and Splenda into a punch bowl or other pretty large bowl. Just before serving, add the ice and club soda. For the garnish, float thin slices of lime, lemon, and oranges on top.

PER SERVING

Calories 40	Fat 0 grams (saturated)
Carbohydrate 10 grams	Fiber 0 grams
Protein 0 grams	Sodium 0 milligrams

Diabetic exchange = ½ Fruit

WW point comparison = 1 point

Green Tea with Ginger and Honey
Serves Eight

Green tea is "in." No longer simply served as a hot tea in Asian restaurants, green tea has found its way into millions of bottles and cans as a "healthy" cold beverage. But even though these cold teas seem like better bets than soft drinks, they often have more sugar. Here is a version that replicates one of the most popular brands, with a touch of ginger replacing the usual ginseng.

INGREDIENTS:

8 cups water

2 green tea bags

2 tablespoons honey

⅔ cup Splenda Granular (or less, depending on taste)

¼ cup freshly squeezed lemon juice

½ teaspoon finely grated fresh ginger

STEPS:

1. Place water in medium saucepan and bring to a boil. Add green tea bags and steep for 1–2 hours.

2. While tea is still warm, stir in honey, Splenda, lemon juice, and ginger. Let mixture cool, then place in a pitcher and refrigerate.

3. Serve cold.

Green tea is a natural antioxidant that has many health benefits. Health experts believe that green tea may reduce your risk of certain cancers, lower your cholesterol and blood pressure, and bolster your immune system. What's more, new evidence suggests it may aid in weight loss and even protect your teeth!

PER SERVING

Calories 25
Carbohydrate 7 grams
Protein 0 grams

Fat 0 grams
Fiber 0 grams
Sodium 0 milligrams

Diabetic exchange = ½ Carbohydrate
WW point comparison = 0 points (for 8 ounces or less)

Creamy Iced Coffee

Serves One

It's amazing how popular coffee drinks have become. Many of my clients use them as an afternoon pick-me-up. The only problem is that these drinks are loaded with calories and sugar. In fact, a small coffeehouse drink often contains more sugar than a can of cola. Quick and easy to make, this version has a fraction of the calories (and cost!). The trick to getting a silky texture without sugar is to use nonfat half-and-half in place of milk.

INGREDIENTS:

½ cup double-strength coffee or
  2 teaspoons instant coffee dissolved
  in 4 ounces of warm water (regular
  or decaffeinated)

¼ cup nonfat half-and-half

2 tablespoons Splenda Granular
  (or 3 Splenda packets)

½ cup crushed ice

STEPS:

1. Pour the coffee, half-and-half, and Splenda into a blender. Blend to mix.
2. Add the ice and blend briefly (about 15 seconds) until ice is incorporated. Pour into an 8-ounce glass.

A 9.5-ounce bottle of Starbucks Frappuccino contains 31 grams of sugar.

PER SERVING

Calories 48	Fat 0.5 grams (0 saturated)
Carbohydrate 8 grams	Fiber 0 grams
Protein 2 grams	Sodium 60 milligrams

Diabetic exchange = ½ Carbohydrate
WW point comparison = 1 point

Frosty Mocha

Serves One

This Frosty Mocha is a delicious twist on Creamy Iced Coffee. In addition to the chocolate, I've added more ice to make this 12-ounce version tall and frosty. Don't forget to have a straw ready.

INGREDIENTS:

½ cup double-strength coffee or 2 teaspoons instant coffee dissolved in 4 ounces of warm water (regular or decaffeinated)

¼ cup + 1 tablespoon nonfat half-and-half

3 tablespoons Splenda Granular (or 4 Splenda packets)

1 teaspoon unsweetened cocoa powder

1 cup crushed ice

STEPS:

1. Pour the coffee, half-and-half, Splenda, and cocoa powder into a blender. Blend to mix.
2. Add half of the ice and blend briefly (about 15 seconds) until ice is incorporated.
3. Add the rest of the ice and blend once more.
4. Pour into a tall 12-ounce glass.

The good news about Au Bon Pain's Frozen Mocha Blast (16 ounces) is that it has only 3 grams of fat. The bad news is that, at 320 calories, it contains more than 60 grams of sugar.

PER SERVING

Calories 61	Fat 0.5 gram (0 saturated)
Carbohydrate 10	Fiber 0 grams
Protein 2 grams	Sodium 67 milligrams

Diabetic exchange = ½ Carbohydrate
WW point comparison = 1 point

Chocolate Frosty

Serves One

My son Stephen is the chocolate lover in our family, and this recipe from Fantastic Food with Splenda is one of his favorites. According to him, it's just as good as the ones from fast-food outlets—but you can enjoy this treat right at home.

INGREDIENTS:

1 individual-serving packet Splenda-sweetened sugar-free hot chocolate mix (Swiss Miss)

½ cup 1% milk

1 tablespoon Splenda Granular (or 2 Splenda packets)

2 teaspoons cocoa powder

½ cup sugar-free light vanilla ice cream

½ cup crushed ice

STEPS:

1. Place hot chocolate mix, milk, Splenda, and cocoa in a blender. Blend to mix.
2. Add vanilla ice cream and ice and blend until thick and frosty.

When choosing a sugar-free ice cream, be sure to look at the fat content and select one that is "light" in fat and reduced in overall calories—not simply sugar-free.

PER SERVING

Calories 200	Fat 5 grams (3 saturated)
Carbohydrate 24 grams	Fiber 4 grams
Protein 13 grams	Sodium 220 milligrams

Diabetic exchange = ½ Milk, 1 Starch
WW point comparison = 4 points

Orange Sunshine Smoothie

Serves One

Reminiscent of a creamsicle, this creamy drink is a wonderful addition to any breakfast. It offers a full day's worth of vitamin C, with less sugar and more protein than even sunny orange juice can deliver.

INGREDIENTS:

½ cup light orange juice

¼ cup plain nonfat yogurt

½ cup crushed (or cubed) ice

1 tablespoon Splenda Granular (or 2 Splenda packets)

STEPS:

1. Place all ingredients in a blender.
2. Blend at high speed for 30–45 seconds.

You may also use freshly squeezed or regular-style orange juice as I did in Unbelievable Desserts with Splenda. This adds 30 calories, 6.5 grams of carbohydrate, and 1 additional Weight Watchers point.

PER SERVING

Calories 70	Fat 0 grams
Carbohydrate 13 grams	Fiber 0 grams
Protein 5 grams	Sodium 145 milligrams

Diabetic exchange = 1 Fruit, ½ Nonfat Milk
WW point comparison = 1 point

Orange Creamsicle Frappe

Serves Two

As a kid, I loved the frothy orange drink called an Orange Julius. This frappe has that same delicious sweet orange/vanilla taste I remember so well. Egg substitute does a great job of giving the drink its characteristic froth and a protein boost without any raw egg worries.

INGREDIENTS:

¾ **cup light orange juice**

¾ **cup 1% milk**

¼ **cup Splenda Granular (or 6 Splenda packets)**

¼ **cup egg substitute (like Egg Beaters)**

¾ **teaspoon vanilla**

1 **cup crushed ice (or 5-6 cubes)**

STEPS:

1. Place all ingredients except ice in a blender and pulse to blend.

2. Add ice and blend until ice is completely incorporated and the drink is frothy.

3. Serve immediately in 8-ounce glasses.

PER SERVING

Calories 90	Fat 1 gram (.5 saturated)
Carbohydrate 13 grams	Fiber 0 grams
Protein 8 grams	Sodium 100 milligrams

Diabetic exchange = ½ Low-Fat Milk, ½ Fruit
WW point comparison = 2 points

Berry Blast Smoothie

Serves Two

In a magazine, I saw a drink similar to this that was touted for its anti-cancer properties (berries have compounds that are powerful foes to tumors). But I love this drink mainly because of its delicious taste. Any combination of berries will do—just make sure one type is frozen.

INGREDIENTS:

½ cup 1% (or skim) milk

1 cup plain nonfat yogurt

½ cup blueberries

½ cup frozen strawberries

¼ cup Splenda Granular (or 6 Splenda packets)

1 cup crushed (or cubed) ice

STEPS:

1. Place milk in a blender. Add remaining ingredients except ice. Pulse.
2. Add ice and blend at high speed until smooth.

By simply switching to lower-fat dairy products, you add 3 grams of protein and save 5 grams of fat (4 saturated) and 20 calories per serving in this lean smoothie.

PER SERVING

Calories 140	Fat 1 gram (.5 saturated)
Carbohydrate 23 grams	Fiber 2 grams
Protein 10 grams	Sodium 145 milligrams

Diabetic exchange = 1 Low-Fat Milk, ½ Fruit
WW point comparison = 2 points

Peachy Vanilla Slender Shake

Serves One

So creamy. So peachy. So slenderizing! This thick 16-ounce shake is sure to fill you up—but not out. Rich in protein, vitamins A and C, and an excellent source of calcium, it's truly a delicious way to start your morning or fuel your afternoon.

INGREDIENTS:

¾ **cup nonfat milk**

¼ **cup plain nonfat yogurt**

¾ **cup frozen sliced peaches**

½ **teaspoon vanilla extract**

¼ **teaspoon almond extract**

2 **tablespoons Splenda Granular (or 3 packets)**

½ **cup ice (if you use fresh peach slices)**

STEPS:

1. In a blender, combine all ingredients. Blend until smooth.
2. Serve in a 16-ounce glass.

PEACHY COCONUT SLENDER SHAKE
  VARIATION: Add ½ teaspoon coconut extract and omit the almond extract.

PER SERVING

Calories 150	Fat .5 grams (0 saturated)
Carbohydrate 28 grams	Fiber 2 grams
Protein 11 grams	Sodium 140 milligrams

Diabetic exchange = 1 Nonfat Milk
WW point comparison = 3 points

Strawberry Banana Smoothie

Serves Two

Whether you like your smoothies thick and creamy or cool and frosty, this recipe fits the bill. Perfect for a snack or as part of a meal, this soothing taste combination is always a winner. It also makes use of those overripe bananas—simply peel them and place them in a plastic bag before freezing. Frozen bananas will keep for a month or more.

INGREDIENTS:

1 cup 1% (or skim) milk

1 cup plain nonfat yogurt

1 cup sliced strawberries (about 8 medium)

2 tablespoons Splenda Granular (or 3 Splenda packets)

½ large banana (frozen)

STEPS:

THICK AND CREAMY:

1. Place milk into a blender. Add yogurt, strawberries, and Splenda. Pulse.
2. Add the banana and blend until thick and creamy.

COOL AND FROSTY:

1. Add 1 additional tablespoon of Splenda and ½ cup crushed ice to the thick and creamy smoothie.
2. Blend on high for 30 seconds longer until ice is incorporated.

Add a scoop of protein powder to make a tasty high-protein shake or enjoy it with a handful of low-fat wheat crackers and a tablespoon of peanut butter for a wholesome low-calorie mini-meal.

PER SERVING

Calories 150	Fat 2 grams (1 saturated)
Carbohydrate 24 grams	Fiber 2 grams
Protein 10 grams	Sodium 65 milligrams

Diabetic exchange = 1 Low-Fat Milk, ½ Fruit

WW point comparison = 3 points

Strawberry Almond Soy Smoothie

Serves Two

Let's face it—tofu doesn't have a very good reputation as a tasty food—good for you, yes, but yummy, no. This shake will change your mind. I've added the delicious combination of strawberries and almond to make a smoothie that's both creamy and tasty. (You may actually forget that it's also good for you.)

INGREDIENTS:

1 cup 1% milk

¾ cup strawberries, fresh, quartered (or frozen, partially defrosted)

⅓ cup firm silken tofu

¼ cup Splenda Granular (or 6 Splenda packets)

¼ teaspoon almond extract

½ cup ice

STEPS:

1. Place all ingredients except ice in a blender and pulse to blend.
2. Add ice and blend until thick and creamy.
3. Serve immediately in 8-ounce glasses.

PER SERVING

Calories 110	Fat 3 grams (1 saturated)
Carbohydrate 14 grams	Fiber 1 gram
Protein 7 grams	Sodium 65 milligrams

Diabetic exchange = ½ Low-Fat Milk, ½ Fruit
WW point comparison = 2 points

Soy is a great source of protein and a healthy addition to any diet. Soy can help lower cholesterol and may also decrease the risk of osteoporosis, heart disease, and some cancers.

Triple Vanilla Breakfast Drink

PER SERVING
Calories 170   Fat .5 gram (0 saturated) Carbohydrate 17 grams   Fiber 0 grams

"Meal replacement drinks" are a relatively new phenomenon, but Carnation Instant Breakfast is one powdered instant breakfast drink that has been around as long as I can remember. Not only did I drink it as a kid, I have ordered it for people who needed extra nutrition when recuperating from an illness. Full of protein, vitamin C, and calcium, this economical copycat mix makes it easy to drink healthy.

INGREDIENTS:

1 small box (3-ounce) vanilla sugar-free pudding mix

¾ cup vanilla-flavor protein powder (0 carbohydrate variety)

3 cups nonfat dry milk

½ cup Splenda Granular

4 ½ teaspoons vanilla

STEPS:

1. Place all ingredients except vanilla in a large plastic container with lid. Shake vigorously until mixed.

2. For each breakfast drink, place ½ cup mix, ½ teaspoon vanilla, 1 cup water, and 1 cup ice in a blender. Blend until thick and smooth.

Serves Nine

Although many canned meal replacements are anything but healthy when it comes to sugar content, they do come in lots of flavors. Just use your imagination on this version and vary the extract and the flavor of sugar-free pudding. You can also drop in a bit of fresh fruit (a chunk of frozen banana is my favorite).

Protein 24 grams   Sodium 450 milligrams

Diabetic exchange = 1 Nonfat Milk, ½ Carbohydrate
WW point comparison = 3 points

Double Chocolate Breakfast Drink

Serves Ten

The only thing better than my Triple Vanilla Breakfast Drink mix is this chocolate variation. Thick, rich, and chocolatey, it will satisfy your kids' cravings for chocolate for breakfast (or your own).

INGREDIENTS:

1 small box (3-ounce) chocolate sugar-free pudding mix

¾ cup unflavored protein powder (0 carbohydrate variety)

3 cups nonfat dry milk powder

1 cup Splenda Granular

½ cup Dutch-process or regular cocoa powder

STEPS:

1. Place all ingredients in a large plastic container with lid. Shake vigorously until mixed.

2. For each breakfast drink, place ½ cup mix, ¾ cup water, and 1 cup ice in a blender. Blend until thick and smooth. Pour into a 16-ounce glass.

After school, my boys love for me to whip this up and throw a scoop of vanilla ice cream in the mix. To them, it's a chocolate shake. To me, it's a quick solution for a healthy snack.

PER SERVING

Calories 160	Fat 1 gram (.5 saturated)
Carbohydrate 17 grams	Fiber 1 gram
Protein 21 grams	Sodium 390 milligrams

Diabetic exchange = 1 Nonfat Milk, ½ Carbohydrate
WW point comparison = 3 points

Chocolate Banana Peanut Butter High-Protein Shake

Serves Two

The name says it all for this rich, thick, creamy, fill-you-up type of drink. Drink alone as a mini-meal or combine this drink with a piece of light whole-wheat toast for a satisfying and nutritious breakfast.

INGREDIENTS:

1 banana, peeled, cut in half and frozen

1 cup cold 1% milk

2 tablespoons peanut butter

3 tablespoons Splenda Granular (or 4 Splenda packets)

2 teaspoons cocoa powder

2 tablespoons protein powder

½ cup crushed ice

STEPS:

1. Place all the ingredients in a blender and blend until thick and smooth.
2. Serve in 8-ounce glasses.

Eating peanut butter is back in style! Although it's dense in both calories and fat, the fat is monounsaturated, which means it's good for you. So eat up—just not too much.

PER SERVING

Calories 250
Carbohydrate 26 grams
Protein 17 grams

Fat 9 grams (3 saturated)
Fiber 3 grams
Sodium 200 milligrams

Diabetic exchange = ½ Low-Fat Milk, 1 Fruit, 2 Medium-Fat Meat
WW point comparison = 5 points

Tempting Hot Beverages and Homemade Dry Mixes

Café Mocha

Café Orange

Hot Vanilla Steamer

Deep Dark Hot Chocolate

Decadent Hot Chocolate

Mexican Hot Chocolate

Indian Chai Tea

(In)Famous Hot Lemonade

Krista's Spiced Tea

Apple Spiced Tea

Old-Fashioned Eggnog

Rich Instant Eggnog for One

Homemade Hot Chocolate Mix

Homemade Chai Spice Mix

Homemade Café Mocha Mix

Homemade French Vanilla
    Coffee Mix

Nothing wards off the cold or brings comfort like a steaming hot beverage. In fact, I enjoy them so much that I've dedicated an entire chapter to them.

I can honestly say that these were some of my favorite recipes to develop. If you're wondering why, it's because I have found that taking time to sip a nice, hot drink, even in the midst of a hectic day, helps me relax and rejuvenate. Even my kids have joined in on the ritual, discovering that a cup of Café Mocha makes homework a bit easier to navigate and that a Hot Vanilla Steamer can soothe you right into bed.

So, it's with great pride that I introduce you to my versions of coffeehouse headliners like Café Mocha and Indian Chai Tea, which have had the sugar dropped but not the taste; rich hot chocolates like Decadent Hot Chocolate that are deep and dark without the fat; and holiday favorites like Old-Fashioned Eggnog that still have all the traditional taste—but not the calories.

For a bit of fun, I suggest you take a peek at—or actually make—my recipe for (In)Famous Hot Lemonade. In addition, I'm excited to offer you several recipes for incredible homemade dry mixes. Now, right at home, you can make your own sugar-free, instant hot beverage mixes like Hot Chocolate and French Vanilla Coffee Mix, thus eliminating the need for pricey store-bought mixes. So, go ahead, relax and indulge—these temptations are delicious and guilt-free.

Café Mocha

Serves One

When I wrote my first book, I developed a recipe for hot chocolate for my son Stephen, who was then eight years old. Now twelve, he has developed a taste for the hot "mochas" that are served at a nationally known coffee chain. So, I have taken his Deep Dark Hot Chocolate and turned it into a perfect mocha (motherhood!).

INGREDIENTS:

1 tablespoon unsweetened Dutch-process cocoa powder

1 tablespoon + 2 teaspoons Splenda Granular (or 3 Splenda packets)

½ cup 1% milk

¾ cup hot double-strength coffee (decaffeinated or regular)

STEPS:

1. Place the cocoa powder and Splenda into a microwaveable mug. Add the milk and whisk until smooth.

2. Microwave on high for 1 ½ minutes or until hot (do not boil).

3. Remove from microwave and add coffee. Stir to combine.

PER SERVING

Calories 80	Fat 2 grams (1 saturated)
Carbohydrate 11 grams	Fiber 2 grams
Protein 5 grams	Sodium 65 milligrams

Diabetic exchange = 1 Low-Fat Milk
WW point comparison = 1 point

Café Orange

Serves Four

I am not usually a fan of flavored coffees, nor do I usually like my coffee sweet, but I do love orange zest. In this unique recipe, orange zest is placed directly into coffee grounds and Splenda into the coffee pot before brewing. The result is positively addictive. This is a wonderful coffee to serve with dessert—or for dessert. Simply add your favorite creamer, steamed milk, or light whipped topping.

INGREDIENTS:

6 tablespoons ground coffee (note: standard coffee scoops often measure 2 tablespoons)

1 small orange

3 tablespoons Splenda Granular (or 4 Splenda packets)

2 teaspoons honey (optional)

4 cups water

STEPS:

1. Place coffee in filter. Grate the zest of the orange into grounds.
2. Measure Splenda and honey into coffee pot. Brew coffee as directed on coffee machine.
3. Add milk or creamer to hot coffee as desired.

Serving this as an after-dinner drink, you can turn it into a superb Orange and Brandy Coffee by simply adding 1 ½ ounces of your favorite brandy to each mug. Top it with some light whipped topping and a curl of orange zest

PER SERVING (WITH HONEY)

Calories 20	Fat 0 grams (0 saturated)
Carbohydrate 5 grams	Fiber 0 gram
Protein 0 grams	Sodium 0 milligrams

Diabetic exchange = 1 Free Food
WW point comparison = 0 points

Hot Vanilla Steamer

Serves One

My youngest son prefers vanilla over chocolate, so this luscious drink was made especially for him. It's amazingly delicious and wonderfully soothing. In fact, this makes the perfect bedtime treat.

INGREDIENTS:

1 cup minus 2 tablespoons 1% milk

2 tablespoons fat-free half-and-half

1 tablespoon Splenda Granular (or 2 Splenda packets)

½ teaspoon vanilla

STEPS:

1. Place milk and half-and-half in a microwaveable 8-ounce mug.
2. Stir in Splenda.
3. Microwave on high for 1 ½ minutes (until hot, not boiling).
4. Remove from microwave and stir in vanilla.

Fat-free half-and-half is the key to making this drink rich and creamy. For an extra treat, top it off with a dollop of light whipped cream.

PER SERVING

Calories 120

Carbohydrate 16 grams

Protein 8 grams

Fat 2 grams (1 saturated)

Fiber 0 grams

Sodium 80 milligrams

Diabetic exchange = 1 Low-Fat Milk

WW point comparison = 3 points (2 points if made with nonfat milk; add an extra tablespoon of nonfat half-and-half)

Deep Dark Hot Chocolate

Serves One

I developed this recipe when my eldest son was eight. He called it "Mom's Special Recipe," and no other hot chocolate would do. There are many specialty sugar-free hot chocolate mixes, but I have yet to find one that wards off the chills with the rich, dark flavor of this original recipe. (This also makes a great cold chocolate milk—no heating required.)

INGREDIENTS:

1 tablespoon unsweetened Dutch-process cocoa powder (like Hershey's European)

1 tablespoon + 2 teaspoons Splenda Granular (or 3 Splenda packets)

2 tablespoons hot water

1 cup 1% milk

STEPS:

1. Place the cocoa powder and Splenda into a microwaveable mug.
2. Add the hot water and stir until smooth.
3. Pour in the milk and stir again.
4. Microwave on high for 1 ½ minutes or until hot. (Do not boil.)

FLAVORED VARIATIONS: Try adding ¼ teaspoon of vanilla, orange, or raspberry extract.

Did you know that an individual packet of hot chocolate can contain as much as 5 teaspoons of sugar?

PER SERVING

Calories 120	Fat 3 grams (2 saturated)
Carbohydrate 16 grams	Fiber 1 gram
Protein 9 grams	Sodium 124 milligrams

Diabetic exchange = 1 Low-Fat Milk

Decadent Hot Chocolate

Serves One

Even darker than my Deep Dark Hot Chocolate, this is comfort food at its best. If you're a chocolate lover (and who isn't?), sipping a steaming cup of this silky, thick hot chocolate will satisfy you to no end. For added decadence, top it off with your favorite light whipped cream.

INGREDIENTS:

1 tablespoon + 2 teaspoons unsweetened cocoa powder

2 tablespoons Splenda Granular

¾ teaspoon cornstarch

¾ cup 1% milk

½ teaspoon vanilla extract

STEPS:

1. In a small saucepan, whisk together the cocoa powder, Splenda, cornstarch, and ¼ cup of the milk until blended. Whisk in remaining milk.

2. Place over medium heat and bring to a low boil, stirring just until chocolate thickens.

3. Remove from heat, whisk in vanilla, and serve.

Although luscious, a 6-ounce cup of Starbucks Chantico Drinking Chocolate contains 390 calories, 21 grams fat, and 51 grams carbohydrate. (For my WW friends, that translates to 10 points or almost 1 point per tablespoon.)

PER SERVING

Calories 130	Fat 3 grams (1.5 saturated)
Carbohydrate 18 grams	Fiber 3 grams
Protein 8 grams	Sodium 95 milligrams

Diabetic exchange = 1 Low-Fat Milk, ½ Carbohydrate
WW point comparison = 2 points

Mexican Hot Chocolate

Serves One

In order to make true Mexican hot chocolate, you need to use solid chocolate. You may have seen "Mexican chocolate" designated for this purpose, but here I have created that same taste with less fat and sugar—plus, this recipe lets you adjust the spiciness to your own taste. By the way, the froth is the best part of this drink. To create it, all you have to do is place a whisk into the hot drink and rapidly roll the handle back and forth between your palms. You'll have instant froth.

INGREDIENTS:

¾ cup 1% milk

½ ounce bittersweet chocolate, chopped★

1 ½ tablespoons Splenda Granular

1 teaspoon cocoa powder

⅛ teaspoon cinnamon

Pinch ground red pepper

¼ teaspoon pure vanilla extract

STEPS:

1. Pour milk into a large microwaveable mug. Microwave on high for 1 minute.

2. Add chocolate, Splenda, cocoa, cinnamon, and red pepper. Whisk well to combine.

3. Microwave on high for an additional minute. Add vanilla. Whisk until frothy.

4. Pour into a 6-ounce coffee cup.

★I use 16 Ghirardelli Double Chocolate Chocolate Chips.

PER SERVING

Calories 160	Fat 7 grams (4 saturated)
Carbohydrate 21 grams	Fiber 1 gram
Protein 8 grams	Sodium 95 milligrams

Diabetic exchange = 1 Low-Fat Milk, ½ Carbohydrate, 1 Fat
WW point comparison = 3 points

Mexican Hot Chocolate, or "chocolatl," was introduced to Spanish explorers by Montezuma, emperor of Mexico, who preferred drinking his rich vanilla-and-spice-flavored chocolate drink out of a golden goblet.

Indian Chai Tea

Serves Three

Legend has it that a chef in India created this tea for a king. The chef wanted a tea with a luxurious fragrance, and so he scented it with cloves, cardamom, and nutmeg. Today you can go to a nearby tea or coffee house to find this sweet and spicy favorite, or you can make this version, which has the same great taste with a fraction of the sugar and calories.

INGREDIENTS:

2 cups water

¼ teaspoon ground cinnamon

¼ teaspoon ground cloves

¼ teaspoon powdered ginger

¼ teaspoon ground cardamom

⅛ teaspoon ground nutmeg

3 tea bags, Darjeeling or black tea

½ teaspoon vanilla

¼ cup Splenda Granular

1 tablespoon honey

1 cup 1% milk

STEPS:

1. Bring water to a boil with the spices in a small saucepan.

2. Add the tea bags and let steep 2–3 minutes.

3. Remove tea bags and stir in vanilla, Splenda, and honey. Strain tea.

4. To serve, measure ⅔ cup tea mixture and ⅓ cup milk into mug and microwave 1 minute or heat tea and milk together in a small saucepan, then pour into mug.

Adjust this recipe to your own taste. It is very sweet, just like the most popular versions. If you like yours not-so-sweet, simply reduce the amount of honey or Splenda. During the holidays, I add a touch more nutmeg, and in the summer I like it over ice.

PER SERVING

Calories 60	Fat 1 gram (.5 saturated)
Carbohydrate 12 grams	Fiber 0 grams
Protein 3 grams	Sodium 40 milligrams

Diabetic exchange = 1 Carbohydrate
WW point comparison = 1 point

(In)Famous Hot Lemonade

Serves Eight

This recipe was inspired by a very famous Martha. I first heard of "Hot Lemonade" when it was widely reported that this was one of the first things she made after her long stay away from home. Now that I have adapted her now-famous recipe, I must agree—on a cold, gray winter's day, this hot, lemony drink is like drinking a cup of sunshine.

INGREDIENTS:

1 cup light orange juice

1 cup freshly squeezed lemon juice

1 ½ cups Splenda Granular

2 teaspoons vanilla

Scant ¼ teaspoon ground cloves

STEPS:

1. Combine all ingredients in a small pitcher. Stir.
2. For 1 cup of Hot Lemonade, combine ¼ cup lemon mixture with ¾ cup of boiling water. Serve hot.

Feeling under the weather with a scratchy throat? Add a teaspoon of honey and a shot of whiskey for a old-fashioned remedy that will make you feel better in no time.

PER SERVING

Calories 35

Carbohydrate 9 grams

Protein 1 gram

Fat 0 grams (0 saturated)

Fiber 0 grams

Sodium 0 milligrams

Diabetic exchange = ½ Fruit

WW point comparison = 1 point

Krista's Spiced Tea

Serves Four

A friend and nutrition colleague of mine is a diabetes educator. She was kind enough to give me the recipe for a hot tea that she and her clients really enjoy. This tea reminds me of hot cider but has fewer calories and no added sugar. You'll find that Krista's Spiced Tea is great on its own, but even better when served with a nice warm scone.

INGREDIENTS:

3 cups boiling water

3 cinnamon flavored tea bags

½ cup light orange juice

1 teaspoon lemon juice

⅓ cup Splenda Granular

STEPS:

1. Steep tea bags in water for 5 minutes. Remove tea bags and discard.

2. Add orange juice, lemon juice, and Splenda.

3. Stir and serve.

VARIATION: Serve cold with ice.

This tea smells wonderful. For holiday entertaining, double or triple the recipe and place in a pot or crockpot to keep warm. Drop in a fresh cinnamon stick and a few twists of fresh orange peel as garnishes.

PER SERVING

Calories 15	Fat 0 grams
Carbohydrate 4 grams	Fiber 0 grams
Protein 0 grams	Sodium 0 milligrams

Diabetic exchange = 1 Free Food

WW point comparison = 0 points

Apple Spiced Tea

Serves Four

While I taught an "Apple Time" cooking class a couple years back for Williams-Sonoma, my students happily sipped on this warm spicy cider. Fot its apple flavor, this tea takes advantage of apple tea bags, which significantly reduce the usual sugar content of this seasonal favorite.

INGREDIENTS:

3 cups boiling water

3 apple (or apple cinnamon) tea bags

1 cup apple cider

1 teaspoon lemon juice

⅓ cup Splenda Granular

¼ teaspoon allspice

2 cinnamon sticks

2 orange slices (each cut in half)

STEPS:

1. Measure water into a medium pot. Bring to a boil; turn off heat and add tea bags. Let steep 3 minutes. Discard tea bags.

2. Add juices, Splenda, allspice, cinnamon sticks, and orange slices.

3. Turn on heat and bring back to a simmer (do not boil), and serve in 8-ounce mugs.

Spiced apple cider made from cider and sugar can easily contain 40 grams or more of sugar in an 8-ounce glass.

PER SERVING

Calories 35	Fat 0 grams
Carbohydrate 9 grams	Fiber 0 grams
Protein 0 grams	Sodium 0 milligrams

Diabetic exchange = ½ Fruit
WW point comparison = 1 point

Old-Fashioned Eggnog

Serves Eight

This recipe was a big hit during the holidays and got "two thumbs up" from everyone who drank it. Although you can buy low-fat eggnogs, I have yet to see one that is also low in sugar. In fact, the light or low-fat versions usually contain more sugar than the regular kind. Once made, this keeps very well for up to a week in the refrigerator.

INGREDIENTS:

3 cups 1% milk, divided

1 ½ cups fat-free half-and-half

1 tablespoon + 1 teaspoon cornstarch

3 large eggs, well beaten

⅔ cup Splenda Granular

2 teaspoons vanilla

½ teaspoon nutmeg

STEPS:

1. In a large saucepan, thoroughly whisk together 1 cup of the milk and the next 4 ingredients (half-and-half, cornstarch, eggs, and Splenda).

2. Place on stove and cook over low heat, stirring constantly, until mixture is thick enough to coat the back of a spoon. Remove from heat.

3. Stir in vanilla and nutmeg. Stir in remaining milk and cool.

4. Chill and store in refrigerator until served.

VARIATION: For a spiked version, substitute ½ to 1 cup brandy or rum for equal amount of milk.

PER SERVING

Calories 100	Fat 3 grams (1.5 saturated)
Carbohydrate 11 grams	Fiber 0 grams
Protein 6 grams	Sodium 80 milligrams

Diabetic exchange = 1 Low-Fat Milk
WW point comparison = 2 points

Watching your weight? Then watch out for traditional eggnogs—they can contain up to 30 grams of fat and sugar each—in a mere ½ cup.

Rich Instant Eggnog for One

Serves One

A perfect mini-meal replacement that is quick and easy, this one-serving eggnog is also rich, filling, and high in protein and nutrients. What it lacks is the sugar, fat, and the high price tag of many brand-name meal-replacement drinks. Try a hot mug of it for breakfast.

INGREDIENTS:

1 large egg

1 cup 1% milk

2 tablespoons Splenda Granular (or 3 Splenda packets)

¼ teaspoon nutmeg

1 teaspoon vanilla

STEPS:

1. Place egg in a large microwaveable mug and beat well.
2. Add milk, Splenda, and nutmeg, and whisk thoroughly (until egg is completely beaten in).
3. Heat in the microwave for 1 minute. Stir. Heat for 30 more seconds or until hot and slightly thickened. Do not boil.
4. Remove from microwave, stir in vanilla, and enjoy.

The egg in this nog is thoroughly cooked; therefore, you don't have to use pasteurized eggs. You may, however, use ¼ cup Egg Beaters if you prefer it to the whole egg.

PER SERVING

Calories 180	Fat 7 grams (3 saturated)
Carbohydrate 13 grams	Fiber 0 grams
Protein 15 grams	Sodium 80 milligrams

Diabetic exchange = 1 Low-Fat Milk, 1 Medium-Fat Meat

WW point comparison = 4 points

Homemade Hot Chocolate Mix

Serves Fourteen

I often recommend low-calorie hot chocolate to chocoholics who want to curb their calories. This is a delicious, inexpensive alternative to individual packets.

INGREDIENTS:

1 cup nonfat dry milk powder

½ cup nondairy dry creamer

⅔ cup Dutch-process cocoa powder

⅔ cup Splenda Granular

STEPS:

1. Thoroughly mix all ingredients together. Place in an airtight container.

2. To serve, stir 3 tablespoons of the dry mix into 6 ounces very hot water.

Try adding a few well-crushed, sugar-free peppermint candies to the mix to create your own peppermint hot chocolate.

PER SERVING (3 TABLESPOONS)

Calories 50	Fat 1.5 grams (1 saturated)
Carbohydrate 8 grams	Fiber 1 gram
Protein 3 grams	Sodium 30 milligrams

Diabetic exchange = ½ Carbohydrate

WW point comparison = 1 point

Homemade Chai Spice Mix

Serves Twelve

Another popular addition to the flavored drink market is chai tea mix. Unfortunately, it's very high in sugar content. This recipe solves that problem. Chai Spice Mix is easy to make, economical, and handy to use for a terrific "gift in a jar."

INGREDIENTS:

¾ cup unsweetened instant ice tea mix

¾ cup Splenda Granular

½ cup nonfat dry milk powder

½ cup nondairy powdered creamer

1 ½ teaspoons cinnamon

1 ½ teaspoons powdered ginger

1 teaspoon ground cloves

¾ teaspoon nutmeg

¾ teaspoon ground cardamom

STEPS:

1. Measure all ingredients into a blender. Blend for 1 minute.

2. Pour mix into a jar or other airtight container.

3. To serve, stir 1 ½ tablespoons dry mix into 6 ounces very hot water.

Blending the mix helps to evenly distribute the spices and concentrates the mix for easier storage. However, you may still find a small amount of spice will settle in the bottom of your cup. Swirling the cup a few times while you drink helps to keep the spices suspended.

PER SERVING

Calories 35	Fat 1 gram (1 saturated)
Carbohydrate 6 grams	Fiber 0 grams
Protein 1 gram	Sodium 15 milligrams

Diabetic exchange = ½ Carbohydrate
WW point comparison = 1 point

Homemade Café Mocha Mix

Serves Fourteen

Café Mocha is clearly one of the most popular coffee drinks, and this mix really fits the bill. Not overly sweet, it has a rich coffee flavor, blended with a touch of chocolate and a hint of cinnamon. Keep a jar of it handy so you can prepare a cup anytime the mood hits.

INGREDIENTS:

- ⅔ **cup instant coffee (regular or decaffeinated)**
- ⅔ **cup Splenda Granular**
- ½ **cup nonfat dry milk powder**
- ½ **cup nondairy creamer**
- ⅓ **cup Dutch-process cocoa powder**
- ¼ **teaspoon cinnamon**

STEPS:

1. Measure all ingredients into a blender. Blend for 1 minute.
2. Pour mix into a jar or other airtight container.
3. To serve, stir 2 tablespoons of the dry mix into 6 ounces very hot water.

Cocoa powder contains all of the heart-healthy antioxidants without the added fat of solid chocolate.

PER SERVING (2 TABLESPOONS)

Calories 45	Fat 1 gram (0 saturated)
Carbohydrate 7 grams	Fiber 1 gram
Protein 2 grams	Sodium 15 milligrams

Diabetic exchange = ½ Carbohydrate
WW point comparison = 1 point

Homemade French Vanilla Coffee Mix

Serves Sixteen

Coffee aisles these days seem to be overflowing with expensive tins of flavored coffees. Here, a wonderful friend of mine created a creamy and very economical version of one of the most popular. For extra vanilla flavor, add one vanilla bean to dry mix and let sit for five days before using.

INGREDIENTS:

½ **cup instant coffee (regular or decaffeinated)**

1 **cup nonfat dry milk powder**

½ **cup nondairy dry creamer**

½ **cup Splenda Granular**

1 **box (1-ounce) sugar/fat-free vanilla pudding mix**

STEPS:

1. Measure all ingredients into a blender. Blend for 1 minute.

2. Pour mix into a jar or other airtight container.

3. To serve, stir 1 tablespoon dry mix into 6 ounces very hot water.

You may want to simply measure all the ingredients into a large tub and shake them together. Use 3 tablespoons of this mix for each serving.

PER SERVING

Calories 45   Fat 1 gram (0 saturated)
Carbohydrate 7 grams   Fiber 0 grams
Protein 2 grams   Sodium 105 milligrams

Diabetic exchange = ½ Carbohydrate
WW point comparison = 1 point

Good Mornings—
Breakfast and Brunch

Great Granola

Baked Oatmeal

Quick Cinnamon Bun Oatmeal Mix

Quick Cinnamon Rolls

Big, Bad Breakfast Cookies

Peanut Butter and Oats Breakfast Bar

Oatmeal Cookie Pancakes

High-Protein Cinnamon Pancakes

Lemon Cottage Cheese Pancakes

Apple Cinnamon Puffed Pancake

Crispy Cornmeal Waffles

Stuffed French Toast

Baked French Toast

Sweet Cinnamon French Toast

Blueberry-Topped Cheese Blintzes

Amazing Flourless Stuffed Crepes

Breakfast, as you probably learned in grade school, literally means to break the fast, and it does. As your first meal, breakfast refuels your body to get it ready for the busy day ahead. So, Mom was right when she told you it wasn't good to skip breakfast.

Studies show that those who eat breakfast are actually smarter (at least in the morning), thinner, lose more weight, and keep the weight off better than those who skip this important first meal of the day.

But I have some even better reasons to not skip breakfast—wonderful, sweet, warm, and delicious taste sensations you can make that are truly worth waking up for. Some of the newest recipes in my breakfast collection are Oatmeal Cookie Pancakes, Crispy Cornmeal Waffles, and Amazing Flourless Stuffed Crepes. All are made with wholesome whole grains, for a slow and steady fuel supply, and a healthy boost of fiber. Moreover, I know mornings can be extra busy, so my Quick Cinnamon Bun Oatmeal Mix can be whipped up in a jiffy, and Big Bad Breakfast Cookies can travel right along with you for an instant breakfast, or a healthy mid-morning snack. With a few more minutes in your morning routine, you can get your family dashing to the table for Sweet Cinnamon French Toast or Quick Cinnamon Rolls. And when you have even more time, I am delighted to be able to suggest beautiful Apple Cinnamon Puffed Pancake or creamy Blueberry-Topped Cheese Blintzes. Still feel like skipping breakfast?

Great Granola

Serves Eighteen

Granola is a "health" food that isn't always so healthy. Depending on how granola is made, it can be high in fat and/or sugar, making it a dense source of both calories and carbohydrates. This reduced-sugar and reduced-fat version is loaded with only with flavor and makes a great crunchy topping for yogurt or fruit.

INGREDIENTS:

3 cups old-fashioned rolled oats

1 ½ cups puffed wheat cereal

½ cup wheat germ

½ cup unsweetened coconut

½ cup sliced almonds

2 teaspoons cinnamon

¼ teaspoon salt

6 tablespoons sugar-free maple syrup

1 cup Splenda Granular

2 tablespoons canola oil

2 teaspoons molasses

2 teaspoons vanilla

2 large egg whites

⅓ cup dried cranberries or raisins

STEPS:

1. Preheat oven to 250°F.

2. Place oats, cereal, wheat germ, coconut, almonds, cinnamon, and salt in a large bowl.

3. In a small bowl, whisk together syrup, Splenda, oil, molasses, vanilla, and egg whites. Pour over cereal mixture and toss.

4. Spread granola onto a baking sheet or jellyroll pan and bake for 30 minutes. Stir and bake an additional 30 minutes.

5. Remove from oven and toss in dried cranberries.

When watching your waistline, granola is better by the handful than by the bowlful. Fill your bowl ¾ full with a lower-calorie, high-fiber cereal like bran flakes, then sprinkle on granola for a sweet crunchy finish.

PER SERVING (⅓ CUP)

Calories 125	Fat 5 grams (1 saturated)
Carbohydrate 16 grams	Fiber 3 grams
Protein 4 grams	Sodium 40 milligrams

Diabetic exchange = 1 Carbohydrate, 1 Fat
WW point comparison = 2 points

Baked Oatmeal

Serves Eight

This is the best oatmeal recipe I know. It puffs up as it bakes like a soufflé and is very creamy. It reminds me a bit of an oatmeal pudding, with the finished dish so sweet and flavorful that you don't need additional butter or sugar— just perhaps a splash of milk to top off each serving.

INGREDIENTS:

OATMEAL

2 cups old-fashioned oats, uncooked

½ cup Splenda Granular

½ cup Craisins★ or dried cranberries

½ teaspoon cinnamon

½ teaspoon salt

2 cups 1% milk

½ cup nonfat half-and-half

½ cup sugar-free maple syrup

4 large egg whites, lightly beaten

2 tablespoons margarine, melted

2 teaspoons vanilla

½ teaspoon orange zest (optional)

TOPPING

1 tablespoon brown sugar

1 tablespoon Splenda Granular

½ teaspoon cinnamon

STEPS:

1. Heat oven to 350°F. Spray 1 ½-quart soufflé dish with cooking spray.

2. In a large bowl, combine the oats, Splenda, Craisins, cinnamon, and salt; mix well.

3. In a medium bowl, combine milk and remaining liquid ingredients. Add milk mixture to dry ingredients and orange zest, stir. Pour into baking dish.

4. Bake for 30 minutes.

5. While baking, prepare topping: Combine brown sugar, Splenda, and cinnamon. Sprinkle on topping and bake for an additional 15-20 minutes or until center puffs slightly and is firm to the touch.

★ You may substitute raisins or eliminate craisins for a savings of 7 grams of carbohydrate and 30 calories per serving.

PER SERVING

Calories 190	Fat 4.5 grams (1 saturated)
Carbohydrate 24 grams	Fiber 2 grams
Protein 8 grams	Sodium 350 milligrams

Diabetic exchange = 1 Carbohydrate, 1 Fat, ½ Low-Fat Milk
WW point comparison = 4 points (3 without craisins)

Oatmeal is a wonderful source of soluble fiber, which helps to blunt the insulin response and lower the glycemic index of this healthful whole grain.

Quick Cinnamon Bun Oatmeal Mix

Serves Twelve

On busy mornings, instant packages of oatmeal can be a lifesaver. Just add boiling water and breakfast is on the table. You do, however, pay for the convenience—with your waist and your wallet. I've discovered it's just as quick and easy to whip up a batch of your own "packets," eliminating the sugar but keeping the sweet flavor you love.

INGREDIENTS:

3 cups instant oatmeal

Pinch salt

1 ½ cups Splenda Granular

3 teaspoons cinnamon

12 small plastic zip-lock bags

water

vanilla

STEPS:

1. In each bag, combine ⅓ cup instant oatmeal, pinch salt, 2 tablespoons Splenda Granular, and ¼ teaspoon cinnamon.

2. To use, combine the contents of one bag with ½ cup boiling water and ½ teaspoon vanilla. Stir and let set one minute to thicken.

PER SERVING

Calories 105

Carbohydrate 20 grams

Protein 3 grams

Fat 1.5 grams (0 saturated)

Fiber 3 grams

Sodium 150 milligrams

Diabetic exchange = 1 ½ Carbohydrate

WW point comparison = 2 points

Quick Cinnamon Rolls

Serves Ten

You won't have a problem getting the family to the breakfast table when you bake a pan full of these fragrant cinnamon rolls. Because you start with store-bought ready-made dough, they are quick and easy breakfast treats.

INGREDIENTS:

1 11-ounce tube of Pillsbury French loaf bread dough (refrigerated)

2 teaspoons flour

⅓ cup Splenda Granular

2 tablespoons dark brown sugar

2 teaspoons cinnamon

3 tablespoons margarine, softened

2 teaspoons powdered sugar

Need to watch the sugar in your diet? Then steer clear of the Cinnabon shop, where one cinnamon roll chocks up close to 100 grams of carbohydrate and 10-12 teaspoons of sugar.

STEPS:

1. Preheat oven to 375°F. Spray 9-inch round pan with nonstick cooking spray.

2. Open tube of bread dough. Set on work surface dusted with flour. Look for seam and unroll dough. Using rolling pin, shape into a 15 x 10-inch rectangle.

3. In a small bowl, combine Splenda, brown sugar, and cinnamon.

4. Spread margarine onto dough and evenly coat with cinnamon/sugar mixture.

5. Using hands, pat sugar mixture into margarine. Roll up jellyroll-style from the short (10-inch) side of dough. Wet the far edge of dough with water to seal roll. Turn dough onto seam, and using a sharp knife, cut into ten 1-inch slices. Place slices cut-side up in prepared pan and pat down slightly.

6. Bake for 18-20 minutes or until nicely browned.

7. Dust rolls with powdered sugar and serve. (Best while warm—reheat any leftover rolls briefly in microwave.)

PER SERVING

Calories 110

Carbohydrate 18 grams

Protein 3 grams

Fat 3 grams (1 saturated)

Fiber 0 grams

Sodium 260 milligrams

Diabetic exchange = 1 Carbohydrate, ½ Fat

WW point comparison = 2 points

Big, Bad Breakfast Cookies

Serves Thirteen

Cookies for breakfast? You bet! I picked up a cereal cookie at the store recently labeled "Breakfast on the Run." Reading the label, I realized I had better be on the run to burn it off. The palm-sized cookie equalled four bowls of cereal or four tall glasses of milk, and was creatively labeled as serving four people! Instead, try these big, ba-a-a-d cookies that do, in fact, make a wholesome meal on the run—even for breakfast.

INGREDIENTS:

1 cup all-purpose flour

1 cup whole-wheat pastry flour

1 ½ cups old-fashioned rolled oats

1 cup Splenda Granular

3 tablespoons brown sugar

1 ½ teaspoons baking soda

1 teaspoon baking powder

1 ½ teaspoons cinnamon

¼ cup chopped dried apricots

¼ cup chopped pecans

**1 2 ½-ounce jar baby food prunes
or ¼ cup prune puree**

3 tablespoons canola oil

3 tablespoons water

3 large egg whites

1 tablespoon molasses

2 teaspoons vanilla

STEPS:

1. Preheat oven to 350°F. Lightly spray a cookie sheet with nonstick cooking spray.

2. In a very large bowl, mix together the first 10 ingredients (flour through pecans). Set aside.

3. In a medium bowl, whisk together remaining 6 ingredients (prunes through vanilla). Pour prune mixture over dry ingredients. Mix with spoon to form a stiff dough.

4. For each cookie, scoop ¼ cup dough (using measuring cup or small ice-cream scoop) onto a cookie sheet and pat flat to form 3 ½- to 4-inch circle.

5. Bake for 12-15 minutes or until bottoms of cookies are dry. Remove from pan and place on wire rack to cool. (You may wrap, freeze, and thaw individual cookies.)

For variety, try different combinations of fruits and nuts. Some suggestions: dried cranberries or cherries and almonds, or raisins with walnuts.

PER SERVING

Calories 180	Fat 4.5 grams (0 saturated)
Carbohydrate 30 grams	Fiber 3 grams
Protein 5 grams	Sodium 190 milligrams

Diabetic exchange = 2 Carbohydrate, 1 Fat
WW point comparison = 3 points

Peanut Butter and Oats Breakfast Bar

Serves Eighteen

Wrapped up and ready-to-go breakfast bars are a popular food convenience. This simple and healthy version not only works for a quick breakfast with a glass of milk, but it also makes a great afternoon snack.

INGREDIENTS:

2 cups old-fashioned rolled oats

1 ½ cups crispy rice cereal (like Rice Krispies)

½ cup whole-wheat flour

⅓ cup chopped raisins

1 teaspoon cinnamon

¼ teaspoon salt

⅓ cup peanut butter

3 tablespoons margarine, melted

3 tablespoons honey

2 teaspoons molasses

1 cup Splenda Granular

4 large egg whites

1 teaspoon vanilla

STEPS:

1. Preheat oven to 350°F. Spray a 9 x 13-inch baking pan with nonstick cooking spray.

2. In a large bowl, mix together the first 6 ingredients (oats through salt). Set aside.

3. In a medium bowl, stir together remaining ingredients. Pour peanut butter mixture over oats and stir until well mixed.

4. Pat mixture into prepared pan and bake for 15 minutes. Cool and cut into 18 bars.

Breakfast bar or candy bar? Some "breakfast bars" get up to 33 percent of their calories (or 32 grams) from sugar and 50 percent (or 12 grams) from fat, with very little protein and fiber. They may be quick, but they're definitely not healthy.

PER SERVING

Calories 125	Fat 4 grams (1 saturated)
Carbohydrate 18 grams	Fiber 2 grams
Protein 4 grams	Sodium 110 milligrams

Diabetic exchange = 1 Carbohydrate, 1 Fat
WW point comparison = 2 points

Oatmeal Cookie Pancakes

Serves Six

Although these pancakes contain no refined flour at all, lots of testing ensured that they are a far cry from the flat, gummy pancakes often made with oatmeal. In fact, served up with sugar-free syrup, these are among my husband's favorite breakfast treats. To ensure the best rise, allow the batter to sit for five minutes before you begin cooking.

INGREDIENTS:

1 ½ cups old-fashioned oatmeal

2 cups + 2 tablespoons low-fat buttermilk

¾ cup whole-wheat pastry flour

⅓ cup Splenda Granular

1 teaspoon baking soda

½ teaspoon baking powder

1 large egg

3 teaspoons cinnamon

½ teaspoon vanilla

¼ teaspoon ground nutmeg

STEPS:

1. In a medium bowl, combine the oatmeal and the buttermilk. Stir in the flour, Splenda, baking soda, and baking powder.

2. Add the egg and stir to combine. Add the cinnamon, vanilla, and nutmeg and stir to combine. Let sit 5 minutes.

3. Spray a nonstick skillet with cooking spray and heat over medium heat.

4. Using ⅓ cup batter per pancake, pour 2 pancakes into the preheated pan. When the bottoms are golden brown and bubbles begin to form on top, flip them over and cook the other side for 3-4 minutes. Don't rush! These pancakes benefit from longer, slower cooking than all-purpose flour pancakes.

5. Remove to a platter and serve immediately with sugar-free syrup if desired.

A handful of banana slices (½ small banana) tastes great on these "cookie" cakes. Add some Canadian bacon and a small glass of low-fat milk, and you have a nutritionally complete breakfast for about 400 calories.

PER SERVING (TWO 4-INCH PANCAKES PER SERVING)

Calories 170	Fat 3 grams (1 saturated)
Carbohydrate 28 grams	Fiber 4 grams
Protein 9 grams	Sodium 350 milligrams

Diabetic exchange = 1 ½ Carbohydrate, ½ Low-Fat Milk
WW point comparison = 3 points

High-Protein Cinnamon Pancakes

Serves Four

I must admit that at first I was pretty skeptical of recipes that use protein powder in place of flour. But when an author I really admire used it in her pancakes, I figured it was worth a try. Much to my surprise, these cakes cooked up nice and light. Upon running the nutritional analysis, I was even more impressed—15 grams of protein in 2 pancakes, and a reduction of carbohydrate by 50 percent. Wow! These are terrific paired with Apple Cider Butter Syrup (page 432).

INGREDIENTS:

½ cup + 2 tablespoons all-purpose flour

½ cup protein powder

¼ cup Splenda Granular

1 teaspoon baking powder

1 teaspoon cinnamon

1 ½ cups buttermilk

1 tablespoon margarine or butter, melted

2 eggs, lightly beaten

I have discovered that the fluffy beige- or yellow-tinged soy-based protein powders found in bins or bags work better as a substitute for flour than the canned varieties, which I like for drinks. I tested these using Bob's Red Mill brand.

STEPS:

1. In a medium bowl, combine the dry ingredients.

2. In a small bowl, whisk together the buttermilk, melted margarine, and eggs. Stir into the dry ingredients, using a spoon or rubber spatula, just until all of the flour is moistened. Do not overmix.

3. Place a griddle or skillet over medium heat. Spray lightly with nonstick cooking spray.

4. Pour ¼ cup batter and spread into 4-inch circle for each pancake. Cook pancake for 3-4 minutes on first side until underside browns. Flip pancake and cook on second side 2-3 minutes.

5. Serve hot with syrup if desired.

PER SERVING (TWO 4-INCH PANCAKES PER SERVING)

Calories 170	Fat 5 grams (1.5 saturated)
Carbohydrate 18 grams	Fiber 1 gram
Protein 15 grams	Sodium 400 milligrams

Diabetic exchange = 2 Lean Meat, 1 Carbohydrate
WW point comparison = 4 points

Lemon Cottage Cheese Pancakes

Serves Three

These sweet lemon-flavored pancakes have a lot less flour than traditional pancakes and don't require additional butter or syrup, although a sprinkling of fresh raspberries is very nice. The cottage cheese adds protein and gives them a soft, pudding-like texture. PS: Thanks to Joe, who says these are now a Sunday tradition in his home.

INGREDIENTS:

2 large eggs

¾ cup low-fat cottage cheese

½ cup flour

⅓ cup Splenda Granular

2 tablespoons margarine, melted

1 tablespoon lemon juice

Zest of 1 lemon

½ teaspoon vanilla

3 teaspoons powdered sugar (optional)

STEPS:

1. In a large bowl, beat eggs. Add remaining ingredients (except powdered sugar) and mix until smooth.

2. Heat a large skillet or griddle and coat lightly with oil or cooking spray. When hot, ladle about 3 tablespoons of batter per pancake onto pan. Spread batter evenly to 3-inch diameter. Cook for 1–2 minutes until bottom is brown and firm. Flip pancake and cook until underside is browned. (For firmer pancakes, press lightly on pancake after turning.)

3. Place 3 pancakes on a plate and dust with 1 teaspoon of powdered sugar. Serve plain or with berries.

Compare: Three 4-inch frozen pancakes, with a mere teaspoon of butter and a tablespoon of syrup on each, contain 550 calories, 19 grams of fat, and 630 milligrams of sodium. They also give you only 6 grams of protein but a whopping 93 grams of carbohydrate.

PER SERVING (3 PANCAKES)

Calories 250   Fat 10 grams (2.5 saturated)
Carbohydrate 21 grams   Fiber 0 grams
Protein 14 grams   Sodium 340 milligrams

Diabetic exchange = 1 ½ Carbohydrate, 2 Fat
WW point comparison = 6 points

Apple Cinnamon Puffed Pancake

Serves Three

This pretty cinnamon-scented pancake "puff" is so delicious and sweet on its own that you only need to add a light dusting of powdered sugar to finish it off. I serve it up with lean ham or sausage and a few slices of fresh orange for an extra-special breakfast.

INGREDIENTS:

2 teaspoons butter

2 teaspoons brown sugar

1 small apple, peeled, cored, and finely diced

⅔ cup 1% milk

2 large eggs + 1 egg white

½ cup flour

¼ cup Splenda Granular

¾ teaspoon cinnamon

½ teaspoon vanilla

1 teaspoon powdered sugar, optional

STEPS:

1. Preheat oven to 425°F. Melt butter in a 10-inch ovenproof skillet.

2. Add brown sugar and diced apple and sauté for 3-4 minutes to soften apple.

3. In a medium bowl, whisk together milk, eggs, flour, Splenda, cinnamon, and vanilla until smooth.

4. Pour into the hot pan over the cooked apple and immediately place in hot oven.

5. Bake for 15 minutes at 425°F, lower oven to 375°F, and bake an additional 10-15 minutes or until pancake has risen and edges are curled up and browned.

6. Dust with powdered sugar if desired and serve.

PER SERVING

Calories 210	Fat 7 grams (2.5 saturated)
Carbohydrate 26 grams	Fiber 2 grams
Protein 9 grams	Sodium 120 milligrams

Diabetic exchange = 1 ½ Carbohydrate, 1 Fat
WW point comparison = 4 points

Just 2 tablespoons of syrup have as much carbohydrate as an entire serving of this flavorful sweetened pancake.

Crispy Cornmeal Waffles

Serves Six

A touch of cornmeal and a beaten egg white that you fold into the batter keeps these waffles crisp and light. To make sure they cook up nice and crisp, allow plenty of time in the waffle maker (to brown, they may take longer than your "done light" setting allows).

INGREDIENTS:

¼ **cup all-purpose flour**

½ **cup cornmeal flour**

¼ **cup cornstarch**

¼ **teaspoon salt**

½ **teaspoon baking powder**

¼ **teaspoon baking soda**

2 **tablespoons Splenda Granular (or 3 packets)**

1 **cup low-fat buttermilk**

3 **tablespoons canola oil**

1 **large egg, separated**

½ **teaspoon vanilla**

STEPS:

1. Preheat the waffle iron.

2. In a medium bowl, combine flour, cornmeal, cornstarch, salt, baking powder, and baking soda. Whisk to combine.

3. In a separate bowl, combine buttermilk, canola oil, egg yolk, and vanilla, and whisk to combine.

4. In a small bowl, beat the egg white to stiff but not dry peaks.

5. Pour the buttermilk mixture into the dry ingredients and stir to combine. Gently fold in the egg white.

6. Using approximately ⅓ cup batter, drop mixture into preheated waffle iron and cook until golden brown on both sides and steam is no longer escaping from the waffle iron.

You'll find lots of terrific low-sugar toppings in the Sweet Embellishments section of the book. I love combining these waffles with the Sweet Cherry Topping or Blueberry Sauce, but these waffles are sweet and delicious even plain.

PER SERVING (ONE 4-INCH WAFFLE)

Calories 170	Fat 8 grams (1 saturated)
Carbohydrate 19 grams	Fiber 1 gram
Protein 4 grams	Sodium 220 milligrams

Diabetic exchange = 1 Carbohydrate, 2 Fat

WW point comparison = 4 points

Stuffed French Toast

Serves Eight

When stuffed with sweet strawberry cream cheese, French toast becomes an extraordinary breakfast. This rich-tasting recipe finished off in the oven serves eight, making it an ideal recipe for a special occasion. Serve with lean ham and fresh strawberries for a beautiful brunch.

INGREDIENTS:

FILLING

8 ounces tub-style light cream cheese

¼ cup Splenda Granular

2 tablespoons low-sugar strawberry (or other fruit) preserves

EGG MIXTURE

2 large eggs + 2 egg whites

½ cup nonfat half-and-half

½ cup 1% milk

¼ cup Splenda Granular

2 tablespoons flour

2 teaspoons baking powder

1 teaspoon vanilla

FRENCH TOAST

16 pieces Italian or French bread (1 ½ pounds)

1 tablespoon powdered sugar (optional)

STEPS:

1. Preheat oven to 400°F. Spray baking sheet with cooking spray. Heat griddle or large skillet coated with nonstick cooking spray to medium.

2. FILLING: In a small bowl, blend together cream cheese, Splenda, and preserves. Set aside.

3. EGG MIXTURE: In a medium bowl, whisk together eggs, half-and-half, milk, Splenda, flour, baking powder, and vanilla. Set aside.

4. Spread 2 tablespoons of cream cheese mixture onto half of the bread slices. Top each slice with another piece of bread and press together. Soak each sandwich in egg mixture until saturated but not falling apart. Place sandwich in hot skillet and cook until one side is golden brown. Turn and cook until second side is golden brown. Transfer each piece to baking sheet.

5. Baked sautéed slices until puffed up and golden brown, about 5 minutes. Dust powdered sugar over tops and serve immediately.

PER SERVING

Calories 270	Fat 7 grams (3 saturated)
Carbohydrate 39 grams	Fiber 2 grams
Protein 12 grams	Sodium 600 milligrams

Diabetic exchange = 2 ½ Carbohydrate, 1 ½ Lean Meat
WW point comparison = 5 points

Baked French Toast

Serves Twelve

I would like to thank Louise Huskins for this recipe—again. She told me that the idea came to her when a friend had made a similar recipe for Christmas breakfast. Louise refined her recipe with techniques she learned from my first Splenda cookbook. She was so pleased with her results that she sent this recipe to me on Christmas morning—what a great Christmas gift!

INGREDIENTS:

4 ounces tub-style light cream cheese

4 ounces tub-style fat-free cream cheese

¾ cup Splenda Granular

3 tablespoons margarine, softened

2 teaspoons vanilla

1 ½ teaspoons cinnamon

1 cup egg substitute (like Egg Beaters)

2 large eggs

3 cups 1% milk

1 pound cinnamon raisin, French, or wheat bread (1-inch slices)

2 teaspoons powdered sugar (optional)

STEPS:

1. Spray a 9 x 13-inch baking dish or 2 smaller (9 x 9-inch) baking pans with nonstick cooking spray.

2. In a large bowl, beat cream cheeses, Splenda, margarine, vanilla, and cinnamon until smooth. Blend in egg substitute (¼ cup at a time) and then eggs.

3. Add milk and mix well. Soak bread slices in egg mixture and place into prepared pan. Pour remaining batter over slices. Cover and refrigerate for at least 1 hour and even overnight.

4. Preheat oven to 350°F. Bake for 40-45 minutes until puffed in center and lightly browned.

5. Remove from oven and lightly dust with powdered sugar if desired.

PER SERVING

Calories 210	Fat 7 grams (0 saturated)
Carbohydrate 24 grams	Fiber 2 grams
Protein 11 grams	Sodium 320 milligrams

Diabetic exchange = 1 Carbohydrate, ½ Low-Fat Milk, 1 Medium-Fat Meat

WW point comparison = 4 points

For my last Christmas Brunch, I served this with Boysenberry Syrup (page 431) and fresh berries along with fresh scrambled eggs, Canadian bacon, and Café Orange (page 60).

Sweet Cinnamon French Toast

Serves Four

Traditional French toast recipes are often made with cream and butter. This version cuts down on the fat and calories while retaining all of the flavor. Serve with one of the new Splenda-sweetened sugar-free syrups or your favorite low-sugar jam.

INGREDIENTS:

1 large egg + 2 egg whites

1 cup 1% milk

2 tablespoons Splenda Granular

¾ teaspoon vanilla

½ teaspoon cinnamon

8 slices cinnamon swirl bread (I use Pepperidge Farm Cinnamon Swirl)

STEPS:

1. Coat griddle or large skillet with nonstick cooking spray and heat to medium.

2. In a shallow bowl, whisk together all ingredients except bread. Soak slices of bread, one by one, in egg mixture until saturated but not falling apart.

3. Place bread into hot skillet and cook until underside is golden brown. Turn and cook until second side is golden brown. Serve immediately.

When made with cream, this recipe contains 30 grams of fat—half of it saturated.

PER SERVING (2 SLICES)

Calories 220	Fat 7 grams (2 saturated)
Carbohydrate 32 grams	Fiber 4 grams
Protein 11 grams	Sodium 300 milligrams

Diabetic exchange = 2 Carbohydrate, 1 Fat
WW point comparison = 4 points

Blueberry-Topped Cheese Blintzes

Serves Eight

A Jewish cousin of French crepes, blintzes also start with a crepe batter. The crepes are filled, and then the loose crepe ends are "tucked" to create a nice, plump package. Like the chefs at many Jewish delis, I stuff these with a sweet cottage-cheese filling and then adorn them with fruit topping.

INGREDIENTS:

1 recipe Blueberry Sauce (page 426)

1 ¼ cups low-fat cottage cheese

3 tablespoons light cream cheese

1 large egg

1 ½ tablespoons Splenda Granular (or 2 Splenda packets)

¼ teaspoon vanilla extract

½ teaspoon lemon zest

Crepe Batter (page 278)

The options for topping these blintzes are endless. In the Sweet Embellishments section (page 419), you will also find Sweet Cherry Topping and a chunky Strawberry Sauce. You may also want to try them with Boysenberry Syrup or a favorite of mine, Hot Lemon Sauce.

STEPS:

1. Make Blueberry Sauce according to directions. Do not strain and set aside.

2. If cottage cheese has a lot of liquid, drain by placing in a colander and pressing on curds to remove excess. Place in a medium bowl and beat with an electric mixer to break up curds.

3. Add cream cheese, egg, Splenda, vanilla, and zest. Continue to beat until curds are mostly broken down and mixture is creamy (you may also use a blender or food processor, but don't overprocess or mixture will become too thin). Refrigerate.

4. Make crepes according to recipe. To assemble, place 3 tablespoons cheese filling down the middle of a crepe, leaving ¾ inch on each end bare. Fold crepe over filling and then fold in sides. Lastly, fold the remaining side up over filling to create filled package. Repeat to form 8 blintzes.

5. Place blintzes in a 9 x 13-inch pan sprayed with cooking spray. At this point, you can cover the blintzes and refrigerate them.

6. Preheat oven to 400°F. Brush blitzes with melted butter and place in oven.

7. Heat for 10 minutes if they're room temperature, 15–18 minutes if cold.

8. Top each blintz with 3 tablespoons warm Blueberry Sauce before serving.

PER SERVING

Calories 155	Fat 6 grams (2 saturated)
Carbohydrate 16 grams	Fiber 1 gram
Protein 9 grams	Sodium 240 milligrams

Diabetic exchange = 1 Lean Meat, ½ Carbohydrate, ½ Fruit, ½ Fat

WW point comparison = 3 points

Amazing Flourless Stuffed Crepes

Serves Two

A crepe without flour? Developed on a whim when a batter was a bit too thin, these delicious stuffed crepes offer another great alternative to refined flour pancakes. It's a bit harder to turn, but you can create one large, dramatic crepe by using a 10-inch nonstick pan and double the batter you normally use for each crepe.

INGREDIENTS:

CREPES

½ **cup oatmeal**

¼ **cup low-fat cottage cheese**

1 **large egg**

¼ **cup water**

1 **tablespoon Splenda Granular**
  (or 2 Splenda packets)

½ **teaspoon cinnamon**

2 **teaspoons butter, melted**

Pinch nutmeg

Pinch salt

FILLING

¾ **cup low-fat cottage cheese**

1 **tablespoon Splenda Granular**
  (or 2 Splenda packets)

½ **cup fresh raspberries**

2 **teaspoons powdered sugar**

STEPS:

1. CREPES: Combine crepe ingredients in a blender and blend until very smooth.

2. Heat a 6-inch nonstick skillet over medium-high heat until hot.

3. For each crepe, pour 3 tablespoons of batter into the skillet and quickly swirl the pan until batter thinly coats the entire bottom. Cook approximately 1 minute or until small bubbles appear on top. Gently turn and cook other side 30 seconds and remove to a plate.

4. FILLING: In a small bowl, combine cottage cheese and Splenda.

5. Spoon 3 tablespoons of sweetened cottage cheese into crepe. Add ¼ of the raspberries. Fold the crepe gently over the top. Repeat to create 4 stuffed crepes. Place on 2 plates and dust with powdered sugar.

PER SERVING

Calories 240	Fat 7 grams (3 saturated)
Carbohydrate 24 grams	Fiber 4 grams
Protein 21 grams	Sodium 460 milligrams

Diabetic exchange = 1 Carbohydrate, 3 Very Lean Meat, ½ Fruit, 1 Fat

WW point comparison = 5 points

For variety, fill crepes with flavored light yogurt or low-fat ricotta sweetened with Splenda, and your own favorite fresh fruit.

Marvelous Muffins and Scrumptious Scones

Oat Bran Apricot Muffins

Oatmeal Muffins

Best Bran Muffins

Banana Bran Muffins

Blueberry Muffins

Blueberry Corn Muffins

Fresh Carrot Muffins

Chocolate Cherry Muffins

Sour Cream Chocolate Chocolate
     Chip Muffins

Spicy Pumpkin Muffins

Strawberry-Filled Cinnamon Muffins

Lemon Cheese Danish Muffins

Cranberry Orange Muffins

Apple Oatmeal Streusel Muffins

Quick Chocolate Chip Muffins

Fresh Blueberry Scones

Pumpkin Scones

Orange Ginger Scones

Maple Oat Scones

Fresh Raspberry Lemon Scones

Muffins are marvelous, and scones are scrumptious. They're both easy to make, don't take long to bake, come in lots of great flavors, are easy to tote or carry, and don't even require utensils to eat them. No wonder they're so popular.

The downside is that the more popular they have become, the larger they have become, literally—in size, fat, sugar, and calories. The ones you now find at the market or coffee shop have more than 500 calories, and up to 30 grams of fat and 75 grams of carbohydrate!

But thanks to Splenda and some innovative ways to cut the fat, you can make your own delicious muffins and scones with a fraction of the fat and sugar in the perfect size to enjoy as a snack or as part of a healthy breakfast. And if you do want to create them oversized—it's no problem—just fill jumbo muffin tins two-thirds full or drop or cut twice the amount of scone dough and bake them an extra 5 to 8 minutes. (But don't forget to double the calories.)

Here are a few additional tips about these very quick "quickbreads" that will keep them consistently marvelous and always scrumptious.

» Never overmix muffin or scone batter, it toughens the dough. Gently stir liquid ingredients into dry ingredients with a large spoon or spatula just until the flour is wet. Small lumps in the batter are normal.

» Don't overknead scone batter. Place barely mixed dough onto a hard surface and lift dough up and over itself only until batter is uniform for rolling or cutting.

» Be careful not to overbake. Splenda creates faster baking, and low-fat batters can be dry if overbaked.

» Cool just-baked muffins and scones in the pan on a wire rack for a few minutes before removing from pans.

» Muffins and scones are best the day they are made. Wrap leftovers tightly or place in airtight containers or freeze. Rewarm briefly in the microwave.

Oat Bran Apricot Muffins

Serves Twelve

Oat bran is a great source of soluble fiber—the kind of fiber that helps to lower cholesterol and control your blood sugar. Here, I've paired oat bran with whole-wheat flour and served it up in a moist yet low-fat muffin that's dotted with pieces of chewy dried apricots and crunchy pecans.

INGREDIENTS:

¾ cup 1% milk

½ cup light orange juice

2 tablespoons canola oil

1 3.5-ounce container strained apricots (like Gerber's baby food)

1 large egg + 1 large egg white

1 ½ cups unprocessed oat bran

1 cup whole-wheat pastry flour

½ cup Splenda Granular

1 tablespoon baking powder

½ teaspoon baking soda

1 ½ teaspoons cinnamon

¼ cup chopped dried apricots

¼ cup chopped pecans

STEPS:

1. Preheat oven to 425°F. Spray standard 12-cup muffin tin with nonstick cooking spray.

2. In a small bowl, whisk together milk, orange juice, canola oil, baby food, and eggs. Set aside.

3. In a large bowl, combine remaining dry ingredients. Stir. Add apricots and pecans and stir. Make a well and add liquid mixture. Using a large spoon or spatula, stir just until dry ingredients are moistened. Let set for 3 minutes to thicken.

4. Spoon batter into prepared muffin tins.

5. Bake for 16–18 minutes or until center springs back when lightly touched. Cool for 5 minutes before removing to a wire rack.

Most oat bran muffins come in one of two varieties—delicious but short on oat bran and high in sugar and fat, or healthful and bran-filled but dry and short on taste. These muffins finally combine the best of both worlds: you get good taste and good health.

PER SERVING

Calories 125	Fat 5 grams (1 saturated)
Carbohydrate 20 grams	Fiber 3 grams
Protein 5 grams	Sodium 135 milligrams

Diabetic exchange = 1 Carbohydrate, 1 Fat
WW point comparison = 2 points

Oatmeal Muffins

Serves Ten

Healthy ingredients like oats and whole-wheat flour are good for you but can weigh muffins down. To counter this, I have updated this recipe with a creaming technique that helps to give this muffin more lift. What I haven't changed is its great taste of oatmeal, with everyone's favorite toppings.

INGREDIENTS:

MUFFIN BATTER

3 tablespoons margarine, room temperature

1 tablespoon brown sugar

⅔ cup Splenda Granular

1 egg + 1 egg white

1 cup uncooked old-fashioned oats (not quick-cooking)

¾ cup all-purpose flour

½ cup whole-wheat pastry flour

¼ cup nonfat dry milk

1 teaspoon baking powder

¾ teaspoon baking soda

1 ½ teaspoons cinnamon

¾ cup 1% milk

TOPPING

1 tablespoon brown sugar

1 tablespoon Splenda Granular

½ teaspoon cinnamon

STEPS:

1. Preheat oven to 350°F. Spray standard 12-cup muffin tin with nonstick cooking spray.

2. BATTER: In a large bowl, with an electric mixer, cream margarine and brown sugar until light and creamy. Beat in Splenda. Beat in egg and then egg white. Set aside.

3. In a medium bowl, combine oats, both types of flour, dry milk, baking powder, baking soda, and cinnamon. Using a large spoon or spatula, lightly stir ½ of the flour mixture into creamed mixture. Stir in ½ of the 1% milk. Repeat with the rest, stirring just until blended.

4. Spoon batter into prepared muffin tins.

5. TOPPING: Combine brown sugar, Splenda, and cinnamon. Sprinkle over muffins. Bake for 20 minutes or until center springs back when lightly touched. Cool for 5 minutes before removing to a wire rack. (These are best served the day they are baked.)

PER SERVING

Calories 140	Fat 4 grams (1 saturated)
Carbohydrate 21 grams	Fiber 2 grams
Protein 5 grams	Sodium 180 milligrams

Diabetic exchange = 1 ½ Carbohydrate, 1 Fat
WW point comparison = 3 points

Oats are a great source of soluble fiber and may help reduce cholesterol when consumed regularly.

Best Bran Muffins

Serves Eight

While everyone assumes bran muffins are good for you, most of them are chock-full of sugar and fat. Bursting with flavor, these dark and moist muffins pack a generous 5 grams of fiber, along with vitamin C and iron, without the stuff you don't want (or need). Like many muffins, they are at their best shortly after they are baked; however, you can make the batter ahead of time.

INGREDIENTS:

2 large egg whites

1 cup low-fat buttermilk

1 ½ cups 100% bran cereal (not flakes)

3 tablespoons molasses

2 tablespoons canola oil

1 teaspoon finely grated orange peel

½ cup all-purpose flour

½ cup whole-wheat flour

½ cup Splenda Granular

1 teaspoon baking soda

1 ½ teaspoons baking powder

½ teaspoon cream of tartar

¼ cup finely chopped dried cranberries, raisins, or nuts★

STEPS

1. Preheat oven to 375°F. Spray 8 muffin cups in standard muffin tin with nonstick cooking spray.

2. In a medium bowl, whip the egg whites and buttermilk until frothy. Add the bran cereal, molasses, oil, orange peel, and cranberries, raisins, or nuts, if desired, and set aside for 5 minutes.

3. Measure flours, Splenda, baking soda, baking powder, and cream of tartar into a large bowl. Stir to mix. Make a well in the center and pour in the bran mixture. Using a large spoon or spatula, stir just until dry ingredients are moistened.

4. Spoon batter into muffin cups, filling ¾ full.

5. Bake for 18 minutes or until a center springs back when lightly touched. Cool for 5 minutes before removing to a wire rack. Store in an airtight container.

PER SERVING

Calories 160	Fat 4.5 grams (.5 saturated)
Carbohydrate 29 grams	Fiber 5 grams
Protein 5 grams	Sodium 325 milligrams

Diabetic exchange = 1 ½ Bread, ½ Fat
WW point comparison = 3 points
★ For dried fruit, add 3 grams carbohydrate and 12 calories per serving. For nuts, add 0.5 grams carbohydrate, 2 grams fat, and 24 calories per serving.

Foods high in fiber help keep blood sugar levels on an even keel. The recommended guideline for fiber intake for adults is 28 grams per day on a 2,000-calorie diet.

Banana Bran Muffins

Serves Twelve

These muffins are so wonderfully moist, light, and loaded with fresh banana that you'd never guess that they are so low in fat and so high in fiber.

INGREDIENTS:

1 cup mashed banana (about 2 medium bananas)

1 cup unsweetened shredded bran cereal (like All-Bran)

¼ cup buttermilk

2 large egg whites

2 tablespoons canola oil

2 teaspoons molasses

1 teaspoon vanilla

1 cup all-purpose flour

¼ cup Splenda Granular

1 teaspoon baking soda

1 teaspoon baking powder

½ teaspoon cream of tartar

STEPS:

1. Preheat oven to 400°F. Spray standard 12-cup muffin tin with nonstick cooking spray.

2. In a medium bowl, stir together the first 7 ingredients (banana through vanilla). Set aside for at least 5 minutes to soften bran.

3. In a large bowl, combine flour, Splenda, baking soda, baking powder, and cream of tartar. Stir; make a well in the center and add the banana mixture. Using a large spoon or spatula, stir just until dry ingredients are moistened.

4. Spoon batter into prepared muffin tins.

5. Bake for 15 minutes or until center springs back when lightly touched. Cool for 5 minutes before removing to a wire rack.

PER SERVING

Calories 110	Fat 3 grams (0 saturated)
Carbohydrate 19 grams	Fiber 3 grams
Protein 3 grams	Sodium 220 milligrams

Diabetic exchange = 1 Carbohydrate, ½ Fat

WW point comparison = 2 points

For these muffins, be sure to use only shredded bran cereal, not bran flakes or powdered unprocessed bran.

Blueberry Muffins

Serves Twelve

The most popular muffin? Why, blueberry, of course. These moist low-fat muffins are a breeze to make and a joy to eat. These can be made with frozen berries but are an extra-special treat when fresh blueberries are available. The lemon yogurt helps to keep them moist and adds a nice flavor.

INGREDIENTS:

1 large egg

3 tablespoons canola oil

½ cup Splenda Granular

1 8-ounce cup low-fat lemon yogurt

6 tablespoons 1% milk

1 ½ teaspoons vanilla

2 cups all-purpose flour

1 tablespoon baking powder

½ teaspoon baking soda

1 cup blueberries (don't thaw if frozen)

1 teaspoon finely grated lemon peel

1 ½ teaspoons sugar (optional, for tops)

STEPS:

1. Preheat oven to 375°F. Spray standard 12-cup muffin tin with nonstick cooking spray.

2. In a small bowl, whisk egg until frothy. Add oil, Splenda, yogurt, milk, and vanilla. Whisk until smooth.

3. In a large bowl, combine flour, baking powder, and baking soda. Stir. Add blueberries and lemon peel. Make a well in the dry ingredients and pour in the yogurt mixture. Using a large spoon or spatula, stir just until dry ingredients are moistened.

4. Spoon batter into muffin tins, filling each cup ⅔ full. If desired, sprinkle sugar lightly over muffins.

5. Bake for 18-20 minutes, or until center springs back when lightly touched. Cool for 5 minutes before removing to a wire rack.

Do not substitute "light" or low-calorie lemon yogurt. The sugar in the regular low-fat yogurt helps the muffin sides and bottoms brown. Remember, each muffin has only a touch of sweetened yogurt in it.

PER SERVING

Calories 145	Fat 4.5 grams (.5 saturated)
Carbohydrate 23 grams	Fiber 0.5 grams
Protein 4 grams	Sodium 200 milligrams

Diabetic exchange = 1 ½ Carbohydrate, ½ Fat
WW point comparison = 3 points

Blueberry Corn Muffins
Serves Twelve

This new addition to my muffin collection is made with Splenda-Sugar Blend for Baking. Bursting with blueberries and a touch of cornmeal, these muffins are truly treats. Better yet, I guarantee no one will ever guess that they contain only half the sugar and fat of their commercial counterparts. Put them out at your next brunch and watch them disappear.

INGREDIENTS:

1 cup + 2 tablespoons buttermilk

1 large egg

3 tablespoons butter, melted

½ teaspoon vanilla

Zest of 1 orange

1 ½ cups flour

½ cup cornmeal

2 teaspoons baking powder

½ teaspoon baking soda

¼ cup Splenda Sugar Blend

1 generous cup blueberries

STEPS:

1. Preheat oven to 425°F. Spray a standard 12-cup muffin tin with nonstick cooking spray.

2. In a medium bowl, combine buttermilk, egg, butter, vanilla, and orange zest. Set aside.

3. In a large bowl, combine flour, cornmeal, baking powder, baking soda, and Splenda. Stir to combine. Gently stir in blueberries. Make a well in the center and add the liquid mixture. Using a large spoon or spatula, stir just until all of the dry ingredients are moistened.

4. Spoon batter into prepared muffin tins.

5. Bake for 15–17 minutes or until center springs back when lightly touched. Cool for 5 minutes before removing to a wire rack.

PER SERVING
Calories 115	Fat 3.5 grams (2 saturated)
Carbohydrate 17 grams	Fiber 1 gram
Protein 3 grams	Sodium 160 milligrams

Diabetic exchange = 1 Carbohydrate, 1 Fat
WW point comparison = 2 points

Fresh Carrot Muffins

Serves Twelve

Moist, sweet, and spicy, these muffins are terrific. I reworked this recipe several times to make sure these muffins were every bit as good as the ones I enjoy from the bakery near my home. When all my tasters loved them as much as I do, I knew I had it right.

INGREDIENTS:

¾ cup buttermilk

3 tablespoons canola oil

1 tablespoon molasses

1 small jar or package baby food prunes
  or ¼ cup prune puree

1 large egg + 1 egg white

1 cup shredded carrots

¾ cup whole-wheat flour

¾ cup all-purpose flour

1 cup Splenda Granular

1 ½ teaspoons baking soda

1 teaspoon baking powder

1 ½ teaspoons cinnamon

½ teaspoon allspice

¼ teaspoon ground cloves

⅓ cup raisins, chopped

STEPS:

1. Preheat oven to 375°F. Spray standard 12-cup muffin tin with nonstick cooking spray.

2. In a medium bowl, stir together the first 7 ingredients (buttermilk through carrots). Set aside.

3. In a large bowl, combine flours, Splenda, baking soda, baking powder, spices, and raisins. Stir; make a well in the center of the dry ingredients and add the liquid mixture. Using a large spoon or spatula, stir just until dry ingredients are moistened.

4. Spoon batter into prepared muffin tin.

5. Bake for 20 minutes or until center springs back when lightly touched. Cool for 5 minutes before removing to a wire rack.

VARIATION: Substitute chopped nuts for the raisins (adds 2 grams fat and 10 calories but subtracts 3 grams of carbohydrate).

PER SERVING

Calories 130	Fat 4 grams (0 saturated)
Carbohydrate 20 grams	Fiber 3 grams
Protein 4 grams	Sodium 180 milligrams

Diabetic exchange = 1 Carbohydrate, 1 Vegetable, 1 Fat
WW point comparison = 2 points

Serving suggestion: Place these on a table with a bowl of Orange Cream Cheese (page 434) or Low-Sugar Marmalade instead of calorie-laden butter.

Chocolate Cherry Muffins

Serves Twelve

My inspiration here was to create a muffin reminiscent of a classic Black Forest cake. The result—a cherry-studded muffin that's wonderfully fudgy and decadent enough to be served as a cupcake.

INGREDIENTS:

1 ½ cups frozen unsweetened dark cherries, partially thawed, cut in half

1 cup + 2 tablespoons Splenda Granular

¾ teaspoon almond extract

¾ cup 1% milk

½ cup unsweetened applesauce

3 tablespoons canola oil

3 tablespoons brown sugar

2 egg whites

1 teaspoon vanilla

1 ½ cups all-purpose flour

⅓ cup Dutch-process cocoa powder

1 ½ teaspoons baking powder

½ teaspoon baking soda

2 teaspoons powdered sugar

STEPS:

1. Preheat oven to 375°F. Spray standard 12-cup muffin tin with nonstick baking spray.

2. In a small bowl, stir together cherries, 2 tablespoons Splenda, and almond extract. Set aside.

3. In a medium bowl, whisk together next 6 ingredients (milk through vanilla). Set aside.

4. In a large bowl, combine flour, 1 cup Splenda, cocoa powder, baking powder, and baking soda. Stir; make a well in the center of the dry ingredients and add liquid mixture. Using a large spoon or spatula, stir just until dry ingredients are moistened. Carefully stir in cherries, taking care not to overmix.

5. Spoon batter into prepared muffin cups.

6. Bake for 18-20 minutes or until center springs back when lightly touched. Cool for 5 minutes before removing to a rack. Dust with powdered sugar by pressing it through a fine mesh strainer.

PER SERVING

Calories 145	Fat 5 grams (0 saturated)
Carbohydrate 22 grams	Fiber 1 gram
Protein 3 grams	Sodium 220 milligrams

Diabetic exchange = 1 ½ Carbohydrate, 1 Fat

WW point comparison = 3 points

Dutch-process cocoa, like Hershey's European or Special Dark brand, is less acidic and therefore less bitter and richer in color than traditional cocoa powder.

Sour Cream Chocolate Chocolate Chip Muffins

Serves Twelve

I must admit just seeing the word "chocolate" twice in the title is enough to make me take notice. This is "dessert for breakfast" at its best. These light-textured muffins are so rich with chocolate my son had me make them for his classroom for birthday treats. Serve them up with a nice glass of cold milk.

INGREDIENTS:

1 ½ cups all-purpose flour

⅓ cup Dutch-process cocoa powder (like Hershey's European or Special Dark)

1 ½ teaspoons baking powder

½ teaspoon baking soda

⅓ cup mini semisweet chocolate chips

3 tablespoons brown sugar

2 egg whites

3 tablespoons canola oil

½ cup unsweetened applesauce

⅔ cup 1% or skim milk

¼ cup light or nonfat sour cream

1 cup Splenda Granular

1 teaspoon vanilla

2 teaspoons powdered sugar

STEPS:

1. Preheat oven to 375°F. Spray standard 12-cup muffin tin with nonstick cooking spray.

2. Sift flour, cocoa powder, baking powder, and baking soda into a large bowl. Stir in chocolate chips. Add brown sugar. Set aside.

3. In a medium bowl, whisk egg whites until frothy. Stir in next 6 ingredients (oil through vanilla). Make a well in the center of the dry ingredients and pour in the liquid mixture. Using a large spoon or spatula, mix just until all the flour is moistened. Do not overmix.

4. Spoon batter into prepared muffin tin. Bake for 15-18 minutes or until center springs back when lightly touched. Cool for 5 minutes before moving to a wire rack.

5. Use a small sifter or mesh strainer to sprinkle powdered sugar over tops of muffins (this accounts for less than ½ gram carbohydrate per muffin).

PER SERVING

Calories 155	Fat 6 grams (1.5 saturated)
Carbohydrate 24 grams	Fiber 2 grams
Protein 4 grams	Sodium 135 milligrams

Diabetic exchange = 1 ½ Carbohydrate, 1 Fat
WW point comparison = 3 points

Two ways to incorporate the great flavor of chocolate into low-fat recipes is to use cocoa powder and mini chocolate chips (they disperse better so you can use less).

Spicy Pumpkin Muffins

Serves Ten

One of my most dog-eared recipes in my dessert book—Unbelievable Desserts with Splenda—is the Pumpkin Pecan Bread. I have been asked many times whether it can be baked up as muffins (and it can), but I have also taken that bread recipe one step further and revised it into a delectable dark and spicier pumpkin muffin, which also works as a quick bread. If you're looking for a recipe to serve during the winter holidays, these delicious muffins are a perfect choice.

INGREDIENTS:

¾ cup pumpkin puree

1 cup Splenda Granular

6 tablespoons buttermilk

3 tablespoons canola oil

3 tablespoons molasses

1 large egg + 1 large egg white

1 ½ cups all-purpose flour

2 teaspoons baking powder

½ teaspoon baking soda

1 ½ teaspoons cinnamon

1 teaspoon ginger

½ teaspoon allspice

¼ teaspoon cloves

¼ teaspoon salt

STEPS:

1. Preheat oven to 375°F. Spray 10 muffin cups in standard muffin tin with nonstick cooking spray.

2. In a medium bowl, stir together the first 7 ingredients (pumpkin through eggs). Set aside.

3. In a large bowl, combine flour, baking powder, baking soda, spices, and salt. Stir; make a well in the center of the dry ingredients and add the pumpkin mixture. With a large spoon or spatula, stir just until blended.

4. Spoon batter into prepared muffin tin.

5. Bake for 20 minutes or until center springs back when lightly touched. Cool in pan for 5 minutes before removing to a wire rack.

PER SERVING

Calories 150	Fat 5 grams (0 saturated)
Carbohydrate 22 grams	Fiber 1 gram
Protein 4 grams	Sodium 180 milligrams

Diabetic exchange = 1 ½ Carbohydrate, 1 Fat
WW point comparison = 3 points

Strawberry-Filled Cinnamon Muffins

Serves Ten

While I was on the Internet one day, I came across this tasty jam-filled muffin by way of Cooking Light magazine. Because it had garnered great compliments, I decided that a low-sugar makeover was in order. It took me a few tries to get it right, but the effort was certainly worth it. A basket of these fresh-baked muffins would be perfect for breakfast guests.

INGREDIENTS:

6-ounce nonfat vanilla yogurt (like Yoplait, not light)

3 tablespoons butter, melted

1 large egg

½ cup 1% milk

1 ¾ cups all-purpose flour

½ cup Splenda Granular

1 tablespoon baking powder

1 ½ teaspoons cinnamon

⅛ teaspoon salt

10 teaspoons low-sugar strawberry jam

1 ½ teaspoons sugar

½ teaspoon cinnamon

I get these ready to bake before guests arrive or awake; and pop them in the oven just before serving so everyone enjoys the wonderful aroma of the cinnamon and sugar as they bake.

STEPS:

1. Preheat oven to 375°F. Spray 10 muffin cups in standard muffin tin with nonstick cooking spray.

2. In a medium bowl, whisk together yogurt, melted butter, egg, and milk. Set aside.

3. In a large bowl, combine flour, Splenda, baking powder, cinnamon, and salt. Stir; make a well in center of dry ingredients and add the liquid ingredients. Using a large spoon or spatula, stir just until dry ingredients are moistened.

4. Place 1 heaping tablespoon of batter into each muffin cup. Press 1 teaspoon jam into the center of batter. Place another heaping tablespoon of batter to cover jam, smoothing to edges. Repeat for remaining muffins.

5. In a very small dish, mix 1 ½ teaspoons of sugar with ½ teaspoon cinnamon. Sprinkle over muffins.

6. Bake for 13-15 minutes or until center springs back when lightly touched. Cool for 5 minutes before removing to a wire rack.

PER SERVING

Calories 160

Carbohydrate 25 grams

Protein 4 grams

Fat 4.5 grams (2.5 saturated)

Fiber 1 gram

Sodium 230 milligrams

Diabetic exchange = 1 ½ Carbohydrate, 1 Fat

WW point comparison = 3 points

Lemon Cheese Danish Muffins

Serves Twelve

These delicious muffins combine the things we like best about muffins and Danish. They are light-textured muffins with a spot of cheese Danish filling hidden in the center, and they are crowned with a touch of powdered sugar. These make a lovely addition to a brunch or luncheon.

INGREDIENTS:

FILLING

4 ounces tub-style light cream cheese

3 tablespoons Splenda Granular

2 teaspoons 1% milk

⅛ teaspoon almond extract

MUFFIN BATTER

1 large egg

3 tablespoons margarine, melted

¼ cup 1% milk

½ teaspoon vanilla extract

8 ounces regular nonfat lemon yogurt (not light)

2 cups + 2 tablespoons cake flour

¾ cup Splenda Granular

1 teaspoon baking powder

1 teaspoon baking soda

Grated zest of 1 lemon (2 teaspoons)

2 teaspoons powdered sugar (optional)

STEPS:

1. Preheat oven to 400°F. Spray standard 12-cup muffin tin with nonstick cooking spray.

2. FILLING: In a small bowl, cream together cream cheese, 3 tablespoons Splenda, milk, and extract. Set aside.

3. BATTER: In another small bowl, whisk together egg, margarine, milk, vanilla, and yogurt. Set aside.

4. In a large bowl, combine flour, ¾ cup Splenda, baking powder, baking soda, and lemon zest. Stir; make a well in center of dry ingredients and add liquid mixture. With a large spoon or spatula stir just until dry ingredients are moistened.

5. Spoon 1 large tablespoon of batter into each muffin cup (about ½ full); place 2 teaspoons cheese mixture over each; fill cups with remaining muffin batter.

6. Bake for 16–18 minutes or until center springs back when lightly touched. Cool in pan 5 minutes before removing to wire rack. Before serving, dust with powdered sugar.

LEMON BERRY MUFFIN VARIATION: Replace cream cheese filling with your choice of low-sugar berry jam. This adds 1 gram of carbohydrate but lowers the fat to 3.5 total grams and the calories to 130.

PER SERVING

Calories 140	Fat 5 grams (2 saturated)
Carbohydrate 20 grams	Fiber 0 grams
Protein 4 grams	Sodium 210 milligrams

Diabetic exchange = 1 ½ Carbohydrate, 1 Fat
WW point comparison = 3 points

Cranberry Orange Muffins

Serves Twelve

The classic combination of orange and cranberries has become one of the most popular for muffins. The orange juice imparts a sweet and bold flavor and is a perfect complement to the tart cranberries. While these are great during the holidays when cranberries are in season, you can enjoy them year-round by keeping a few bags of cranberries in your freezer or substituting blueberries in the summer.

INGREDIENTS:

2 cups all-purpose flour

2 teaspoons baking powder

½ teaspoon baking soda

¼ teaspoon salt

1 ¼ cups fresh cranberries

1 large egg

¼ cup canola oil

¾ cup light orange juice

½ cup 1% or skim milk

1 cup + 2 tablespoons Splenda Granular

1 tablespoon orange zest

1 tablespoon reduced-sugar orange marmalade (optional)

Watch out for "no-sugar-added" cranberry juice. It may contain lots of added sugar in the form of fruit juice concentrates that technically are not counted as "added sugars."

STEPS:

1. Preheat oven to 375°F. Spray standard 12-cup muffin tin with nonstick cooking spray.

2. In a large bowl, combine flour, baking powder, soda, salt, and cranberries. Set aside.

3. In a small bowl, whisk the egg, oil, ½ cup orange juice, milk, 1 cup Splenda, and zest together. Make a well in the center of the dry ingredients and pour in the milk mixture. Using a large spoon or spatula, mix just until all the flour is moistened.

4. Spoon batter into the prepared tin and bake for 18-20 minutes or until center springs back when lightly touched.

5. While muffins are baking, place ¼ cup orange juice and 2 tablespoons of Splenda (and marmalade) into a small pot or microwaveable bowl. Heat gently until mixture reduces by half.

6. Remove muffins from the oven and brush each muffin with the orange mixture. Cool in the tin 5 minutes before removing to wire rack.

PER SERVING

Calories 150	Fat 5 grams (.5 saturated)
Carbohydrate 22 grams (3 sugar)	Fiber 1 gram
Protein 3 grams	Sodium 250 milligrams

Diabetic exchange = 1 ½ Carbohydrate, 1 Fat
WW point comparison = 3 points

Apple Oatmeal Streusel Muffins

Serves Twelve

These are so good and good for you. I have made a few adjustments, but these tender muffins are still made with fresh apple and whole-wheat flour and topped with a streusel of oats and brown sugar. What a great way to start the day!

INGREDIENTS:

MUFFIN BATTER

1 large egg

1 cup low-fat buttermilk

3 tablespoons canola oil

¾ cup Splenda Granular

1 cup peeled, grated cooking apple

1 ½ cups all-purpose flour

½ cup whole-wheat pastry flour

1 teaspoon baking powder

1 teaspoon baking soda

2 teaspoons cinnamon

¾ teaspoon nutmeg

STREUSEL TOPPING

2 tablespoons all-purpose flour

4 tablespoons rolled oats

2 tablespoons Splenda Granular

1 tablespoon brown sugar

½ teaspoon cinnamon

1 tablespoon butter

STEPS:

1. Preheat oven to 375°F. Spray standard 12-cup muffin tin with nonstick cooking spray.

2. STREUSEL TOPPING: Place all of the streusel ingredients in a small bowl except butter and stir until thoroughly mixed. Cut in butter until crumbly. Set aside.

3. BATTER: In a separate bowl, beat the egg and egg white with the buttermilk until foamy. Whisk in the oil, Splenda, and grated apple. Set aside.

4. In a large bowl, combine flour, baking powder, baking soda, cinnamon, and nutmeg. Make a well in the center and pour in the apple mixture. With a large spoon or spatula, stir just until dry ingredients are moistened.

5. Spoon batter into prepared muffin tin. Divide streusel evenly among muffin tops.

6. Bake for 15 minutes or until a toothpick comes out clean when placed into the center of the muffin. Remove from baking tin and cool on wire rack.

PER SERVING

Calories 150

Carbohydrate 22 grams

Protein 4 grams

Fat 5 grams (.5 saturated)

Fiber 1 gram

Sodium 180 milligrams

Diabetic exchange = 1 ½ Carbohydrate, 1 Fat

WW point comparison = 3 points

Quick Chocolate Chip Muffins

Serves Ten

Here is another quick and easy kid favorite. As usual, I tested these on my own kids; I simply left the muffins out on the counter when they arrived home from school and watched. Each child quickly dove towards them, ate one, and wanted another. That's two thumbs up in my house.

INGREDIENTS:

¾ cup 1% milk

¼ cup applesauce

1 egg

2 tablespoons canola oil

1 tablespoon brown sugar

½ teaspoon vanilla

1 ½ cups low-fat baking mix (like Reduced-Fat Bisquick)

½ cup Splenda Granular

⅓ cup mini chocolate chips

¼ cup nonfat dry milk

½ teaspoon baking powder

½ teaspoon cinnamon

STEPS:

1. Preheat oven to 375°F. Spray 10 muffin cups in standard muffin tin with nonstick cooking spray.

2. In a small bowl, whisk together milk, applesauce, egg, canola oil, brown sugar, and vanilla (be sure to dissolve any brown sugar lumps). Set aside.

3. In a large bowl, combine remaining dry ingredients. Stir; make a well in center and add milk mixture. With a large spoon or spatula, stir just until dry ingredients are moistened.

4. Spoon into prepared muffin cups.

5. Bake for 12-15 minutes or until center springs back when lightly touched. Cool for 5 minutes before removing to a wire rack.

Powdered milk adds protein and calcium to these muffins and helps maintain their structure. You may note its distinct flavor in the raw batter but not in the baked muffins.

PER SERVING

Calories 150	Fat 6 grams (1 saturated)
Carbohydrate 20 grams	Fiber 1 gram
Protein 4 grams	Sodium 250 milligrams

Diabetic exchange = 1 ½ Carbohydrate, 1 Fat
WW point comparison = 3 points

Fresh Blueberry Scones

Serves Thirteen

Scones are made from sweetened biscuit dough and can vary quite a bit in richness. Most of the ones found in bakeries and coffee shops are quite rich and usually oversized, meaning that they contain large amounts of carbohydrates, fat, and calories. Try to use fresh blueberries in this recipe to give these scones their best appearance; frozen berries will color the dough, giving you a "blue" berry scone.

INGREDIENTS:

2 cups all-purpose flour

⅓ cup Splenda Granular

2 teaspoons baking powder

½ teaspoon baking soda

¼ teaspoon salt

1 cup fresh blueberries

1 cup buttermilk

3 tablespoons margarine, melted

1 large egg

½ teaspoon almond extract

2 teaspoons granulated sugar

STEPS:

1. Preheat oven to 425°F. Spray a cookie sheet with nonstick cooking spray.

2. In a large bowl, mix together the flour, Splenda, baking powder, baking soda, and salt. Stir in blueberries; set aside.

3. In a small bowl, whisk together the buttermilk, margarine, egg, and almond extract. Pour wet mixture over dry ingredients and stir just until dry ingredients are moistened (do not overmix).

4. Drop by heaping spoonfuls (about ¼ cup) onto prepared cookie sheet, making 13 mounds. Sprinkle scones with granulated sugar.

5. Bake for 12-15 minutes until lightly browned. Transfer to a wire rack to cool slightly before serving.

If you want big bakery-style scones, use ½ cup batter for each—they will be 230 calories each, with 36 grams of carbohydrate and 6 grams of fat. Still a far cry from a popular coffeehouse favorite, with 550 calories and 28 grams of fat.

PER SERVING

Calories 115	Fat 3 grams (0 saturated)
Carbohydrate 18 grams	Fiber 1 gram
Protein 3 grams	Sodium 220 milligrams

Diabetic exchange = 1 Carbohydrate, 1 Fat
WW point comparison = 2 points

Pumpkin Scones

Serves Twelve

No longer just a seasonal special, you now find pumpkin scones year-round at coffee shops and bakeries. Though tasty, these regrettably have enough calories to be considered a meal rather than a snack. So, to satisfy your urge for pumpkin scones, I created these healthful, square-shaped versions that are absolutely terrific with a nice cup of hot coffee or tea.

INGREDIENTS:

1 ¾ cups all-purpose flour

1 cup old-fashioned rolled oats

⅔ cup Splenda Granular

2 teaspoons baking powder

1 teaspoon baking soda

1 ½ teaspoons cinnamon

¾ teaspoon nutmeg

¼ teaspoon cloves

4 tablespoons butter, cold

¾ cup pumpkin puree

6 tablespoons low-fat buttermilk

2 teaspoons molasses

2 teaspoons granulated sugar (or brown sugar pushed through a sieve onto scones)

STEPS:

1. Preheat oven to 425°F. Spray cookie sheet with nonstick cooking spray.

2. In a large bowl, mix together the flour, oats, Splenda, baking powder and soda, cinnamon, nutmeg, and cloves. Using your fingertips or a pastry blender, cut butter into flour mixture until crumbly; set aside.

3. In a small bowl, whisk pumpkin, buttermilk, and molasses. Pour over dry ingredients and stir just until dry ingredients are moistened.

4. Coat your hands with flour and place moist dough onto lightly floured surface. Gently mix dough over and onto itself until all dry ingredients are incorporated. Shape dough into a 12 x 4-inch rectangle. Cut rectangle in half lengthwise, then each piece into 6 scones (2 x 2-inch squares). Transfer to cookie sheet and sprinkle scones with sugar.

5. Bake for 14–16 minutes until tops are browned. Transfer to a wire rack to cool slightly before serving.

To make slightly larger scones, pat dough into a 6 x 8-inch rectangle. Cut down length and then cut each piece into 4 scones. You will have 8 scones, each with 210 calories, 2 carbohydrate exchanges, and the equivalent of 4 WW points.

PER SERVING

Calories 140	Fat 5 grams (3 saturated)
Carbohydrate 21 grams	Fiber 2 grams
Protein 3 grams	Sodium 200 milligrams

Diabetic exchange = 1 ½ Carbohydrate, 1 Fat
WW point comparison = 3 points

Orange Ginger Scones

Serves Ten

The orange-ginger combination not only makes these taste wonderful, but it also gives them a lovely aroma. These triangular-cut scones are terrific served with low-sugar orange marmalade.

INGREDIENTS:

2 cups all-purpose flour

¼ cup Splenda Granular

2 teaspoons baking powder

½ teaspoon baking soda

¼ teaspoon salt

¾ teaspoon ginger

½ teaspoon allspice

3 tablespoons margarine, cold

¾ cup buttermilk

1 large egg

1 tablespoon orange zest

1 tablespoon 1% milk

1 teaspoon granulated sugar

STEPS:

1. Preheat oven to 400°F. Spray a cookie sheet with nonstick cooking spray.

2. In a large bowl, mix together the flour, Splenda, baking powder, baking soda, salt, ginger, and allspice. Using your fingertips, two knives, or a pastry blender, cut margarine into flour mixture until crumbly; set aside.

3. In a small bowl, whisk together buttermilk, egg, and zest. Pour over dry ingredients and stir just until dry ingredients are moistened.

4. Coat your hands with flour and place dough onto lightly floured surface. Knead gently once or twice to pull dough together and pat into an 8-inch round. Using a sharp knife, cut into 10 equal wedges and transfer to cookie sheet.

5. Brush wedges with milk and sprinkle with sugar. Bake for 12–15 minutes or until lightly browned. Transfer to a wire rack to cool slightly before serving.

Southern cooks have known all along that buttermilk makes biscuits nice and tender. The acid gives buttermilk its tenderizing properties and works just as well in the sweetened biscuits we call scones.

PER SERVING

Calories 140   Fat 4 grams (1 saturated)
Carbohydrate 22 grams   Fiber 1 gram
Protein 4 grams   Sodium 260 milligrams

Diabetic exchange = 1 ½ Carbohydrate, 1 Fat
WW point comparison = 3 points

Maple Oat Scones

Serves Eight

Nutty oats and a slight hint of maple make these hearty sweetened biscuits great additions to your breakfast table. Enjoy them warm with a touch of light butter or your favorite low-sugar marmalade.

INGREDIENTS:

1 cup all-purpose flour

½ cup whole-wheat pastry flour

1 cup rolled oats

⅓ cup Splenda Granular

2 teaspoons baking powder

½ teaspoon baking soda

¼ teaspoon salt

3 tablespoons margarine

⅔ cup buttermilk

1 large egg

1 tablespoon sugar-free maple syrup

1 tablespoon 1% milk

2 teaspoons granulated sugar

STEPS:

1. Preheat oven to 425°F. Spray a cookie sheet with nonstick cooking spray.

2. In a large bowl, mix together flours, oats, Splenda, baking powder, baking soda, and salt. Using your fingertips, a pastry blender, or two knives, cut margarine into flour mixture until crumbly.

3. In a small bowl, whisk together buttermilk, egg, and maple syrup. Pour over dry ingredients and stir just until moistened.

4. Coat your hands with flour and place the dough onto a lightly floured surface. Knead dough gently once or twice just to bring together and pat into an 8-inch round. Using a sharp knife, cut into 8 wedges and transfer to cookie sheet.

5. Brush scones with milk and sprinkle with sugar.

6. Bake for 12-14 minutes until tops are lightly browned. Transfer to wire rack to cool slightly before serving.

PER SERVING

Calories 165	Fat 5 grams
Carbohydrate 25 grams	Fiber 2 grams
Protein 5 grams	Sodium 90 milligrams

Diabetic exchange = 1 ½ Carbohydrate, 1 Fat
WW point comparison = 3 points

The oats in the scone give them a nice crunchy quality. I have often seen oat-based scones referred to as Scottish scones.

Fresh Raspberry Lemon Scones

Serves Ten

After having a particularly lovely scone with fresh raspberries, I had to come up with one of my own. I've added a bit of lemon zest and use a touch of powdered sugar to adorn these rather than a heavy powdered sugar icing. I think you will find them lovely as well.

INGREDIENTS:

2 cups all-purpose flour

⅓ cup Splenda Granular

1 teaspoon cream of tartar

½ teaspoon baking soda

⅛ teaspoon salt

4 tablespoons margarine

¾ cup + 2 tablespoons buttermilk

1 large egg

1 ½ teaspoons lemon zest

1 cup fresh raspberries

2 teaspoons powdered sugar

STEPS:

1. Preheat oven to 425°F. Spray cookie sheet with nonstick cooking spray.

2. In a large bowl, mix together the flour, Splenda, cream of tartar, baking soda, and salt. Using your fingertips or a pastry blender, cut margarine into flour mixture until crumbly; set aside.

3. In a small bowl, whisk together buttermilk, egg, and zest. Pour over dry ingredients and stir just until dry ingredients are moistened. Stir in raspberries very gently.

4. Drop by moundfuls (about ⅓ cup) onto prepared cookie sheet, making 10 mounds. Bake for 12-15 minutes or until lightly browned. Transfer to wire rack to let cool.

5. Just prior to serving, press powdered sugared through small mesh strainer and dust onto scones.

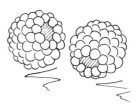

PER SERVING

Calories 150	Fat 5 grams (2 saturated)
Carbohydrate 23 grams	Fiber 2 grams
Protein 4 grams	Sodium 170 milligrams

Diabetic exchange = 1 Carbohydrate, ½ Fruit, 1 Fat
WW point comparison= 3 points

Easy Quick Breads and Classic Coffee Cakes

Lemon Blueberry Bread

Pumpkin Pecan Bread

Zucchini Walnut Bread

Wholesome Banana Bread

Mediterranean Banana Bread

Cranberry Orange Tea Bread

Chocolate Loaf

Sour Cream Almond Poppy Seed Loaf

Irish Soda Bread

Quick Cake with Coconut and Almonds

Buttermilk Pecan Crumb Cake

Gingerbread Coffee Cake

Raspberry Almond Crumb Cake

Simple Cinnamon Coffee Cake

S'More Crumb Cake

Blueberry Buckle

Cinnamon Streusel Coffee Cake

The very first thing I ever baked with Splenda was a Cranberry Orange Tea Bread. It was (for those who watch Oprah) my "a-ha" or lightbulb moment. That was the moment I knew that I could make wonderful baked goods, like coffee cakes and quick breads, for those who want to cut sugar but still eat the foods they love. That was also the moment I knew I could go back to the chefs whom I'd taught nutrition and finally tell them how to bake successfully even without sugar.

Since then, I have developed many recipes for quick breads and coffee cakes because they are such a pleasure to make—and to eat. Simple by design, most quick breads require no more than a bowl and a spoon. They're called "quick" because they use baking soda and/or baking powder, not yeast, for leavening. But best of all, they are sweet and moist, can be made with different ingredients for great variety, and are universally enjoyed.

With so many recipes to choose from, I'm confident that you'll find the perfect quick bread or coffee cake. If "quick" is what you truly need, try the wholesome Mediterranean Banana Bread, made healthy with olive oil, or sample the Simple Cinnamon Coffeecake. If you love chocolate, you'll love the Deep, Dark Chocolate Loaf, and kids of all ages will revel in the mini-morsel-topped S'More Crumb Cake. Plus, your Sunday mornings are guaranteed to get even better when you put Buttermilk Pecan Crumb Cake on the table. Last, I'm never one to leave out a holiday—so why not serve Gingerbread Coffee Cake for Christmas, Pumpkin Pecan Bread for Thanksgiving, and Irish Soda Bread for St. Pat's. Making one of these recipes may even prove to be your "a-ha!" moment.

Lemon Blueberry Bread

Serves Twelve

This blueberry-studded, lemon quick bread is one of my favorites. It's simple to make, beautiful to look at, and incredibly delicious. You'll find that this bread is great with a cup of coffee or tea and rich enough to serve as dessert when you top it with a dollop of light whipped topping.

INGREDIENTS:

⅔ cup 1% milk

1 large egg

1 teaspoon vanilla

4 tablespoons margarine, melted

6 ounces low-fat lemon yogurt
 (I use Yoplait)

Grated zest of 1 lemon

1 cup Splenda Granular

2 cups all-purpose flour

2 teaspoons baking powder

½ teaspoon baking soda

1 cup fresh blueberries (½ pint)

1 teaspoon granulated sugar

STEPS:

1. Preheat oven to 350°F. Coat a 9 x 5-inch loaf pan with nonstick cooking spray.

2. In a medium bowl, whisk together milk, egg, vanilla, margarine, yogurt, zest, and Splenda. Set aside.

3. In a large bowl, combine flour, baking powder, baking soda, and blueberries. Stir; make a well in the center and pour in wet ingredients. Mix gently with a spoon until batter is just smooth.

4. Spoon batter into prepared pan. Smooth top and sprinkle with sugar.

5. Bake for 45 minutes or until toothpick or cake tester inserted into center comes out clean. Cool on rack 10-15 minutes and then remove from pan.

Scientists at the Human Nutrition Center on Aging in Boston ranked blueberries as number one in antioxidant activity when compared to more than forty other fruits and vegetables.

PER SERVING

Calories 150

Carbohydrate 23 grams

Protein 4 grams

Fat 4.5 grams (1 saturated)

Fiber 1 gram

Sodium 190 milligrams

Diabetic exchange = 1 ½ Carbohydrate, 1 Fat

WW point comparison = 3 points

Pumpkin Pecan Bread

Serves Twelve

This holiday favorite is sure to please the most discerning of your guests. Serve it like I always do, with the crowd-pleasing Orange Cream Cheese on page 434 for a delicious taste treat.

INGREDIENTS:

¼ cup canola oil

1 cup pumpkin purée

1 large egg

1 large egg white

½ cup low-fat buttermilk

2 tablespoons molasses

1 cup + 2 tablespoons Splenda Granular

1 ¾ cups all-purpose flour

1 teaspoon baking powder

½ teaspoon baking soda

1 ½ teaspoons cinnamon

½ teaspoon ginger

¼ teaspoon cloves

⅓ cup chopped pecans

STEPS:

1. Preheat oven to 350°F. Coat a 9 x 5-inch loaf pan with nonstick cooking spray.

2. In a medium bowl, whisk together the oil, pumpkin, whole egg, egg white, buttermilk, molasses, and Splenda.

3. In a large bowl, measure the flour, baking powder, baking soda, spices, and nuts. Stir; make a well in the center and pour in the pumpkin mixture. With a large spoon or spatula, stir just until blended. Do not overmix.

4. Spoon the batter into the prepared pan and smooth surface.

5. Bake for 40-45 minutes until a toothpick or cake tester inserted into the center comes out clean. Cool on rack for 10-5 minutes and then remove from pan.

Did you know that one large bagel can have as much as 70 grams of carbohydrate?

PER SERVING

Calories 165	Fat 7 grams (.5 saturated)
Carbohydrate 21 grams	Fiber 1 gram
Protein 4 grams	Sodium 170 milligrams

Diabetic exchange = 1 ½ Carbohydrate, 1 Fat
WW point comparison = 4 points
(omit nuts and subtract 1 point)

Zucchini Walnut Bread

Serves Twelve

If you have ever grown zucchini, you know how prolific this summer squash can be. The first zucchini bread was surely created by someone who was looking for ways to use it up. My variation on this popular bread uses pineapple to keep it wonderfully moist while allowing the spices and nuts to really stand out. Who said eating your fruits and vegetables couldn't be fun?

INGREDIENTS:

½ cup 1% milk

1 large egg + 1 egg white

4 tablespoons canola oil

1 cup grated zucchini (unpeeled)

¾ cup drained crushed pineapple

2 teaspoons vanilla

¾ cup whole-wheat pastry flour

¾ cup all-purpose flour

¾ cup Splenda Granular

1 teaspoon baking powder

1 ½ teaspoons baking soda

1 ½ teaspoons cinnamon

½ teaspoon nutmeg

¼ teaspoon allspice

⅓ cup chopped walnuts

STEPS:

1. Preheat oven to 350°F. Coat a 9 x 5-inch loaf pan with nonstick cooking spray.

2. In a medium bowl, stir together milk, eggs, oil, zucchini, pineapple and vanilla. Set aside.

3. In a large bowl, combine flours, Splenda, baking powder, baking soda, spices, and nuts. Stir; make a well and add the liquid mixture. Using a large spoon or spatula, stir just until blended.

4. Spoon into prepared pan and smooth surface.

5. Bake for 35–40 minutes or until toothpick or cake tester inserted into the center comes out clean. Cool on rack for 10–15 minutes and then remove from pan.

I use equal parts whole-wheat pastry flour and all-purpose flour to make this bread wholesome without weighing it down. You can vary this ratio, noting that more whole-wheat flour will make it denser (yet higher in fiber) and more all-purpose flour will lighten it up.

PER SERVING

Calories 140

Carbohydrate 16 grams

Protein 4 grams

Fat 7 grams (.5 saturated)

Fiber 2 grams

Sodium 200 milligrams

Diabetic exchange = 1 Carbohydrate, 1 Fat

WW point comparison = 3 points

Wholesome Banana Bread

Serves Twelve

This banana bread is incredibly sweet, dense, and moist. It is sturdy enough to pack and makes a great addition to anyone's lunch.

INGREDIENTS:

1 ⅓ cups mashed ripe bananas (about 3 medium whole ripe bananas)

¼ cup low-fat buttermilk

1 cup all-purpose white flour

½ cup whole-wheat pastry flour

1 teaspoon baking soda

½ teaspoon baking powder

4 tablespoons margarine

2 tablespoons prune purée

1 ½ teaspoons vanilla

¾ cup Splenda Granular

1 egg

Fruit purées are great for adding moistness to quick breads without fat. Bananas have the additional benefit of being a great source of potassium.

STEPS:

1. Preheat oven to 350°F. Spray one 9 x 5-inch loaf pan or two 6 x 3 ½-inch mini-loaves with nonstick cooking spray.

2. Mash the bananas in a small bowl by hand or with electric mixer. Stir in buttermilk. Set aside. In a medium bowl, sift together flours with baking soda and powder. Set aside.

3. In a large bowl, cream the margarine with an electric mixer on medium speed. Add the prune purée and beat well. Beat in the vanilla and the Splenda. Beat in the egg. On very low speed, alternate adding the banana mixture and the flour mixture, adding half of the flour and mixing until just incorporated and then half the banana. Repeat once.

4. Turn mixture into prepared pan(s) and smooth top.

5. Bake for 35-40 minutes for a 9 x 5-inch pan and 30 to 35 minutes for 2 mini-loaves or until a toothpick or cake tester inserted into the middle of the loaf comes out dry. Cool for 10-15 minutes on a rack and then remove from pan.

PER SERVING

Calories 130	Fat 4 grams (1 saturated)
Carbohydrate 21 grams	Fiber 2 grams
Protein 3 grams	Sodium 170 milligrams

Diabetic exchange = 1 Carbohydrate, ½ Fruit, 1 Fat
WW point comparison = 3 points

Mediterranean Banana Bread

Serves Twelve

Surprisingly, this banana bread is made with olive oil. But don't worry—you won't be able to taste the olive flavor, but you will reap the many health benefits this oil provides. This banana bread is simple to make and requires only a few basic ingredients (in addition to those old bananas you need to use up).

INGREDIENTS:

1 ½ cups mashed bananas (about 4 medium or 3 large bananas)

¼ cup olive oil (not extra-virgin)

2 large eggs

1 ½ teaspoons vanilla

2 cups all-purpose flour

1 cup Splenda Granular

1 ½ teaspoons baking soda

STEPS:

1. Preheat oven to 350°F. Spray one 9 x 5 inch loaf pan with nonstick cooking spray.

2. In a medium bowl, with an electric mixer, beat together bananas and olive oil. Add eggs and vanilla, beating well to combine ingredients. Set aside.

3. In a large bowl, stir together flour, Splenda, and baking soda. Stir and make a well. Add banana mix and stir just until blended. Do not overmix.

4. Pour batter into prepared pan and smooth.

5. Bake for 45–55 minutes until a toothpick or cake tester inserted into the middle of the loaf comes out dry. Cool on rack for 10–15 minutes and then remove from pan.

PER SERVING

Calories 160

Carbohydrate 24 grams

Protein 3 grams

Fat 6 grams (1 saturated)

Fiber 2 grams

Sodium 170 milligrams

Diabetic exchange = 1 Carbohydrate, ½ Fruit, 1 Fat

WW point comparison = 3 points

Extra-virgin olive oil is minimally processed and thus has the strongest olive flavor. Regular olive oil and light olive oil have been further processed, which reduces the olive flavor and color. The nutrition content, including fat and calories, is the same for all olive oils.

Cranberry Orange Tea Bread

Serves Twelve

The classic pairing of orange and cranberries makes this holiday bread a year-round favorite. With its orange glaze and orange-tinted crumb flecked with bright red cranberries, this is a gorgeous loaf for giving and for eating.

INGREDIENTS:

LOAF BATTER

½ cup light orange juice

⅓ cup 1% milk

3 tablespoons canola oil

1 large egg + 1 egg white

1 tablespoon orange zest (zest of 1 orange)

1 teaspoon vanilla

2 cups all-purpose flour

1 cup Splenda Granular

2 teaspoons baking powder

½ teaspoon baking soda

¼ teaspoon salt

1 ⅓ cups fresh cranberries, chopped

GLAZE

¼ cup light orange juice

¼ cup Splenda Granular

STEPS:

1. Preheat oven to 350°F. Coat a 9 x 5-inch loaf pan with nonstick cooking spray.

2. BATTER: In a medium bowl, stir together orange juice, milk, oil, eggs, zest and vanilla. Set aside.

3. In a large bowl, combine flour, Splenda, baking powder, baking soda, salt, and cranberries. Stir; make a well and add the liquid mixture, stirring just until blended.

4. Spoon into prepared pan and smooth.

5. Bake for 50 minutes or until a toothpick or cake tester inserted into the middle of the loaf comes out dry.

6. GLAZE: While bread is baking, combine orange juice and Splenda in a small saucepan. Place on medium heat and reduce by one half. Brush glaze onto warm loaf immediately after removing from oven. Cool on rack for 15 minutes; then remove from pan.

GIFT LOAF VARIATION: Makes 2–3 small loaves—fill mini-loaf pans ⅔ full and bake for 30–35 minutes.

Cranberries freeze incredibly well. Just buy an extra bag or two when they're on sale at Thanksgiving and pop them into the freezer. You'll have them on hand to make this bread any time of year.

PER SERVING

Calories 140	Fat 4 grams (0 saturated)
Carbohydrate 22 grams	Fiber 1 gram
Protein 3 grams	Sodium 170 milligrams

Diabetic exchange = 1 ½ Carbohydrate, 1 Fat
WW point comparison = 3 points

Chocolate Loaf

Serves Twelve

Here is a breakfast/snack loaf for all of you chocolate lovers. After you let it cool, this moist quick bread is sturdy enough to be cut into slices. Enjoy it just as it is, or spread heated or toasted slices with one of the sweet cream cheese spreads in the Sweet Embellishments Chapter. Wrap up tight (if you have any left) to keep from drying out.

INGREDIENTS:

¼ **cup margarine, softened**

¼ **cup brown sugar**

¾ **cup Splenda Granular**

1 large egg

2 large egg whites

½ **cup applesauce**

1 teaspoon vanilla

1 ½ cups all-purpose flour

½ **cup Dutch-process cocoa powder**

1 teaspoon baking powder

¾ **teaspoon baking soda**

¾ **cup low-fat plain yogurt**

STEPS:

1. Preheat oven to 350°F. Coat a 9 x 5-inch loaf pan with nonstick cooking spray.

2. In a large bowl, with an electric mixer, cream together margarine and brown sugar. Beat in Splenda, and then eggs. On low speed, blend in applesauce and vanilla.

3. In a medium bowl, combine flour, cocoa powder, baking powder, and baking soda. With a large spoon or spatula, stir in ½ the yogurt and then ½ of the flour mixture. Repeat, mixing just until blended. Do not overmix.

4. Spoon mixture into prepared pan and smooth.

5. Bake for 50-55 minutes or until a toothpick or cake tester inserted into the middle of the loaf comes out dry. Cool in pan on wire rack for 10-15 minutes; then remove from pan.

PER SERVING

Calories 150	Fat 4.5 grams (1 saturated)
Carbohydrate 22 grams	Fiber 2 grams
Protein 5 grams	Sodium 190 milligrams

Diabetic exchange = 1 ½ Carbohydrate, 1 Fat

WW point comparison = 3 points

Sour Cream Almond Poppy Seed Loaf

Serves Twelve

I never know which recipes will tickle people's taste buds. This one certainly did for several of my tasters. Its cake-like texture melts in your mouth, and this loaf is superb when sliced and topped with fresh berries as a dessert.

INGREDIENTS:

¼ cup margarine, softened

1 cup Splenda Granular

1 large egg + 2 egg whites

⅓ cup unsweetened applesauce

1 cup light sour cream

2 tablespoons poppy seeds

Zest of 1 lemon

1 teaspoon almond extract

½ teaspoon vanilla

2 cups all-purpose flour

1 teaspoon baking powder

1 teaspoon baking soda

STEPS:

1. Preheat oven to 350°F. Coat a 9 x 5-inch loaf pan with nonstick cooking spray.

2. In a large bowl, cream together margarine and Splenda with an electric mixer. Beat in egg and egg whites. On slow speed, blend in applesauce, sour cream, poppy seeds, zest, and almond and vanilla extracts.

3. Sift together flour, baking powder, and baking soda. With a large spoon or spatula, stir flour mixture into poppy seed mixture just until flour is incorporated, being careful not to overmix.

4. Spoon into prepared pan and smooth.

5. Bake for 45 minutes or until a toothpick or cake tester inserted into the middle of the loaf comes out dry. Cool in pan on wire rack for 10-15 minutes; then remove from pan.

PER SERVING

Calories 170	Fat 8 grams (2 saturated)
Carbohydrate 19 grams	Fiber 1 gram
Protein 5 grams	Sodium 180 milligrams

Diabetic exchange = 1 ½ Carbohydrate, 2 Fat
WW point comparison = 4 points

Although poppy seeds appear black, they are actually kidney-shaped and slate blue (if you look real close). They are a bit hard to count, but it's reported that it takes 900,000 of them to make a pound.

Irish Soda Bread

Serves Twelve

A week before St. Patrick's Day and a week before my Irish mother-in-law came to visit, I started working on this recipe. One version came out too dark, another a bit dry. On the morning of St. Pattie's Day, though, I threw one last combination in the oven, and that night my mother-in-law ate several servings of my Irish Soda Bread, declaring it "just right."

INGREDIENTS:

2 ½ cups all-purpose flour

⅓ cup Splenda Granular

1 ½ teaspoons baking powder

½ teaspoon baking soda

½ teaspoon salt

2 teaspoons caraway seeds, crushed

2 tablespoons butter

⅓ cup currants

Scant 1 cup buttermilk

1 tablespoon milk (for brushing)

STEPS:

1. Preheat oven to 375°F. Spray an 8-inch round cake pan with nonstick cooking spray.

2. In a medium bowl, combine flour, Splenda, baking powder, baking soda, salt, and caraway seeds. Stir to combine.

3. Cut in butter until texture resembles fine meal. Add currants. Stir in buttermilk and pull dough together to form a ball. (Dough will be a bit soft.) Flour your hands and gently place dough on lightly floured board and knead for about 1 minute. Create a rounded loaf with a flat bottom about 6 ½ inches in diameter.

4. Tuck in or remove any currants that are sticking out (or they will burn in the oven). Brush loaf with 1 tablespoon of milk for browning.

5. Place in prepared pan. With a sharp knife, slice an X about ¼-inch-deep across the middle of the loaf.

6. Bake for 30–35 minutes or until browned and a toothpick or cake tester inserted in the middle comes out clean.

PER SERVING

Calories 135

Carbohydrate 25 grams

Protein 4 grams

Fat 2.5 grams (1.5 saturated)

Fiber 1 gram

Sodium 250 milligrams

Diabetic exchange = 1 ½ Carbohydrate, ½ Fat

WW point comparison = 3 points

Quick Cake with Coconut and Almonds

Serves Nine

This coffeecake is really quick! Light and tender, it takes advantage of a low-fat baking mix. The cake is mixed in one bowl and then topped with a yummy mixture of coconut and almonds before baking. Just add a Sunday morning paper and a cup of coffee and you're all set.

INGREDIENTS:

1 ½ cups reduced-fat baking mix
    (like Reduced-Fat Bisquick)

½ cup + 2 tablespoons Splenda Granular

½ teaspoon baking powder

⅔ cup 1% or skim milk

1 large egg, lightly beaten

1 tablespoon canola oil

½ teaspoon vanilla

6 tablespoons shredded coconut

1 tablespoon brown sugar

3 tablespoons sliced almonds

1 tablespoon melted margarine

STEPS:

1. Preheat oven to 350°F. Spray an 8-inch square baking pan with nonstick cooking spray.

2. Measure the baking mix, ½ cup Splenda, and baking powder into a large mixing bowl. Add the milk, egg, oil, and vanilla. Stir just until smooth. Spoon into prepared pan.

3. Place the coconut, 2 tablespoons Splenda, brown sugar, and almonds in a small bowl. Add the margarine and mix. Sprinkle this mixture over the top of the cake.

4. Bake for 20 minutes or until the center springs back when gently touched. Cool on rack.

Switching to low-fat baking mix is an easy way to cut back on unnecessary fat.

PER SERVING

Calories 160	Fat 7 grams (2 saturated)
Carbohydrate 20 grams	Fiber 1 gram
Protein 3 grams	Sodium 270 milligrams

Diabetic exchange = 1 ½ Carbohydrate, 1 Fat
WW point comparison = 4 points

Buttermilk Pecan Crumb Cake

Serves Eight

My husband is a fan of coffee cakes with traditional crumb topping, but he had given up on them because they're full of butter and sugar. However, this moist crumb cake with its crunchy, sweet topping has a great taste yet is low in fat and sugar. Now, he can indulge at will.

INGREDIENTS:

CAKE BATTER

¾ **cup buttermilk**

1 **large egg**

2 **tablespoons canola oil**

⅔ **cup Splenda Granular**

1 **teaspoon orange zest**

½ **teaspoon vanilla**

1 ½ **cups all-purpose flour**

1 ½ **teaspoons baking powder**

½ **teaspoon baking soda**

½ **teaspoon cinnamon**

¼ **teaspoon nutmeg**

¼ **teaspoon salt**

Traditional crumb-topped coffee cake can easily have more than 500 calories and 25 grams of fat per piece.

TOPPING

¼ **cup pecans**

¼ **cup all-purpose flour**

2 **tablespoons brown sugar**

2 **tablespoons Splenda Granular**

1 **tablespoon butter, melted**

½ **teaspoon cinnamon**

STEPS:

1. Preheat oven to 350°F. Coat an 8-inch round baking pan with nonstick cooking spray.

2. Batter: In a medium bowl, whisk together buttermilk, egg, oil, Splenda Granular, orange zest, and vanilla. Set aside.

3. In a large bowl, combine flour, baking powder and soda, spices, and salt. Stir; make a well in the center and pour in buttermilk mixture. Mix gently with a large spoon until batter is smooth. Spoon batter into prepared pan.

4. Topping: In a small bowl, mix together pecans, flour, brown sugar, Splenda, butter, and cinnamon. Sprinkle over top of cake.

5. Bake for 25 minutes or until center springs back when lightly touched. Cool on rack.

PER SERVING

Calories 195	Fat 6 grams (2 saturated)
Carbohydrate 28 grams	Fiber 1 gram
Protein 5 grams	Sodium 200 milligrams

Diabetic exchange = 2 Carbohydrate, 1 Fat

WW point comparison = 4 points

Gingerbread Coffeecake

Serves Eight

This tender and very light-textured cake may become your next Christmas classic. Not overly sweet, but with a subtle taste of gingerbread, it makes a fine treat after a hard day of holiday shopping.

INGREDIENTS:

1 cup all-purpose flour, sifted

½ cup + 1 tablespoon Splenda Granular

1 ¾ teaspoons cinnamon

¾ teaspoon ginger

¼ teaspoon allspice

4 tablespoons margarine

¾ teaspoon baking powder

½ teaspoon baking soda

½ cup buttermilk

1 tablepoon + 2 teaspoons molasses

1 large egg, lightly beaten

STEPS:

1. Preheat oven to 350°F. Spray an 8-inch round cake pan with nonstick cooking spray.

2. In a large bowl, combine flour with ½ cup Splenda, ¾ teaspoon cinnamon, ginger and allspice. Cut in the margarine using a pastry blender or fork until the mixture resembles small crumbs. Measure out ⅓ cup into a small bowl and set aside.

3. To the large bowl of flour, add the baking powder, baking soda, buttermilk, molasses, and egg. Beat with a spoon or on low speed with a mixer until smooth. Spoon into the prepared pan.

4. Add last tablespoon of Splenda and 1 teaspoon cinnamon to the reserved crumb mixture. Sprinkle mixture over the top of the cake. Bake for 25 minutes or until the center of the cake springs back when touched lightly. Cool on rack.

Watch out for that cinnamon roll at the mall. It weighs in at almost 700 calories, with 34 grams of fat and more than 80 grams of carbohydrate. That's more than eating half this Gingerbread Coffeecake all by yourself.

PER SERVING

Calories 130	Fat 6 grams (1.5 saturated)
Carbohydrate 17 grams	Fiber 0.5 grams
Protein 3 grams	Sodium 200 milligrams

Diabetic exchange = 1 Carbohydrate, 1 Fat
WW point comparison = 3 points

Raspberry Almond Crumb Cake

Serves Eight

This cake is picture perfect. Inspired by Cooking Light magazine, I retooled this delightful cream cheese and raspberry crumb cake. Splenda helped me to lower the sugar to only 3 grams. Make it when you can get fresh raspberries and have a little extra time to put it together. This coffeecake is definitely worth it.

INGREDIENTS:

1 cup all-purpose flour, sifted

½ cup + 1 tablespoon + 1 teaspoon Splenda Granular

4 tablespoons margarine

2 tablespoons sliced almonds

2 egg whites

1 teaspoon baking powder

¾ teaspoon baking soda

2 tablespoons 1% or skim milk

1 teaspoon vanilla

½ teaspoon almond extract

¼ cup low-fat cottage cheese

2 tablespoons tub-style light cream cheese

¼ cup low-sugar raspberry preserves

½ cup fresh raspberries

For egg whites to beat fluffy, be sure bowl and beaters are clean and grease-free and that yolk gets into the whites. No don't need to wash the beaters before re-using them to beat the batter.

STEPS:

1. Preheat oven to 350°F. Spray an 8-inch round springform or cake pan with nonstick cooking spray.

2. In a large bowl, combine flour and ½ cup Splenda. Cut in the margarine, using a pastry blender or fork, until the mixture resembles small crumbs. Measure out 6 tablespoons into a small bowl; add almonds and set aside.

3. Place the egg whites into a bowl and beat with an electric mixer until soft peaks form. Set aside.

4. To the large bowl of flour, add the baking powder and soda, milk, and extracts. Use mixer on low speed and beat until blended. Fold in the beaten egg whites with a spatula or large spoon and spoon batter into prepared pan.

5. Purée cottage cheese until smooth in a food processor. Add cream cheese and remaining Splenda and pulse again until thick and creamy. Spread evenly over the cake batter. Dot the cheese mixture with the preserves and top with the raspberries.

6. Sprinkle almond crumb mixture over entire cake. Bake for 20 minutes or until cake springs back when touched lightly in the center. Cool on rack.

PER SERVING

Calories 140	Fat 6 grams (1.5 saturated)
Carbohydrate 17 grams	Fiber 1 gram
Protein 4 grams	Sodium 230 milligrams

Diabetic exchange = 1 Carbohydrate, 1 Fat
WW point comparison= 3 points

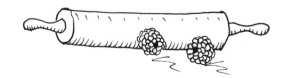

Simple Cinnamon Coffeecake

Serves Eight

Here is another quick-to-make coffeecake—no mixer required. In fact, this can be made and out of the oven in 30 minutes—just enough time to whip up some eggs, heat up some ham, and cut up some fruit for a nice Sunday breakfast.

INGREDIENTS:

1 ½ cups all-purpose flour

⅔ cup Splenda Granular

½ teaspoon baking powder

4 tablespoons margarine

1 ¼ teaspoons cinnamon

⅔ cup buttermilk

1 large egg

¾ teaspoon baking soda

1 ½ tablespoons brown sugar

STEPS:

1. Preheat oven to 350°F. Coat an 8-inch round or square pan with nonstick cooking spray.

2. In a large bowl, combine flour, Splenda, and baking powder. Using a pastry blender or fork, cut in the margarine until the mixture resembles small crumbs. Measure out 3 tablespoons into a small bowl and set aside.

3. To the large bowl of flour, add ½ teaspoon cinnamon. Measure buttermilk into large glass measuring cup. Whisk in egg and baking soda. Pour over flour mixture and stir with a large spoon just until blended. Spoon into prepared pan.

4. Add ¾ teaspoon cinnamon and brown sugar to small bowl. Mix and sprinkle over top of cake. Bake for 20–22 minutes or until the center of the cake springs back when lightly touched. Cool on rack.

PER SERVING

Calories 165	Fat 6 grams (1 saturated)
Carbohydrate 23 grams	Fiber 0 grams
Protein 4 grams	Sodium 210 milligrams

Diabetic exchange = 1 ½ Carbohydrate, 1 Fat

WW point comparison = 4 points

S'More Crumb Cake

Serves Nine

This crumb cake makes a great afternoon snack. My kids love it, as do many others according to the emails I have received. The fun combination of graham crackers and chocolate chips makes it easy to see where the name came from.

INGREDIENTS:

CAKE BATTER

3 tablespoons margarine, melted

¾ cup buttermilk

1 large egg

1 teaspoon vanilla

¾ cup Splenda Granular

1 ½ cups all-purpose flour

1 ½ teaspoons baking powder

½ teaspoon baking soda

½ teaspoon cinnamon

TOPPING

⅓ cup graham-cracker crumbs

¼ cup Splenda Granular

¼ cup mini chocolate chips

2 teaspoons powdered sugar

STEPS:

1. Preheat oven to 350°F. Coat an 8-inch square baking pan with nonstick baking spray.

2. BATTER: In a medium bowl, whisk together margarine, buttermilk, egg, vanilla, and Splenda. Set aside.

3. In a large bowl, combine flour, baking powder, baking soda, and cinnamon. Stir; make a well in the center and pour in buttermilk mixture. Mix gently with a large spoon until batter is smooth. Spoon batter into prepared pan.

4. TOPPING: Combine graham cracker crumbs, Splenda, and chocolate chips. Sprinkle over cake.

5. Bake for 20 minutes or until the center of the cake springs back when lightly touched.

6. Cool slightly on rack. Sift powdered sugar over cake.

Kids love to help cook, especially when you're making goodies like this. Having kids involved in choosing and preparing healthy foods will foster good lifelong eating habits.

PER SERVING

Calories 180	Fat 7 grams (2 saturated)
Carbohydrate 24 grams	Fiber 1 gram
Protein 4 grams	Sodium 240 milligrams

Diabetic exchange = 1 ½ Carbohydrate, 1 Fat

WW point comparison = 4 points

Blueberry Buckle

Serves Nine

This is the perfect coffeecake for your next brunch. Bursting with blueberries, it's topped with a streusel flecked with orange rind and just a touch of sugar for a glistening appearance. Make it in the height of summer when blueberries are in season. Your guests will surely thank you.

INGREDIENTS:

CAKE BATTER

1 ½ cups all-purpose flour, sifted

1 ½ teaspoons baking powder

½ teaspoon baking soda

½ cup Splenda Granular

1 cup blueberries (½ pint)

2 tablespoons canola oil

1 large egg

¾ cup buttermilk

TOPPING

⅓ cup all-purpose flour

¼ cup Splenda Granular

1 teaspoon orange rind

3 tablespoons light butter, chilled

2 teaspoons granulated sugar

STEPS:

1. Preheat oven to 350°F. Spray an 8-inch square baking pan with nonstick cooking spray.

2. Batter: In a large bowl, combine 1 ½ cups flour, baking powder, and baking soda. Stir. Add ½ cup Splenda and blueberries.

3. In a small bowl, whisk the oil, egg, and buttermilk. Make a well in the center of the dry ingredients and pour in the buttermilk mixture. Stir briefly just to combine. Spoon into the prepared pan and smooth the top.

4. TOPPING: In another small bowl, place ⅓ cup flour, ¼ cup Splenda, and orange rind. Cut in the light butter until mixture resembles small crumbs. Sprinkle over the top of the cake. Sprinkle sugar over topping.

5. Bake for 20-23 minutes or until center springs back when lightly touched. Cool on rack.

Just a touch of sugar, when spread on top, goes a long way and adds only 1 gram of carbohydrate per piece.

PER SERVING

Calories 160

Carbohydrate 26 grams

Protein 4 grams

Fat 4.5 grams (1 saturated)

Fiber 2 grams

Sodium 190 milligrams

Diabetic exchange = 1 ½ Carbohydrate, 1 Fat

WW point comparison = 3 points

Cinnamon Streusel Coffeecake

Serves Sixteen

This is the granddaddy of all coffeecakes. With streusel in the middle and on top, no wonder it's a favorite. The original has a stick or two of butter, sour cream, sugar, and nuts—so I knew I had my work cut out for me. But I finally came up with the big, showy cake I wanted. Wrap up this cake to seal in the moisture after you cut it. Less fat causes it to dry out faster.

INGREDIENTS:

STREUSEL

⅔ cup graham-cracker crumbs

⅔ cup Splenda Granular

⅓ cup chopped nuts

2 tablespoons cinnamon

1 tablespoon canola oil

1 tablespoon brown sugar

CAKE BATTER

3 cups cake flour

1 tablespoon baking powder

¾ teaspoon baking soda

⅓ cup margarine

1 ⅓ cups Splenda Granular

1 large egg

4 large egg whites

2 teaspoons vanilla

½ cup unsweetened applesauce

1 ½ cups light sour cream

STEPS:

1. Preheat oven to 350°F. Spray a 10-inch tube pan (angel food pan) or nonstick bundt pan with cooking spray.

2. STREUSEL: In a medium bowl, combine all the ingredients except the oil and brown sugar in a bowl. Set aside.

3. BATTER: Sift the cake flour, baking powder, and soda into a medium bowl. Set aside.

4. In a large mixing bowl, cream the margarine with an electric mixer. Add the Splenda and then the egg and continue to beat until smooth. Add the egg whites and vanilla. Beat briefly to incorporate. (It will not be smooth.) Beat in the applesauce. Add the sifted flour mixture and beat on low speed just until smooth. Add the sour cream and mix just until blended.

5. Spoon half of batter into the bottom of the prepared pan. Spread with a spoon to smooth. Sprinkle half of the streusel mixture over the batter. Drop the remaining batter by spoonfuls over the streusel and carefully spread. (Using the back of a spoon coated with cooking spray will help.)

6. Add the oil and brown sugar to the remaining streusel. Sprinkle on top.

7. Bake for 35-40 minutes or until a toothpick inserted near the center comes out clean. Cool on rack.

PER SERVING

Calories 195	Fat 8.5 grams (3 saturated)
Carbohydrate 24 grams	Fiber 1 gram
Protein 5 grams	Sodium 250 milligrams

Diabetic exchange = 1 ½ Carbohydrate, 1 ½ Fat
WW point comparision = 4 points

Sensational Side and Entree Salads

Sweet and Sour Party Slaw

Creamy Coleslaw

Waldorf Slaw

Asian Peanut Slaw

Old-Fashioned Seven-Layer Salad

Fresh and Crunchy Broccoli Salad

Creamy Carrot and Raisin Salad

Classic Triple Bean Salad

Southwest Black Bean and Corn Salad

Creamy Dilled Cucumber Salad

Oriental Cucumber Salad

Greek Hearts of Palm Salad

Sweet Italian Tomato Salad

Sweet and Sour Zucchini Salad

Romaine and Orange Salad

Marinated Beet and Red Onion Salad

Orange-Pineapple Layered Gelatin Mold

Holiday Cranberry Jello Salad

Sweet Tabbouleh Salad

Mandarin Spinach Salad

Spinach Salad with Hot Bacon Dressing

Entrée Salads

Thai Beef Salad

Chinese Chicken Salad

Rotisserie Chicken and Avocado Salad

We all think of salads as healthy, but an analysis of many of their ingredients (mayonnaise, oil, cheese, bacon, nuts, croutons, and, let's not forget, sugar) proves this theory wrong. Let's face it, the traditional salad may have a bit of lettuce here and a few veggies there, but anything healthy is often drowned out by all the tasty accoutrements or "add-ons." In fact, bacon bits, nuts, cheese, dressings, and the like can easily produce a salad of more than 1,000 calories—yep, that's 1,000.

But I've changed all that. In this chapter, you'll find recipes that have lightened up the fat, slashed the sugar, and cut the calories in salads we all love. In fact, I give you two dozen different ways to satisfy the salad lover in you. You'll find several great slaws to choose from—from Sweet and Sour Party Slaw to Asian Peanut Slaw—all perfect for entertaining. They're great especially when you're grilling out, whether it's your turn to cook or your turn to tote.

Old-fashioned and deli favorites, like broccoli salad, Classic Triple-Bean Salad, and Creamy Carrot and Raisin, have been given fresh and healthy makeovers, turning them into everyday favorites again. Also refreshed are some great dinnertime classics. Spinach Salad with Hot Bacon Dressing is back and, dare I say, better than ever; and so is Creamy Dilled Cucumber Salad, draped in luscious sour cream.

If you're looking for gelatin salads made with Splenda, I think you'll be delighted with the results of my refreshing Pineapple-Layered Gelatin Mold.

And last, for all you salad lovers (like me) who consider the salad "the meal," I've created three fabulous entrée salads, including my brand-new favorite—Thai Beef Salad.

Sweet and Sour Party Slaw

Serves Eight

When I think of picnic food, I think slaws. Slaws are shredded vegetable salads. Not all but most of them include shredded cabbage as a main ingredient. Slaws are great for picnics because they are easy to make (even when you're serving a crowd) and, more important, easy to tote. This is one of my favorites—you use both green and red cabbage for great color, and and toss it up with a sweet and tangy oil-based dressing.

INGREDIENTS:

6 cups shredded green cabbage (about 1 ½ pounds cabbage)

2 cups shredded red cabbage

1 cup shredded carrot (use large-holed grater)

½ sweet onion, peeled

¼ cup fresh chopped parsley (or cilantro)

¼ cup cider vinegar

3 tablespoons Splenda Granular (or 4 Splenda packets)

3 tablespoons virgin olive oil

1 tablespoon creamy mustard (like Dijonnaise)

2 teaspoons celery seed

½ teaspoon minced garlic

½ teaspoon salt

Pepper to taste

STEPS:

1. Place cabbages and carrot in a large bowl.

2. Quarter onion lengthwise. Cut into thin slices, making long, thin slivers of onion. Add to bowl. Toss in parsley.

3. In a small bowl, whisk together remaining ingredients. Pour over slaw and toss. Chill before serving.

To beautifully shred cabbage, use a knife— not a food processor or grater. Remove outer leaves and cut cabbage in half. Cut each half in half again lengthwise to create four cabbage wedges. Place one wedge on its side onto a cutting board. Then with a long sharp stainless-steel knife (like a chef's knife), remove core and slice off thin vertical slices of cabbage to create long julienned shreds.

PER SERVING (1 CUP)

Calories 70	Fat 5 grams (.5 saturated)
Carbohydrate 7 grams	Fiber 2 grams
Protein 1 gram	Sodium 180 milligrams

Diabetic exchange = 1 Vegetable, 1 Fat
WW point comparison = 1 point

Creamy Coleslaw

Serves Eight

If you enjoy the famous slaw found at KFC, you'll enjoy this. The big difference is not the taste but that my recipe contains half the fat of the Colonel's and no sugar at all.

INGREDIENTS:

8 cups very finely chopped cabbage

1 medium carrot, peeled and shredded

6 tablespoons light mayonnaise

6 tablespoons light sour cream

¼ cup 1% milk

¼ cup Splenda Granular

2 tablespoons vinegar

1 tablespoon lemon juice

1 teaspoon bottled horseradish

Generous ¼ teaspoon salt

STEPS:

1. Place cabbage and carrot in a large bowl. Set aside.

2. Whisk together remaining ingredients and toss with cabbage.

3. Chill for at least 2 hours for flavors to penetrate cabbage.

This slaw is an excellent source of both vitamins A and C.

PER SERVING (³/4 CUP)

Calories 80	Fat 4.5 grams (.5 saturated)
Carbohydrate 8 grams	Fiber 2 grams
Protein 1 gram	Sodium 210 milligrams

Diabetic exchange = 1 Vegetable, 1 Fat
WW point comparison = 2 points

Waldorf Slaw

Serves Six

The original Waldorf salad was created at New York's Waldorf-Astoria Hotel in the late 1890s. It contained simply apples, celery, and mayonnaise. Inspired by the original recipe, I have created a Waldorf slaw significantly lower in carbs and fat. I especially like the great crunch, twist, and beautiful color added by the red cabbage.

INGREDIENTS:

2 cups shredded* red cabbage

1 cup diced, peeled apples

1 cup diced celery

⅓ cup chopped walnuts

5 tablespoons light mayonnaise

6 tablespoons low-fat plain yogurt

1 tablespoon Splenda Granular
   (or 2 Splenda packets)

¼ teaspoon salt

STEPS:

1. Place cabbage, apples, celery, and nuts in a large bowl.
2. Whisk together remaining ingredients and toss with cabbage mixture. Refrigerate to chill and serve.

* See page 137 for tip on shredding cabbage.

PER SERVING (¾ CUP)

Calories 100	Fat 8 grams (1 saturated)
Carbohydrate 8 grams	Fiber 2 grams
Protein 2 grams	Sodium 190 milligrams

Diabetic exchange = 1 Vegetable, 1 ½ Fat
WW point comparison = 2 points

Red cabbage adds more than color and crunch to this salad. It also adds fiber, twice as much vitamin C as green cabbage, and phytochemicals known for cancer prevention.

Asian Peanut Slaw

Serves Five

Every time I take this to a picnic or potluck, someone asks for the recipe. This is definitely not your usual slaw, but it's incredibly delicious, especially to peanut-butter fans. With its Asian flair, this slaw complements fish or meat, including good ol' American favorites like hamburgers and hot dogs.

INGREDIENTS:

5 cups shredded* green cabbage
   (about 1 pound)

⅓ cup green onion, sliced on diagonal

1 medium carrot, peeled and shredded

3 tablespoons natural rice vinegar

2 ½ tablespoons peanut butter

2 tablespoons Splenda Granular
   (or 3 Splenda packets)

1 tablespoon brown sugar

2 teaspoons light soy sauce

2 teaspoons sesame oil

1 tablespoon water

⅛ teaspoon red pepper flakes (or to taste)

2 ½ tablespoons chopped, unsalted peanuts
   for garnish

Fresh cilantro (optional for garnish)

* See page 137 for tip on shredding cabbage.

STEPS:

1. Place cabbage, onion, and carrot in a large bowl.

2. Vigorously whisk together remaining ingredients in a small bowl until smooth.

3. Pour dressing over cabbage and toss. (It's best if you serve it within an hour or so of tossing. Take the dressing in a separate bottle if you are "toting" it and toss at serving location.)

4. Garnish with peanuts and cilantro.

For a picnic, double the recipe, place in a large bowl, and garnish with cilantro. Portion sizes here are generous at 1 cup; doubled, it will serve 12-16 people as part of a buffet.

PER SERVING (1 CUP)

Calories 120	Fat 8 grams (1 saturated)
Carbohydrate 11 grams	Fiber 3 grams
Protein 4 grams	Sodium 120 milligrams

Diabetic exchange = 2 Vegetable, 1 ½ Fat
WW point comparison = 2 points

Old-Fashioned Seven-Layer Salad

Serves Six

Another "oldie but goodie" found in my recipe archives, this crunchy, easy-to-tote salad has always been fun. Out with the old heavy grated cheddar and bacon layers, its made-over version has more fresh vegetables and a sprinkling of Parmesan.

INGREDIENTS:

1 small head iceberg lettuce, cut in cubes

1 large bell pepper, chopped

3 large stalks celery, chopped

4-6 green onions, sliced

1 cup frozen peas

½ cup light sour cream

½ cup light mayonnaise (like Best Foods or Hellman's)

2 tablespoons Splenda Granular

2 tablespoons grated Parmesan cheese

STEPS:

1. In a small bowl, mix together sour cream, mayonnaise, and Splenda. Set aside.

2. Starting with the lettuce and ending with the peas, carefully layer the first 5 ingredients in a bowl, being sure to spread ingredients to the rim each time.

3. Spread dressing over the top of the salad and sprinkle with Parmesan cheese.

4. Cover and refrigerate at least ½ hour (or up to overnight).

A pretty glass bowl with straight sides is ideal for layering and showing off the layers of this salad. Once finished, simply wrap the top tight with Saran Wrap, and you're all set to transport with no fuss upon arrival.

PER SERVING

Calories 140	Fat 9 grams (2.5 saturated)
Carbohydrate 10 grams	Fiber 3 grams
Protein 5 grams	Sodium 135 milligrams

Diabetic exchange = 2 Vegetable, 2 Fat

WW point comparison = 3 points

Fresh and Crunchy Broccoli Salad

Serves Six

You won't be able to take just one bite. If you've ever had a salad like this, you know that it is absolutely addictive. It has the perfect combination of crunchy nuts, sweet raisins, and crisp broccoli, all served up with a creamy dressing. In a hurry? Check to see if your produce department carries the florets ready to go in pre-packaged bags.

INGREDIENTS:

4 cups fresh broccoli florets, cut into bite-sized florets

½ cup chopped celery

½ cup thinly sliced red onion

⅓ cup packed raisins

3 tablespoons cider vinegar

2 tablespoons Splenda Granular

⅓ cup light mayonnaise

3 tablespoons light sour cream

¼ cup sunflower seeds

2 tablespoons real bacon bits (optional; these add 10 calories and 1 gram fat)

STEPS:

1. In a large bowl, mix together broccoli, celery, red onion, and raisins.

2. In a small bowl, whisk together vinegar, Splenda, mayonnaise, sour cream, and bacon (if desired).

3. When thoroughly mixed, pour dressing over broccoli and other ingredients and toss lightly. Place in refrigerator for at least 6 hours or overnight.

4. Just before serving, sprinkle sunflower seeds across top of salad.

Broccoli has been named one of today's "super foods." But there's nothing super about the original recipe for this salad, which contained 50 grams fat, 30 grams carbohydrate (25 of them from sugar), and more than 500 calories per serving.

PER SERVING

Calories 130	Fat 8 grams (2 saturated)
Carbohydrate 13 grams	Fiber 3 grams
Protein 4 grams	Sodium 120 milligrams

Diabetic exchange = 1 Vegetable, 1 ½ Fat, ½ Fruit
WW point comparison = 3 points

Creamy Carrot and Raisin Salad

Serves Five

My editor requested this one. She says this good old-fashioned deli favorite is making a comeback in her area. I'm not sure it ever left.

INGREDIENTS:

⅓ cup raisins

2 cups peeled, coarsely grated carrots (or 10-ounce bag freshly shredded carrots)

¼ cup chopped celery

¼ cup light mayonnaise

¼ cup nonfat plain yogurt

3 tablespoons Splenda Granular (or 4 Splenda packets)

2 tablespoons orange juice

1 tablespoon lemon juice

¼ teaspoon salt

STEPS:

1. In a small bowl, pour ½ cup very hot water over raisins. Let sit 5 minutes, drain, and transfer to a medium bowl. Add carrots and celery.

2. Whisk together remaining ingredients and toss with carrot mixture. Serve immediately at room temperature or refrigerate.

Pick this up at the deli, and you will also be picking up twice the sugar and carbohydrates and four times the fat in a ½-cup serving.

PER SERVING (¹/2 CUP)

Calories 90	Fat 3 grams (1 saturated)
Carbohydrate 15 grams	Fiber 2 grams
Protein 2 grams	Sodium 210 milligrams

Diabetic exchange = 1 Vegetable, ½ Fruit, 1 Fat
WW point comparison = 2 points

Classic Three Bean Salad

Serves Six

My mother loves this salad-bar staple. She buys it in large jars yet is careful to watch her portions because of the sugar content. Now she can make her own using my recipe, which contains ½ the carbohydrates and calories and about ⅓ the fat of commercially prepared versions. In her honor, I have designated an ample ¾-cup portion.

INGREDIENTS:

1 15-ounce can cut green beans, drained

1 15-ounce can yellow wax beans, drained

1 15-ounce kidney beans, drained and rinsed

1 small green pepper, diced

1 small red pepper, diced

1 small red onion, diced

½ cup red wine vinegar

⅔ cup Splenda Granular

¼ cup tomato juice

3 tablespoons canola oil

¾ teaspoon salt

½ teaspoon pepper

STEPS:

1. In a large bowl, gently mix together beans, green and red peppers, and red onion.
2. In a small bowl (or jar with lid), whisk (or shake) remaining ingredients.
3. Pour dressing over bean mixture and toss to coat. Cover and refrigerate at least 6 hours. or preferably overnight, before serving.

Not all carbs are created equal. This salad is chock-full of fiber and high in protein—in other words, these carbs are good for you.

PER SERVING (³/₄ CUP)

Calories 165	Fat 6.5 grams (.5 saturated)
Carbohydrate 22 grams	Fiber 7 grams
Protein 6 grams	Sodium 360 milligrams

Diabetic exchange = 2 Vegetable, 1 Fat, 1 Very Lean Meat, ½ Carbohydrate

WW point comparison = 3 points (½ cup = 2 points)

Southwest Black Bean and Corn Salad

Serves Eight

This is a great side dish salad. It's healthy, colorful, and always a hit. In my family, it's referred to as "Marlene's Black Bean Salad," and everyone has made it at one time or another, most often for entertaining. Personally, I find it's another perfect potluck dish because it goes well with just about anything that can be thrown on a grill.

INGREDIENTS:

1 15-ounce can black beans, drained and rinsed

1 15-ounce can corn niblets, drained

½ cup garbanzo beans or chickpeas, drained

½ cup frozen peas (do not thaw)

½ cup sliced black olives

1 medium red pepper, diced

½ medium red onion, diced

½ cup diced jicama (optional)

6 tablespoons red wine vinegar

3 tablespoons olive oil

1 ½ tablespoons Splenda Granular (or 2 packets)

2 teaspoons crushed garlic

¾ teaspoon cumin

¼ teaspoon salt

¼ teaspoon red pepper

½ cup fresh cilantro, chopped

STEPS:

1. Place black beans, corn, garbanzo beans, peas, olives, pepper, onion, and jicama in a large bowl.

2. In a small bowl, whisk together vinegar, oil, Splenda, garlic, cumin, salt, and red pepper. Pour over salad and stir to coat. Add fresh cilantro and stir once more.

3. Refrigerate for at least 1 hour. Keeps well for several days.

When you're trying to eat more fiber, you can't do much better than beans. Each ½ cup has a whopping 5 grams of fiber. That's a big hit toward the 25 grams or more recommended daily.

PER SERVING

Calories 155	Fat 6 grams (.5 saturated)
Carbohydrate 22 grams	Fiber 7 grams
Protein 6 grams	Sodium 350 milligrams

Diabetic exchange = 1 Carbohydrate, 1 Vegetable, 1 Fat
WW point comparison = 3 points

Creamy Dilled Cucumber Salad

Serves Six

Cucumbers draped in luscious sour cream are an Old World tradition. Here I have cut the fat by using "light" sour cream, and I've added some fresh dill along with red onion to add a new fresh taste. Because the cukes will "water out," serve this salad the day you make it or crisp them up by using the tip in the following recipe.

INGREDIENTS:

½ cup reduced-fat sour cream

2 tablespoons Splenda Granular

2 tablespoons apple cider vinegar

2 teaspoons chopped fresh dill

Pinch salt

4 cups thinly sliced, peeled cucumber

½ cup thinly sliced red onion

STEPS:

1. In a large bowl, combine sour cream, Splenda, vinegar, dill, and a pinch of salt.

2. Add the cucumbers and onion and stir gently to coat.

3. Cover and refrigerate for 30 minutes to allow the flavors to meld and the cukes to soften slightly. Stir again gently just before serving.

"Light" and reduced-fat sour creams vary widely in quality. The best ones, like Knudsen Light Sour Cream, are wonderful replacements for their full-fat counterparts. But others can be gummy or gelatinous and lack flavor. So, if your first try doesn't yield one that you like, be sure to sample another brand.

PER SERVING

Calories 40

Carbohydrate 5 grams

Protein 2 grams

Fat 2 grams (1.5 saturated)

Fiber 1 gram

Sodium 65 milligrams

Diabetic exchange = 1 Vegetable, ½ Fat

WW point comparison = 1 point

Oriental Cucumber Salad

Serves Four

A cool and refreshing salad brimming with flavor, this is often served with Asian dishes as it offers a nice balance to their spiciness. Serve it with grilled teriyaki chicken or fish.

INGREDIENTS:

½ **cup hot water**

¼ **cup Splenda Granular**

¼ **cup natural rice wine vinegar**

2 **tablespoons sliced green onion**

2 **tablespoons minced fresh cilantro**

½ **teaspoon freshly grated ginger**

½ **teaspoon salt**

1 **small jalapeno, seeded and finely diced (optional)**

1 ½ **pounds cucumbers, peeled, seeded, and sliced (2 ½ cups)**

1 **medium carrot, peeled and shredded**

STEPS:

1. In a large shallow bowl, whisk together all ingredients except cucumbers and carrot. When thoroughly mixed, toss with the cucumbers and carrot.

2. Refrigerate until cool (at least 30 minutes). Serve in lettuce cups if desired.

To keep cucumbers crisp, sprinkle slices with 2 teaspoons of salt and let sit for 1 hour. Rinse well before adding to recipe and eliminate ½ teaspoon salt added to dressing.

PER SERVING (¹/₂ CUP)

Calories 35	Fat 0 grams (0 saturated)
Carbohydrate 8 grams	Fiber 2 grams
Protein 1 gram	Sodium 260 milligrams

Diabetic exchange = 1 Vegetable
WW point comparison = 0 points

Greek Hearts of Palm Salad

Serves Four

Hearts of palm have a delicate flavor similar to that of artichoke hearts. Here, they are used in place of high-fat olives to lower the fat in this twist on a Greek Salad. With its piquant mustard dressing, this is delicious served on lettuce leaves or all by itself as a side dish.

INGREDIENTS:

1 14.5-ounce can hearts of palm, sliced ¼- to ½-inch thick

12 cherry tomatoes, halved

½ cucumber, peeled, cut in half, seeded, and sliced in half-moon pieces

½ small red onion, sliced and separated into rings

¼ cup white wine vinegar

1 ½ tablespoons Splenda Granular

1 tablespoon Dijon mustard

1 clove garlic, crushed

½ teaspoon ground oregano

½ teaspoon dried basil

Pinch salt

$\frac{1}{8}$ teaspoon pepper

2 tablespoons olive oil

4 green- or red-leaf lettuce leaves

4 tablespoons crumbled feta cheese

STEPS:

1. In a large bowl, combine hearts of palm, tomatoes, cucumber, and onion.

2. In a small bowl, whisk together vinegar, Splenda, Dijon, garlic, spices, salt, and pepper. Continue whisking and slowly drizzle olive oil into the mixture.

3. Pour dressing over salad and toss to combine. Chill for 1 hour.

4. Spoon onto lettuce leaves and top each salad with feta cheese.

Hearts of palm are the "heart" of the young leaf shoots found on a cabbage palm tree. Low in carbohydrates and free of fat, they can be found next to canned artichoke hearts in most grocery stores.

PER SERVING

Calories 130	Fat 9 grams (2.5 saturated)
Carbohydrate 9 grams	Fiber 3 grams
Protein 4 grams	Sodium 350 milligrams

Diabetic exchange = 2 Vegetable, 2 Fat
WW point comparison = 3 points

Sweet Italian Tomato Salad

Serves Six

This salad tastes best when you use tomatoes at the peak of their season—ones that are firm and full of flavor. It's so good that even people who don't usually eat tomatoes enjoy it. Served either cold or at room temperature, it's a great buffet dish.

INGREDIENTS:

⅓ cup white wine (or cider) vinegar

⅓ cup Splenda Granular

3 tablespoons extra-virgin olive oil

¾ teaspoon dried basil (or 2 teaspoons fresh, minced)

½ teaspoon minced garlic

¼ teaspoon salt (or to taste)

8 medium tomatoes (about 2 ½ pounds), quartered and seeded

STEPS:

1. In a large bowl, whisk together all the ingredients except tomatoes.
2. When thoroughly mixed, gently stir in tomatoes. Will keep several days covered in the refrigerator.

Tomatoes are an excellent source of potassium and vitamin C. You can add buffalo mozzarella or goat cheese to this salad for extra flavor and texture.

PER SERVING (³/4 CUP)

Calories 100	Fat 7 grams (1 saturated)
Carbohydrate 10 grams	Fiber 2 grams
Protein 1 gram	Sodium 110 milligrams

Diabetic exchange = 2 Vegetable, 1 Fat
WW point comparison = 2 points

Sweet and Sour Zucchini Salad

Serves Eight

This very simple salad is packed with fresh flavors and crunch, making it a great addition to any table. I serve it in a large flat bowl with additional Italian parsley garnishing the rim, to give this ordinary vegetable an extraordinary presentation.

INGREDIENTS:

¾ **cup cider vinegar**

⅔ **cup Splenda Granular**

1 **teaspoon salt**

1 **teaspoon black pepper, freshly ground**

¼ **cup canola oil**

4 **medium zucchini, thinly sliced (about 1 pound)**

1 **medium red onion, thinly sliced**

1 **red bell pepper, diced**

1 **cup celery, diced**

2 **tablespoons chopped Italian parsley**

STEPS:

1. Whisk together cider vinegar, Splenda, salt, pepper, and canola oil.

2. Place zucchini, red onion, red bell pepper, and celery in a medium bowl or large ziplock bag. Pour in dressing. Cover or "zip," and place in refrigerator to marinate for 4–8 hours.

3. Just before serving, toss in chopped parsley.

PER SERVING

Calories 80	Fat 2 grams (1 saturated)
Carbohydrate 11 grams	Fiber 2 grams
Protein 5 grams	Sodium 65 milligrams

Diabetic exchange = 2 Vegetable, ½ Fat
WW point comparison = 1 point

Romaine and Orange Salad

Serves Eight

This light and sweet salad is the perfect complement to a heavy or spicy entrée. Don't skip toasting the nuts, as it crisps them up and brings out their flavor.

INGREDIENTS:

½ cup sliced almonds

2 oranges, peeled and sectioned

8 cups chopped or torn romaine lettuce

¼ cup rice wine vinegar

¼ cup Splenda Granular

3 tablespoons canola oil

3 tablespoons orange juice

½ teaspoon prepared mustard

Fresh ground pepper to taste

STEPS:

1. Preheat oven to 325°F.

2. Spread almonds onto ungreased baking sheet and bake for 5 minutes. Shake sheet to toss nuts and bake 2-3 minutes longer until nuts darken in color. Set aside to cool.

3. Cut orange sections in half and place in large bowl. Add romaine and toss.

4. In a small bowl, whisk together remaining ingredients.

5. Just prior to serving, pour dressing over salad and toss lightly. Sprinkle almonds on top.

PER SERVING

Calories 110

Carbohydrate 7 grams

Protein 2 grams

Fat 8 grams (0 saturated)

Fiber 2 grams

Sodium 45 milligrams

Diabetic exchange = 1 Vegetable, 2 Fat

WW point comparison = 2 points

Marinated Beet and Red Onion Salad

Serves Three

This low-calorie salad is a refreshing and colorful change from the usual slaws and potato salads. You can double or triple the recipe.

INGREDIENTS:

1 16-ounce can sliced beets

¼ cup beet juice (reserved from sliced beets)

½ medium red onion, peeled and sliced thin

¼ cup white wine (or cider) vinegar

3 tablespoons Splenda Granular (or 4 Splenda packets)

½ teaspoon dry mustard

½ teaspoon cornstarch

STEPS:

1. Drain beets, reserving ¼ cup liquid, and julienne to make ½-inch strips. Place in a large bowl and add onion. Set aside.

2. In a small saucepan, mix together the reserved juice and remaining ingredients.

3. Place over medium heat and cook until sauce comes to a boil, thickens slightly, and clears.

4. Pour marinade over beets and red onion. Cool; then refrigerate for several hours before serving.

For a picnic, triple the recipe, place in a medium bowl, and garnish with 2 teaspoons fresh orange zest (will serve 10–12 as part of a buffet).

PER SERVING (¹/2 CUP)

Calories 40

Carbohydrate 10 grams

Protein 1 gram

Fat 0 grams (0 saturated)

Fiber 2 grams

Sodium 170 milligrams

Diabetic exchange = 2 Vegetable

WW point comparison = 0 points

Orange-Pineapple Layered Gelatin Mold

Serves Eight

Old-fashioned molded gelatin salads never lose their appeal. Made from scratch, this gelatin has a cleaner, fresher flavor and a more natural color than packaged gelatins. This is not hard to make but takes a couple steps, and you use most ingredients more than once, so keep your measuring cups handy.

INGREDIENTS:

2 packets unflavored gelatin

2 ¼ cups low-sugar orange juice (like Tropicana Light 'n Healthy)

½ cup Splenda Granular

2 tablespoons lemon juice

1 8-ounce can crushed pineapple, drained and juice reserved

1 cup low-fat cottage cheese

¼ cup low-fat cream cheese

"Old-fashioned" is not merely a saying when it comes to gelatin. The first patent for gelatin sold in boxes was in 1845, and Jell-O brand gelatin is now more than 100 years old.

STEPS:

1. Sprinkle one packet of gelatin over ¼ cup of the orange juice in a small bowl. Let sit for 3 minutes to soften.

2. Bring another ½ cup of the orange juice to a boil in the microwave. Pour over gelatin and stir to dissolve. Add ¼ cup Splenda, lemon juice, ¾ cup orange juice, and reserved pineapple juice. Mix thoroughly and pour into 4-cup gelatin mold or glass bowl and refrigerate until completely set.

3. When first layer is set, sprinkle second packet of gelatin over ¼ cup of orange juice in a small bowl. Let set as above to soften. Bring last ½ cup of orange juice to a boil, pour over softened gelatin, and stir to dissolve.

4. In the food processor or blender, blend the cottage cheese until smooth and creamy. Add last ¼ cup Splenda and gently pulse in the cream cheese just until blended. Whisk cheese mixture into gelatin mixture. Fold in the crushed pineapple.

5. Spoon pineapple mixture over molded gelatin mixture. Smooth pineapple layer and chill until completely set.

6. To unmold, immerse outside of gelatin mold or bowl briefly in hot water to loosen gelatin. Place a large plate on top of mold or bowl and quickly invert gelatin onto plate.

PER SERVING

Calories 80	Fat 1.5 grams (1 saturated)
Carbohydrate 10 grams	Fiber 1 gram
Protein 6 grams	Sodium 135 milligrams

Diabetic exchange = 1 Lean Meat, ½ Fruit
WW point comparison = 2 points

Holiday Cranberry Jello Salad

Serves Ten

Gelatin salads are like having a touch of dessert with your dinner, which is probably why they are served at festive occasions. This particular type of gelatin salad is a holiday staple, but my version also leaves you room for dessert.

INGREDIENTS:

1 12-ounce bag fresh cranberries, washed and picked over

1 ½ cups Splenda Granular

2 cups boiling water

1 6-ounce box sugar-free cherry gelatin dessert mix

¼ cup granulated sugar

1 cup cold water

1 ½ cups crushed pineapple (packed in light juice), drained

½ cup finely chopped celery

½ cup chopped nuts

STEPS::

1. Finely chop cranberries in food processor or by hand and place in medium bowl. Add Splenda and stir. Set aside.

2. In a large bowl, pour boiling water over gelatin and sugar to dissolve. Add cold water. Stir in cranberries, pineapple, celery, and nuts.

3. Pour into 2-quart serving container, mold, or 9 x 13-inch glass pan, and place in refrigerator for several hours or until firm.

If you're eating the traditional version and are watching your carbs, beware—it packs 63 grams a serving. (That's as much as eating a big piece of fruit pie.)

PER SERVING (¹/₂ CUP)

Calories 110	Fat 3.5 grams (2 saturated)
Carbohydrate 17 grams	Fiber 2 grams
Protein 3 grams	Sodium 45 milligrams

Diabetic exchange = 1 Carbohydrate, ½ Fat
WW point comparison = 2 points

Sweet Tabbouleh Salad

Serves Eight

This refreshing and energizing salad is a classic vegetarian dish in the Middle East. Made in true Middle Eastern style, tabbouleh's two main ingredients are fresh parsley and lemon, not bulgur, which is minimized. This makes a nice salad or side dish and can be spooned into whole-wheat pita bread.

INGREDIENTS:

½ cup bulgur wheat, dry

4 cups parsley, chopped

4 roma tomatoes, seeded and chopped

½ medium cucumber, peeled, seeded, and chopped

⅔ cup chopped green onions

2 tablespoons chopped fresh mint (or 1 tablespoon dry)

2 tablespoons extra-virgin olive oil

1 tablespoon Splenda Granular

Juice of 2-3 lemons, about ½ cup

½ teaspoon salt

¼ teaspoon black pepper

STEPS:

1. In a small bowl, add dry bulgur wheat to 1 cup of boiling water. Let stand 5-10 minutes until bulgur softens.

2. In a large bowl, mix together parsley, tomatoes, cucumber, onions, mint, and softened bulgur.

3. In a small bowl, whisk together olive oil, Splenda, fresh lemon juice, salt, and pepper.

4. Toss vegetable-bulgur mix with dressing. Chill.

Bulgur wheat is an excellent source of vitamins, minerals, phytochemicals, and fiber.

PER SERVING

Calories 95	Fat 4 grams (1 saturated)
Carbohydrate 13 grams	Fiber 4 grams
Protein 2 grams	Sodium 160 milligrams

Diabetic exchange = 1 Vegetable, 1 Fat, ½ Carbohydrate
WW point comparison = 1 point

Mandarin Spinach Salad

Serves Eight

The delicious dressing that adorns this salad is very unique and absolutely makes the dish. To create this unusual sweet and tangy dressing, you use grated red onion. You can also turn this into an entrée for four by topping it with cooked, thinly sliced top sirloin marinated in Teriyaki Sauce (page 173).

INGREDIENTS:

8 cups fresh spinach leaves (about 8 ounces)

1 8-ounce can sliced water chestnuts, drained

1 11-ounce can mandarin oranges, drained

8 ounces sliced mushrooms

1 small red onion, grated

3 tablespoons canola oil

2 tablespoons ketchup

2 tablespoons Splenda Granular

2 tablespoons apple cider vinegar

2 tablespoons water

2 teaspoons Worcestershire sauce

2 teaspoons soy sauce

Freshly ground black pepper

⅓ cup sliced almonds or crispy rice noodles (optional)

STEPS:

1. In a large salad bowl, gently combine spinach, water chestnuts, mandarin oranges, and mushrooms. Set aside.

2. In a small bowl, stir together next 8 ingredients. Gently toss dressing with salad just prior to serving.

3. Add pepper and sprinkle almonds or crispy noodles on top as desired.

Pop the onion into the refrigerator an hour or so before you grate it and you'll be less likely to tear up. The vapors, when cold, do not travel as readily. To prepare the grated onion, peel and trim the onion and then grate it with a medium-holed grater the way you would a carrot.

PER SERVING

Calories 100   Fat 5 grams (0 saturated)
Carbohydrate 12 grams   Fiber 4 grams
Protein 3 grams   Sodium 180 milligrams

Diabetic exchange = 2 Vegetable, 1 Fat
WW point comparison = 2 points

Spinach Salad with Hot Bacon Dressing

Serves Eight

Of spinach salad variations, this is my all-time favorite. I have seen some recipes that start out with as much as a ½ pound of bacon for four servings—probably why it is often reserved for special occasions. But you can enjoy this healthful yet delicious version anytime.

INGREDIENTS:

4 slices center-cut lean bacon

½ cup diced onion

½ cup water

⅓ cup cider vinegar

3 tablespoons Splenda Granular (or 4 Splenda packets)

Salt (to taste if desired)

1 teaspoon cornstarch mixed with 2 teaspoons water

12 ounces prewashed, bagged spinach leaves (or 1 pound fresh)

1 red onion, peeled and sliced into thin rings

1 cup sliced mushrooms

STEPS:

1. In a large skillet, cook bacon over moderate heat, turning until crisp. Transfer to a paper-towel-lined plate, blot off excess fat, and crumble. Set aside.

2. Add onion to drippings (you should have about 2 tablespoons—if more, discard excess). Cook for 3 minutes or until softened and golden. Add water, vinegar, Splenda, and salt if desired. Stir, scraping bottom to incorporate drippings.

3. Bring to low boil and add cornstarch mixture. Heat until thickened and clear.

4. In a large bowl, combine spinach, onion, and mushrooms.

5. Pour hot dressing over spinach mixture and toss. Sprinkle with crumbled bacon and serve.

Using prewashed bagged spinach makes whipping up a great spinach salad a snap.

PER SERVING

Calories 100

Carbohydrate 12 grams

Protein 3 grams

Fat 5 grams (1 saturated)

Fiber 4 grams

Sodium 180 milligrams

Diabetic exchange = 2 Vegetable, 1 Fat

WW point comparison = 2 points

Thai Beef Salad

Serves Four

This colorful salad is simply bursting with flavor. It's terrific year-round, but I find it especially nice in the summer, when tomatoes are at their peak and the weather is perfect for outdoor grilling.

INGREDIENTS:

1 pound flank steak

8 cups mixed greens (such as spring mix)

2 medium tomatoes, cut in wedges

½ cup sweet onion, thinly sliced

¼ cup mint leaves, julienned or chopped

¼ cup cilantro, coarsely chopped

½ cucumber peeled, halved, seeded, and sliced into half-moons

¼ cup green onion, thinly sliced (white and green) for garnish

MARINADE AND DRESSING

½ cup light soy sauce

½ cup lime juice

2 tablespoons fish sauce

½ cup Splenda Granular

1 tablespoon Thai or serrano chiles, seeded, minced

1 tablespoon garlic, minced

⅓ cup green onion, thinly sliced (white and green)

2 tablespoons fresh ginger, minced or grated

1 tablespoon cilantro, finely chopped

1 tablespoon canola oil

1 teaspoon sesame oil

STEPS:

1. MARINADE: Combine soy sauce, lime juice, and fish sauce, and stir in Splenda. Add chiles, garlic, onion, ginger, and cilantro.

2. Reserve ⅓ cup of the mixture for the salad dressing. Pour the remainder (about 1 cup) over the steak and marinate for 1–2 hours.

3. Grill the steak over a hot fire, about 7–8 minutes for medium rare, or to desired level of doneness. Cover with foil or place in a warm oven to rest for 5–10 minutes before carving.

4. Toss the mint, cilantro, cucumber, and sweet onion gently into the salad greens.

5. Whisk the oils into the reserved marinade (or shake in a tightly covered jar) to finish the dressing. Pour over the greens and toss to coat evenly.

6. Add the tomatoes and toss gently.

7. Arrange the salad on dinner plates, with the bright tomatoes around the edges.

8. Carve the steak into thin slices, cutting across the grain of the meat on the diagonal. Arrange the slices on top of the salads; garnish with green onion and serve.

You can julienne broad-leafed herbs such as mint and basil in a jiffy. Stack the leaves, roll them up, and slice thinly across the roll. Gently toss cut pieces to tease the strips apart.

PER SERVING

Calories 310	Fat 14 grams (4.5 saturated)
Carbohydrate 19 grams	Fiber 4 grams
Protein 29 grams	Sodium 1420 milligrams

Diabetic exchange = 4 Lean Meat, 2 Vegetable, ½ Carbohydrate, ½ Fat

WW point comparison = 6 points

Chinese Chicken Salad

Serves Four

I simply had to include this recipe because I love Chinese Chicken Salad. While chicken salad sounds light, most are anything but. In fact, a popular fast-food chain's oriental-inspired chicken salad with sesame dressing contains more than 35 grams of fat and uses no fewer than four types of sugar to sweeten the dressing—for more than 50 grams of carbohydrate per serving. This flavorful, large-meal-sized salad packs in more protein and great nutrition, with a lot fewer carbs and calories.

INGREDIENTS:

4 cups spring salad mix

1 cup shredded Napa cabbage

1 medium red pepper, julienned

1 medium yellow pepper, julienned

2 ounces fresh snow peas, trimmed and cut in half on diagonal

½ cup sliced green onions

4 cups thin strips or shredded cooked chicken breast (about 1 pound)

3 tablespoons natural rice wine vinegar

1 ½ tablespoons Splenda Granular (or 2 Splenda packets)

1 tablespoon light soy sauce

½ teaspoon fresh grated ginger

2 tablespoons canola oil

1 ½ tablespoons sesame oil

Freshly ground pepper

½ cup crispy rice noodles (or sliced almonds★)

STEPS:

1. In a large bowl, toss together the salad mix, cabbage, peppers, snow peas, and green onions. Add chicken to bowl. Set aside.

2. Whisk together remaining ingredients except rice noodles and pour into bowl. Toss lightly and portion onto 4 plates. Top each salad with 2 tablespoons noodles (or nuts).

★If you are severely restricting your carbs, choose almonds instead of noodles and the carbohydrates decrease to 10 grams and the fiber increases to 5 grams, making the net carbs 5. This, however, also increases calories by 40 and fat by 5 grams.

PER SERVING

Calories 320	Fat 15 grams (2 saturated)
Carbohydrate 13 grams	Fiber 3 grams
Protein 33 grams	Sodium 390 milligrams

Diabetic exchange = 4 Lean Meat, 1 Vegetable, ½ Carbohydrate, 1 Fat

WW point comparison = 7 points (a packet of fast-food dressing alone is 8 points)

Rotisserie Chicken and Avocado Salad

Serves Two

This hearty entrée salad is not low-fat, but it's quite healthy. I created it while looking for low-carb entrées that featured "good" fats and lean meats, and found it quite popular, even with non-salad-loving men. It seems the hearty portion of meat and creamy avocado hit a chord. For women, my use of store-bought rotisserie chicken sealed the deal.

INGREDIENTS:

4 cups mixed lettuce

1 small red pepper cut in strips

8 ounces rotisserie chicken breast meat

½ cup thinly sliced cucumber

½ avocado, pitted and sliced

¼ cup Mustard Vinaigrette (page 165)

½ cup sliced green onion

Fresh cilantro (for garnish)

STEPS:

1. Divide lettuce onto two large plates. Sprinkle with red pepper strips, and place ½ of chicken breast meat in center of each salad.

2. Decoratively place cucumbers around edge of plates and fan avocado on either side of chicken.

3. Drizzle each salad with 2 tablespoons vinaigrette and top with green onion. Garnish with cilantro if desired.

When compared to the Asian chicken salad from a popular fast-food eatery, this recipe gives you 9 extra grams of protein, with 28 fewer grams carbohydrate and 36 fewer grams sugar. You also still save 180 calories.

PER SERVING

Calories 430	Fat 26 grams (2.5 saturated)
Carbohydrate 12 grams	Fiber 6 grams
Protein 39 grams	Sodium 320 milligrams

Diabetic exchange = 4.5 Lean Meat, 3 Fat, 2 Vegetable
WW point comparison = 10 points

Dressings and Marinades

Dressings

Raspberry Vinaigrette
Sweet Balsamic Vinaigrette
Sweet Mustard Vinaigrette
Thousand Island Dressing
Fat-Free Catalina Dressing
Old World Sour Cream Dip
    and Dressing
Creamy Poppy Seed Dressing
Sesame Ginger Dressing
Spinach Salad Dressing
Strawberry Yogurt Fruit Salad Dressing

Marinades

Teriyaki Sauce
Spicy Teriyaki Sauce
Fresh Citrus Marinade
Spicy Thai Marinade
    and Dipping Sauce

Salads may make the meal, but dressings make the salad. Because I'm a cooking instructor, people often assume I make everything from scratch. But the truth is, I don't. I often use packaged and convenience products just like you do, but not for my salad dressings.

Here's why. Just read the label. A typical regular bottled dressing can contain more than 200 calories, 20 grams of fat, and 10 grams of carbohydrate in just two tablespoons. The same goes for restaurant dressings, only their idea of what constitutes one serving is at least twice that much!

With these facts, it's easy to see why salad dressings are highlighted as a major source of fat in our diets. And although I am aware that there are many low-fat, no-fat, and even "low-carb" dressings on the market, honestly, when it comes to dressings, I make my own because healthy-homemade tastes so much better. I'm sure you'll agree after you've sampled some of these recipes.

Just try the lovely Raspberry Vinaigrette on a salad of assorted greens or Creamy Poppy Seed Dressing on fresh fruit or luscious Old World Sour Cream Dressing over a crisp wedge of iceberg. I also recommend that you check out the dressings in the Side and Entrée Salad section because even though those dresssings are parts of complete salad recipes, you can easily "borrow" them. For example, you'll find a nice basic sweet and sour dressing in the Sweet and Sour Party Slaw, recipe and there's a wonderful marinade dressing in the Classic Three-Bean Salad. Simply make the dressing alone and use on anything you choose.

In this section you'll also find four terrific marinades and a dipping sauce to perk flavor and keep lean meats tender. Use these to "dress" anything from beef and pork to poultry and seafood—from easy teriyakis to a brand-new authentic Spicy Thai Marinade and Dipping Sauce.

Raspberry Vinaigrette

Serves Five

Many raspberry vinaigrettes start with raspberry vinegar. After searching for it in my local markets, I realized that it can be hard to find and expensive. My solution is to use whole raspberries to impart a wonderful distinctive raspberry taste. An added bonus is the thickness you get from pureeing the whole raspberries in this flavorful reduced-fat dressing.

INGREDIENTS:

4 tablespoons natural rice vinegar

2 tablespoons canola oil

¼ cup fresh or frozen raspberries

1 tablespoon Dijon mustard

1 tablespoon each lime (or lemon) juice and water

1 tablespoon Splenda Granular (or 2 Splenda packets)

Fresh ground pepper to taste

STEPS:

1. Puree all ingredients in a food processor or blender until smooth.
2. Adjust pepper.

This is delicious over grilled chicken and mixed greens, garnished with toasted pecans.

PER SERVING (2 TABLESPOONS)

Calories 60	Fat 6 grams (0 saturated)
Carbohydrate 1 gram	Fiber 1 gram
Protein 0 grams	Sodium 40 milligrams

Diabetic exchange = 1 Fat
WW point comparison = 1 point

Sweet Balsamic Vinaigrette

Serves Six

This sweet vinaigrette is a lovely dressing for salads containing fruit. I like it drizzled over baby greens and sliced strawberries, spinach with fresh orange sections, or red leaf lettuce and thin pear slices.

INGREDIENTS:

3 tablespoons red wine vinegar

2 tablespoons balsamic vinegar

2 tablespoons orange juice

2 tablespoons Splenda Granular (or 3 Splenda packets)

1 clove garlic, minced

3 tablespoons extra-virgin olive oil

2 teaspoons Dijon mustard

Freshly ground pepper

STEPS:

1. Whisk first 5 ingredients together in a small bowl.

2. Whisk in olive oil, 1 tablespoon at a time, to incorporate thoroughly.

3. Whisk in mustard. Add pepper to taste.

Traditional vinaigrette recipes use 3 parts oil to 1 part vinegar, giving them up to 20 grams fat in 2 tablespoons.

PER SERVING (2 TABLESPOONS)

Calories 70	Fat 7 grams (1 saturated)
Carbohydrate 2 grams	Fiber 0 grams
Protein 0 grams	Sodium 0 milligrams

Diabetic exchange = 1 ½ Fat
WW point comparison = 2 points

Sweet Mustard Vinaigrette

Serves Six

Classic vinaigrettes usually have three parts oil to one part vinegar. The oil's job is to cut the bite of the vinegar and to emulsify the dressing. In this tangy dressing, I use mustard and sugar to tone down the vinegar and a touch of xantham gum to emulsify it, which reduced the fat content by 75 percent. If you can't find xantham gum, cut the water to 1 tablespoon and pour the dressing over your salad as soon as it's whisked.

INGREDIENTS:

⅓ cup natural rice wine vinegar

3 tablespoons water

1 tablespoon prepared yellow mustard

1 ½ tablespoons Splenda Granular (or 2 packets)

2 tablespoons finely chopped cilantro

⅛ teaspoon salt

¼ cup canola or olive oil

Scant ¼ teaspoon xantham gum

Freshly ground pepper to taste

STEPS:

1. In a small glass bowl or measuring cup, whisk together first 6 ingredients (vinegar to salt). Whisk in oil.

2. Sprinkle xantham gum over dressing and quickly whisk in. Refrigerate until you're ready to use.

I purposely choose easy-to-find ingredients for my recipes. Manufacturers commonly use xantham gum and guar gum to thicken, stabilize, and emulsify foods (like dressings), and just a pinch does the trick. Xantham gum is easy to find at natural food stores and regular markets that carry brands like Bob's Red Mill.

PER SERVING (2 TABLESPOONS)

Calories 60	Fat 7 grams (0 saturated)
Carbohydrate 0 grams	Fiber 0 grams
Protein 0 grams	Sodium 80 milligrams

Diabetic exchange = 1 ½ Fat
WW point comparison = 2 points

Thousand Island Dressing

Serves Five

One of my all-time favorite salads is Crab Louie. The truth is, what I adore is the Thousand Island Dressing customarily served with it. I'm happy to report that this healthy version has a taste that's just as good.

INGREDIENTS:

½ cup light mayonnaise (I prefer
  Best Foods or Hellmann's)

2 tablespoons chili sauce

1 tablespoon Splenda Granular
  (or 1 Splenda packet)

2 tablespoons finely chopped celery

1–2 teaspoons 1% milk

STEPS:

1. Whisk all ingredients together in a
   small bowl.

2. For consistency that's less thick, thin
   with milk.

PER SERVING (2 TABLESPOONS)

Calories 45   Fat 3.5 grams (0 saturated)
Carbohydrate 4 grams   Fiber 1 gram
Protein 0 grams   Sodium 180 milligrams

Diabetic exchange = 1 Fat
WW point comparison = 1 point

Fat-Free Catalina Dressing

Serves Eight

Traditionally, this dressing is a sweet and tangy blend of oil, ketchup, and sugar, so it's basically fat and sugar—no wonder it's so popular! Luckily, it can be made without fat or sugar and still taste great. You must taste it to believe it.

INGREDIENTS:

1 cup cold water

⅓ cup Splenda Granular

3 tablespoons tomato paste

1 ½ teaspoons cornstarch

½ teaspoon salt

⅛ teaspoon garlic powder

⅛ teaspoon chili powder (optional)

STEPS:

1. Place all the ingredients in a small saucepan and whisk until the cornstarch is completely dissolved.

2. Place over low heat and cook until dressing comes to a boil and thickens and clears. Remove from heat and cool. Cover and refrigerate.

Two tablespoons of bottled Honey French dressing will set you back 170 calories, 13 grams of fat, and 12 grams of carbohydrate.

PER SERVING (2 TABLESPOONS)

Calories 10	Fat 0 grams (0 saturated)
Carbohydrate 3 grams	Fiber 0 grams
Protein 0 grams	Sodium 180 milligrams

Diabetic exchange = 1 Fat
WW point comparison = 1 point

Old World Sour Cream Dip and Dressing

Serves Eight (Dressing) Serves Seven (Dip*)

Many European cuisines have sour cream dressings, which commonly contain vinegar or lemon juice and sugar to balance the acid. The addition of mustard, chives, and garlic makes this a nice dressing to use on a cold green salad or as a dip for vegetables.

Ingredients

1 cup light sour cream

3 tablespoons cider vinegar

2 tablespoons Splenda Granular

2 teaspoons fresh minced chives

½ teaspoon dry mustard

½ teaspoon garlic powder

⅛ teaspoon salt

3 tablespoons 1% milk

Steps:

1. For DIP: In a small bowl, whisk together all ingredients except milk. Refrigerate for 30 minutes to allow flavors to meld.

2. For DRESSING: Add milk to dip mix and whisk until smooth.

Per Serving (2 Tablespoons)

Calories 45	Fat 2.5 grams (2 saturated)
Carbohydrate 3 grams	Fiber 0 grams
Protein 2 grams	Sodium 65 milligrams

Diabetic exchange = ½ Fat
WW point comparison = 1 point

* Add 5 calories and ½ gram fat per serving.

Creamy Poppy Seed Dressing

Serves Eight

If you like a very creamy dressing, this one is for you. It is perfect to drizzle over delicate lettuces, such as butter or Bibb, or to toss with fresh fruit.

INGREDIENTS:

½ **cup buttermilk**

½ **cup light sour cream**

3 **tablespoons Splenda Granular (or 4 Splenda packets)**

2 **teaspoons lemon juice**

1 **teaspoon poppy seeds**

STEPS:

1. In a small bowl, whisk together all ingredients.

Add a touch of orange zest to the dressing and serve it over fresh strawberries for a sweet finish to your meal.

PER SERVING (2 TABLESPOONS)

Calories 10	Fat 0 grams (0 saturated)
Carbohydrate 3 grams	Fiber 0 grams
Protein 0 grams	Sodium 180 milligrams

Diabetic exchange = 1 Fat
WW point comparison = 1 point

Sesame Ginger Dressing

Serves Six

Oil creates the emulsion in most dressings. When you cut back on the oil, the result is a thinner dressing. This cooked, oriental-inspired dressing uses cornstarch as a thickener instead of a lot of oil.

INGREDIENTS:

⅓ cup chicken broth

¼ cup pineapple juice

3 tablespoons natural rice vinegar

2 tablespoons sesame oil

1 tablespoon light soy sauce

2 tablespoons Splenda Granular
  (or 3 Splenda packets)

1 ½ teaspoons fresh ginger, minced

½ teaspoon garlic, minced

1 teaspoon cornstarch mixed with
  1 tablespoon water

STEPS:

1. Place all ingredients except cornstarch mixture in a small saucepan and bring to medium heat.

2. Stir in cornstarch mixture, bring to a boil, and cook until dressing is thick and clear. Remove from heat and cool. Cover and refrigerate.

3. Shake or stir before using.

PER SERVING (2 TABLESPOONS)

Calories 55	Fat 4.5 grams (0 saturated)
Carbohydrate 3 grams	Fiber 1 gram
Protein 0 grams	Sodium 140 milligrams

Diabetic exchange = 1 Fat
WW point comparison = 1 point

Spinach Salad Dressing

Serves Eight

Recently I picked up a "Spinach Salad Dressing" made by a very popular restaurant chain and found six—yes, six—different sources of sugar in the ingredients. No wonder most of the calories were from sugar! Here, I give you a spinach dressing that is simple and has only a touch of real sugar for clarity. Refrigerate until you're ready to use.

INGREDIENTS:

1 ½ tablespoons canola oil

½ cup diced onion

½ teaspoon liquid smoke

⅔ cup water

⅓ cup cider vinegar

2 tablespoons Splenda Sugar Blend for Baking★

Scant ¼ teaspoon salt

1 ½ teaspoons cornstarch dissolved in 1 tablespoon water

2 tablespoons real bacon bits

STEPS:

1. In a small pot, heat oil over medium heat. Add onion and cook for 3-5 minutes or until onions are translucent and soft.

2. Add liquid smoke, water, vinegar, Splenda, and salt, and stir.

3. Bring mixture to low boil and add cornstarch mixture. Stir for 1 minute or until dressing thickens and clears.

4. Whisk in bacon bits. Cook an additional 30 seconds and remove from heat. Use immediately or place in a container and refrigerate.

★ I use Splenda/Sugar Blend for this dressing. If you substitute Splenda Granular, use ¼ cup.

PER SERVING (2 TABLESPOONS)

Calories 50	Fat 3 grams (1 saturated)
Carbohydrate 5 grams	Fiber 0 gram
Protein 1 gram	Sodium 95 milligrams

Diabetic exchange = 1 Fat

WW point comparison = 1 point

Strawberry Yogurt Fruit Salad Dressing

Serves Twelve

Here is a simple little dressing with just a hint of honey to top off a cup or bowl of fresh fruit. I like to serve it with a complementary combination of fresh strawberries and oranges, but any mixture of fresh fruit tastes great.

INGREDIENTS:

½ **cup sliced strawberries**

½ **teaspoon orange zest**

¾ **cup nonfat or low-fat plain yogurt**

6 **tablespoons light sour cream**

2 **tablespoons Splenda Granular**

2 **teaspoons honey**

STEPS:

1. In a food processor, pulse together strawberries and orange zest until crushed (not liquid).
2. Place crushed strawberries in a medium bowl. Whisk in yogurt, sour cream, Splenda, and honey. Mix well. Chill until serving.

Fresh berries are great. They are low in carbohydrates and high in fiber and nutrients. Also good for fruit cups are melons, like cantaloupe, watermelon, and honeydew (their high water content keeps their caloric density low).

PER SERVING (2 TABLESPOONS)

Calories 25	Fat .5 gram (.5 saturated)
Carbohydrate 3 grams	Fiber 0 grams
Protein 2 grams	Sodium 15 milligrams

Diabetic exchange = Free Food

WW point comparison = 1 point (up to ¼ cup)

Teriyaki Sauce

Serves Ten

I love teriyaki sauce because it is so versatile and tastes great as a marinade for all types and cuts of beef, pork, chicken, and seafood; a dipping sauce for cooked meats; and a stir-fry sauce when thickened with a touch of cornstarch.

INGREDIENTS:

⅓ **cup light soy sauce**

¼ **cup dry sherry**

2 **tablespoons natural rice vinegar**

3 **tablespoons Splenda Granular**

1 **tablespoon brown sugar**

2 **teaspoons sesame oil**

1 **teaspoon freshly grated ginger**

½ **teaspoon minced garlic**

STEPS:

1. Whisk all ingredients together in a small bowl.
2. Store covered in the refrigerator.

Natural rice vinegar contains no sugar. Seasoned rice vinegar is rice vinegar seasoned with sugar. Each tablespoon of vinegar contains about 1 teaspoon of sugar.

PER SERVING (1 TABLESPOONS)

Calories 20	Fat 1 gram (0 saturated)
Carbohydrate 2 grams	Fiber 0 grams
Protein 1 gram	Sodium 260 milligrams

Diabetic exchange = Free Food
WW point comparison = 0 points

Spicy Teriyaki Sauce

Serves Ten

Instead of ginger, this sauce uses more garlic and red pepper flakes to add some heat. I especially like to use this teriyaki sauce as a stir-fry sauce.

INGREDIENTS:

⅓ cup light soy sauce

¼ cup dry sherry

2 tablespoons natural rice vinegar

3 tablespoons Splenda Granular

1 tablespoon brown sugar

1 tablespoon sesame oil

1 teaspoon minced garlic

⅛ teaspoon red pepper flakes

STEPS:

1. Whisk all ingredients together in a small bowl.
2. Store covered in the refrigerator.

After marinating meat, boil the leftover marinade and reduce the volume by half to use as a glaze on the cooked meat.

PER SERVING (1 TABLESPOON)

Calories 25	Fat 1.5 grams (0 saturated)
Carbohydrate 2 grams	Fiber 0 grams
Protein 1 gram	Sodium 260 milligrams

Diabetic exchange = Free Food

WW point comparison = 1 point

Fresh Citrus Marinade

Serves Ten

This recipe is great for grilling fish, chicken, or shrimp. To marinate on-the-go, place the marinade in a large ziploc bag and throw in your choice of protein. Place it into a cooler with some ice, and by the time you are ready to grill, your meat will be tender and flavorful.

INGREDIENTS:

⅓ cup reduced-sugar orange juice (like Tropicana Light 'n Healthy)

Juice and zest of 1 lemon

Juice of 1 lime

2 tablespoons Splenda Granular

2 cloves garlic, minced

½ teaspoon red pepper flakes (optional)

Pinch salt

⅛ teaspoon black pepper

STEPS:

1. Mix all ingredients together and let rest at room temperature for 1 hour.
2. Add your favorite fish, chicken, or shrimp, and place in refrigerator or cooler for up to 2 hours.

Watching the sodium in your diet? The bright citrus flavors eliminate the need for lots of salt in this marinade.

PER SERVING

Calories 5

Carbohydrate 1 grams

Protein 0 grams

Fat 0 grams (0 saturated)

Fiber 0 grams

Sodium 35 milligrams

Diabetic exchange = Free Food

WW point comparison = 0 points

Spicy Thai Marinade and Dipping Sauce

Serves Six

Thai cuisine is defined by four primary flavors—hot, sweet, salty, and spicy. Like many Thai sauces, this one features all four flavors. It's a great marinade for steak, chicken, and fish and a nice dipping sauce for everything from grilled food to egg rolls. You may also add a tiny pinch of guar or xantham gum to thicken it and brush it onto food as a glaze.

INGREDIENTS:

¼ cup light or reduced-sodium soy sauce

¼ cup lime juice

1 tablespoon fish sauce

¼ cup Splenda Granular

2 tablespoons green onion, finely sliced (white and green)

1 ½ teaspoons Thai or serrano chiles, seeded and minced

1 ½ teaspoons garlic, minced

STEPS:

1. Combine liquid ingredients.
2. Stir in Splenda. Add green onion, chiles, and garlic.

Fish sauce, made from the liquid of salted, fermented fish, is an essential ingredient in Thai cooking. Pungent and strong, it adds a distinct aroma and flavor that cannot be replaced. In Thailand, you find it on tables the way you find table salt here. In your local market, look for fish sauce (also known as Nam Pla) in the Asian food aisle.

PER SERVING (2 TABLESPOONS)

Calories 15	Fat 0 grams
Carbohydrate 3 grams	Fiber 0 grams
Protein 1 gram	Sodium 570 milligrams

Diabetic exchange = Free Food
WW point comparison = 0 points

Versatile Vegetables

Onions and Apples

Glazed Carrots with Fresh Dill

Sesame Green Beans

Orange-Sauced Beets

Asian Pepper Medley

Silly Carrots

Marinated Mushrooms

Asparagus with Lemon Tarragon
Vinaigrette

Sweet and Sour Red Cabbage

Boston Baked Beans

Butternut Squash Soufflé

Sweet Potatoes with Apple
Cider Syrup

Stovetop Maple Sugar Baked Beans

German Potato, Green Bean, and
Mushroom Salad

Buttermilk Cornbread

Cheesy Jalapeno Cornbread

Sweet Southwestern-Style Corn Pudding

We all know that vegetables are good for us, and the scientific evidence just keeps mounting—vegetables have the power to protect us from various cancers, lower blood pressure, protect eyesight, and even keep us looking young. So, follow the current recommendation and eat 5 servings (or 2 ½-3 cups), or more, of a variety of vegetables each day. But, to get the best of the benefits, you do need to lose the butter and sugar. On that note, I've got wonderful news—you won't even miss it because I've taken a nice variety of colorful, good-for-you vegetables and sweetly seasoned them to tickle your taste buds—without messing with Mother Nature's natural goodness.

For instance, a great example is my Butternut Squash Soufflé; high in vitamin A and antioxidants, it has only a slim 130 calories (and no added-sugar) in each serving. Try this creamy, sweet, mile-high traditional holiday casserole with its crunchy pecan topping as an alternative to the traditional sweet potato puff that delivers more than 400 calories, 20 grams of fat, and 40 grams of sugar a serving—and you will be amazed that something this good is actually good for you.

Beyond this holiday classic (which, of course, should not be confined to just the holidays), you will find many other great versatile vegetable recipes, from Boston Baked Beans, to colorful Sweet and Sour Red Cabbage, Asian-tinged Sesame Green Beans, and even Silly Carrots for the kids. With vegetables this good, 5 servings just got easier.

Onions and Apples

Serves Two

Here's another dish from my Splenda-loving friend Fran. I have found this 15-minute sauté of apples and onions a great complement to quick lean broiled pork chops.

INGREDIENTS:

1 large onion, sliced

1 large cooking apple, about ⅓ pound, peeled, cored, and sliced in wedges

1 tablespoon cider vinegar

2 tablespoons Splenda Granular

1 teaspoon brown sugar

¼ teaspoon caraway seeds (optional)

Pinch salt

Pepper to taste

STEPS:

1. Using a large nonstick skillet, add apples, onions, cider vinegar, Splenda, and brown sugar. Stir gently to combine.

2. Cover and cook over medium heat until the apples and onions are soft but not mushy— approximately 15 minutes.

3. Season to taste with salt and pepper.

I choose to add caraway seeds to complement pork, but you may substitute a variety of savory flavors. Think rosemary instead of caraway seeds for chicken and beef, or fresh dill for grilled salmon.

PER SERVING

Calories 90	Fat 0 grams
Carbohydrate 22 grams	Fiber 4 grams
Protein 1 grams	Sodium 125 milligrams

Diabetic exchange = 1 Fruit, 1 Vegetable
WW point comparison = 1 point

Glazed Carrots with Fresh Dill

Serves Six

Glazed carrots seem to pair well with almost any dish—maybe that's why they are so popular. Although carrots sometimes get a bad rap for their "high sugar content," they are actually low in carbohydrate and fit easily into most diets. The problem with glazed carrots is the glaze, not the carrots. Some recipes call for up to ½ cup of sugar and ½ cup of butter (for six servings or less). This recipe uses just enough sweetener and butter to enhance the natural goodness of the carrots. The crowning touch is the fresh dill.

INGREDIENTS:

¼ cup regular or light orange juice

¼ cup water

1 pound carrots (about 6 large), trimmed, peeled, and sliced

2 tablespoons light butter, melted

3 tablespoons Splenda Granular

1 teaspoon fresh minced dill

Salt and pepper to taste

STEPS:

1. Place orange juice and water in a medium saucepan. Add carrots and simmer, covered, for 15 minutes until carrots are tender and liquid is absorbed.

2. In a small bowl, combine melted butter, Splenda, and dill. Pour over hot carrots and toss.

3. Adjust salt and pepper to taste.

Carrots are good for you—½ cup of boiled carrots has only 8 grams of carbohydrate (with 2 grams of fiber) and an entire day's worth of vitamin A.

PER SERVING (¹/2 CUP)

Calories 60	Fat 2 grams (1 saturated)
Carbohydrate 9 grams	Fiber 2 grams
Protein 1 gram	Sodium 45 milligrams

Diabetic exchange = 1 ½ Vegetable, ½ Fat

WW point comparison = 1 point

Sesame Green Beans

Serves Four

Parboiling green beans brightens their color and keeps them plump. It also lets you prepare the beans in advance, leaving only a last-minute sauté prior to serving. I like to serve these dark and fragrant beans with Asian Barbecued Pork Tenderloin (page 228).

INGREDIENTS:

1 pound fresh green beans, trimmed

1 tablespoon sesame seeds

2 teaspoons sesame oil

2 tablespoons light soy sauce

2 tablespoons Splenda Granular

1 tablespoon natural rice wine vinegar

Pinch red pepper flakes

STEPS:

1. Place beans in a large pot of boiling water with 2 teaspoons salt and cook for 4 minutes or until tender but still slightly firm. Drain and place in ice water until beans are cool. Drain and pat dry. Set aside.

2. In a large nonstick sauté pan, toast sesame seeds until golden over low heat. Remove from pan and set aside.

3. Add oil to pan and heat until very hot (but not smoking). Add beans and sauté for 1–2 minutes or until hot.

4. Mix together remaining ingredients and add to pan. Sauté until beans are coated and sauce is hot. Pour onto serving platter and top with toasted sesame seeds.

While sesame oil is remarkably stable, sesame seeds can turn rancid due to their high oil content. Kept in a cool, dark place, they will stay fresh for 3 months, in the refrigerator for 6 months, and in the freezer for up to 12 months.

PER SERVING

Calories 70

Carbohydrate 9 grams

Protein 2 grams

Fat 3.5 grams (0 saturated)

Fiber 3 grams

Sodium 250 milligrams

Diabetic exchange = 1 ½ Vegetable, 1 Fat

WW point comparison = 1 point

Orange-Sauced Beets

Serves Four

I must confess, before developing this recipe, I had never cooked fresh beets. What a mistake. While canned beets work just fine for this recipe, I highly recommend fresh—you can't beat their texture. This richly colored side dish is versatile enough to complement both simple and elegant meals.

INGREDIENTS:

1 pound fresh beets or 2 15-ounce cans whole beets in juice, drained

¼ cup regular or light orange juice

¼ cup Splenda Granular

2 tablespoons white or cider vinegar

1 teaspoon cornstarch

1 teaspoon orange zest

Dash salt

1 tablespoon margarine or butter

You may want to wear gloves to peel the beets because the pigment will temporarily stain your hands (and anything else it touches).

STEPS:

1. To prepare fresh beets, scrub and trim the stem down to 1 inch (tail can be left intact). Place in boiling water and boil for 40-60 minutes or until tender when pierced all the way through with a sharp knife. Drain and plunge them into cold water until cooled. Rub beets between your hands to remove peels and chop into large bite-sized cubes.

2. In a medium saucepan, whisk together remaining ingredients, except margarine. Heat over medium heat until sauce comes to a boil and thickens.

3. Turn down heat and swirl in margarine. Add beets to sauce and heat until coated and hot.

PER SERVING

Calories 85
Carbohydrate 14 grams
Protein 2 grams

Fat 2.5 grams (.5 saturated)
Fiber 2 grams
Sodium 150 milligrams

Diabetic exchange = 2 Vegetable, ½ Fat
WW point comparison = 1 point

Asian Pepper Medley

Serves Four

This medley of colorful sweet peppers makes a terrific accompaniment to any grilled meat or fish. The sesame oil in this dish adds an exotic flavor.

INGREDIENTS:

2 teaspoons canola oil

1 teaspoon minced garlic

3 large bell peppers—1 red, 1 green, 1 orange or yellow, seeded and sliced in ¼-inch strips

3 tablespoons natural rice wine vinegar

1 tablespoon light soy sauce

1 tablespoon sesame oil

1 tablespoon Splenda Granular

¼ teaspoon minced or grated ginger

Fresh ground pepper

STEPS:

1. In a large nonstick sauté pan, heat oil; add garlic and then pepper strips. Sauté over high heat for 3 minutes.
2. Mix remaining ingredients together and pour over peppers.
3. Cook for 3–5 more minutes until peppers are tender but not limp.
4. Season with pepper to taste.

PER SERVING (¹/2 CUP)

Calories 70	Fat 4.5 grams (0 saturated)
Carbohydrate 8 grams	Fiber 2 grams
Protein 1 gram	Sodium 130 milligrams

Diabetic exchange = 1 Vegetable, 1 Fat
WW point comparison = 1 point

Silly Carrots

Serves Ten

When I told my mom I was including vegetable recipes in my book, she immediately told me about a recipe for carrots that could use a "sugar makeover." She said that this recipe was a huge hit at potlucks quite a few years back. I went on to find that Silly Carrots were actually a "My Best Recipe" winner in 1981 in the Los Angeles Times newspaper. The original "retro" recipe has a terrific sweet sauce that really makes them special. Now, here's my version, which also has the same great taste.

INGREDIENTS:

6 cups carrots, peeled and sliced (2 pounds raw carrots)

1 10-ounce can tomato soup (Campbell's Healthy Selections)

⅔ cup Splenda Granular

⅔ cup vinegar

2 tablespoons canola oil

1 ½ teaspoons prepared mustard

1 medium onion, diced

1 medium green pepper, diced

½ cup celery, chopped

⅛ teaspoon salt

STEPS:

1. In a medium saucepan, cook carrots in boiling water just until tender (about 10 minutes). Drain and set aside.

2. Combine remaining ingredients in saucepan and cook over medium heat until boiling. Reduce heat and simmer for 10 minutes. Pour over drained carrots. Serve hot, or refrigerate and serve cold.

These could get just about anyone to eat carrots, which is a good thing considering the fact that a single serving of Silly Carrots provides a whopping 420 percent of the Recommended Daily Allowance for vitamin A.

PER SERVING (½ CUP)

Calories 90	Fat 3.5 grams (0 saturated)
Carbohydrate 15 grams	Fiber 3 grams
Protein 2 grams	Sodium 180 milligrams

Diabetic exchange = 2 ½ Vegetable, 1 Fat
WW point comparison = 1 point

Marinated Mushrooms

Serves Six

Low in calories and carbohydrates and virtually free of fat, mushrooms are perfect for any diet. Once you've marinated them, these sweet and savory morsels can go several ways, complementing an entrée like grilled steak, topping your favorite salad, or serving as delicious hors d'oeuvres. When you're serving a crowd, simply double the recipe.

INGREDIENTS:

1 pound fresh mushrooms (button-size or small white)

¼ cup light soy sauce

½ cup red wine

¼ cup sherry

¼ cup Splenda Granular

1 cup finely minced onion

¼–½ teaspoon fresh cracked pepper

STEPS:

1. Wash and dry mushrooms (if mushrooms are large, cut in half); set aside.

2. Mix remaining ingredients in saucepan and bring to a boil.

3. Remove from heat and pour over mushrooms. Refrigerate overnight. Serve cold or at room temperature.

A mushroom is actually a fungus, not a vegetable, which puts it in a class of its own. Nutritionally, mushrooms stand out for being "vegetables" that are high in protein, B vitamins, minerals, and fiber, with only a few slim calories.

PER SERVING

Calories 35	Fat 0 grams
Carbohydrate 4 grams	Fiber 1 grams
Protein 3 grams	Sodium 200 milligrams

Diabetic exchange = 1 Vegetable

WW point comparison = 1 point

★ Analysis is based on an estimate of consuming one-half the marinade.

Asparagus with Lemon Tarragon Vinaigrette

Serves Six

Although asparagus is now available almost year-round, this vegetable clearly makes its mark each spring at the peak of its season. In this simple yet upscale presentation, you get the beauty and fresh flavor of asparagus as well as the healthy-food payoff.

INGREDIENTS:

1 ½ pounds fresh asparagus, washed (ends trimmed)

2 tablespoons Dijon mustard

2 tablespoons Splenda Granular

2 tablespoons fresh lemon juice

2 tablespoons virgin or extra-virgin olive oil

1 tablespoon finely chopped fresh tarragon, divided in half (or ¾ teaspoon dried tarragon and ½ tablespoon chopped fresh parsley for garnish)

Asparagus may be low in calories, but it's high in nutrients such as fiber, folic acid, and vitamins A and C. It is also a natural detoxifier, diuretic, and cancer fighter.

STEPS:

1. Steam or microwave spears by placing them in a glass dish with a small amount of water, covering tightly with Saran Wrap, and microwaving on high for 4 minutes or until spears are tender crisp. Immediately submerge in ice water to stop cooking process. (You may eliminate this step if you want the asparagus to cook longer or you're serving warm immediately.)

2. Drain and arrange on a large flat serving dish or platter.

3. In a small mixing bowl, whisk together mustard, Splenda, lemon juice, olive oil, and ½ tablespoon fresh tarragon or ¾ teaspoon crushed dried tarragon.

4. Drizzle vinaigrette over asparagus. Sprinkle the other half of the chopped tarragon or parsley over asparagus just before serving.

5. Serve cold or at room temperature.

PER SERVING

Calories 60	Fat 5 grams (1 saturated)
Carbohydrate 4 grams	Fiber 1 gram
Protein 2 grams	Sodium 130 milligrams

Diabetic exchange = 1 Vegetable, 1 Fat
WW point comparison = 1 point

Sweet and Sour Red Cabbage

Serves Six

I remember how, when I was a child, my German father was so delighted every time my mother served red cabbage. Now, when the weather turns cool in the fall, I serve this beautiful sugar-free rendition with pork loin— and my husband, too, is delighted.

INGREDIENTS:

2 teaspoons olive or canola oil

½ cup diced red onion

1 medium red cabbage (about 2 pounds), cored, quartered, and thinly sliced

1 apple, peeled and grated (optional)★

½ cup red wine

¼ cup cider vinegar

1 cup water

¼ cup Splenda Granular

½ teaspoon salt

3–4 drops liquid smoke

Pepper to taste

STEPS:

1. Heat oil in a medium-sized saucepan.

2. Add onion and sauté 4-5 minutes or until translucent. Add cabbage, apple, wine, vinegar, water, and Splenda. Cover and simmer for 20 minutes, stirring occasionally.

3. Stir in salt and liquid smoke and cook for 10 more minutes or until tender but still firm.

★Apple adds a delicious taste, 10 calories, and 3 grams of carbohydrate to each serving.

PER SERVING (³/₄-1 CUP)

Calories 80	Fat 2 grams (.5 saturated)
Carbohydrate 10 grams	Fiber 2 grams
Protein 2 grams	Sodium 220 milligrams

Diabetic exchange = 2 Vegetable, ½ Fat
WW point comparison = 1 point

Liquid smoke is a seasoning made from hickory smoke concentrate via a natural process. It has no calories and imparts a smoky taste, reminiscent of bacon. Use sparingly, though, because it's quite concentrated.

Boston Baked Beans

Serves Twelve

A very kind retired policeman wrote me after receiving my cookbooks Christmas gifts. He told me he loved to cook, has diabetes (under control, of course), and, more importantly, that he was famous for his slow-cooker baked beans—made with lots of brown sugar. Yet he decided to give my recipe a try, cooking them like hi, in his slow cooker for 8 hours. His final declaration that mine were actually "better" than his more than made my day, and now you have a cooking option—the oven or a slow cooker.

INGREDIENTS:

**1 pound dried navy beans, rinsed
and picked clean of stones or debris**

1 large onion, chopped

½ cup tomato juice

½ cup sugar-free maple syrup

⅔ cup Splenda Granular

3 tablespoons molasses

2 tablespoons cider vinegar

2 teaspoons dry mustard

¾ teaspoon salt

½ teaspoon ginger

**Liquid smoke (optional, if you like
'em smokey)**

STEPS:

1. Bring 2 quarts of water and beans to boil in a large pot and simmer 2 minutes. Remove from heat, cover, and soak for at least 1 hour (or up to 8 hours).

2. Preheat oven to 300°F. Drain beans and put them in a pot, casserole, or slow cooker. Add remaining ingredients.

3. Stir and thoroughly cover beans with hot water (about 2 cups).

4. Cover and bake 5-6 hours or until beans are tender and the sauce is bubbly. Check midway to see if more water is needed.

Fiber blunts the rapid rise in blood sugar associated with refined carbohydrates. Beans are an incredible source of fiber (and a nice protein source as well), making them very good carbs.

PER SERVING (¹/₂ CUP)

Calories 140	Fat 0 grams (2 saturated)
Carbohydrate 26 grams	Fiber 7 grams
Protein 8 grams	Sodium 180 milligrams

Diabetic exchange = 1 ½ Carbohydrate
WW point comparison = 2 points

Butternut Squash Soufflé

Serves Eight

If you want a lower-carb alternative to sweet potatoes, look no further. This simple-to-make yet sumptuous side dish tastes creamy, rich, and sweet and yet has a fraction of the sugar, fat, and calories of traditional versions. Don't worry—I have even included the nut-studded crunchy topping. I promise you that no one will think this is low in anything.

INGREDIENTS:

SOUFFLÉ

3 cups cooked mashed butternut squash (about 2 pounds, whole)

⅔ cup Splenda Granular

1 large egg

3 egg whites

⅓ cup light sour cream

1 tablespoon margarine, melted

¾ teaspoon cinnamon

½ teaspoon vanilla

1 teaspoon baking powder

¼ teaspoon salt

TOPPING

2 tablespoons flour

3 tablespoons Splenda Granular

3 tablespoons pecans, finely chopped

1 tablespoon margarine, melted

¼ teaspoon cinnamon

STEPS:

1. Preheat oven to 350°F. Coat a 2-quart casserole or soufflé dish with nonstick cooking spray.

2. SOUFFLÉ: Prick squash with a knife in several places and place in microwave. Microwave on high for 8-10 minutes. Remove and cut squash in half lengthwise. When cool enough to handle, scoop out seeds. Place halves, cut-side down, in a glass baking dish; add ¼ cup of water, cover tightly with plastic wrap (or lid), and place back in microwave for 10 more minutes or until flesh is very soft. Scoop out flesh into large bowl.

3. Add remaining soufflé ingredients and beat until well blended. Spoon into baking dish and smooth top.

4. In a small bowl, combine all topping ingredients and mix with fork or fingers until crumbly. Cover top of soufflé with crumb mixture.

5. Bake for 30-35 minutes until soufflé puffs up in center and top is well browned.

When whipped up into this soufflé, the taste difference between sweet potatoes and butternut squash is indistinguishable. However, ½ cup of the squash contains only 13 grams of carbohydrate whereas ½ cup of mashed sweet potatoes contains 40.

PER SERVING (¹/₂ CUP)

Calories 120	Fat 5 grams (2 saturated)
Carbohydrate 15 grams	Fiber 3 grams
Protein 4 grams	Sodium 180 milligrams

Diabetic exchange = 1 Carbohydrate, 1 Fat
WW point comparison = 2 points

Sweet Potatoes with Apple Cider Syrup

Serves Six

If you have had enough of over-the-top-sweet marshmallow-and-brown sugar sweet potato recipes, try this one. I took the classic pairing of apples and sweet potatoes and added apple cider to create a delicious butter syrup that complements the sweet potatoes instead of overpowering them.

INGREDIENTS:

4 large sweet potatoes or yams (about 1 ½ pounds)

¾ cup apple cider

½ cup Splenda Granular

2 tablespoons butter

STEPS:

1. Preheat oven to 350°F. Coat a baking dish with nonstick cooking spray.

2. Boil sweet potatoes for 20–25 minutes or until nearly tender when pierced with a knife. Drain potatoes and let stand until cool enough to handle. Peel and cut potatoes into ¼-inch rounds and layer in rectangular baking dish.

3. In a small saucepan, heat apple cider over medium heat until mixture reduces by ⅓ to ½. Stir in Splenda and heat 1 more minute. Remove from heat and stir in butter.

4. Pour syrup over potatoes, cover, and bake 30 minutes until very soft and hot.

Although sweet potatoes may taste like they contain more sugar than their white cousins, they actually affect blood sugar much more slowly. Top them with ½ cup or more of brown sugar and a slew of marshmallows and that all changes. In fact, one serving of the traditional sweet potato casserole has more than 60 grams of carbohydrate (more than 30 of them from sugar).

PER SERVING (¹/₂ CUP)

Calories 150	Fat 4.5 grams (3 saturated)
Carbohydrate 27 grams	Fiber 2 grams
Protein 2 grams	Sodium 50 milligrams

Diabetic exchange = 2 Vegetable, ½ Fat
WW point comparison = 3 points

Stovetop Maple Sugar Baked Beans

Serves Six

In today's fast-paced world, "quick" and "easy" are very welcome words indeed. In the time it takes to make the rest of your meal, you can have "homemade" baked beans. These beans are truly quick and easy.

INGREDIENTS:

1 teaspoon canola oil

1 small onion, finely chopped

½ cup tomato sauce

¼ cup sugar-free maple syrup

¼ cup Splenda Granular

1 tablespoon molasses

2 teaspoons prepared mustard

1 teaspoon vinegar

4-5 drops liquid smoke

2 15-ounce cans pinto beans, drained and rinsed (you can vary type of beans)

STEPS:

1. In a large saucepan, heat oil, add onions, and sauté for 3-4 minutes until softened slightly.
2. Add remaining ingredients and stir.
3. Simmer on low for 25-30 minutes.

Sweet baked beans are a great way to get your kids to eat more fiber. The recommended allowance for fiber in children is their age plus 5. With 5 grams of fiber per serving, this dish hits the jackpot.

PER SERVING

Calories 145	Fat 2 grams (2 saturated)
Carbohydrate 26 grams	Fiber 5 grams
Protein 8 grams	Sodium 160 milligrams

Diabetic exchange = 1 ½ Carbohydrate
WW point comparison = 2 points

German Potato, Green Bean and Mushroom Salad

Serves Six

German potato salad, dense in starchy white potatoes and bacon, isn't on anyone's healthy-food list. But, boy, can it taste good! To put it back on the menu, I lightened the density, I added lower-carb vegetables, took out the sugar, and only used enough bacon for the classic taste. Enjoy it anytime, or pair it with reduced-fat sausage or brats for a German feast.

INGREDIENTS:

8 ounces fresh green beans, trimmed

1 pound red potatoes, scrubbed

3 slices center-cut bacon

1 small onion, diced

½ teaspoon dry mustard

½ teaspoon crushed thyme

2 teaspoons flour

⅔ cup chicken broth

⅓ cup white wine vinegar or cider vinegar

2 tablespoons Splenda Granular

⅛ teaspoon salt (or more to taste)

4 ounces fresh mushrooms, cut in wide ¼-inch slices

Black pepper to taste

STEPS:

1. Boil green beans in a large pot of water with 1 teaspoon salt for 6-8 minutes until tender but still crisp. Remove with slotted spoon into a large covered bowl and add potatoes (with skins) to water. Boil for 20 minutes or until potatoes are tender when pierced with a fork. Drain, slice, and place in covered bowl with green beans.

2. While potatoes are boiling, cook bacon until crisp in a large skillet. Remove bacon; drain off fat with paper towels, crumble, and set aside.

3. Pour all but 2 tablespoons of drippings out of pan. Add onion and sauté until soft. Stir in mustard and thyme and then flour.

4. Whisk in broth, vinegar, Splenda, and salt. Stir until thickened.

5. Add mushrooms briefly to heat, not cook, and pour hot sauce over potato mixture. Toss, add crumbled bacon, and adjust seasonings.

PER SERVING

Calories 130	Fat 3.5 grams (.5 saturated)
Carbohydrate 20 grams	Fiber 3 grams
Protein 5 grams	Sodium 290 milligrams

Diabetic exchange = 1 Carbohydrate, 1 Vegetable, ½ Fat
WW point comparison = 2 points

Buttermilk Cornbread

Serves Twelve

Entire books have been written to pay homage to this seemingly simple side dish. More than just a bread to many, cornbread is comfort. And like most comfort foods, lots of styles will satisfy. I have fashioned mine as a healthier version of one from a famous pie shop that became even more famous for its cornbread (Marie Callender's, for those of you who are still guessing). Loved by y'all, this cornbread is moist, sweet, and not too heavy. Serve it up warm for a real treat.

INGREDIENTS:

1 large egg + 2 egg whites

3 tablespoons margarine, melted

1 ¼ cups buttermilk

1 teaspoon vanilla

1 cup cornmeal

1 cup all-purpose flour

½ cup Splenda Granular

4 teaspoons baking powder

½ teaspoon baking soda

Pinch salt

STEPS:

1. Preheat oven to 375°F. Spray an 8-inch square pan or 9-inch round pan with nonstick cooking spray.

2. In a medium bowl, whisk together first 4 ingredients (eggs through vanilla). Set aside.

3. In a large bowl, combine the dry ingredients. Stir. Make a well in the center and pour in buttermilk mixture. Mix gently with a spoon just until all dry ingredients are wet.

4. Spoon batter into prepared pan. Bake for 20-25 minutes or until center springs back when lightly touched.

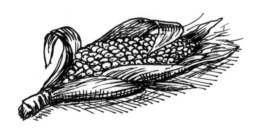

Have you ever heard the saying "as common as corn?" Well, you can find this ubiquitous vegetable in more than 3,000 grocery store products. I'd call that pretty common.

PER SERVING

Calories 125   Fat 3.5 grams (2 saturated)
Carbohydrate 19 grams   Fiber 1 gram
Protein 4 grams   Sodium 295 milligrams

Diabetic exchange = 1 Carbohydrate, 1 Fat
WW point comparison = 2 points

Cheesy Jalapeno Cornbread

Serves Twelve

Served as a side dish for brunch, lunch, or dinner, these yummy, cheesy muffins have quite a kick. After testing them several times, I found that the cheese gives the most flavor and eye appeal when sprinkled on top; however, you can simply stir it into the muffins if you prefer.

INGREDIENTS:

1 cup cornmeal

1 cup flour

¼ cup Splenda Granular

1 tablespoon baking powder

1 teaspoon baking soda

1 ¼ cups buttermilk

1 egg

3 tablespoons butter or margarine, melted

1 tablespoon chopped jalapeno pepper (fresh or from a jar)

12 tablespoons grated low-fat sharp cheddar cheese

STEPS:

1. Preheat oven to 375°F. Lightly spray a 12-cup muffin tin with cooking spray.

2. In a medium bowl, mix together cornmeal, flour, Splenda, baking powder, and baking soda.

3. In a large measuring cup, mix together buttermilk, egg, and melted butter.

4. Make a well in the center of the dry ingredients. Add the wet ingredients and gently stir just to combine. Stir in the chopped jalapeno pepper.

5. Divide batter into 12 muffin cups.

6. Top each muffin with 1 tablespoon of the grated cheddar cheese.

7. Bake for approximately 15-17 minutes, or until toothpick inserted in muffin comes out clean.

PER SERVING

Calories 140	Fat 5 grams (1 saturated)
Carbohydrate 19 grams	Fiber 1 grams
Protein 5 grams	Sodium 330 milligrams

Diabetic exchange = 1 Carbohydrate, 1 Fat
WW point comparison = 3 points

Sweet Southwestern-Style Corn Pudding

Serves Six

Corn pudding recipes vary, but all are high in calories, fat, and carbohydrates. Some are more like custards, while others are so heavy with cornmeal that they can be cut into squares. My version has a nice "middle of the road" texture and a sweet and rich flavor. Sautéed onion and green chiles make it a fantastic side dish that is perfect with Mexican food or food grilled with Southwest spices. If you prefer a more classic version, simply use the traditional version below.

INGREDIENTS:

1 small onion, diced

2 tablespoons margarine or butter

1 cup buttermilk

1 large egg + 2 egg whites

1 4.5-ounce can chopped green chiles

1 15-ounce can corn, drained

½ cup cornmeal

2 tablespoons all-purpose flour

½ teaspoon baking powder

½ cup Splenda Granular

STEPS:

1. Preheat oven to 350°F. Spray a 1-quart casserole dish with nonstick cooking spray.

2. In a small sauté pan, cook onion in margarine until soft. Scrape onions into large bowl and add buttermilk, egg, egg whites, and chiles.

3. Place corn into food processor or blender. Pulse or blend briefly to coarsely chop corn. Add corn to bowl.

4. In a small bowl, blend remaining dry ingredients. Pour into liquid mixture and stir. Spoon batter into prepared dish and bake for 45–50 minutes or until puffed and browned.

TRADITIONAL SWEET CORN PUDDING: Eliminate the onions and chiles. Melt margarine or butter and add to liquid mixture. (No significant change in calories, fat, or carbohydrate.)

PER SERVING

Calories 140	Fat 4 grams (2 saturated)
Carbohydrate 18 grams	Fiber 2 grams
Protein 5 grams	Sodium 270 milligrams

Diabetic exchange = 1 Carbohydrate, 1 Fat
WW point comparison = 2 points

Winning Condiments

Tomato Ginger Jam

Thai Peanut Sauce

Sweet Horseradish Sauce

Sweet Mustard Sauce and Dip

Quick Smooth Barbecue Dipping Sauce

Sweet Smoky Barbecue Sauce

Sweet and Spicy Cajun Rub

Two-Way Cranberry Sauce

Sensational No-Cook Cranberry Relish

Zucchini and Corn Relish

Cranberry Chutney

Peach Chutney

Southwest Peach Chutney

Quick and Fresh Mint Chutney

Bread and Butter Pickles

Easy Re-Pickled Pickles

Apple Butter

Low-Sugar Strawberry Freezer Jam

Microwave Cinnamon Applesauce

Want to add some quick zip to your food? Then add a condiment. Whether sweet, spicy, savory, chunky, or creamy, it's often the sauce, topping, or tasty garnish that makes a dish memorable.

Unfortunately, by their very nature many condiments are laden with sugar, fat, or calories, and they can leave you with more than just a memory (like extra pounds on your scale or high blood sugar on your meter), and that's why most nutritionists will ask you to leave it off! But not me; I'm here to tell you that you can have it all—the winning combination of great, flavorful condiments *and* healthy food.

This chapter will show you how to add big, bold flavors to all your meals. From makeovers of traditional favorites like Two-Way Cranberry Sauce (with 8 instead of the usual 45 grams of carbohydrate per serving), to Sweet Smoky Barbecue Sauce and old-fashioned Apple Butter, these condiments are sure to liven up all your meals. I've also given you new taste sensations like Southwest Peach Chutney and Thai Peanut Sauce, along with a clever way to make a sour pickle turn sweet—without sugar! It's a snap with my Easy Re-Pickled Pickles. Finally, I've also included lots of ideas in the recipe introductions where I've paired these great flavors to help get you started in creating your own winning taste sensations.

Tomato Ginger Jam

Serves Ten

Several years ago I attended a "Holiday Gifts" class at a local cooking school, where I learned to make a delectable chutney-like jam with tomatoes and ginger similar to those found at upscale gourmet markets. This version retains the flavor and tangy quality of the original without the copious sugar. Use it on grilled meats or as a topping for crackers spread with light cream cheese for a delicious and festive-looking treat.

INGREDIENTS:

1 28-ounce can plum or diced tomatoes

⅔ cup Splenda Granular

⅔ cup cider vinegar

2 tablespoons corn syrup

1 ¼ teaspoons ground ginger

1 teaspoon minced garlic

½ teaspoon salt

⅛ teaspoon cayenne pepper or ¼ teaspoon red pepper flakes

STEPS:

1. Combine all ingredients in a heavy saucepan.

2. Bring to a boil over high heat; then lower heat and simmer, stirring occasionally, until liquid evaporates and jam thickens, about 1 hour.

3. Cool, cover, and store in refrigerator. Keeps for up to 1 month.

Amid the usual store-bought goodies and cookie trays, this bold-flavored "jam" stands out as a heartfelt and unique holiday hostess gift. Bottle it up in a pretty jar tied with raffia or a festive holiday ribbon.

PER SERVING (3 TABLESPOONS)

Calories 35	Fat 0 grams (0 saturated)
Carbohydrate 8 grams	Fiber 2 grams
Protein 1 gram	Sodium 0 milligrams

Diabetic exchange = 1 Vegetable
WW point comparison = 0 points

Thai Peanut Sauce

Serves Eight

Peanut sauces are as common in Asia as barbecue sauce is here. In my version, I have eliminated the excess fat and, of course, the sugar. What I have not eliminated, although it does contain a bit of sugar, is the hoisin sauce. Hoisin sauce provides a rich flavor that no other ingredient can duplicate. You can find jars of it in the Asian section of your supermarket.

INGREDIENTS:

2 tablespoons light soy sauce

3 tablespoons natural rice vinegar

2 tablespoons hoisin sauce

2 tablespoons Splenda Granular

1 teaspoon sesame oil

½ cup water

Pinch red pepper flakes

3 tablespoons smooth peanut butter

**½ teaspoon cornstarch dissolved in
   1 teaspoon water**

STEPS

1. Whisk all ingredients except peanut butter and cornstarch mixture together in a small saucepan.

2. Add peanut butter and place over low heat. Heat, stirring with a whisk until smooth. Bring to a low boil and add cornstarch mixture. Stir until sauce thickens and clears.

This sauce is used for the satay on page 239. I also use it as a stir-fry sauce or toss leftover sauce with pasta, chicken, and vegetables for a healthy Asian noodle bowl.

PER SERVING (2 TABLESPOON)

Calories 55	Fat 4 grams (1 saturated)
Carbohydrate 4 grams	Fiber 0 grams
Protein 2 grams	Sodium 220 milligrams

Diabetic exchange = 1 Fat
WW point comparison = 1 point

Sweet Horseradish Sauce

Serves Twelve

I still remember my brother raving about a sandwich sauce called Horsey Sauce. This sweetened mayonnaise concoction flavored with horseradish definitely gives great zip to sandwiches such as roast beef. In my own version, I use a fat-lowering technique I teach to chefs— how to successfully substitute cottage cheese for mayonnaise.

INGREDIENTS:

½ cup low-fat cottage cheese

3 tablespoons light sour cream

2 tablespoons horseradish

1 tablespoon Splenda Granular

STEPS:

1. Place cottage cheese in food processor or blender and puree until completely smooth (like mayonnaise).

2. Add sour cream, horseradish, and Splenda, and blend again. Cover and refrigerate.

You may substitute plain pureed low-fat cottage cheese in any spread, dip, or dressing recipe for part or all of the mayonnaise or sour cream. Not only does it lower the fat and calories, it adds protein and calcium.

PER SERVING (1 TABLESPOON)

Calories 15

Carbohydrate 1 gram

Protein 1 gram

Fat 1 gram (1 saturated)

Fiber 0 grams

Sodium 45 milligrams

Diabetic exchange = Free Food

WW point comparison = 0 points

Sweet Mustard Sauce and Dip

Serves Ten

This recipe is similar to the honey mustard sauce found at T.G.I. Friday's restaurant. I've used reduced-fat products and Splenda to cut the calories, fat, and carbohydrate by half. You can thin this sauce with a few tablespoons of hot water and use it as a sweet mustard salad dressing.

INGREDIENTS:

¼ cup reduced-fat mayonnaise (not nonfat)

¼ cup light sour cream

2 tablespoons Splenda Granular

1 tablespoon hot water

1 tablespoon + 1 teaspoon Dijon mustard

1 ½ teaspoons vinegar

2 teaspoons honey

STEPS:

1. Place all ingredients in small bowl and whisk together.

2. Cover and refrigerate to thicken. If you want to use immediately as a sandwich spread, eliminate the hot water.

Although regular mayonnaise doesn't contain sugar, it's a fat splurge few of us can afford at 100 calories per tablespoon.

PER SERVING (1 TABLESPOON)

Calories 35	Fat 2.5 grams (1 saturated)
Carbohydrate 2 grams	Fiber 0 grams
Protein 0 grams	Sodium 70 milligrams

Diabetic exchange = ½ Fat
WW point comparison = 1 point

Quick Smooth Barbecue Dipping Sauce

Serves Six

Easy to make and loved by kids, this sauce is great on anything you would put barbecue sauce on, like barbecued chicken or ribs.

INGREDIENTS:

1 8-ounce can tomato sauce

2 tablespoons water

1 tablespoon Worcestershire sauce

1 tablespoon cider vinegar

¼ cup Splenda Granular

1 teaspoon honey

Pinch onion powder

Pinch salt

STEPS:

1. Place all ingredients in a small saucepan, stir, and cook for 5 minutes over low heat.

2. For a thicker sauce, cook an additional 5 minutes.

One packet of Wendy's barbecue sauce contains 45 calories and 10 grams of carbohydrate; use two and that's 90 calories and 20 grams carb.

PER SERVING (2 TABLESPOONS)

Calories 15

Carbohydrate 4 grams

Protein 0.5 grams

Fat 0 grams (0 saturated)

Fiber .5 grams

Sodium 210 milligrams

Diabetic exchange = Free Food

WW point comparison = 0 points

Sweet Smoky Barbecue Sauce

Serves Twelve

Traditional American barbecue sauce is versatile and extremely popular. But no matter what the style—hickory, smoky, honey, or spicy—sugar is one ingredient all these sauces have in common. And while a tablespoon may easily fit into your diet, many of us eat far more than a tablespoon (or two) at a sitting. Try this simple-to-make sauce as a great low-sugar alternative. It makes a great complement to beef, pork, and chicken.

INGREDIENTS:

2 teaspoons canola oil

1 teaspoon minced garlic

1 cup finely chopped onion

1 6-ounce can tomato paste

1 cup water

2 tablespoons apple cider vinegar

3 tablespoons Worcestershire sauce

⅓ cup Splenda Granular

2 teaspoons molasses

1 teaspoon chili powder

1 teaspoon dry mustard

3-4 drops liquid smoke

Few drops Tabasco sauce (optional, to taste)

STEPS:

1. In a medium saucepan, heat oil and garlic over medium heat for 1 minute. Add onion and cook for 10 minutes, until onion is soft and translucent.

2. Add the remaining ingredients, stir well, and simmer for 20 minutes over low heat.

3. Remove from heat and blend in a blender to smooth and meld flavors.

4. Cool, cover, and refrigerate (keeps for 2 weeks).

Tomato paste is rich in lycopene, a powerful antioxidant that may be beneficial in fighting certain forms of cancer and heart disease.

PER SERVING (2 TABLESOONS)

Calories 25	Fat .5 grams (0 saturated)
Carbohydrate 5 grams	Fiber .5 grams
Protein 1 gram	Sodium 105 milligrams

Diabetic exchange = ½ Carbohydrate (for up to 3 tablespoons)

WW point comparison = 0 points

Sweet and Spicy Cajun Rub

Serves Twenty-Four

Meat rubs are a simple way to add flavor and color to meats without added fat. The best rubs mix flavors like sweet and salty with savory and spicy, to tickle all your taste buds. You may use this rub on any meat, poultry, or fish. Single-serving pieces should be "rubbed" about one hour before cooking or grilling—and large pieces several hours or even overnight—to allow the rub to mix with the juices from the meat.

INGREDIENTS:

2 tablespoons paprika

1 ½ tablespoons Splenda Granular

1 tablespoon salt

1 tablespoon freshly ground pepper

1 tablespoon garlic powder

1 tablespoon onion powder

1 tablespoon oregano

1 tablespoon thyme

1 to 1 ½ teaspoons cayenne pepper (1 ½ teaspoons make this quite spicy)

STEPS:

1. Thoroughly mix all ingredients together.

2. Use immediately or place in a tightly sealed jar (stays good for several months).

If you are on a low-sodium diet, cut the salt in half or use a low-sodium salt substitute like Nu-Salt in place of some or all of the salt.

PER SERVING (1 TEASPOON)

Calories 8	Fat 0 grams
Carbohydrate 2 grams	Fiber 1 gram
Protein 0 grams	Sodium 300 milligrams

Diabetic exchange = Free Food
WW point comparison = 0 points

Two-Way Cranberry Sauce

Serves Ten (¼ cup whole or 2 tablespoons jellied)

The thing I've come to realize about holiday cooking is that no one accepts a new dish (healthy or not) if it doesn't compare favorably to a traditional recipe. I guarantee that if you try this recipe, no one will know you have taken out more than 75 percent of the sugar needed to make a traditional cranberry sauce recipe because this one tastes just as sweet. You may choose to leave the berries whole (as I do), or strain the sauce to make a jellied cranberry sauce by using the variation below.

INGREDIENTS:

¼ cup regular or light orange juice

1 teaspoon unflavored gelatin

12 ounces fresh cranberries, washed and picked over

1 cup water

¾ cup Splenda Granular

3 tablespoons granulated sugar

Red food color (optional)

STEPS:

1. Place orange juice into a small bowl. Add gelatin. Let set 3 minutes.

2. Combine cranberries, water, Splenda, and sugar in a medium skillet. Bring to a boil.

3. Add softened gelatin. Simmer for 10 minutes or until most of the cranberries pop open.

4. Adjust color by adding 2-3 drops of red food color if desired.

JELLIED CRANBERRY SAUCE: Increase gelatin to 2 teaspoons. Strain sauce by using the back of a spoon to press berries and juice through a sieve. Refrigerate sauce overnight.

Traditional homemade cranberry sauce can have as much as 35 grams of sugar in a ¼-cup serving. That's more sugar than you'll find in any dessert recipe in this book.

PER SERVING (¹/4 CUP WHOLE OR 2 TABLESPOONS JELLIED)

Calories 30	Fat 0 grams (0 saturated)
Carbohydrate 8 grams	Fiber 2 grams
Protein 1 gram	Sodium 0 milligrams

Diabetic exchange = ½ Fruit
WW point comparison = 1 point

Sensational No-Cook Cranberry Relish

Serves Eight

In recent years, cranberry relishes have become increasingly popular. In this tart and refreshing version, I include a few added touches that really make it stand out. Prepare at least a day ahead of time to allow the flavors to meld.

INGREDIENTS:

1 12-ounce bag cranberries, washed and picked over

1 orange, peeled and seeded (reserve ¼ of rind)

2 tablespoons brown sugar

2 tablespoons orange liqueur

¾ cup Splenda Granular

Cranberries (originally called crane berries) are full of antioxidants and flavonoids that may help you ward off everything from ulcers to heart disease and cancer.

STEPS;

1. Place ½ the cranberries, the orange, and the orange rind in a food processor and pulse until mixture is finely chopped (not pureed). Pour into a large bowl.

2. Repeat process with second half of cranberries and brown sugar. Add to bowl.

3. Stir orange liqueur and Splenda into cranberry mixture. Cover and refrigerate overnight or longer before serving (holds well up to 2 weeks).

PER SERVING

Calories 35

Carbohydrate 7 grams

Protein 0 grams

Fat 0 grams (0 saturated)

Fiber 1 gram

Sodium 0 milligrams

Diabetic exchange = ½ Fruit

WW point comparison = 1 point

Zucchini and Corn Relish

Serves Sixteen

For this cookbook, a lifelong friend of mine adapted her grandmother's fresh alternative to pickle relish. Originally chock-full of sugar, in this revised version Zucchini and Corn Relish is a dieter's delight that's low in fat and calories and full of flavor. My friend Nancie uses it to perk up her tuna salad, but it's also great for sprucing up reduced-fat hot dogs and lean burgers.

INGREDIENTS:

2 ½ cups grated zucchini

1 cup minced onion

¾ cup grated green pepper

¾ cup grated red pepper

1 tablespoon salt

¼ teaspoon tumeric

¼ teaspoon curry powder

¼ teaspoon celery seed

¼ teaspoon pepper

½ teaspoon cornstarch

1 cup Splenda Granular

⅔ cup vinegar

STEPS:

1. In a large bowl, mix zucchini, onion, green pepper, red pepper, and salt. Let stand in the refrigerator overnight.

2. In the morning, rinse thoroughly in cold water and drain well.

3. Add remaining ingredients and cook over medium heat for 30 minutes. Store in an airtight container in the refrigerator. Keeps 1-2 weeks.

If you decide to can this relish, sterilize jars properly and heat per canner instructions to ensure jars are sealed. Check by pressing on tops, making sure they don't pop up (if they do, the relish isn't sealed well enough for cupboard storage).

PER SERVING (2 TABLESPOONS)

Calories 20	Fat 0 grams
Carbohydrate 4 grams	Fiber 1 gram
Protein 1 gram	Sodium 40 milligrams

Diabetic exchange = 1 Vegetable
WW point comparison = 0 points

Cranberry Chutney

Serves Twelve

Every year during the holidays, I make cranberry chutney to serve with turkey. Chutneys combine vinegar with sugar for a balance of sweet and sour flavors, but this one also has a touch of heat from red pepper flakes, along with a lovely hint of orange. Make another batch or use leftover chutney as a great spread for cold turkey sandwiches. This chutney also really dresses up pork tenderloin.

INGREDIENTS:

1 teaspoon canola oil

1 large shallot, finely chopped (⅓ cup)

1 12-ounce package cranberries

½ cup Splenda Granular

½ cup regular or light orange juice

⅓ cup cider vinegar

1 tablespoon brown sugar

½ teaspoon ground ginger

Scant ¼ teaspoon red pepper flakes

1 tablespoon orange zest

STEPS:

1. In a large saucepan, heat oil and sauté shallot 3-4 minutes or until softened.

2. Add remaining ingredients except zest and bring to a boil. Lower heat and simmer for 15 minutes, stirring occasionally.

3. Add zest and cook 15 more minutes or until thickened.

4. Cool and store in refrigerator. Serve cool or at room temperature.

I usually add a couple drops of red food color to give a deep red color to the chutney, especially if I spoon it into jars to give as gifts during the holidays.

PER SERVING (2 TABLESPOONS)

Calories 35	Fat 0 grams (0 saturated)
Carbohydrate 8 grams	Fiber 1 gram
Protein 0 grams	Sodium 0 milligrams

Diabetic exchange = ½ Fruit
WW point comparison = 1 point

Peach Chutney

Serves Eight

My next-door neighbor, a gracious beneficiary of many of my recipe trials, was delighted the day she received a container of this scrumptious Peach Chutney. In fact, she mentioned it for weeks! It makes a wonderful accompaniment for grilled meat or fish.

INGREDIENTS:

6 fresh medium peaches (1 ½ pounds)

1 tablespoon lemon juice

½ cup chopped onion

½ cup chopped red pepper

1 teaspoon oil

½ cup Splenda Granular

⅓ cup cider vinegar

1 teaspoon freshly grated ginger

2 teaspoons honey

⅛ teaspoon cinnamon

⅛ teaspoon red pepper flakes

STEPS:

1. Plunge peaches into boiling water for 1 minute. Immediately drop into cold water and cool. Peel, pit, and chop into medium-sized pieces (about 3 cups). Sprinkle with lemon juice.

2. In a medium saucepan, sauté onion and pepper in oil until slightly softened.

3. Add peaches and remaining ingredients and bring to low boil. Reduce heat to simmer and cook for 30 minutes, stirring occasionally until cooked down and thickened.

You can use many types of fruits and vegetables to make chutneys. You can make them fresh like this one or canned like jelly. Refrigerated, fresh chutneys are good for as long as one month.

PER SERVING (¼ CUP)

Calories 45	Fat 0 grams (0 saturated)
Carbohydrate 11 grams	Fiber 2 grams
Protein 1 gram	Sodium 0 milligrams

Diabetic exchange = 1 Fruit
WW point comparison = 1 point

Southwest Peach Chutney

Serves Eight

Cumin and tumeric bring a bit of the Southwest into this savory-style chutney. Try it over grilled chicken with a big green salad and either Sweet Southwestern-Style Corn Pudding (page 195) or Cheesy Jalapeno Cornbread (page 194). Then wash it all down with a tall glass of Sparkling Limeade (page 39).

INGREDIENTS:

6 fresh medium peaches (1 ½ pounds)

1 tablespoon lime juice

1 teaspoon oil

½ cup chopped onion

½ cup chopped red pepper

1 small jalapeno pepper, seeded and finely diced

½ cup Splenda Granular

⅓ cup cider vinegar

2 teaspoons honey

½ teaspoon cumin

⅛ teaspoon tumeric

STEPS:

1. Plunge peaches into boiling water for 1 minute. Immediately drop into cold water and cool.

2. Peel, pit, and chop into medium-sized pieces (about 3 cups). Sprinkle with lemon juice.

3. In a medium saucepan, sauté onion and peppers until slightly softened. Add remaining ingredients and bring to low boil. Reduce heat to simmer and cook for 30 minutes, stirring occasionally until cooked down and thickened.

PER SERVING (¼ CUP)

Calories 45	Fat 0 grams (0 saturated)
Carbohydrate 11 grams	Fiber 2 grams
Protein 1 gram	Sodium 0 milligrams

Diabetic exchange = 1 Fruit
WW point comparison = 1 point

Quick and Fresh Mint Chutney

Serves Four

Most often, you'll find chutney made with cooked fruits or vegetables (like the Cranberry Chutney on page 209), but this one is a bit different. Quick and Fresh Mint Chutney hails from India and is more akin to pesto, in which fresh herbs are blended into a thick paste. The wonderful combination of mint and lemon creates a very flavorful accompaniment (or spread) for lamb, chicken, and seafood.

INGREDIENTS:

1 cup loosely packed fresh mint leaves

¼ cup fresh cilantro

¼ cup green onions (white and green parts)

1 tablespoon chopped jalapeno pepper

Zest of 1 lemon

1 teaspoon Splenda Granular (or ½ Splenda packet)

1 teaspoon freshly minced ginger

Pinch salt

3 tablespoons fresh lemon juice

1 tablespoon canola oil

1 tablespoon water

STEPS:

1. Place mint leaves, cilantro, onion, jalapeno, lemon zest, Splenda, ginger, and salt in a food processor or blender. Pulse to chop leaves.

2. Add lemon juice, oil, and water, and pulse briefly to combine.

This recipe doubles easily, and you can make it a day or two ahead of time. Keep in an airtight container in the refrigerator until you serve it.

PER SERVING (2 TABLESPOONS)

Calories 45	Fat 3.5 grams (0 saturated)
Carbohydrate 3 grams	Fiber 1 gram
Protein 1 gram	Sodium 90 milligrams

Diabetic exchange = 1 Fat, ½ Vegetable
WW point comparison = 1 point

Bread and Butter Pickles

Serves Ten

I was delighted with the outcome of these pickles; they taste even better than the commercial brands that are loaded with sugar. Small pickling cukes or gherkins are ideal, but regular salad cucumbers work just fine, too. You can also "pickle" mixed vegetables as seen in the Pickled Mixed Vegetables variation.

INGREDIENTS:

1 ½ pounds of cucumbers, ends trimmed and sliced (unpeeled)

1 medium onion, thinly sliced

1 tablespoon pickling salt

1 ½ cups vinegar

1 cup Splenda Granular

1 ½ teaspoons mustard seed

1 teaspoon cornstarch

¾ teaspoon turmeric

½ teaspoon celery seed

STEPS:

1. Place cucumbers and onion in a large bowl and toss with pickling salt. Cover and refrigerate for 1–2 hours.

2. Rinse well in colander under running water, drain, and place in large bowl.

3. In a medium pot, combine the remaining ingredients and bring to boil over high heat. Stir until slightly thickened and clear.

4. Pour hot marinade over cucumbers and onions. Cool to room temperature, cover, and refrigerate. Keeps up to 1 month.

PICKLED MIXED VEGETABLES: Marinate up to 5 cups mixed blanched carrots, peppers, cauliflower, and onions. Add a touch of crushed red pepper for zing.

These sweet and crunchy pickles can really satisfy a sweet tooth when that afternoon craving strikes. If you crave them with ice cream, go ahead (Splenda is even safe for use by pregnant women).

PER SERVING (½ CUP)

Calories 20	Fat 0 grams (0 saturated)
Carbohydrate 5 grams	Fiber .5 grams
Protein 0 grams	Sodium 120 milligrams

Diabetic exchange = 1 Vegetable
WW point comparison = 0 points

Easy Re-Pickled Pickles

Serves Ten to Twelve

When I saw this idea in an old charity cookbook, I just couldn't resist giving it a try. To be honest, I'm not sure why anyone would change a jarred dill pickle to a sweet one using regular sugar (because manufacturers are pros at adding it for you), but what inspiration for those of us who enjoy sweet pickles but want to avoid sugar. So simple yet so sweet!

INGREDIENTS:

1 16-ounce jar baby or mini kosher dill pickles

¾ cup apple cider vinegar

¾ cup Splenda Granular

½ teaspoon dried dill

STEPS:

1. Remove lid from pickle jar and pour out all of the juice (leaving pickles intact).

2. In a small saucepan, heat vinegar, Splenda, and dill until warm.

3. Pour mixture over pickles. Replace lid and let cool to room temperature.

4. Place in refrigerator for 24 hours before serving.

If you're watching your sodium, I suggest you select a reduced-sodium pickle to "re-pickle," or make the Bread and Butter Pickles found next door on page 213.

PER SERVING (1 PICKLE)

Calories 5	Fat 0 grams
Carbohydrate 1 gram	Fiber 0 grams
Protein 0 gram	Sodium 260 milligrams

Diabetic exchange = Free Food
WW point comparison = 0 points

Apple Butter

Serves Forty-Eight

Dark, thick, and smooth, this apple butter is a delicious alternative to butter and sugary fruit jams for use on toast and sandwiches. Don't omit the sieve step because it's essential to achieve the smooth, "buttery" texture that gives apple butter its name and differentiates it from applesauce.

Ingredients:

4 pounds cooking apples, washed, unpeeled, uncored, cut into quartered chunks

2 cups water

½ cup fresh lemon juice

2 teaspoons ground cinnamon

½ teaspoon allspice

¾ cup Splenda Granular (or more, to taste)

Pinch salt

Steps:

1. Put apples (about 12 cups), lemon juice, and water in a saucepan. Cover and bring to a boil. Turn heat down to medium-low, and cook until apples are quite soft (about 30 minutes).

2. Place sieve (chinois or food mill) over a large bowl and ladle apple mixture into sieve 2 cups at a time. Using a hard rubber spatula, press apples through sieve into a large bowl.

3. Preheat oven to 275°F.

4. Stir spices, Splenda, and salt into apples. Pour apple mixture into an ovenproof dish and bake in oven until the mixture is thickened (about 1 hour). When it's thick enough, apple butter should stay well mounded when scooped onto a spoon.

5. Spoon into containers or jars and refrigerate (keeps 1 month).

After you sieve the apple mixture, you may use a crockpot instead of the oven for thickening. Place in crockpot and cook 3–4 hours; check as needed until mixture stays mounded when scooped with spoon.

Per Serving (1 Tablespoon)

Calories 20	Fat 0 grams
Carbohydrate 5 grams	Fiber 0 grams
Protein 0 grams	Sodium 0 milligrams

Diabetic exchange = 1 Free Food
WW point comparison = 0 points

Low-Sugar Strawberry Freezer Jam

Serves Forty-Eight

An award-winning strawberry jam recipe I found on the Internet called for 5 cups of crushed strawberries and 7 cups of sugar. This recipe uses a fraction of the sugar—a mere ⅓ cup—to make 4 cups of jam. You can omit the sugar altogether, but granulated sugar helps to add clarity and improves the overall quality. Be sure to use "no-sugar-needed" pectin in order for the jam to gel.

INGREDIENTS:

2 quarts fresh strawberries, washed, and stemmed (4 cups crushed)

1 package (1 ¾-ounce) no-sugar-needed pectin

2 ½ cups Splenda Granular

⅓ cup granulated sugar

3-4 drops red food coloring

STEPS:

1. Crush berries and mix with pectin in a large saucepan. Stir and let stand 10 minutes.

2. Turn heat to medium; add Splenda and sugar and cook until mixture comes to a boil. Cook for 1 minute. Stir in desired amount of food coloring and skim foam off top.

3. Place in containers and refrigerate (to use within 1 month) or freeze (for up to 1 year).

PEACH FREEZER JAM: Substitute 4 cups fresh, sliced skinless peaches for strawberries.

When choosing pectin, be sure to get no-sugar-needed, not the low-sugar pectin, to ensure your jam gels. And if the powdered pectin has hardened, mix in a blender to turn it back into a powder before adding it to the fruit.

PER SERVING (1 TABLESPOON)

Calories 15	Fat 0 grams (0 saturated)
Carbohydrate 4 grams	Fiber .5 gram
Protein 0 grams	Sodium 0 milligrams

Diabetic exchange = Free Food
WW point comparison = 0 points

Microwave Cinnamon Applesauce

Serves Six

*Fresh applesauce, especially served chunky, makes a great
side dish. This recipe tastes like the old-fashioned kind, but
it's made with a very modern appliance—the microwave.*

INGREDIENTS:

**6 medium apples (1 ½ pounds),
  peeled, halved, and cored**

⅔ cup water

1 tablespoon lemon juice

½ cup Splenda Granular

½ teaspoon cinnamon

1 tablespoon brown sugar

STEPS:

1. Cut apples into either thick slices or 1-inch chunks. Place apples in a deep, microwave-safe casserole dish.

2. Add water, lemon juice, Splenda, and cinnamon to apples.

3. Cook, uncovered, on high for 5 minutes. Stir, mashing apples with a fork into the liquid.

4. Cook for an additional 5-8 minutes or until apples are tender. Mash apples again, mixing with liquid, until desired texture.

5. With a spoon, stir brown sugar into hot apple mixture. Serve hot or cool and store in refrigerator until ready to use. Keeps about 3-4 days.

For the best applesauce, mix a couple of kinds of apples together—like Gravenstein or Pippin blended with Macintosh and/or Golden Delicious.

PER SERVING (½ CUP)

Calories 70	Fat 0 grams (0 saturated)
Carbohydrate 18 grams	Fiber 2 grams
Protein 0 grams	Sodium 0 milligrams

Diabetic exchange = 1 Fruit
WW point comparison = 1 point

Protein-Packed Entrees

Sloppy Joes

Spicy Orange Beef

Grandma Claire's Stuffed Cabbage

Barbecued Meat Loaf Muffins

Cocktail Meatballs with Quick
      Sweet and Sour Sauce

Barbecued Pork Sandwiches

Maple Glazed Ham Steaks

Asian Barbecued Pork Tenderloin

Brined Breast of Turkey

Bourbon Chicken

Sweet and Sour Chicken

Caribbean Chicken

Minced Chicken Lettuce Wraps

Zesty Chicken Strips with Sweet Mustard Dip

Simple Southwest Salmon

Scallops with Mango Salsa

Baked Fish with Oriental Pesto

Grilled Salmon with Mustard Dill Sauce

Shrimp Satay Sticks with Thai Peanut Sauce

Soba Noodle Bowl with Peanut Garlic Sauce

Marlene's Pasta Marinara Dinner

In the restaurant business, the entrée is known as the "center of the plate" because when someone sits down to a meal, the entrée is front and center—the main attraction. Of course, it's this part of the meal where you'll find most of the protein, too. Protein not only fills you up and satisfies you, but is essential for maintaining your health—everything from your muscle mass to keeping your immune system healthy.

And although not everyone agrees with the "high-protein diet theory," everyone agrees with the fact that you need protein, especially during times when you're trying to lose weight. As I told my students in a Low-Carb Done Right cooking class, the key to eating protein in a healthy diet is to keep it lean and to serve it clean (without the usual rich or sugary sauces). In this section, I am happy to provide you with countless and interesting ways to fill the center of your plate with lean, healthy entrees that have the great, sweet embellishments you love—without the sugar. Ranging from popular classics like amazing Sweet and Sour Chicken and Barbecued Pork Sandwiches to hot newcomers like Minced Chicken Lettuce Wraps and Scallops with Mango Salsa, these recipes are set to satisfy. Kids, too, will rally around for Zesty Chicken Strips with Sweet Mustard Dip and Marlene's Pasta Marinara Dinner, while other fantastic dishes like Grilled Salmon with Mustard Dill Sauce and Asian Barbecued Pork Tenderloin are too good not to be shared with friends as well as family. But whatever your taste, these protein-packed dishes will definitely be at the center of everyone's attention, as well as their plates.

Sloppy Joes

Serves Six

As the story goes, Sloppy Joes were created during World War II as a way to extend precious beef rations. Although admittedly messy, these simple-to-make, lean ground sirloin Joes will always give you a hearty, healthy meal.

INGREDIENTS:

1 pound lean ground beef or sirloin

1 small onion, diced

1 green pepper, diced

4 stalks celery, diced

1 cup water

1 6-ounce can tomato paste

3 tablespoons Splenda Granular

1 tablespoon vinegar

1 tablespoon Worcestershire sauce

½ teaspoon chili powder

½ teaspoon paprika

Pinch salt

6 light or reduced-carb wheat buns

STEPS:

1. In a medium skillet, over medium heat, brown beef, onion, green pepper, and celery.

2. Add remaining ingredients except buns; mix thoroughly. Reduce heat, and simmer for 20–30 minutes.

3. Serve scant ½ cup on each bun.

Worcestershire sauce adds great flavor and a bit of bite to beef. Quite exotic, it contains not only anchovies but tamarind, molasses, vinegar, garlic, cloves, chiles, onions, and sometimes fruit.

PER SERVING

Calories 290	Fat 12 grams (5 saturated)
Carbohydrate 26 grams	Fiber 4 grams
Protein 20 grams	Sodium 500 milligrams

Diabetic exchange = 1 ½ Carbohydrate, 3 Lean Meat, 1 Fat
WW point comparison = 6 points

Spicy Orange Beef

Serves Four

Stir-frying rather than deep-frying the beef in this popular dish cuts the fat but not the flavor because it's the sweet and spicy orange sauce that really makes the dish. Slicing the meat while it's slightly frozen makes it easy to cut very thin, uniform slices for stir-frying.

INGREDIENTS

1 pound top sirloin or flank steak, partially frozen

2 tablespoons sherry

2 tablespoons light soy sauce

1 tablespoon cornstarch

1 tablespoon canola or peanut oil

1 medium onion, cut into ½-inch dice

2 small yellow peppers, cut into strips

1 cup sliced water chestnuts

2 green onions, chopped (white and green)

SAUCE

1 teaspoon cornstarch

¼ cup regular or light orange juice

3 tablespoons Splenda Granular

2 tablespoons light soy sauce

2 tablespoons low-sugar orange marmalade

2 teaspoons vinegar

1 teaspoon sesame oil

¼ or ½ teaspoon red pepper flakes

STEPS:

1. Slice steak thinly across the grain. Place in medium bowl.

2. Add sherry, soy sauce, and cornstarch and toss to coat meat. Set aside.

3. SAUCE: Combine sauce ingredients in a small bowl. Set aside.

4. Heat wok until hot. Add the caola or peanut oil. When oil is very hot, add beef. (It should sizzle as it hits wok.) Stir-fry for 3–4 minutes until no longer pink. Remove from wok.

5. Add onion to wok and stir 1 minute. Add peppers and water chestnuts. Stir-fry an additional 2–3 minutes.

6. Add sauce mixture; stir well.

7. Add beef to hot sauce. Toss in green onions. Stir just until beef is coated and serve.

This recipe is a favorite of kids. I've even been told of kids who didn't like meat actually gobbling up this dish, much to Mom's delight. For a healthy whole-grain choice, serve it with brown rice.

PER SERVING

Calories 310	Fat 15 grams (3.5 saturated)
Carbohydrate 16 grams	Fiber 2 grams
Protein 27 grams	Sodium 610 milligrams

Diabetic exchange = 1 Vegetable, 4 Lean Meat, ½ Carbohydrate, ½ Fat
WW point comparison = 7 points

Grandma Claire's Stuffed Cabbage

Serves Ten

One of my recipe testers learned this sweet-and-sour stuffed cabbage recipe from her grandmother. This version of stuffed cabbage originated in Poland, where cinnamon, ginger, and allspice are common ingredients in cooking as well as baking. It works both with ground beef or ground turkey and is delicious the day after it's made when the flavors have had more time to meld. A great idea is to tuck a couple of cabbage rolls aside for lunch the next day.

INGREDIENTS:

1 medium head of cabbage (8-10 whole leaves, plus 2 cups chopped cabbage)

2 pounds lean ground beef or lean ground turkey

2 cups cooked rice

1 tablespoon onion powder

1 egg

½ teaspoon salt (or more to taste)

Ground pepper to taste

1 28-ounce can crushed tomatoes with tomato puree

1 medium yellow onion, diced

Juice of 1 lemon

2 tablespoons cider vinegar

2 tablespoons Splenda Granular

½ teaspoon allspice

½ teaspoon cinnamon

Pinch ground ginger

Salt and pepper to taste

STEPS:

1. In a microwave-safe bowl, place the head of cabbage and 2 tablespoons of water. Cover with plastic wrap and microwave on high for 7 minutes. Remove from microwave.

2. When cool enough to handle, gently peel off 10 whole cabbage leaves, taking care not to tear them. Set aside.

3. In a medium bowl, combine ground beef, rice, onion powder, egg, salt, and pepper. Set aside.

4. In a large saucepan, combine tomatoes, onion, lemon juice, cider vinegar, Splenda, allspice, cinnamon, and ginger. Bring to a simmer over medium heat.

5. While sauce is simmering, spread out one cabbage leaf on a flat surface, stem side toward you. Place about ½ cup meat filling onto the leaf close to the stem end. Roll cabbage leaf over meat once. Fold the sides inward as if you were making a burrito; then finish rolling. Repeat with remaining leaves and meat.

6. Place the cabbage rolls, nestled together, into the simmering sauce on the stovetop. Add 2 cups of chopped cabbage on top, cover, and simmer for 30 minutes, or until meat is cooked through and cabbage is soft.

7. Carefully place cabbage rolls onto platter, covering them with the sauce and extra cabbage.

PER SERVING

Calories 240	Fat 9 grams (3.5 saturated)
Carbohydrate 17 grams	Fiber 3 grams
Protein 22 grams	Sodium 260 milligrams

Diabetic exchange = 3 Lean Meat, 1 Carbohydrate
WW point comparison = 5 points

Barbecued Meat Loaf Muffins

Serves Twelve

Fun to make and even more fun to eat, these muffins are a great way to get your kids involved in cooking dinner. Small fry can easily make the barbecue sauce (while you do the chopping), and then enjoy the fun of mixing it into the meat, finishing it off with their hands, of course. Using muffin tins adds to the fun by giving everyone an individual meat loaf—fast!

INGREDIENTS:

BARBECUE SAUCE

⅔ cup reduced-sugar ketchup
 (like Heinz One Carb)★

2 tablespoons water

1 ½ tablespoons Splenda Granular

1 tablespoon Worcestershire sauce

1 tablespoon vinegar

½ teaspoon liquid smoke

½ teaspoon chili powder

⅛ teaspoon onion powder

⅛ teaspoon garlic powder

MEAT LOAF

1 ¾ pounds lean ground beef or sirloin

½ small yellow onion, finely diced

½ green pepper, finely diced

½ red pepper, finely diced

1 large egg plus 1 egg white

1 cup plain bread crumbs

½ teaspoon onion powder

½ teaspoon garlic powder

½ teaspoon salt

Pepper to taste

STEPS:

1. Preheat oven to 450°F. Coat regular-sized muffin tins, with nonstick cooking spray.

2. SAUCE: Combine all ingredients in small saucepan and stir to combine. Simmer on low for 5 minutes. Set aside.

3. MEATLOAF: Place ground beef in a medium bowl. Add all remaining meat-loaf ingredients and ½ cup barbecue sauce. Combine but don't overmix. Adjust salt and pepper to taste.

4. Divide meat evenly into 12 muffin tins, mounding slightly (scant ½ cup each)

5. Bake 20-25 minutes or until done.

6. Remove from oven and brush muffins with remainder of barbecue sauce. Let sit for 10 minutes before serving.

Getting kids involved in cooking ratchets up their appetite for new foods. Let them chop the peppers, crack the eggs, and measure ingredients in order to learn cooking skills and fractions.

PER SERVING

Calories 165	Fat 7 grams (2.5 saturated)
Carbohydrate 9 grams	Fiber 1 gram
Protein 16 grams	Sodium 380 milligrams

Diabetic exchange = 2 Lean Meat, ½ Carbohydrate, ½ Fat
WW point comparison = 4 points
★ Add 2.5 grams of carb and 10 calories to each serving if you use regular ketchup.

Cocktail Meatballs with Quick Sweet and Sour Sauce

Serves Ten

Make these for a party and watch them disappear. I've provided a recipe here for meatballs, but in a pinch, you can buy prepared ones from your grocer's freezer. Be sure to check the labels—they can be full of both fat and fillers.

INGREDIENTS:

MEATBALLS

½ **pound lean ground beef or lean ground turkey**

⅓ **cup unseasoned bread crumbs**

1 **large egg**

2 **tablespoons dry minced onion**

2 **tablespoons fresh parsley, minced**

½ **teaspoon salt**

¼ **teaspoon pepper**

½ **cup 1% milk**

SAUCE

⅓ **cup ketchup**★

¼ **cup cider vinegar**

¼ **cup Splenda Granular**

2 **teaspoons Worcestershire sauce**

⅔ **cup cold water**

1 **tablespoon + 1 teaspoon cornstarch**

STEPS:

1. Preheat oven to 350°F.

2. MEATBALLS: In a large bowl, mix all ingredients.

3. Using hands, roll mixture into 1-inch balls and place on ungreased baking sheet.

4. Bake for 15 minutes or until center is no longer pink.

5. SAUCE: In a small saucepan, combine ingredients.

6. Place over medium heat and simmer until thickened and clear.

7. Pour sauce over meatballs. Serve hot.

How popular are cocktail-style meatballs? Extremely. If you want to check this out, do a Web search and you'll find literally thousands of recipes.

PER SERVING (3-4 MEATBALLS, PLUS SAUCE)

Calories 130	Fat 5 grams (2 saturated)
Carbohydrate 9 grams	Fiber 0 grams
Protein 12 grams	Sodium 580 milligrams

Diabetic exchange = 2 Lean Meat, ½ Carbohydrate
WW point comparison = 3 points
★ If you use reduced-sugar ketchup (1 gram carb per tablespoon), subtract 1.5 grams carb and 8 calories per serving.

Barbecued Pork Sandwiches

Serves Twelve

This soft, shredded pork smothered in sweet tangy barbecue sauce is all served up on a bun for fewer than 250 calories. The recipe also yields a dozen sandwiches, making it perfect for entertaining. The Sweet and Sour Party Slaw (page 137) would make a great low-carbohydrate accompaniment.

INGREDIENTS:

2-2 ¼ pounds boneless pork loin roast, trimmed of excess fat

1 8-ounce can tomato sauce

1 6-ounce can tomato paste

¼ cup vinegar

½ cup Splenda Granular

2 tablespoons molasses

2 tablespoons Worcestershire sauce

2 teaspoons onion powder

12 light wheat hamburger buns

STEPS:

1. Place pork loin in a 4-quart Dutch oven or large pot; add 2 cups water. Cover and cook for 2 ½ hours or until meat shreds when tested with fork.

2. Remove meat from liquid and pull apart with fork; set aside.

3. Drain cooking liquid, reserving 1 cup, and skim fat.

4. Return 1 cup of liquid to pot. Add remaining ingredients (except buns) to pot and stir.

5. Gently add meat to sauce (overstirring will turn meat to mush). Cover and simmer on low for 30 minutes.

6. Scoop ¼ cup barbecue pork onto each bun and serve.

Look for reduced-carb buns or light wheat buns. The one my local market carries contains 90 calories, 18 grams of carbohydrate, and 3 grams of fiber per bun. Pepperidge Farm makes a nice one called Pepperidge Farm Carb-Style Hamburger Rolls.

PER SERVING

Calories 245 — Fat 7 grams (2 saturated)
Carbohydrate 27 grams — Fiber 4 grams
Protein 21 grams — Sodium 510 milligrams

Diabetic exchange = 1 ½ Carbohydrate, 3 Lean Meat
WW point comparison = 5 points

Maple-Glazed Ham Steaks

Serves Four

While whole hams are usually reserved for special occasions and entertaining, lean ham steaks provide a quick and tasty anyday supper. This unusual glaze uses sugar-free maple syrup as its base. Choose one of the many brands that is made with Splenda.

INGREDIENTS:

2 fully cooked ¾- to 1-inch-thick lean ham steaks (12 ounces each)

SAUCE

⅓ cup sugar-free maple syrup

2 tablespoons unsweetened applesauce

2 tablespoons Splenda Granular

1 tablespoon ketchup

1 teaspoon Dijon mustard

½ teaspoon salt

Pinch garlic powder

STEPS:

1. SAUCE: In a small saucepan over medium heat, whisk together all ingredients. Cook for 5 minutes over low heat.

2. Place ham steaks on baking sheet. Spoon ½ of the sauce over steaks.

3. Broil (2 inches from heating element) for 5 minutes. Turn steaks, spoon on remaining sauce, and broil for 5 minutes more or until steaks are heated throughout.

Salt is an essential ingredient in the processing of curing ham; therefore, it's always high in sodium. If you are on a sodium-restricted diet, you may want to reduce your portion size.

PER SERVING

Calories 230

Carbohydrate 9 grams

Protein 33 grams

Fat 8 grams (2 saturated)

Fiber 0 grams

Sodium 1,980 milligrams

Diabetic exchange = 5 Lean Meat

WW point comparison = 5 points

Asian Barbecued Pork Tenderloin

Serves Four

Hoisin is a thick, sweet, spicy condiment used extensively in Asian cuisine. In addition to being spread on pancakes for mu shu pork, it can be used for delicious stir-fries or barbecue sauces like this one.

INGREDIENTS:

¼ cup regular or light orange juice

3 tablespoons Splenda Granular

2 tablespoons light soy sauce

2 tablespoons hoisin sauce

2 teaspoons sesame oil

½ teaspoon grated ginger

1 ¼ pounds pork tenderloin

STEPS:

1. In a small bowl, combine all ingredients except pork.

2. Place pork in shallow dish and coat with sauce. Cover and marinate for several hours or overnight.

3. Preheat oven to 425°F.

4. Remove pork from sauce and place on baking sheet covered with foil. Brush with marinade and cook for 20 minutes or until internal temperature reaches 145-150°F.

5. While meat is cooking, place marinade into a small saucepan and bring to a boil. Simmer for 5 minutes until reduced to a glaze. Remove meat from oven and coat with glaze.

6. Let meat rest 5-10 minutes. Slice thinly across the grain to serve.

Hoisin is made from soybeans, chiles, garlic, ginger, and sugar. Brands vary quite a bit from one another so be sure to choose hoisin that's very dark and has a complex flavor. Koon Chun and Lee Kum Kee are two good brands.

PER SERVING

Calories 210

Carbohydrate 5 grams

Protein 30 grams

Fat 7 grams (2 saturated)

Fiber 0 grams

Sodium 490 milligrams

Diabetic exchange = 4 Very Lean Meat, ½ Carbohydrate

WW point comparison = 5 points

Brined Breast of Turkey

Serves Eight

Lean turkey breasts are a quick and healthful way to enjoy the great taste of turkey, but they can easily cook up dry. A simple and flavorful solution to this cooking dilemma is to "brine" the breast by soaking it in a flavored salt solution that will assure you flavorful, moist turkey breast every time.

INGREDIENTS:

1 turkey breast, about 5 pounds

10 cups water

½ cup kosher salt

½ cup Splenda Granular

2 tablespoons honey

2 tablespoons Dijon mustard

1 teaspoon red pepper flakes

2 sprigs fresh rosemary

Paprika

STEPS:

1. Place 8 cups of cold water in a container large enough to hold the turkey breast and all the brining liquid.

2. In a small saucepan, combine 2 cups water, salt, Splenda, honey, mustard, red pepper flakes, and rosemary. Cook over medium heat until salt has dissolved. Pour into the cold water.

3. Add the turkey breast; cover and refrigerate for 4-8 hours.

4. Preheat oven to 425°F.

5. Remove turkey from brine and pat dry. Place on large roasting pan and sprinkle all over with paprika. Do not salt. Cook until thermometer inserted in largest part of breast reads 170°F, approximately 1 ½ hours.

Brines add moisture and tenderness to meats because salt helps the muscle fibers absorb more liquid, making the meat juicier. It also denatures and dissolves some of the proteins, making the meat tenderer. Spices and sweeteners tag along for the ride and add flavor.

PER SERVING

Calories 240	Fat 2 grams (.5 saturated)
Carbohydrate 2 grams	Fiber 0 grams
Protein 51 grams	Sodium 950 milligrams

Diabetic exchange = 6 Very Lean Meat

WW point comparison = 5 points

Bourbon Chicken

Serves Four

Whenever I take my boys to the shopping mall, they head straight for the food court looking for a sample of a dish named Bourbon Chicken. It doesn't actually contain alcohol, but this delicious version does.

INGREDIENTS:

⅓ cup light soy sauce

⅓ cup Splenda Granular

⅓ cup bourbon whiskey

2 tablespoons dried minced onion

1 teaspoon molasses

1 teaspoon powdered ginger

½ teaspoon garlic powder

1 pound boneless chicken tenderloins

STEPS:

1. In a large bowl, combine all ingredients except chicken and stir to mix.
2. Add chicken and stir to coat. Cover and refrigerate for several hours or overnight.
3. Preheat oven to 350°F. Place chicken and marinade in baking dish.
4. Bake for 30 minutes, basting occasionally with marinade.
5. Remove from oven. Baste chicken with remaining marinade and serve.

Although most of the alcohol content dissipates after ½ hour in the oven, I have had a few readers ask about good substitutions for bourbon. Either ¼ cup unsweetened pineapple juice or orange juice with ½ teaspoon vanilla extract may be substituted. The taste will be a bit different but equally delicious.

PER SERVING

Calories 180	Fat 2.5 grams (1 saturated)
Carbohydrate 3 grams	Fiber 0 grams
Protein 23 grams	Sodium 1,060 milligrams

Diabetic exchange = 4 Very Lean Meat
WW point comparison = 4 points

Sweet and Sour Chicken

Serves Four

When you think of entrées with lots of sugar, traditional Asian sweet and sour dishes certainly come to mind. I didn't have to look far for a model for this recipe as my mom always made great sweet and sour chicken. I am thrilled to tell you that my Splenda version is indistinguishable from hers. Thanks, Mom.

INGREDIENTS:

1 tablespoon vegetable oil

1 pound boneless, skinless chicken breast, cut into bite-size pieces

2 teaspoons cornstarch

1 tablespoon sherry

½ teaspoon salt

½ teaspoon grated ginger (optional)

½ cup peeled carrots, cut in ¼-inch slices

½ cup green pepper, cut in 1-inch pieces

½ cup pineapple chunks, well drained

½ cup Splenda Granular

¼ cup reduced-sugar ketchup (like Heinz One Carb)

1 tablespoon light soy sauce

⅓ cup cider vinegar

2 tablespoons cornstarch + ¼ cup water

STEPS:

1. In a medium bowl, combine chicken, cornstarch, sherry, salt, and ginger. Toss to coat meat and set aside.

2. Put carrots in small saucepan with ½ cup water. Bring to boil. Boil for 1 minute.

3. Add green pepper and boil for 1 more minute. Drain vegetables and rinse thoroughly in cold water. Add pineapple and set mixture aside.

4. In a small saucepan, combine Splenda, ketchup, soy sauce, and vinegar. Bring to low simmer.

5. Add cornstarch mixture and cook, stirring, until thickened and clear. Stir in vegetables.

6. Heat wok until hot. Add oil. When oil is very hot, add chicken. (It should sizzle as it hits the wok.) Stir-fry for 2–3 minutes until no longer pink. Remove from wok.

7. Combine sweet and sour sauce with chicken. Serve over brown or white rice if desired.

Heinz One Carb Ketchup has 1 gram of carbohydrate and 5 calories instead of the usual 4 grams of carbohydrate and 16 calories per tablespoon. It is made with sucralose (Splenda) and offers a great ketchup option for ketchup lovers who want to reduce sugar. Look for it in your local market or online at www.ketchupworld.com.

PER SERVING

Calories 200	Fat 5 grams (1 saturated)
Carbohydrate 14 grams	Fiber 1 gram
Protein 24 grams	Sodium 370 milligrams

Diabetic exchange = 4 Very Lean Meat, 1 Carbohydrate
WW point comparison = 4 points

Caribbean Chicken

Serves Four

This tropics-inspired dish brings back pleasing memories of time spent in the Caribbean. The piquant sauce has a fresh citrus taste that is both sweet and savory.

INGREDIENTS:

4 5-ounce skinless, boneless chicken breasts

¼ cup unsweetened pineapple juice

2 tablespoons lime juice

3 tablespoons Splenda Granular

2 tablespoons low-sugar peach jam

1 tablespoon light soy sauce

½ teaspoon crushed dry thyme leaves

¼ teaspoon powdered ginger

¼ teaspoon nutmeg

3-4 drops Tabasco

The enzyme bromelain found in pineapple juice is a powerful tenderizer, making it an excellent addition to marinades.

STEPS:

1. In a small bowl, whisk together all ingredients except chicken.

2. Pound chicken between sheets of plastic wrap or wax paper to ¼-inch thickness. Place in shallow dish and cover with sauce. Marinate 1 hour (or longer).

3. Heat grill or broiler. Remove chicken from sauce.

4. Pour sauce into a small saucepan. Place over medium heat and bring to a low boil. Turn down and simmer until reduced by ½.

5. Grill or broil chicken 4-5 minutes per side or until juices run clear. Spoon sauce over chicken and serve.

PER SERVING

Calories 240	Fat 8 grams (2.5 saturated)
Carbohydrate 8 grams	Fiber 0 grams
Protein 31 grams	Sodium 240 milligrams

Diabetic exchange = 4 Lean Meat, ½ Carbohydrate
WW point comparison = 5 points

Minced Chicken Lettuce Wraps

Serves Four

Without a doubt, people who want to "shed the bread" have pushed the popularity of lettuce wraps in chain restaurants. But, actually, these tasty wraps have long been a part of Asian cuisine. Often found on appetizer menus, they make a great lunch or light dinner.

INGREDIENTS:

SAUCE

¼ cup water

3 tablespoons Splenda Granular

3 tablespoons light soy sauce

2 tablespoons natural rice vinegar

2 tablespoons hoisin

2 teaspoons sesame oil

2 teaspoons red chili paste

1 teaspoon Chinese-style hot mustard

1 ½ teaspoons cornstarch

1 tablespoon water

FILLING

1 tablespoon canola oil

1 pound ground chicken breast

1 8-ounce can water chestnuts, drained and minced

1 cup minced brown mushrooms

½ cup minced red bell pepper

½ thinly sliced green onions, white and green part

½ medium carrot, grated

2 small or 1 large head butter lettuce, washed and dried

STEPS:

1. SAUCE: In a small saucepan, combine all ingredients except cornstarch and 1 tablespoon of water. Heat gently and stir to combine.

2. Combine cornstarch and 1 tablespoon water in a small bowl and stir to combine. When the sauce begins to simmer, add the cornstarch. Bring to a boil. Cook until sauce has thickened and is shiny. Set aside.

3. FILLING: In a large nonstick skillet, heat oil until hot but not smoking. Add ground chicken and sauté, using a fork to break up the meat, until chicken is barely cooked through. Add water chestnuts, mushrooms, red pepper, and green onion and heat through.

4. Add warm sauce to chicken. Stir to combine. Toss in grated carrot and remove from heat.

5. Spoon meat into lettuce leaves or serve on decorative platter as suggested.

Serving suggestion: Line the edges of a large platter with lettuce leaves. Add thin slices of cucumber, fresh mint leaves, and additional shredded carrot to the platter. Pile the warm chicken filling in the middle and let guests make their own wraps.

PER SERVING (4 WRAPS)

Calories 275	Fat 8 grams (1 saturated)
Carbohydrate 18 grams	Fiber 5 grams
Protein 34 grams	Sodium 920 milligrams

Diabetic exchange = 4 Lean Meat, 2 Vegetable

WW point comparison = 5 points

Zesty Chicken Strips with Sweet Mustard Dip

Serves Four

Whether served as an appetizer or an entrée, chicken strips are definitely crowd-pleasers. I serve them here as an entrée with a dipping sauce that's patterned after the honey mustard sauces most restaurants offer.

INGREDIENTS:

1 pound boneless chicken breast or tenders

1 large egg white

1 teaspoon Dijon mustard

½ cup plain bread crumbs

4 tablespoons cornmeal

4 tablespoons grated Parmesan cheese

½ teaspoon garlic powder

½ teaspoon each crushed thyme, oregano, and basil leaves

Black pepper to taste

Sweet Mustard Sauce and Dip (page 202)

STEPS:

1. Preheat oven to 450°F. Coat baking sheet with nonstick cooking spray. Place baking sheet in oven to preheat.

2. Pound chicken breasts to flatten slightly. Slice into ½-inch strips.

3. In a small bowl, beat egg white and mustard. Coat strips.

4. In a medium bowl, stir together remaining ingredients, except Sweet Mustard Dip. Thoroughly coat each piece of chicken with bread crumbs. When all pieces are coated, remove prepared pan from oven and lay chicken fingers on hot baking sheet.

5. Bake 8 minutes, turn, and bake an additional 7 minutes until brown and crisp.

6. While baking, prepare Sweet Mustard Dip (page 202). Serve strips with dip.

PER SERVING

Calories 280	Fat 11 grams (3 saturated)
Carbohydrate 15 grams	Fiber 1 gram
Protein 27 grams	Sodium 300 milligrams

Diabetic exchange = 4 Very Lean Meat, 1 ½ Fat, 1 Carbohydrate

WW point comparison = 6 points

Simple Southwest Salmon

Serves Four

This dish may be simple to make but the flavor is anything but simple. Sweet, spicy, and savory, it will definitely perk up your taste buds. Terrific hot, it's also great at room temperature or cold, making leftovers a bonus.

INGREDIENTS:

4 5-ounce salmon fillets

2 tablespoons pineapple juice

1 tablespoon lime or lemon juice

3 tablespoons Splenda Granular

2 teaspoons chili powder

¾ teaspoon ground cumin

¼ teaspoon salt

⅛ teaspoon cinnamon

STEPS:

1. Place salmon in shallow dish. Pour pineapple and lemon juice over salmon, cover, and place in refrigerator for 30 minutes.

2. Preheat oven to 400°F.

3. In a small bowl, combine remaining ingredients.

4. Remove salmon from marinade. Pat spice mixture onto fillets.

5. Place fillets in baking dish and cook for 15–20 minutes or until the fish flakes easily when tested with a fork.

6. Serve hot or at room temperature.

Did you know that wild salmon not only has fewer pollutants but up to 6 grams less fat in a 5-ounce portion, compared to farm-raised salmon?

PER SERVING

Calories 225★	Fat 12 grams (1.5 saturated)
Carbohydrate 2 grams	Fiber 0 grams
Protein 28 grams	Sodium 220 milligrams

Diabetic exchange = 4 Lean Meat
WW point comparison = 5 points
★Average of wild and farm-raised salmon

Scallops with Mango Salsa

Serves Four

Here, I provide directions for pan-grilling scallops. This is a wonderful (and quick) technique for times when you can't grill outdoors, and works great with shellfish. Once "grilled," the scallops are topped with a colorful salsa made from sweet mango and spicy jalapeno. Shrimp or fresh tuna are good seafood substitutes for scallops.

INGREDIENTS:

1 mango, peeled, pitted, and
   coarsely chopped

½ cup chopped red bell peppers

½ small jalapeno pepper, finely chopped

⅓ cup diced red onion, rinsed
   and drained

¼ cup chopped fresh cilantro

3 tablespoons fresh lime juice

1 tablespoon Splenda Granular

Pinch salt

Pinch cayenne pepper

1 ½ pounds sea or bay scallops

1 tablespoon olive oil

STEPS:

1. Mix all ingredients except scallops and olive oil in a small bowl. (You can do this ahead of time—just cover and chill.)

2. Drizzle oil over scallops. Heat a large heavy skillet over high heat until very hot. (Be sure to turn on the exhaust fan.)

3. Add scallops, making sure there is room for all of them to lie flat on the hot surface. Cook for 1 ½-2 minutes or until bottoms are brown (some smoking of pan is normal). Turn and cook second side for an additional 1 ½-2 minutes. Turn down heat for 1-2 minutes to finish cooking through, if needed.

4. Place immediately on serving dish or 4 plates.

5. Garnish with mango salsa and additional cilantro if desired.

Like avocados, ripe mangoes should feel soft when pressed. To hasten ripening, place in a sealed paper bag. Once they are ripe, you may store them in the refrigerator for several days before using.

PER SERVING

Calories 220	Fat 5 grams (1 saturated)
Carbohydrate 16 grams	Fiber 2 grams
Protein 29 grams	Sodium 350 milligrams

Diabetic exchange = 4 Very Lean Meat, ½ Fruit, ½ Carbohydrate

WW point comparison = 4 points

Baked Fish with Oriental Pesto

Serves Four

This Oriental Pesto, as I call it, truly is one of my favorite sauces. Over the years I have taught it in my cooking classes and served it to many guests in my home. Because you make more than you need, save the rest for the next day, when you can make it seem like a different meal by using chicken instead of fish.

INGREDIENTS:

2 tablespoons fresh lime juice

1 tablespoon light soy sauce

1 tablespoon sherry

1 teaspoon sesame oil

1 teaspoon Splenda Granular

4 5-ounce fish fillets (sea bass, halibut, salmon, or other preferred fish fillets)

PESTO

1 teaspoon canola oil

1 teaspoon garlic, minced

2 teaspoons fresh ginger, minced finely

3 tablespoons each fresh lemon juice, rice vinegar, and rice wine

2 tablespoons light soy sauce

2 tablespoons Splenda Granular

¼ cup green onion (white and green), minced finely

¼ cup fresh cilantro, minced finely

1 teaspoon cornstarch + 2 teaspoons cold water

STEPS:

1. Preheat grill or oven to 350°F.

2. In a small bowl, mix together the first 5 ingredients (lime juice through Splenda) and pour over fish; set aside for 20-30 minutes to marinate.

3. PESTO: Heat oil in a small saucepan until very hot; add garlic and ginger. Heat for 20 seconds.

4. Add remaining ingredients, except cornstarch mixture, and stir well. Bring sauce to simmer and stir in cornstarch mixture. Cook, stirring, until pesto thickens and clears.

5. To bake fish, cover fish with foil and bake for 20 minutes, or until fish flakes easily when tested with fork.

6. Serve fish draped with 2 tablespoons sauce (you will have sauce left over).

PER SERVING (WITH SEA BASS OR OTHER WHITE FISH)

Calories 190	Fat 6 grams (1 saturated)
Carbohydrate 2 grams	Fiber 0 grams
Protein 30 grams	Sodium 520 milligrams

Diabetic exchange = 4 Very Lean Meat, 1 Fat
WW point comparison = 4 points

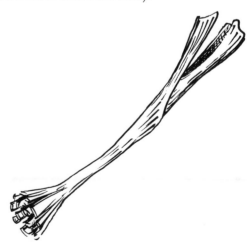

Grilled Salmon with Mustard Dill Sauce

Serves Four

This dill sauce is a real winner. It's equally delicious served with gravlax (cold cured, smoked salmon) or over grilled salmon fillets. If you'd like to create your own signature dish, simply substitute your favorite fish.

INGREDIENTS:

3 tablespoons creamy Dijon mustard (like Dijonnaise)

2 tablespoons Splenda Granular

1 ½ tablespoons white wine vinegar

1 tablespoon minced fresh dill

Scant ½ teaspoon dry mustard

3 tablespoons virgin olive oil

Fresh pepper to taste

4 salmon fillets (4 to 5 ounces each)

STEPS:

1. In a small bowl, whisk together the first 5 ingredients (Dijon mustard through dry mustard).

2. Continue to whisk while drizzling in olive oil 1 tablespoon at a time. Add pepper to taste.

3. Set sauce aside for at least 30 minutes to mellow dry mustard (you can do this ahead of time).

4. Grill salmon over high heat, cooking each side approximately 5 minutes (for 1-inch fillets), or until fish flakes apart easily when teased with a fork.

5. Place fillets on plates or serving tray and spoon sauce over top.

This is a lovely dish to serve guests. Be sure to garnish with additional fresh dill and lemon slices. If you are really watching the fat (or WW points), you can save an extra 6 grams of fat and 50 calories (2 points' worth) by switching from salmon to a white fish, like snapper or cod.

PER SERVING

Calories 285

Carbohydrate 2 grams

Protein 24 grams

Fat 19 grams (2 saturated)

Fiber 0 grams

Sodium 310 milligrams

Diabetic exchange = 4 Lean Meat, 1 ½ Fat

WW point comparison = 7 points

Shrimp Satay Sticks with Thai Peanut Sauce

Serves Four

Widely cooked throughout Asia, sate, or satay, is marinated meat, fish, or fowl threaded onto wooden or bamboo skewers. However, these tasty shrimp satay sticks served with Thai Peanut Sauce are universally welcomed.

INGREDIENTS:

8 bamboo or wooden skewers

1 tablespoon olive oil

1 tablespoon lime juice

1 tablespoon each light soy sauce and sherry

1 tablespoon Splenda Granular

2 cloves garlic. minced

1 ½ pounds large to extra-large shrimp (21–26 count), peeled and deveined

Thai Peanut Sauce (page 200)

STEPS:

1. Presoak bamboo or wooden skewers in cold water for 30-60 minutes to prevent burning.

2. Mix together all ingredients (except Thai Peanut Sauce) in a large bowl and add shrimp. Refrigerate and marinate for 30 minutes (or longer).

3. Thread shrimp (to lie flat) onto skewers.

4. Cook shrimp on hot grill or place 4-6 inches under broiler for 4-6 minutes, turning once.

5. Serve with Thai Peanut Sauce.

You may substitute chicken breast for the shrimp or add fresh vegetables to your skewers. You can expect 1 pound of boneless, skinless breast to yield approximately 8 skewers.

PER SERVING (1 STICK PLUS 2 TABLESPOONS SAUCE)

Calories 175	Fat 3.5 grams (.5 saturated)
Carbohydrate 4 grams	Fiber 0 grams
Protein 24 grams	Sodium 450 milligrams

Diabetic exchange = 3 Lean Meat
WW point comparison = 4 points

Soba Noodle Bowl with Peanut Garlic Sauce

Serves Four

In Japan, just about everyone everywhere eats soba noodles made from buckwheat and wheat flour. Used for snacks and meals, they are served hot or cold, depending on the season or time of day. These healthy noodles are higher in protein and fiber than traditional pasta and make a tasty base for vegetables and peanut sauce in this simple one-dish noodle bowl (that also can be served hot or cold).

INGREDIENTS:

SAUCE

⅔ **cup chicken broth**

¼ **cup light soy sauce**

3 **tablespoons natural rice wine vinegar**

2 **tablespoons sherry**

2 **tablespoons Splenda Granular**

2 **tablespoons smooth peanut butter**

½ **teaspoon each garlic and cornstarch**

¼ **teaspoon red pepper flakes**

6 **ounces soba noodles**

1 **red pepper, cut in strips**

1 **cup sliced mushrooms**

4 **ounces snow peas**

4 **green onions, chopped**

12 **ounces cooked, coarsely chopped chicken breast**

1 **medium carrot, shredded**

Fresh chopped cilantro

STEPS:

1. SAUCE: In a small pot, whisk together sauce ingredients (peanut butter will not dissolve).

2. Set over medium heat and bring to simmer, stirring until smooth. Set aside.

3. In a large pot, cook soba noodles according to package directions (about 5–7 minutes).

4. While noodles are cooking, pour sauce into a large sauté pan and bring to a simmer.

5. Add red pepper, mushrooms, snow peas, and onions to sauce and saute for 1 minute.

6. Drain noodles and add to sauce with chicken. Stir just to coat and immediately divide into bowls. Top each bowl with shredded carrot and chopped cilantro.

You can find lots of ways to personalize this dish. Look in the produce department for cut-up, bagged vegetables, or substitute cooked shrimp or tofu for the chicken. You may also want to serve this cold on a bed of lettuce as a soba noodle salad.

PER SERVING

Calories 350	Fat 7 grams (1 saturated)
Carbohydrate 40 grams	Fiber 4 grams
Protein 32 grams	Sodium 690 milligrams

Diabetic exchange = 2 Carbohydrate, 4 Very Lean Meat, 1 Vegetable, 1 Fat

WW point comparison = 7 points

Marlene's Pasta Marinara Dinner

Serves Four

Pasta, has been demonized for its high carb content, however, the problem is really not the pasta, but the portion size. To fix this, try one of the new whole-grain-blend pastas, and decrease serving size to 1-cup and top it with a 4-ounce seasoned breast of chicken. Then add a nice, big green salad with my Sweet Balsamic Vinaigrette (page 164). This still leaves room for a chewy piece of Italian bread or a serving of Tiramisu (page 270). Thanks go to Julie, my website developer, for the marinara.

INGREDIENTS:

1 ½ tablespoons olive oil

1 small white onion, chopped

2 cloves garlic, minced

1 28-ounce can crushed tomatoes

1 6-ounce can tomato paste

1 8-ounce can tomato sauce

½ cup dry red wine

2 tablespoons Splenda Granular

2 tablespoons dried basil leaves

1 tablespoon oregano leaves

½ teaspoon black pepper

1 pound skinless, boneless chicken breasts

1 teaspoon each garlic salt, dried basil, and oregano leaves

8 ounces pasta (like Barilla Plus or Healthy Harvest Whole-Wheat Blend)

¼ cup Parmesan

For a healthy change, top cooked spaghetti squash with marinara and Parmesan cheese.

STEPS:

1. Add olive oil to a large pot and heat. Add onion and sauté until slightly soft. Add garlic and sauté until onions are very soft. Add remaining ingredients through black pepper and 1 ½ cups water and bring to a boil. Reduce heat to low and simmer for a minimum of 1 hour (or several hours if time permits).

2. Prepare chicken by pounding breasts between sheets of wax paper or Saran Wrap until ¼-inch-thick. Sprinkle each breast with garlic salt, dried basil, and oregano leaves (crushing leaves between your fingers as you sprinkle them on). Set aside.

3. Bring a large pot of water to a boil. Add salt if preferred and cook pasta according to package directions.

4. While pasta is cooking, grill or pan fry chicken breasts on one side until browned (1-2 minutes). Turn over and sear second side, again cooking for about 2 minutes. Let cook 1-2 minutes longer or until done.

5. Drain pasta and divide among plates. Top pasta with ⅓ cup marinara and then chicken breast. Dust each with 1 tablespoon Parmesan cheese.

PER SERVING

Calories 390	Fat 4.5 grams (1 saturated)
Carbohydrate 44 grams	Fiber 5 grams
Protein 36 grams	Sodium 660 milligrams

Diabetic exchange = 4 Very Lean Meat,
2 ½ Carbohydrate, 1 Vegetable
WW point comparison = 7 points

Puddings and Custards

Vanilla Pudding

Light Butterscotch Pudding

Double Chocolate Pudding

Creamy Italian Pudding

Traditional Egg Custard

Fabulous Custard Variations

Chocolate Custard

Pumpkin Custard Cups

Flan

Ginger-Infused Flan with Orange Sauce

Tapioca Pudding

Creamy Rice Pudding

Baked Brown Rice Pudding

New Orleans Bread Pudding
        with Bourbon Sauce

Pastry Cream

When it comes to good ole'-fashioned sweet comfort food, you don't have to look much further than puddings and custards. However, in our fast-paced world, homemade creamy puddings and custards have all but been replaced by boxed mixes and packaged containers. This makes me sad, because they really are simple to make, and nothing beats the taste of homemade pudding or custard. What's more, these treats rank as two of the most nutritious desserts. High in both calcium and protein, they offer a solid dose of nutrition in a creamy, sweet package, making them perfect not only for dessert, but also as snacks, bedtime treats, and, admittedly, for me— sometimes breakfast.

Some of you may already be familiar with my Double Chocolate and Vanilla Puddings, but now I am delighted to offer you a dozen and a half different variations on pudding and custard. Some of my new favorite puddings are Light Butterscotch Pudding, a unique Creamy Italian Pudding made with ricotta cheese, and a New Orleans Bread Pudding with Bourbon Sauce that I promise will amaze even the most diehard low-fat, low-sugar skeptics. For custards, you will find not one but two terrific flan recipes, plus a Traditional Egg Custard that you can whip up for an any-day treat. You will also find many variations, such as pumpkin and eggnog custards for the holidays and Creamy Chocolate Custard for your next Sunday dinner. And just for you java junkies, there's even a special Coffee Custard. Mmmm...

Vanilla Pudding

Serves Five

When it comes to pudding at my house, we have the vanilla camp versus the chocolate camp. I definitely belong to the first camp, especially when it comes to smooth, sweet, creamy puddings like this one. This rich vanilla pudding stands on its own as a prized homestyle dessert, but it can also be used in your favorite parfait recipes, or as filling for a vanilla cream pie.

INGREDIENTS:

3 tablespoons cornstarch

⅔ cup Splenda Granular

½ cup nonfat half-and-half

1 large egg + 1 egg yolk, slightly beaten

1 ¾ cups 1% milk

1 ½ teaspoons vanilla

STEPS:

1. In a medium saucepan, combine the cornstarch, Splenda, half-and-half, and beaten egg. Whisk until smooth. Whisk in 1% milk.

2. Cook and stir over medium heat until the pudding is thick and bubbly. Cook for 1 minute more. Remove from heat. Stir in the vanilla.

3. Pour into medium bowl or divide among 5 dessert dishes. Cover with plastic wrap. Cool and refrigerate until served.

VANILLA PIE FILLING: Add 1 additional tablespoon of cornstarch to recipe to fill a 9-inch pie.

Nonfat half-and-half adds richness without fat to this pudding; you may substitute evaporated skim milk or additional 1% milk for nonfat half-and-half if preferred.

PER SERVING

Calories 110

Carbohydrate 15 grams

Protein 4 grams

Fat 3 grams (1 saturated)

Fiber 0 grams

Sodium 60 milligrams

Diabetic exchange = ½ Low-Fat Milk, ½ Carbohydrate

WW point comparison = 2 points

Light Butterscotch Pudding

Serves Four

The newest addition to the Splenda line is Splenda Brown Sugar Blend which is half brown sugar and half Splenda, giving each cup twice the sweetening power of regular brown sugar. I developed this recipe prior to the new Splenda product's release, but you can substitute ¼ cup of the new blend (if you choose) and omit both the brown sugar, and the Splenda Granular in this recipe.

INGREDIENTS:

⅓ cup egg substitute (or 1 large egg)
1 large egg yolk
2 tablespoons cornstarch
¼ cup dark brown sugar
¼ cup Splenda Granular
2 cups 1% milk
½ teaspoon vanilla
1 tablespoon light butter

STEPS:

1. In a small bowl, whisk together egg substitute and egg yolk. Set aside.
2. In a medium saucepan, combine cornstarch, brown sugar, and Splenda. Whisk in milk.
3. Place over medium heat and cook, stirring, until hot. Whisk a spoonful of hot milk into egg mixture to temper eggs. Add one more spoonful and then quickly whisk egg mixture into pot.
4. Continue to cook, stirring, until pudding reaches low boil. Cook and stir pudding for 1 minute until pudding is thick and smooth. Remove from heat and stir in vanilla and butter.
5. Pour pudding into a medium bowl or divide among 4 dessert dishes.
6. Cover with plastic wrap. Cool and refrigerate until served.

Because you are using less, you need to use dark brown sugar (not light brown) to give this recipe its characteristic flavor and color. But, to create brown sugar, don't add molasses (although some recipes suggest that) because its flavor is too overpowering for this pudding.

PER SERVING

Calories 155
Carbohydrate 23 grams
Protein 7 grams

Fat 4 grams (2 saturated)
Fiber 0 grams
Sodium 110 milligrams

Diabetic exchange = 1 Carbohydrate, ½ Low-Fat Milk, ½ Fat
WW point comparison = 3 points

Double Chocolate Pudding

Serves Six

This pudding is for the chocolate lovers in your household. A rich and creamy chocolate version, this pudding puts packaged sugar-free counterparts to shame. A special occasion is not a requirement, but this pudding will make any day seem out of the ordinary.

INGREDIENTS:

3 tablespoons cornstarch

¾ cup Splenda Granular

2 tablepoons Dutch-process cocoa powder (like Hershey's European)

½ cup nonfat half-and-half

1 large egg, slightly beaten

1 ¾ cups 1% milk

⅓ cup chocolate chips

1 ½ teaspoons vanilla

STEPS:

1. In a medium saucepan, combine the cornstarch, Splenda, cocoa powder, half-and-half, and beaten egg. Whisk until smooth. Whisk in 1% milk.

2. Cook and stir over medium heat until the pudding is thick and bubbly. Cook for 1 minute more. Remove from heat.

3. Stir in the chocolate chips, whisking until melted. Stir in vanilla.

4. Pour into a medium bowl or divide among 6 dessert dishes. Cover with plastic wrap. Cool and refrigerate until served.

Double the treat: In a tall glass, alternate layers of chocolate and vanilla pudding for a "zebra" parfait.

PER SERVING

Calories 130	Fat 4.5 grams (2.5 saturated)
Carbohydrate 18 grams	Fiber 0 grams
Protein 4 grams	Sodium 65 milligrams

Diabetic exchange = ½ Low-Fat Milk,
½ Carbohydrate, ½ Fat
WW point comparison = 3 points

Creamy Italian Pudding

Serves Six

High in protein, this light and creamy pudding is easy to make and delightful to eat. It's lovely topped off with a few fresh berries or the Quick Raspberry Sauce found on page 423.

INGREDIENTS:

1 ½ cups fat-free half-and-half

1 envelope unflavored gelatin

2 cups low-fat ricotta cheese

½ cup Splenda Granular

1 teaspoon vanilla

Zest of 1 lemon

Low-fat ricotta adds a nice boost of protein to this pudding making it not only delicous, but nutritious.

STEPS:

1. Place ½ cup of the half-and-half into a small saucepan. Sprinkle gelatin over the top and let set for 5 minutes.

2. Place ricotta cheese into blender or food processor.

3. Stir remaining 1 cup half-and-half, Splenda, vanilla, and lemon zest into gelatin mixture. Place over low heat and cook, stirring, until gelatin dissolves. (Do not boil.)

4. Slowly add hot milk mixture to ricotta cheese, while blending, until completely smooth.

5. Divide evenly into 6 ramekins. Chill at least 2 hours or until set.

PER SERVING

Calories 140	Fat 4 grams (2 saturated)
Carbohydrate 13 grams	Fiber 0 grams
Protein 12 grams	Sodium 125 milligrams

Diabetic exchange = 1 Lean Meat, ½ Skim Milk, ½ Carbohydrate
WW point comparison = 3 points

Traditional Egg Custard

Serves Six

You can make custards that are very rich (like crème brulée) or very lean (using only skim milk and egg whites), but I've chosen to balance good taste with good nutrition in developing this traditional custard, by using reduced-fat milk and a combination of whole eggs and egg whites. Additionally, as is the case when you're making traditional custard, it's important to strain the milk mixture and bake it in a water bath to ensure the custard's proper texture.

INGREDIENTS:

2 large eggs

2 large egg whites

⅔ cup Splenda Granular

2 teaspoons vanilla

2 cups 1% milk

1 cup evaporated low-fat or skim milk

Freshly grated or ground nutmeg

If you are trying to add more lean protein to your diet, this is the perfect snack or dessert. Like a Balance Bar, the nutrient ratio is approximately 35 percent protein, 30 percent fat, and 40 percent carbohydrate.

STEPS:

1. Preheat oven to 325°F.

2. In a medium bowl, whisk together eggs, egg whites, Splenda, and vanilla. Set aside.

3. In a small saucepan, bring milks to a low simmer. Whisk a small amount of hot milk into egg mixture to temper eggs. Whisk in remaining milk. Strain mixture into a large measuring cup with pouring lip or bowl.

4. Pour or ladle mixture into six 6-ounce custard cups or ramekins. Sprinkle with nutmeg.

5. Place cups in large baking dish and place in oven. Pour very hot water into baking dish until it reaches halfway up the sides of the custard cups.

6. Bake custards 45-55 minutes or until edges are set and centers jiggle slightly when shaken. Cool and refrigerate to set.

PER SERVING (½ CUP)

Calories 110	Fat 3.5 grams (2 saturated)
Carbohydrate 11 grams	Fiber 1 gram
Protein 9 grams	Sodium 125 milligrams

Diabetic exchange = 1 Low-Fat Milk
WW point comparison = 2 points

Fabulous Custard Variations

If you like custard, you'll surely enjoy these delightful variations. Simply use the Traditional Egg Custard (page 249) as a base and make the changes as directed.

Extra Creamy Custard

Substitute fat-free half-and-half for evaporated milk. Use 3 whole eggs plus 2 egg whites. Bake 80-90 minutes.

Coconut Custard

Use only 1 teaspoon vanilla and add ½ teaspoon coconut extract. Sprinkle 1 teaspoon toasted coconut into each cup with milk mixture. Eliminate nutmeg and garnish each cup with 1 additional teaspoon toasted coconut after baking (adds 20 calories, 1.5 grams fat, 1 gram protein).

Coffee Custard

Add 1 tablespoon instant coffee powder to milk. Increase Splenda to ¾ cup. Eliminate nutmeg.

Eggnog

Use only 1 teaspoon vanilla and add ½ teaspoon rum extract. Use 3 whole eggs and eliminate egg whites.

Chocolate Custard

Serves Six

For a special treat that's a departure from traditional vanilla custard, try this chocolate version. The light, creamy chocolate texture will remind you of your favorite chocolate pudding. Serve with a dollop of light whipped topping.

INGREDIENTS:

2 large eggs

1 large egg white

⅔ cup Splenda Granular

1 teaspoon vanilla

1 ½ cups fat-free half-and-half

1 cup 1% milk

½ cup cocoa powder

1 tablespoon brown sugar

Six-ounce soufflé-style ramekins are easy to find and not too expensive. They come in handy, not only for custards but for creating individual portions of everything from puddings and soufflés to serving up the perfect single scoop of ice cream.

STEPS:

1. Preheat oven to 325°F.

2. In a medium bowl, whisk together eggs, egg whites, Splenda, and vanilla. Set aside.

3. In a small saucepan, bring half-and-half and milk to a low simmer. Turn off heat and whisk in cocoa and brown sugar until smooth. Whisk a small amount of hot milk into egg mixture to temper eggs. Whisk in remaining milk. Strain chocolate mixture through mesh strainer into a large bowl or large measuring cup with pouring lip.

4. Pour or ladle mixture into six 6-ounce custard cups or ramekins.

5. Place cups in large baking dish and place in oven. Pour very hot water into baking dish until it reaches halfway up the sides of the custard cups.

6. Bake for 35–40 minutes or until edges are set and centers jiggle slightly. Cool and refrigerate to set.

PER SERVING

Calories 125	Fat 3.5 grams (1 saturated)
Carbohydrate 17 grams	Fiber 2 grams
Protein 8 grams	Sodium 115 milligrams

Diabetic exchange = 1 Low-Fat Milk
WW point comparison = 2 points

Pumpkin Custard Cups

Serves Seven

The best part of pumpkin pie is the rich pumpkin filling, of course. Here is a recipe that gives you that delicious filling without the added calories and work of a crust. Another bonus—adding an extra egg yolk and baking the filled cups in a water bath are two steps that produce an even creamier custard texture than you achieve with a pie.

INGREDIENTS:

1 recipe Pumpkin Pie Filling, page 330
1 egg yolk

STEPS:

1. Preheat oven to 350°F. Spray seven 6-ounce custard or soufflé cups with nonstick cooking spray.

2. Prepare the pie filling according to the directions (eliminating the crust and the beaten egg white wash) using 1 additional egg yolk (you can simply substitute 1 additional large whole egg for 1 of the egg whites).

3. Pour the filling into the cups, and place cups in a large, deep baking pan. Pour boiling water into the baking pan until it reaches halfway up the sides of the cups.

4. Bake for 40 minutes or until a knife inserted near the centers of the custards comes out clean.

Individual servings not only make desserts easy to serve, but they're also great for portion control.

PER SERVING

Calories 120
Carbohydrate 17 grams
Protein 8 grams

Fat 1.5 grams (.5 saturated)
Fiber 2 grams
Sodium 100 milligrams

Diabetic exchange = ½ Carbohydrate,
½ Low-Fat Milk, ½ Vegetable
WW point comparison = 2 points

Flan

Serves Six

Here is a favorite dessert inspired by Spain and Mexico. If you haven't tried flan before, here is your chance. It's so light and creamy, and when flipped over, offers a sweet, syrupy surprise!

INGREDIENTS:

CUSTARD:

2 cups 1% milk

2 teaspoons vanilla extract

2 eggs

2 egg whites

⅓ cup Splenda Granular

CARAMEL:

6 tablespoons Splenda Sugar Blend for Baking

3 tablespoons water

Don't substitute Splenda Granular for Splenda Sugar Blend for Baking for the caramel topping because it won't melt or carmelize. You can however, substitute regular granulated sugar if you chose. You will also have a small amount of the sugar stick to both the pot and the ramekins: nutrition information takes this into account.

STEPS:

1. CUSTARD: Preheat oven to 350°F. In a medium pot, heat milk until it simmers. Stir in vanilla and set aside.

2. CARAMEL: In another small pot, place Splenda Sugar Blend and water. Cover pot with lid. Heat mixture over medium-high heat for approximately 5 minutes or until amber colored.

3. Meanwhile, in a large bowl, whisk eggs, egg whites, and Splenda. Slowly pour hot milk into egg mixture while continuing to whisk. Strain mixture through a fine mesh strainer.

4. When caramel is done, pour into 6 four-ounce ramekins (ceramic dishes) or small heat-proof glass bowls. Quickly swirl mixture around the bottom of each ramekin to coat.

5. Ladle egg-milk mixture over caramel coated ramekins. Place ramekins into a large baking pan and place in oven. Pour hot water into large pan to create water bath.

6. Bake custards for 18-20 minutes or until set, with a slight jiggle still in centers.

7. Remove from water bath to cool. Place in refrigerator for at least 1 hour before serving. To serve, loosen edge of custard with a sharp knife and invert flan onto a plate.

PER SERVING

Calories 110	Fat 2.5 grams (1 saturated)
Carbohydrate 16 grams	Fiber 0 grams
Protein 6 grams	Sodium 80 milligrams

Diabetic exchange = ½ Low-Fat Milk, ½ Carbohydrate
WW point comparison = 2 points

Ginger-Infused Flan with Orange Sauce

Serves Six

East meets West in this traditional Mexican flan infused with ginger and served draped in sweet orange sauce. Nice and light, it makes a great finish to a meal that features Asian Barbecued Pork Tenderloin (page 228), steamed brown rice, and Sesame Green Beans (page 181).

INGREDIENTS:

CUSTARD

1 cup 1% milk

1 cup fat-free half-and-half

1 2-inch piece fresh ginger, peeled

2 eggs

2 egg whites

½ cup Splenda Granular

ORANGE SAUCE

1 cup reduced-calorie orange juice (like Tropicana Light 'n Healthy)

1 tablespoon Splenda Granular

2 teaspoons cornstarch

2 teaspoons water

To prepare ginger, cut off and peel one of the "fingers." Slice open to expose its flavor and place in milk. Wrapped, unpeeled ginger keeps in the refrigerator for up to three months and in the freezer for six months.

STEPS:

1. Preheat oven to 350°F. In a medium pot, heat milk and half-and-half until boiling. Turn off heat and add ginger. Let steep for 15 minutes. Strain out ginger.

2. In a mixing bowl, combine eggs, egg whites, and Splenda; whisk until combined but not frothy. Slowly add eggs to milk mixture while whisking. Strain mixture through a fine mesh strainer. Ladle into a 2-quart ceramic baking dish or 9-inch glass pie plate.

3. Place dish in a large baking pan and place in oven. Pour hot water into large pan halfway up sides of the dish to create water bath. Bake for 30 minutes or until set but with slight jiggle still in center. Remove from water bath and cool.

4. Refrigerate for at least 1 hour or overnight.

5. While flan is cooking, place orange juice in a small pot and simmer over medium heat for 5 minutes or until juice concentrates to ¾ cup. Add Splenda. Mix together cornstarch and water. Whisk into orange juice and continue stirring over medium heat until mixture comes to a boil and clears.

6. Serve flan cold with warm or cold orange sauce.

PER SERVING

Calories 90	Fat 2 grams (1 saturated)
Carbohydrate 12 grams	Fiber 0 grams
Protein 6 grams	Sodium 100 milligrams

Diabetic exchange = ½ Nonfat Milk, ½ Carbohydrate
WW point comparison = 2 points

Tapioca Pudding

Serves Six

A couple of simple changes were all it took to lighten up this old-fashioned favorite. The most difficult thing about this pudding is not eating the entire pot!

INGREDIENTS:

2 ½ cups 1% milk

1 large egg, separated

½ cup Splenda Granular

3 ½ tablespoons quick-cooking tapioca

1 ½ teaspoons vanilla

¼ teaspoon cream of tartar

2 teaspoons sugar

STEPS:

1. In a medium saucepan, combine milk, egg yolk, Splenda, and tapioca; let sit for 5 minutes to soften tapioca.

2. Whisk milk mixture thoroughly and place on stove. Bring to a boil while stirring. Remove from heat, stir in vanilla, and let set (it will thicken as it cools).

3. In a small bowl, beat egg white and cream of tartar until foamy. Sprinkle in sugar and beat to soft peaks. Gently fold egg white into hot pudding.

4. Let cool at least 20 minutes before serving or pouring into bowl or serving dishes. If not served warm, refrigerate.

Tapioca does not respond well to "overdoing." Overcooking or overstirring tapioca (once it thickens) will create a gluey pudding.

PER SERVING (½ CUP)

Calories 90	Fat 2 grams (1 saturated)
Carbohydrate 14 grams	Fiber 0 grams
Protein 4 grams	Sodium 100 milligrams

Diabetic exchange = ½ Low-Fat Milk, ½ Carbohydrate
WW point comparison = 2 points

Creamy Rice Pudding

Serves Eight

I can't tell you how many pots of rice pudding I have made. I've added a couple more tablespoons of rice to this version to be sure it thickens up nicely.

INGREDIENTS:

1 cup cold water

⅔ cup medium-grain uncooked white rice

3 cups 1% milk

1 cup fat-free half and half

½ cup Splenda Granular

1 tablespoon butter

⅛ teaspoon salt

2 teaspoons cornstarch + 1 tablespoon water

1 ½ teaspoons vanilla

¼ teaspoon almond extract

½ teaspoon lemon zest

STEPS:

1. In a medium saucepan, bring water to a boil and stir in rice. Reduce to simmer, cover, and cook for 15-20 minutes or until water is absorbed.

2. Stir in milk, half-and-half, Splenda, butter, and salt. Cook, uncovered, over medium heat for 30 minutes, stirring frequently.

3. Add cornstarch mixture, heat until bubbling, and cook just until pudding thickens. Stir in vanilla, almond extract, and lemon zest. Pour into serving bowl or dessert dishes.

OLD-FASHIONED VARIATION: Eliminate lemon zest and top pudding with cinnamon.

For a lovely summer dessert, top each serving with ¼ cup fresh blueberries (adds 20 calories and 1 gram of fiber but doesn't change the diabetic exchange or WW points).

PER SERVING

Calories 135	Fat 2.5 grams (1.5 saturated)
Carbohydrate 22 grams	Fiber 0.5 grams
Protein 4 grams	Sodium 100 milligrams

Diabetic exchange = ½ Low-Fat Milk, 1 Carbohydrate
WW point comparison = 3 points

Baked Brown Rice Pudding

Serves Six

Compared to white rice, brown rice is higher in protein and fiber and has a lower glycemic index (the rate at which carbohydrates convert to sugar in the body). Brown rice also makes a nutritious and delicious rice pudding.

INGREDIENTS:

1 ¼ cups water

½ teaspoon cinnamon

¼ teaspoon salt

½ cup brown rice

2 ½ cups 1% milk

2 eggs, beaten

1 ½ teaspoons vanilla

1 teaspoon orange zest

⅓ cup Splenda Granular

½ teaspoon cinnamon

STEPS:

1. Preheat oven to 325°F.

2. In a medium saucepan, bring water, ½ teaspoon cinnamon, and salt to a boil. Stir in rice. Cover and cook for 35–45 minutes or until most of the water is absorbed.

3. Stir milk, eggs, vanilla, orange zest, and Splenda into rice. Bring mixture to a simmer and transfer to a 2-quart casserole or baking dish.

4. Bake, uncovered, for 30 minutes; stir. Bake additional 30 minutes and stir again. Remove from oven and swirl in last ½ teaspoon cinnamon. Pudding will continue to thicken as it cools. Serve warm or chilled.

A touch of healthful sliced almonds makes a nice garnish for this pudding.

PER SERVING (¹/₂ CUP)

Calories 135	Fat 2 grams (1 saturated)
Carbohydrate 18 grams	Fiber 1 gram
Protein 7 grams	Sodium 120 milligrams

Diabetic exchange = ½ Low-Fat Milk,
½ Carbohydrate, ½ Lean Meat
WW point comparison = 3 points

New Orleans Bread Pudding with Bourbon Sauce

Serves Six

Bread puddings are the quintessential comfort food. Maybe that's why, in these stressful times, we have seen a resurgence in their popularity. The Bourbon Sauce, a New Orleans tradition, complements the bread pudding beautifully, both in taste and appearance.

INGREDIENTS:

5 cups slightly dried-out French or Italian bread, cubed (1- to 2-inch pieces)

1 ½ cups 1% milk

1 cup fat-free half-and-half

¾ cup Splenda Granular

2 large eggs

2 large egg whites

1 ½ teaspoons cinnamon

1 tablespoon vanilla

2 teaspoons granulated sugar

½ teaspoon cinnamon

Bourbon Sauce (page 422)

STEPS:

1. Preheat oven to 350°F. Spray 8-inch square baking pan with nonstick cooking spray. Spread bread cubes in pan.

2. In medium bowl, whisk together next 7 ingredients (milk through vanilla). Pour over bread cubes. Let set about 10 minutes, pressing top cubes down to saturate.

3. Mix together granulated sugar and cinnamon. Sprinkle on top of pudding. Bake for 1 hour until center of pudding puffs.

4. Cool at least 15 minutes or entirely before serving. Serve warm (reheat briefly in microwave) or at room temperature with warmed Bourbon Sauce.

PER SERVING (¹/₂ CUP WITH 1 ¹/₂ TABLESPOONS SAUCE)

Calories 185	Fat 4.5 grams (2 saturated)
Carbohydrate 24 grams	Fiber 1 gram
Protein 8 grams	Sodium 125 milligrams

Diabetic exchange = ½ Low-Fat Milk, 1 Carbohydrate, 1 Fat
WW point comparison = 4 points

Bread pudding is thought to have originated in England in the late 1600s. But in the United States, the city that has adopted this dessert as its own is New Orleans, now renowned for bread puddings.

Pastry Cream

Serves Eight

Pastry cream is customarily very rich (due to lots of egg yolks). It is most often used as a spread for tarts and a filling for éclairs and cake layers. This version is still rich and creamy-tasting, with less than half of the fat. I developed it for the Fresh Fruit Tart on page 359, but it can be used anytime a pastry cream is called for.

INGREDIENTS:

1 large egg

1 large egg yolk

⅓ cup Splenda Granular

2 tablespoons cornstarch

¾ cup 1% milk

½ cup nonfat half-and-half

¾ teaspoon vanilla

STEPS:

1. In a medium bowl, thoroughly whisk together the egg, egg yolk, and Splenda. Whisk in the cornstarch until very smooth. Set aside.

2. In a small to medium pot, heat milk and half-and-half until simmering. Ladle a small amount of the hot milk into the eggs, while whisking constantly. Add several more ladles until eggs are warm and tempered. Whisk egg mixture into pot with milk and place back on heat. Bring to boil while stirring, and then cook for 1 minute or until very thick. Remove from heat and whisk in vanilla.

3. Spoon out of pot into a small bowl to cool. Cover surface with plastic wrap and refrigerate until use.

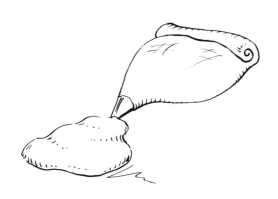

PER SERVING (2 TABLESPOONS)

Calories 45	Fat 1.5 grams (.5 saturated)
Carbohydrate 6 grams	Fiber 0 grams
Protein 2 grams	Sodium 35 milligrams

Diabetic exchange = ½ Carbohydrate
WW point comparison = 1 point

Mousses and Other Creamy Delights

Orange Snow

Strawberry Fool

Yogurt Parfait

Amazing Cream Puffs

Cold Strawberry Souffle

Sicilian Berry Dessert

Tiramisu in a Glass

"Marvel"ous Lemon Mousse

Dark Chocolate Mousse

Chocolate Mousse Cake

Pumpkin Mousse with Gingersnaps

French Cream with Raspberry Sauce

Creamy Orange Crepes

Decadent thoughts come to mind when we think of mousses, soufflés, and all things creamy because we know for a fact that these are indeed very rich. For example, a single serving of a traditional chocolate mousse made with butter, eggs, sugar, and lots of heavy cream contains more than 450 calories and 35 grams of fat, with 20 of them saturated. The good news is, with the help of some creative ingredient substitutions, like nonfat half-and-half, light whipped topping, rich cocoa powder, and, of course, Splenda for the sugar, you can dramatically slash the sugar, fat, and calories of these rich favorites.

You're in for a big treat with the recipes in this chapter, starting with the lightest of light, a lovely Orange Snow, to Dark Chocolate Mousse and French Cream with Raspberry Sauce (and no recipe contains more than 200 calories). But these treats are not just about keeping the calories low—they are delicious and not pale imitations of the originals because I took great care to not skimp on the details. For example, Amazing Cream Puffs are light and airy, filled with a rich vanilla pudding and topped with Chocolate Fudge Sauce; Tiramisu in a Glass is made with mascarpone and ricotta cheeses spooned onto ladyfingers soaked with sweetened coffee and topped with cocoa and grated chocolate; and Strawberry Souffle is made with fresh, crushed strawberries and light whipped topping and then piled high to dazzle your guests. Need I say more...

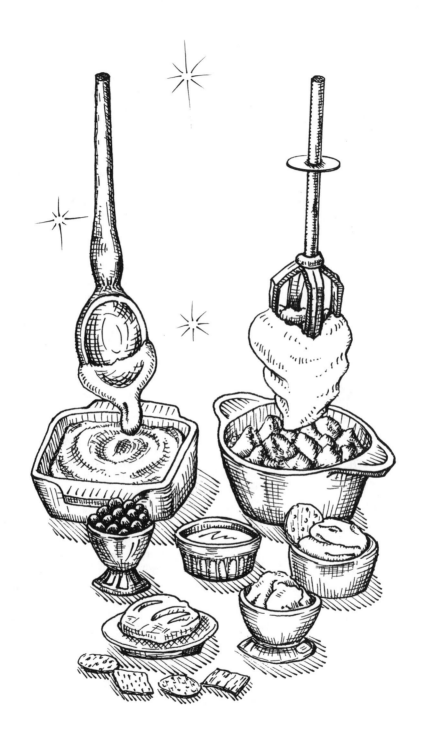

Orange Snow

Serves Four

This is truly a sweet nothing. Very low in calories, fat, and carbs, Orange Snow is quite light and refreshing. I find it the perfect treat for a hot summer's day.

INGREDIENTS:

1 ½ teaspoons unflavored gelatin

2 tablespoons cold water

1 egg yolk

1 cup buttermilk

½ cup + 2 tablespoons Splenda Granular

¼ cup regular or light orange juice

1 tablespoon orange zest

2 egg whites

STEPS:

1. Place gelatin in a small bowl and add water. Set aside.

2. In a medium saucepan, whisk together egg yolk, buttermilk, and ½ cup Splenda. Heat mixture until it thickens slightly (enough to coat a spoon).

3. Stir in softened gelatin, orange juice, and zest. Remove from heat, pour into bowl, and cool mixture in refrigerator until it reaches the consistency of raw egg whites.

4. Whip egg whites until foamy. Add 2 tablespoons Splenda and beat to soft peaks. Fold into orange mixture.

5. Refrigerate until ready to serve.

While the word "butter" is in buttermilk, there is no butter, per se, in buttermilk. Old-fashioned buttermilk was the milk remaining after butter was churned—hence, its name. Today most buttermilk is made from culturing skim or low-fat milk with active lactic acid bacteria.

PER SERVING (½ CUP)

Calories 65	Fat 2 grams (1 saturated)
Carbohydrate 8 grams	Fiber 0 grams
Protein 5 grams	Sodium 95 milligrams

Diabetic exchange = ½ Low-Fat Milk
WW point comparison = 1 point

Strawberry Fool

Serves Four

A fool is an old-fashioned English dessert made by swirling pureed fruit into whipped cream. This lighter version uses a small amount of real whipped cream, combined with yogurt, to lighten it up. The result? A not-so-foolish reduction of fat and calories.

INGREDIENTS:

1 ½ cups low-fat plain yogurt

8 tablespoons Splenda Granular, divided

½ teaspoon almond extract (optional)

12 ounces fresh strawberries, washed and stemmed

4 tablespoons heavy whipping cream

STEPS:

1. In a small bowl, combine yogurt, 4 tablespoons Splenda, and extract, if desired. In a separate bowl, mash berries with 2 tablespoons Splenda. Chill both at least 1 hour.

2. Whip cream with remaining 2 tablespoons Splenda until moderately stiff. Fold cream into yogurt mixture. Swirl strawberry mixture into yogurt/cream mixture. Serve.

Fools date all the way back to the sixteenth century, and the name is believed to have come from the French word fouler, which means "to crush." You should adjust the actual amount of Splenda needed based on the sweetness of the fruit.

PER SERVING (¾ CUP)

Calories 140

Carbohydrate 16 grams

Protein 6 grams

Fat 6 grams (3 saturated)

Fiber 2 grams

Sodium 70 milligrams

Diabetic exchange = ½ Low-Fat Milk, ½ Fruit, 1 Fat

WW point comparison = 3 points

Yogurt Parfait

Serves Two

If you have been to "the golden arches" lately, you know where I got the idea for this recipe. After enjoying a yogurt parfait at just such a place, I realized there had to be a lot of sugar in all of those layers, so I decided to make a healthier version. These parfaits are really simple to make; just get ready to layer.

INGREDIENTS:

2 6-ounce cups plain nonfat yogurt (or 1 ½ cups)

6 teaspoons Splenda Granular (or 3 packets)

½ cup frozen unsweetened strawberries, thawed

½ cup fresh blueberries

¼ cup Great Granola (page 77) or your favorite low-sugar granola or cereal

STEPS:

1. Select two glasses (I like 8-ounce wine glasses).

2. Mix 4 teaspoons Splenda into yogurt. Place ⅓ cup in the bottom of each glass.

3. In a small bowl, mix 2 teaspoons Splenda into strawberries. Spoon ¼ cup of this mixture atop yogurt in each glass. Top each with ¼ cup blueberries.

4. Cover fruit with remaining yogurt. Top each glass with granola or cereal.

(Wrapped parfaits will keep 1 day in the refrigerator; add granola right before eating.)

PER SERVING

Calories 160	Fat 2 grams (0 saturated)
Carbohydrate 27 grams	Fiber 4 grams
Protein 8 grams	Sodium 115 milligrams

Diabetic exchange = 1 Nonfat Milk, 1 Fruit
WW point comparison = 3 points

Amazing Cream Puffs

Serves Eight

Cream puffs are extraordinary treats and although not difficult to make, they require three steps: the puff, the cream filling, and the chocolate fudge topping. You can make the puffs a day ahead or earlier and freeze them. The filling keeps for one day, and the Chocolate Fudge Sauce keeps for a week (unless you eat it sooner). You may prepare the puffs in separate steps if you prefer. However, they are best eaten within a day, which is rarely a problem.

INGREDIENTS:

PUFFS

½ **cup water**

3 **tablespoons butter**

¼ **teaspoon salt**

½ **cup all-purpose flour**

1 **large egg**

3 **large egg whites**

FILLING

1 **recipe Vanilla Pudding (omitting ½ cup nonfat half-and-half) (page 145)**

½ **cup light whipped topping**

TOPPING

⅓ **cup Chocolate Fudge Sauce (page 430)**

STEPS:

1. Preheat oven to 300°F. Spray a baking sheet with nonstick cooking spray.

2. PUFFS: In a medium saucepan, bring the water, butter, and salt to a boil. Add flour, all at once, and stir until the mixture is smooth and pulls away from the sides to form a ball. Remove from heat. Let cool 3 minutes. Add egg and then egg whites, beating vigorously after each addition until mixture is smooth and shiny again. Using a tablespoon, spoon dough onto prepared baking pan, making 8 mounds. Place pan in lower third of oven and turn heat up to 450°F. Bake 15 minutes, until dough is well puffed and brown. Reduce temperature to 300°F and bake 15 more minutes. Cut a small slit on the side of each puff to allow steam to escape; turn off heat and allow puffs to dry for 5 minutes in the oven. Remove and place on rack to cool. Once cool, puffs can be kept 1 day in an airtight container or wrapped well and frozen.

PER SERVING

Calories 170	Fat 8 grams (4 saturated)
Carbohydrate 18 grams	Fiber 0 grams
Protein 6 grams	Sodium 70 milligrams

Diabetic exchange = 1 Carbohydrate, 1 Lean Meat, 1 Fat
WW point comparison = 4 points

3. To PREPARE FILLING: Prepare pudding according to directions. Chill. When cold, fold in whipped topping ¼ cup at a time. Fold in rest of topping. The filling can be kept covered and refrigerated for 1 day.

4. TOPPING: Prepare chocolate fudge sauce according to directions. If prepared in advance, heat lightly to a pourable consistency before using.

5. To ASSEMBLE CREAM PUFFS: Cut top off each puff. Remove any wet or loose dough to create a clean cavity. Fill with ¼ cup cream filling and replace top. Drizzle 2 teaspoons of Chocolate Fudge Sauce over the top of each cream puff.

Starting the puffs in a moderate temperature oven and increasing the heat allows the puffs to reach their maximum height. They rise along with the temperature in the oven.

Cold Strawberry Soufflé

Serves Eight

This is one of the first recipes I developed with Splenda. I made it and took it to a dinner party, and everyone loved it. My friends commented on how light and creamy it was. They also noted the fresh strawberry flavor. What they didn't comment on was the fact that the sugar was replaced with Splenda. This told me what I really wanted to know—that Splenda could sweeten my favorite desserts with the same wonderful taste of sugar.

INGREDIENTS:

2 pints of fresh strawberries (approximately 2 pounds)

2 envelopes unflavored gelatin (2 ½ teaspoons each)

½ cup Splenda Granular

1 tablespoon lemon juice

6 large egg whites or 9 pasteurized egg whites + ½ teaspoon cream of tartar

1 8-ounce container light whipped topping, thawed

Using regular egg whites achieves the greatest egg white volume with the fewest eggs. Be sure eggs are fresh and clean, and have no cracks. For extra safety, when making this dessert for kids, the elderly, or those with compromised immune systems, use egg white powder or pasteurized egg whites.

STEPS:

1. Set aside a 2-quart soufflé dish or bowl.

2. Clean, stem, and halve berries. You should have about 5 cups. Reserve four berries for garnish.

3. Purée the remaining berries in a food processor or blender. Place 1 cup of purée in a medium saucepan. Add gelatin and ¼ cup Splenda. Heat until gelatin dissolves. Add the rest of the purée and the lemon juice. Remove from heat and chill for 20 minutes.

4. While purée is chilling, beat egg whites until foamy. Add remaining Splenda and continue to beat until stiff but not dry. Fold ¼ of the egg whites into the cooled purée. Gently fold in the remaining egg whites. Fold in the light whipped topping.

5. Spoon into the soufflé dish and chill in the refrigerator for at least 4 hours before serving.

6. Just before serving, garnish the top of the soufflé with the reserved berries.

PER SERVING

Calories 120
Carbohydrate 16 grams
Protein 5 grams

Fat 4 grams (3.5 saturated)
Fiber 1 gram
Sodium 45 milligrams

Diabetic exchange = 1 Medium-Fat Meat, ½ Fruit
WW point comparison = 2 points

Sicilian Berry Dessert

Serves Four

Ricotta is a light-textured, mild Italian cheese with a soft texture. It is a staple in many Italian households because it's used to make everything from sweet cannolis to savory lasagna. My Italian friend Chris, a nutrition expert who studies berries and their anticancer qualities, created this very delicious, very healthy dessert, by pairing creamy sweetened ricotta with a mix of fresh berries. Bellissimo!

INGREDIENTS:

¾ cup low-fat ricotta cheese

6 tablespoons light sour cream

⅓ cup Splenda Granular

¼ teaspoon almond extract (or ½ shot amaretto liquor)

1 scant teaspoon orange zest

3 cups fresh berries (blackberries, raspberries, boysenberries, and/or strawberries)

½ ounce white chocolate, grated (optional)★

STEPS:

1. In a food processor or blender, pulse together ricotta cheese, light sour cream, Splenda, and almond extract just until smooth (processing too long will thin topping too much). Spoon into a bowl and stir in orange zest. Cover and chill.

2. Place ¾ cup berries in each of 4 pretty glass bowls or glasses (wine glasses work well). Spoon topping over berries (about ¼ cup each).

3. Garnish with grated white chocolate if desired.

★ White chocolate garnish adds 1 gram of fat, 2 grams of carbohydrate, and 20 calories per serving–and 1 WW point.

This pretty dessert is high in protein, calcium, vitamin C, and fiber and low in added sugars, fat, sodium, and calories. When it comes to good food that's good for you, it doesn't get much better than this!

PER SERVING

Calories 140	Fat 4.5 grams (2 saturated)
Carbohydrate 18	Fiber 6 grams
Protein 7 grams	Sodium 50 milligrams

Diabetic exchange = 1 Fruit, 1 Medium-Fat Meat
WW point comparison = 2 points

Tiramisu in a Glass

Serves Six

Tiramisu is a beloved Italian dessert that contains a rich, smooth, Italian cream cheese called mascarpone that is loaded with fat. Combine this with the cream, egg yolks, and sugar traditionally used to make tiramisu, and you have one heavy dessert. In this recipe, I've kept some of the mascarpone for its unique flavor, but lightened the additional ingredients. I have also chosen a unique and contemporary way to serve it by assembling individual portions in martini glasses. You may also layer ingredients in a large serving dish as described below.

INGREDIENTS:

4 ounces mascarpone cheese★

4 ounces nonfat cream cheese

¼ cup low-fat ricotta cheese

2 tablespoons light sour cream

½ cup Splenda Granular

¾ cup light whipped topping

¾ cup water

1 tablespoon instant coffee

3 tablespoons Splenda Granular

1 tablespoon brandy (optional)

1 3-ounce package ladyfingers
(you need 12 split fingers)

1 teaspoon Dutch-process cocoa powder
(like Hershey's European)

½ ounce semisweet chocolate,
shaved (optional)

★You can substitute 4 ounces tub-style light cream cheese and 2 tablespoons light sour cream.

PER SERVING

Calories 160	Fat 11 grams (4.5 saturated)
Carbohydrate 9 grams	Fiber 0 grams
Protein 5 grams	Sodium 135 milligrams

Diabetic exchange = ½ Carbohydrate,
1 Very Lean Meat, 2 Fat
WW point comparison = 4 points

STEPS:

1. Gather 6 standard martini glasses (about 6 ounces each) or a 1-quart serving dish. In a medium mixing bowl, beat the mascarpone and the next 4 ingredients with an electric mixer until creamy and smooth. Fold in the light whipped topping. Set aside.

2. Place the water in a small microwaveable bowl or saucepan. Add the instant coffee and Splenda—and brandy, if desired—and heat for 2 minutes.

3. TO ASSEMBLE INDIVIDUAL TIRAMISUS: For each tiramisu, lightly dip the outside of 4 ladyfinger pieces (2 whole ladyfingers, each split in half), in coffee mixture and place standing up against the sides of the martini glass. Brush the inside of the ladyfingers with more coffee. Place ½ cup of cheese mixture in the center of the ladyfingers. Sift small amount (⅛ teaspoon) of the cocoa powder over the cheese mixture. Top with a touch of shaved chocolate, if desired. Wrap glass with plastic wrap and refrigerate for 6 hours before serving.

4. To ASSEMBLE IN A SINGLE DISH: Place half
   of the ladyfingers on the bottom of the dish.
   Brush ladyfingers with half of the coffee
   mixture. Top with half of the cheese mixture
   and smooth.

5. Repeat. Sift the cocoa powder over the
   top of the tiramisu. Top with the shaved
   chocolate, if desired. Refrigerate for 6 hours
   before serving.

*I have featured
this recipe many times
while teaching cooking classes.
It has concluded classes on pasta,
healthy low-carb cooking, and sugar-
free baking, and every time, it's a hit.
Students have told me they made it for
friends, and their friends have gone
on to make it for their friends, and
that's the sincerest compliment
of all.*

"Marvel"ous Lemon Mousse

Serves Six

I call this "marvel-ous" because this recipe is a marvel of good nutrition. It is filled with things that are good for you, like protein, vitamin C, and calcium— all packed into 100 slim calories. Cool, creamy, and sweet with a nice tart touch of lemon, "Marvel"ous Lemon Mousse is good for you but so tasty you'll find it hard to believe it.

INGREDIENTS:

1 envelope unflavored gelatin

⅔ cup lemon juice

¾ cup Splenda Granular

Finely grated zest of 1 lemon

2 drops yellow food coloring (optional)

½ cup cottage cheese

8 ounces nonfat plain yogurt

1 egg white (pasteurized or powdered if preferred)

1 tablespoon sugar

¾ cup light whipped topping

STEPS:

1. Place the gelatin in a small saucepan. Add ⅓ cup of the lemon juice and let stand for 3 minutes. Place on low heat and add remaining ⅓ cup of lemon juice, Splenda, zest and food coloring if desired. Heat for 3-4 minutes until gelatin is completely dissolved. Transfer mixture to a bowl.

2. Set aside and allow to cool slightly. Stir occasionally so mixture does not gel. Purée cottage cheese and yogurt until completely smooth (like sour cream).

3. Whisk purée into the lemon-gelatin mixture. Place mixture in the refrigerator to cool, whisking occasionally to prevent lumps. Beat the egg white to soft peaks. Add 1 tablespoon of sugar and beat until stiff, but not dry. Fold into the cooled lemon mixture. Fold in light whipped topping and pour into desired serving dish or serving cups.

Although light and creamy, this mousse is firm enough to be spooned into bite-sized tart shells, like those made from filo dough found in your grocer's freezer case, or a pie shell to make a Lemon Mousse Pie. Any way you serve it, it is beautiful when garnished with fresh berries and mint leaves.

PER SERVING

Calories 100

Carbohydrate 13 grams

Protein 9 grams

Fat 1.5 grams (1 saturated)

Fiber 0 grams

Sodium 55 milligrams

Diabetic exchange = 1 Very Low-Fat Milk

WW point comparison = 2 points

Dark Chocolate Mousse

Serves Six

This recipe is for the "reader from Philadelphia" who so kindly gave my first book a five-star review on Amazon.com and requested a creamy, dark, dense chocolate mousse. I hope this is what you were looking for!

INGREDIENTS:

1 teaspoon unflavored gelatin

2 tablespoons water

¾ cup fat-free half-and-half

1 teaspoon orange zest

2 eggs, separated

⅔ cup Splenda Granular

⅓ cup unsweetened Dutch-process cocoa powder

2 ounces semisweet chocolate, chopped

1 teaspoon vanilla

1 tablespoon sugar

¾ cup light whipped topping

STEPS:

1. In a small saucepan, combine gelatin and water. Let set for 3 minutes. Add nonfat half-and-half and orange zest. Whisk in 2 egg yolks, Splenda, and cocoa powder.

2. Place on medium heat and cook, stirring, until mixture is smooth and thickened (3-4 minutes).

3. Add chopped chocolate and vanilla and stir until smooth. Let cool to room temperature (about 30 minutes).

4. In a large bowl, beat egg whites until frothy. Beat in sugar until soft peaks form. Gently fold egg white into chocolate mixture. Fold in light whipped topping.

5. Refrigerate until very cold.

Cocoa powder is naturally acidic. When treated with an alkali to reduce this acidity, it is called Dutch-processed. Dutch-process cocoa is darker in color and less bitter than natural cocoa. Hershey's sells this as "European Style" and also "Special Dark."

PER SERVING (½ CUP)

Calories 150

Carbohydrate 18 grams

Protein 4 grams

Fat 5.5 grams (3.5 saturated)

Fiber 2 grams

Sodium 25 milligrams

Diabetic exchange = 1 Nonfat Milk, ½ Carbohydrate, 1 Fat

WW point comparison = 3 points

Chocolate Mousse Cake

Serves Eight

My parents happened to be in town the day I made this cake. After dinner, I served it to my father, a lover of all things rich, sweet, and fattening. When I asked him what he thought, he answered with one word—"decadent." Unlike most cakes, this incredible dessert has the light, creamy, rich texture of mousse. It sits on a chocolate crumb crust, but unlike mousse, can be sliced like a cake. Thus, I call it a mousse "cake." My dad prefers to call it delicious.

INGREDIENTS:

CRUST

¾ cup chocolate graham cracker crumbs

1 tablespoon Splenda Granular

1 teaspoon unsweetened Dutch-process cocoa powder (like Hershey's European)

2 tablespoons margarine

FILLING

1 envelope unsweetened gelatin (2 ½ teaspoons)

¼ cup water

1 cup 1% milk

1 large egg, lightly beaten

⅓ cup unsweetened Dutch-process cocoa powder

⅔ cup Splenda Granular

⅓ cup semisweet chocolate chips

1 teaspoon vanilla

¼ teaspoon orange extract or 1 tablespoon orange liqueur

2 large egg whites (or 3 pasteurized, if preferred)

1 tablespoon sugar

1 cup light whipped topping, thawed

½ ounce chocolate shavings (optional)

PER SERVING

Calories 175

Carbohydrate 24 grams

Protein 5 grams

Fat 7.5 grams (3.5 saturated)

Fiber 1.5 grams

Sodium 130 milligrams

Diabetic exchange = 1 Carbohydrate, 1 Lean Meat, 1 Fat
WW point comparison = 4 points

STEPS:

1. Preheat oven to 350°F. Spray a 9-inch springform pan with nonstick cooking spray.

2. CRUST: In a small bowl, combine the graham cracker crumbs, Splenda, and cocoa powder. Add the margarine and stir to mix.

3. Press crumbs onto bottom and 1 ½ inches up the sides of the prepared pan (pressing with plastic wrap will help with the sides). Bake for 8 minutes. Cool.

4. FILLING: In a medium saucepan, sprinkle gelatin over ¼ cup of water. Let stand 3 minutes.

5. Whisk in milk, beaten egg, cocoa powder, and Splenda. Place on stove and turn heat to medium. Cook, stirring until thickened and smooth. Add chocolate chips and stir until melted. Stir in vanilla and orange extract. Remove from heat. Pour into a large bowl and let cool.

6. Refrigerate for 30 minutes, stirring occasionally until mixture is cold and begins to mound when dropped from a spoon.

7. Beat egg whites until frothy. Add sugar and continue to beat until stiff, but not dry. Fold egg whites into chocolate mixture. Fold in light whipped topping. Pour mousse into crust and smooth. Refrigerate for at least 2 hours. Garnish with a touch of chocolate shavings, if desired.

Pumpkin Mousse with Gingersnaps

Serves Eight

The original version of this recipe originally appeared in Fantastic Food with Splenda; now, I've made several major changes. This new version is similar to a pumpkin mousse that was featured on The Food Network and then lightened up by Oprah's chef, Art Smith. I opted out of using the pureed banana in that recipe as well as eliminating a thick graham-cracker crust for a lighter topping of crushed gingersnaps. The result is an improved pumpkin mousse I am sure you will enjoy.

INGREDIENTS:

1 envelope unflavored gelatin

¾ cup nonfat half-and-half

1 15-ounce can pumpkin (not pie filling)

¾ cup Splenda Granular

2 large eggs, separated

2 teaspoons cinnamon

1 teaspoon nutmeg

2 tablespoons granulated sugar

1 cup light whipped topping

6 gingersnap cookies (like Nabisco Old-Fashioned), finely crushed

STEPS:

1. Sprinkle gelatin over ¼ cup of the nonfat half-and-half in a small bowl. Let set for 3 minutes.

2. Meanwhile, in a medium saucepan, whisk together remaining half-and-half, pumpkin, Splenda, egg yolks, and spices. Place on medium heat. Add softened gelatin and stir until mixture heats up and gelatin dissolves. Cook mixture 3-4 minutes or until bubbling. Remove from heat; spoon into large bowl and cool.

3. In a small bowl, whip egg whites until frothy. Add sugar and whip until stiff but not dry. Fold whipped topping and then egg whites carefully into pumpkin mixture.

4. Spoon mousse into desired serving bowl. Sprinkle with crushed gingersnaps.

5. Refrigerate for at least 2 hours.

PER SERVING

Calories 115	Fat 2 grams (1.5 saturated)
Carbohydrate 17 grams	Fiber 2 grams
Protein 4 grams	Sodium 80 milligrams

Diabetic exchange = 1 Vegetable, 1 Carbohydrate
WW point comparison = 2 points

French Cream with Raspberry Sauce

Serves Six

French Cream is a creamy concoction made of sweetened heavy cream, sour cream, and cream cheese. This lightened version is elegant and delicious enough for the fanciest of celebrations and yet easy enough to make anytime.

INGREDIENTS:

1 8-ounce tub-style light cream cheese

1 cup fat-free sour cream

1 ¼ cups fat-free half-and-half

1 envelope unflavored gelatin

¾ cup + 2 tablespoons Splenda Granular

2 tablespoons vanilla

¼ teaspoon almond extract

1 cup raspberries

1 tablespoon orange liqueur or water

Classic French coeur a la crème ("hearts filled with cream") can contain as much as 48 grams of fat per serving (30 of them saturated).

STEPS:

1. Set aside six 4- to 6-ounce custard cups or ramekins.

2. In a medium bowl, beat cream cheese and sour cream until smooth.

3. In a small saucepan, combine half-and-half and gelatin. Let set 3 minutes.

4. Whisk in ¾ cup Splenda and place over medium heat. Cook, stirring, until gelatin dissolves (1–2 minutes).

5. Pour gelatin mixture, vanilla, and almond extract into cream cheese mixture and beat until completely smooth.

6. Divide mixture evenly among the custard cups. Cover and refrigerate.

7. Pulse berries, 2 tablespoons Splenda, and liqueur in food processor or blender until smooth. Strain if desired. Unmold French Cream by dipping cups quickly in warm water and loosening edges with tip of knife.

8. Invert onto serving plate and drizzle with raspberry sauce.

PER SERVING (¹/₂ CUP)

Calories 200	Fat 6 grams (4 saturated)
Carbohydrate 21 grams	Fiber 1 gram
Protein 8 grams	Sodium 210 milligrams

Diabetic exchange = 1 Low-Fat Milk, ½ Carbohydrate
WW point comparison = 4 points

Creamy Orange Crepes

Serves Four

Deceptively rich-tasting and unbelievably pretty, these crepes are one surefire way to make someone feel special. Their high protein content also makes them a good choice for an elegant breakfast or brunch entrée. Use a handful of fresh raspberries and a sprig of mint to dress each plate beautifully.

INGREDIENTS:

CREPE BATTER

½ cup flour

½ cup 1% milk

¼ cup water

1 egg

2 egg whites

1 ½ tablespoons margarine, melted

2 tablespoons Splenda Granular

Pinch salt

FILLING

¼ cup light cream cheese

1 cup low-fat cottage cheese

1 egg yolk

2 ½ tablespoons Splenda Granular

⅛ teaspoon almond extract

1 teaspoon orange zest

2 teaspoons powdered sugar (optional)

Crepe batter is quite easy, and a good nonstick pan makes for an easy release. I simply stack them, but you may find placing wax paper between each one guarantees no sticking problems.

STEPS:

1. BATTER: In a small bowl, whisk together crepe ingredients; set aside and let mixture stand at room temperature for 30 minutes.

2. FILLING: In a food processor or blender, combine cream cheese, cottage cheese, egg yolk, Splenda, and almond extract. Blend until smooth (about 1 minute). By hand, stir in orange zest. Set aside.

3. Spray a nonstick 6-inch skillet with cooking spray. Heat skillet over medium heat. Spoon scant ¼ cup crepe batter into hot pan. Swirl pan quickly to coat bottom with batter. Let crepe cook for 2–3 minutes until underside is lightly browned. Remove crepe, without turning, and place on plate. Continue with remaining batter, stacking crepes. (At this point, you may cover and refrigerate crepes for later use.)

4. Fill crepes by placing 2 heaping tablespoons of filling along the middle center (leaving last ½ inch to edge bare). Fold sides together across filling.

5. Carefully place crepes back into pan coated with cooking spray and cook for 2 minutes on each side until lightly golden brown.

6. Dust with powdered sugar if desired.

PER SERVING (2 CREPES)

Calories 235	Fat 10 grams (4 saturated)
Carbohydrate 18 grams	Fiber 0 grams
Protein 15 grams	Sodium 420 milligrams

Diabetic exchange = 2 Lean Meat, 1 Carbohydrate, 1 Fat
WW point comparison = 5 points

Frozen Desserts

Berry Sorbet

Lemon Lime Sorbet

Chocolate Sorbet

Coffee Granita

Peach Frozen Yogurt

Strawberry Frozen Yogurt

Buttermilk Boysenberry Sherbet

Café au Lait Ice Cream

Rich Chocolate Ice Cream

Lemon Cheesecake Ice Cream

High-Protein Vanilla Soft Serve

Creamy French Vanilla Frozen Custard

Vanilla Ice Cream in a Baggie

Double Cherry Ice Pops

Fresh Strawberry Lime Ice Pops

Have you been to the ice-cream section of your local store lately? There are so many options—from the super-indulgent premium ice creams packed with fat and sugar, to reduced-fat yet high-sugar choices, and now, low-carb, low-sugar selections (many of which are still full of fat)—it's hard to know *what* to choose.

One terrific option is to not choose at all, but to make your own frozen desserts. This way, you control what goes into it and, best of all, you can mix and match your own flavors and have a great time doing it. It's also easier than ever, thanks to new countertop-sized ice-cream makers that don't require any salt or ice. You simply prefreeze the bucket and off you go—30 minutes to healthy homemade ice cream, sorbet, frozen yogurt, and even sherbet.

You'll find that I have covered not only the most popular flavors, ranging from rich chocolate and creamy vanilla to fresh strawberry and smooth coffee, but I've also come up with new ones that add bursts of flavor from real fruit like lemons, limes, peaches, and boysenberries. My hope is that you'll take my lead and use these recipes as a basis to invent some flavors of your own by varying the type of fruit or simply adding any variety of mix-ins.

Please note that all of the recipes in this section are at their best texture when just churned. Because of their low sugar content and because they lack the addition of sugar alcohols (like commerically prepared sugar-free versions), they will freeze very hard. To soften before serving, simply place the container on the counter or in the refrigerator for about 30 minutes.

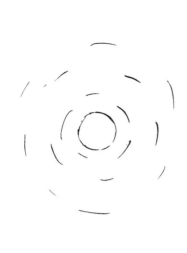

Berry Sorbet

Serves Six

Bursting with the flavor of fresh berries, this beautiful ruby red sorbet is truly a delight to the taste buds. Very or use a combination of berries to create a variety of flavors.

INGREDIENTS:

1 quart fresh strawberries or raspberries, stemmed, washed, and sliced

2 tablespoons orange juice

1 teaspoon orange zest

⅔ cup Splenda Granular

½ cup water

STEPS:

1. Puree berries with orange juice and zest in food processor or blender. Set aside.

2. In a small saucepan, bring Splenda and water to a boil. Reduce heat and simmer for 5 minutes until slightly thickened. Add syrup to berries. Cool.

3. Pour sorbet into ice-cream maker and freeze according to manufacturer's directions. Serve immediately or place into container and freeze.

4. Before serving, place sorbet in refrigerator for 30 minutes to soften.

Marco Polo is credited for bringing the first recipes for fruit ices or sorbets to Europe from the Orient.

PER SERVING (½ CUP)

Calories 35	Fat 0 grams (0 saturated)
Carbohydrate 8 grams	Fiber 2 grams
Protein 0 grams	Sodium 0 milligrams

Diabetic exchange = ½ Fruit

WW point comparison = 0 points (can have up to 1 ½ cups for 1 point)

Lemon-Lime Sorbet

Serves Six

Sweet and tart, this is a refreshing and excellent palate cleanser. I made it using an electric ice-cream maker with a bowl you freeze, but I'm told it's better-aerated and freezes more solidly in a traditional ice-cream maker. To fill this larger maker, use 3 cups water, ¾ cup lemon juice, ½ cup lime juice, 2 ½ cups Splenda, and 1 tablespoon corn syrup.

INGREDIENTS:

2 cups cold water

½ cup fresh lemon juice

⅓ cup fresh lime juice

1 ¾ cups Splenda Granular

2 teaspoons corn syrup

STEPS:

1. Combine all ingredients in a medium bowl and stir to dissolve the Splenda.

2. Chill in the refrigerator for at least 1 hour.

3. Pour sorbet into ice-cream maker and freeze according to manufacturer's directions. Serve immediately or place into container and place in freezer. Stir again 30 and 60 minutes later to help keep sorbet aerated.

4. Before serving, place sorbet in refrigerator for 30 minutes or so to soften.

Noting that lime juice requires a bit more sweetening power, adjust the ratio of lemon and lime juice to your taste.

PER SERVING (½ CUP)

Calories 45	Fat 0 grams
Carbohydrate 11 grams	Fiber 0 grams
Protein 0 grams	Sodium 0 milligrams

Diabetic exchange = 1 Fruit
WW point comparison = 1 point

Chocolate Sorbet

Serves Six

Just a little goes a long way with this intense, dark chocolate sorbet. A mere tablespoon of corn syrup really helps to smooth both the texture and the flavor.

INGREDIENTS:

1 cup Splenda Granular

⅔ cup Dutch-process cocoa powder

1 ½ cups water

1 tablespoon light corn syrup

1 teaspoon vanilla

When made with granulated sugar, one serving of this sorbet contains 30 grams of carbohydrate.

STEPS:

1. Combine Splenda and cocoa powder in medium saucepan. Whisk in water and corn syrup. Place over medium heat and bring to a boil. Reduce heat and simmer 4-5 minutes or until slightly thickened.

2. Remove from heat, pour into bowl, and stir in vanilla. Chill 30 minutes.

3. Pour sorbet into ice-cream maker and freeze according to manufacturer's directions. Serve immediately or place into container and freeze.

4. Place sorbet in refrigerator for 30 minutes to soften before serving.

PER SERVING (⅓ CUP)

Calories 60	Fat 1 gram (.5 saturated)
Carbohydrate 10 grams	Fiber 3 grams
Protein 2 grams	Sodium 10 milligrams

Diabetic exchange = ½ Carbohydrate
WW point comparison = 1 point

Coffee Granita

Serves Four

You don't need an ice-cream maker to make this truly "iced" coffee. It's easy but takes a few "scrapings" to keep it light, so prepare Coffee Granita when you plan to be home for a bit. Serve it up tall in a nice martini or cocktail glass.

INGREDIENTS:

2 cups strong coffee or espresso

½ cup Splenda Granular

1 ½ teaspoons vanilla extract

2 large pieces lemon or orange peel, zest only

STEPS:

1. Stir all ingredients together. Pour into a 9-inch metal baking pan and place in freezer.

2. Every 30 minutes, scrape the mixture with a fork to break up the ice crystals. Do this 3 more times (total of 2 hours in the freezer).

3. Remove into a metal bowl, remove the zest, and freeze for 30 minutes more. Beat well with a fork to get a smooth texture.

4. Serve cold with a garnish of lemon or orange zest.

PER SERVING (¹/₂ CUP)

Calories 20	Fat 0 (0) grams
Carbohydrate 5 grams	Fiber 0 grams
Protein 0 grams	Sodium 0 milligrams

Diabetic exchange = Free Food
WW point comparison = 0 points

Peach Frozen Yogurt

Serves Eight

While nothing beats the taste of a fresh peach in season, you have the option of using frozen peaches in this recipe so you can enjoy the fresh taste of summer all year long.

INREDIENTS:

2 cups peeled peach slices, fresh or frozen, thawed

1 ½ cups Splenda Granular

1 ½ teaspoons unflavored gelatin

¾ cup fat-free half-and-half

1 ½ cups low-fat plain yogurt

½ teaspoon vanilla

To peel the skin off fresh peaches easily, dip whole peaches into boiling water for 30 seconds. Immediately plunge into cold water to cool; then simply slip the skins off the flesh.

STEPS:

1. In a food processor, puree peaches and ¾ Splenda. Set aside.

2. Combine gelatin and ¼ cup half-and-half. Let set 3 minutes. Whisk in remaining half-and-half and Splenda. Heat just until gelatin dissolves. Cool slightly and stir in yogurt and vanilla.

3. Pour yogurt into ice-cream maker and freeze according to manufacturer's directions. Serve immediately or place into container and freeze.

4. Place yogurt in refrigerator for 30 minutes to soften before serving.

PER SERVING (½ CUP)

Calories 100	Fat 1 gram (.5 saturated)
Carbohydrate 16 grams	Fiber 1 gram
Protein 4 grams	Sodium 45 milligrams

Diabetic exchange = ½ Fruit, ½ Low-Fat Milk

WW point comparison = 2 points

Strawberry Frozen Yogurt

Serves Six

It doesn't get any easier than this—and of course any type of berry will do. Adjust sweetness depending on fruit.

INGREDIENTS:

1 quart fresh strawberries, stemmed, washed, and halved

1 tablespoon lemon juice

¾ cup Splenda Granular

1 cup low-fat plain yogurt

¾ cup 1% milk

STEPS:

1. Place berries on a cookie sheet and partially freeze (15-30 minutes).

2. Remove from freezer and coarsely puree berries with lemon juice.

3. In a large bowl, combine Splenda, yogurt, low-fat milk, and berries.

4. Pour yogurt into ice-cream maker and freeze according to manufacturer's directions. Serve immediately or place into container and freeze.

5. Place yogurt in refrigerator for 30 minutes to soften before serving.

To create a richer mouth feel, you may use nonfat half-and-half for part or all of the milk. If you fully replace it, add 5 calories and 2 grams of carbohydrate to each serving.

PER SERVING (½ CUP)

Calories 70	Fat 1 gram (.5 saturated)
Carbohydrate 11 grams	Fiber 2 grams
Protein 3 grams	Sodium 45 milligrams

Diabetic exchange = ½ Nonfat Milk, ½ Fruit
WW point comparison = 1 point

Buttermilk Boysenberry Sherbet

Serves Four

The tartness of buttermilk combines beautifully with fresh or frozen boysenberries for a delicious sherbet low in sugar as well as fat.

INGREDIENTS:

1 teaspoon unflavored gelatin

1 teaspoon orange juice

1 ½ cups fresh or thawed frozen boysenberries

⅔ cup Splenda Granular

⅔ cup water

1 cup buttermilk

STEPS:

1. In a small bowl, sprinkle gelatin over orange juice. Set aside.

2. In a medium saucepan, combine boysenberries, Splenda, and water. Place over medium heat and simmer for 5 minutes. Remove from heat and add gelatin. Stir to dissolve. Strain mixture through a sieve to remove seeds.

3. Combine berry syrup with buttermilk. Pour sherbet into ice-cream maker and freeze according to manufacturer's directions. Serve immediately or place into container and freeze.

4. Place sherbet in refrigerator for 30 minutes to soften before serving.

Boysenberries are quite seedy. When straining, you will need to use a large spoon to press on and mash the berries to force some of the flavor-intense pulp through the sieve or strainer.

PER SERVING (½ CUP)

Calories 60

Carbohydrate 12 grams

Protein 3 grams

Fat 0.5 gram (0 saturated)

Fiber 2 grams

Sodium 55 milligrams

Diabetic exchange = ½ Fruit, ½ Nonfat Milk

WW point comparison = 1 point

Café au Lait Ice Cream

Serves Six

You don't have to be a coffee drinker to enjoy the great taste of this cool treat. Cornstarch and just a handful of mini-marshmallows go a long way in adding a nice, silky texture.

INGREDIENTS:

2 eggs, beaten

¾ cup Splenda Granular

1 ½ cups 1% milk

2 teaspoons cornstarch

2 tablespoons instant coffee granules

¼ cup miniature marshmallows

1 cup fat-free half-and-half

STEPS:

1. In medium saucepan, whisk together first 4 ingredients (eggs through cornstarch) and heat until mixture reaches a low boil. Add coffee granules. Stir in marshmallows. Set aside to cool for 15 minutes. Add half-and-half and cool.

2. Pour mixture into ice-cream maker and freeze according to manufacturer's directions. Serve immediately or place into container and freeze.

3. Place ice cream in refrigerator for 30 minutes to soften before serving.

For an interesting flavor combination, a pastry chef I know always dusts her coffee ice cream with ground cinnamon just before serving. Another terrific topping is the Dark Chocolate Sauce on page 429, spiked with a touch of orange zest.

PER SERVING (½ CUP)

Calories 100	Fat 2.5 grams (1 saturated)
Carbohydrate 13 grams	Fiber 3 grams
Protein 5 grams	Sodium 60 milligrams

Diabetic exchange = ½ Low-Fat Milk, ½ Carbohydrate
WW point comparison = 2 points

Rich Chocolate Ice Cream

Serves Six

This unusual recipe is for my cooking school friends and fans of Alice Medrich, a well-known and talented chocolatier and author. To make her chocolate ice cream, she uses the nib of the cocoa bean. Here, I have lightened up her unique recipe by using Splenda Sugar Blend and nonfat half-and-half for a creamy delight that's best when first churned.

INGREDIENTS:

1 ½ cups whole milk

1 ½ cups nonfat half-and-half

¼ cup cocoa nibs, chopped

¼ cup Splenda Sugar Blend for Baking

1 tablespoon Dutch-process cocoa powder

Pinch salt

STEPS:

1. In a medium saucepan, combine milk, half-and-half, cocoa nibs, Splenda Sugar Blend, and salt. Bring to a boil, remove from heat, and cover. Let steep for 20 minutes.

2. Strain the mixture into a bowl.

3. Chill thoroughly and make according to the directions on your ice-cream maker.

Cocoa nibs are the "nibs" left when you roast and break off the outer hull of a cocoa bean. They are the most valuable (and delicious) part of the bean because they contain all of the chocolate flavor. Used to make chocolate, they are available at many specialty stores. You can crush the leftovers to put in cookies or sprinkle lightly on ice cream for a bit of added crunch.

PER SERVING (½ CUP)

Calories 150

Carbohydrate 19 grams

Protein 6 grams

Fat 5 grams (1.5 saturated)

Fiber 1 gram

Sodium 115 milligrams

Diabetic exchange = 1 Reduced-Fat Milk, ½ Carbohydrate

WW point comparison = 3 points

Lemon Cheesecake Ice Cream

Serves Six

This recipe is for me because I love ice cream, I enjoy cheesecake, and lemon is one of my favorite flavors—and this recipe satisfies all three. The warmed milk mixture helps to cream the ricotta in order to give this ice cream a smoother texture than that of a traditional ricotta cheesecake. Enjoy.

INGREDIENTS:

½ cup low-fat ricotta

¼ cup light cream cheese

¼ cup light sour cream

¼ cup lemon juice

Zest of 1 lemon

½ teaspoon vanilla

¼ teaspoon almond extract

1 ½ cups fat-free half-and-half

¾ cup Splenda Granular

2 eggs, beaten

STEPS:

1. Place ricotta, cream cheese, sour cream, lemon juice, zest and extracts in food processor or blender.

2. In a medium saucepan, combine half-and-half, Splenda, and eggs. Place on medium heat and cook 4–5 minutes until mixture thickens and coats a spoon. Slowly pour mixture into ricotta mixture and blend for several minutes until smooth. Chill 20–30 minutes.

3. Pour into ice-cream maker and freeze according to manufacturer's directions. Serve immediately or place in container and freeze.

4. Once frozen, place ice cream in refrigerator for 30 minutes to soften before serving.

PER SERVING (½ CUP)

Calories 135
Carbohydrate 12 grams
Protein 7 grams

Fat 6 grams (2.5 saturated)
Fiber 0 grams
Sodium 110 milligrams

Diabetic exchange = 1 Low-Fat Milk, 1 Fat
WW point comparison = 3 points

High-Protein Vanilla Soft Serve

Serves Six

My boys really enjoy eating this easy-to-make, delicious, soft-serve-style ice cream. Little do they know it is actually a good source of calcium. Like all vanilla ice creams, it makes a great base for your favorite toppings, too.

INGREDIENTS:

1 teaspoon unflavored gelatin

1 tablespoon water

1 cup 1% milk

¼ cup egg substitute

½ cup nonfat dry milk

⅔ cup Splenda Granular

1 ½ cups whole milk

1 teaspoon vanilla extract

STEPS:

1. In a medium saucepan, sprinkle gelatin over water. Let set 3 minutes.

2. Add low-fat milk and place over low heat until gelatin dissolves. Remove from heat and add remaining ingredients.

3. Pour ice cream into ice-cream maker and freeze according to manufacturer's directions. Serve immediately or place into container and freeze.

4. Once frozen, place ice cream in refrigerator for 30 minutes to soften before serving.

The choices in sugar-free and low-sugar ice creams at the markets have really exploded. Be careful, however, to read labels. Look for "light" or reduced-fat versions of those with reduced sugar. Also be cautious of ice creams with a lot of sugar alcohol. They can be responsible for GI distress, especially in children.

PER SERVING

Calories 100

Carbohydrate 11 grams

Protein 7 grams

Fat 3.5 grams (2 saturated)

Fiber 0 grams

Sodium 100 milligrams

Diabetic exchange = 1 Low-Fat Milk

WW point comparison = 2 points

Creamy French Vanilla Frozen Custard

Serves Six

The pasteurized egg substitute works beautifully to create a "no-cook" creamy custard base for this simple yet delicious, rich-tasting frozen custard. The high egg ratio gives this "French" custard not only its name but also its characteristic yellow color.

INGREDIENTS:

1 cup light cream

1 cup 1% milk

1 cup Splenda Granular

**¾ cup egg substitute
    (I prefer Egg Beaters)**

2 teaspoons vanilla

STEPS:

1. In a large container, whisk together light cream, milk, Splenda, egg substitute, and vanilla.

2. Pour custard into ice-cream maker and freeze according to manufacturer's directions. Serve immediately or place into container and store in freezer.

3. Before serving, place frozen custard in refrigerator for at least 30 minutes to soften.

To keep this recipe simple, I have used pure vanilla extract. If you scrape the inside of a vanilla bean into the custard in place of the extract, it will produce a lovely, vanilla bean-flecked frozen custard.

PER SERVING (¹/₂ CUP)

Calories 120   Fat 7 grams (4 saturated)
Carbohydrate 8 grams   Fiber 0 grams
Protein 5 grams   Sodium 85 milligrams

Diabetic exchange = ½ Low-Fat Milk, 1 Fat
WW point comparison = 3 points

Vanilla Ice Cream in a Baggie

Serves Four

"Baggie Ice Cream" is an old standby for campouts with the kids. A colleague of mine uses this version for her kids at diabetes camp each summer, but it will also work well in your own backyard or as something the kids can do on a rainy afternoon.

INGREDIENTS:

1-gallon freezer bag, zip-type
Cubed or crushed ice
6 tablespoons salt
2 cups fat-free half-and-half
½ cup Splenda Granular (or 12 packets)
1 teaspoon vanilla
1-quart freezer bag, zip-type

STEPS:

1. Fill half the gallon-sized bag with cubed or crushed ice; add 6 tablespoons salt to the ice.
2. Mix the half-and-half, Splenda, and vanilla in the 1-quart freezer bag and zip closed. Place it inside the larger bag; zip closed.
3. Squish and shake for about 5 minutes or until the ice cream thickens.

PER SERVING (½ CUP)

Calories 90
Carbohydrate 15 grams
Protein 2 grams
Fat 0 grams (0 saturated)
Fiber 0 grams
Sodium 80 milligrams

Diabetic exchange = 1 Carbohydrate
WW point comparison = 2 points

Double Cherry Ice Pops

Serves Sixteen

I have to admit that I hesitated as I came across a recipe made with Jell-O and Kool-Aid, but I knew that if these dripless pops worked, my children would be in kiddie heaven. So I tested it several times, with both Splenda Granular and Splenda Sugar Blend for Baking, and I discovered that the sugar blend resulted in a much clearer frozen pop. These have far less sugar than normal ice pops, and kids do love them.

INGREDIENTS:

1 small (4-serving) box sugar-free cherry gelatin

1 package unsweetened cherry Kool-Aid mix

½ cup Splenda Sugar Blend for Baking

1 cup water + 3 cups cold water

16 3-ounce paper cups or Popsicle molds

16 Popsicle sticks

STEPS:

1. Place gelatin and Kool-Aid mix in a large pitcher (bigger than 1 quart).
2. Bring 1 cup of water to a boil; pour over gelatin mix and stir until dissolved. Add remaining 3 cups cold water and stir.
3. Pour 2 ounces or ¼ cup of mix into each cup or mold.
4. Freeze for 1 hour or until firm enough to hold stick.
5. Place a stick in each pop and freeze until hard (about 1 additional hour).

Kids love making these and experimenting with flavors. Any combination of sugar-free gelatin and Kool-Aid can be used.

PER SERVING

Calories 25
Carbohydrate 6 grams
Protein 0 grams

Fat 0 grams
Fiber 0 grams
Sodium 15 milligrams

Diabetic exchange = ½ Carbohydrate
WW point comparison = ½ point

Fresh Strawberry Lime Ice Pops

Serves Six

Made with whole strawberries and freshly squeezed lime juice, these "pops" are definitely not just for kids. Another fun idea is to freeze them in ice cube trays and drop them into the Sparkling Limeade on page 39.

INGREDIENTS:

2 cups washed, hulled, and halved strawberries

½ cup fresh lime juice

½ cup Splenda Granular

¼ cup water

1 tablespoon light corn syrup

Zest of 1 lime

3 drops red food color (optional)

6 3-ounce paper cups or Popsicle molds

6 Popsicle sticks

STEPS:

1. Place all ingredients in a blender and blend until smooth. Strain mixture by pressing through a fine mesh sieve.

2. Pour 2 ounces or ¼ cup of mix into each cup or mold. Freeze for 1 hour or until firm enough to hold stick.

3. Place a stick in each pop and freeze until hard (about 1 additional hour).

You can substitute any of your favorite berries and use lemon juice or light orange juice for the lime juice (like boysenberry and orange-yum). For berries with seeds, you will want to strain the juice just before placing it in the molds.

PER SERVING

Calories 40	Fat 0 grams
Carbohydrate 10 grams	Fiber 0 grams
Protein 0 grams	Sodium 0 milligrams

Diabetic exchange = ½ Fruit
WW point comparison = 1 point

Everyone's Favorite Cookies

Chocolate Chip Cookies

Sugar Blend Chocolate Chip Cookies

Old-Fashioned Peanut Butter Cookies

Chocolate Chocolate Chip Cookies

Great Oatmeal Cookies

Lacy Orange Oatmeal Cookies

Sugar Blend Snickerdoodles

Soft Sour Cream Sugar Cookies

Sliced Lemon Coconut Wafers

Coconut Crispy Macaroons

Chocolate Chip Meringue Cookies

Italian Meringue Cookies

Molasses Cutouts

Zebra Bars

Chocolate Brownies

Frosted Pumpkin Bars

High-Protein Peanut Butter Oat Bars

Apricot Oat Bars

Old-Fashioned Lemon Squares

Creamy Lemon Cheesecake Bars

Raspberry Shortbread Triangles

Chocolate Almond Biscotti

Orange Ginger Pecan Biscotti

One of the most interesting and educational food science articles I ever read was about one of my favorite treats to make—cookies! The article by Shirley O. Corriher, author of *Cookwise: The Hows and Whys of Successful Cooking*, specifically outlined how each of the major ingredients affected the finished cookie. And (of course) two of the most critical components that make a cookie—well, a cookie—are sugar and fat. In addition to sweetening, the amount and type of sugar and fat affect the cookie's color, texture, and height (or the amount of spread). That's why you often find low-fat cookies contain more sugar and vice versa. My challenge was to find a way to reduce the fat *and* the sugar—in the same recipe!

Thanks to Shirley, I had a clue as to what awaited me, but I can honestly tell you that to reach my goal, I had to bake lots and lots of cookies.

Here's what I learned: Something as simple as including a few judicious tablespoons (instead of cups) of the right type of sugar (when necessary) often made the difference between a cookie recipe succeeding or failing.

To that end, I am sincerely pleased to be able to offer you two dozen wonderful cookie recipes. If you prefer bar cookies, you can choose from Frosted Pumpkin Bars and Apricot Oat Bars. You'll also find the cookie-jar staples like Old-Fashioned Peanut Butter and Great Oatmeal Cookies. For the holidays, you can bake batches of Molasses Cutouts and Orange Ginger Biscotti, and get your kids to help you make Chocolate Chocolate Chip Cookies and Zebra Bars.

I'm also delighted to tell you that now, with the help of Splenda Sugar Blend for Baking, I can share with confidence some amazing recipes for some of my all-time low-sugar, low-fat cookie challenges—Chocolate Brownies, Old-Fashioned Lemon Bars, and Sugar Blend Snickerdoodles. Enjoy!

Chocolate Chip Cookies

Serves Eighteen

These chocolate chip cookies look and taste like the real McCoy. They are slightly soft, sweet, and full of chocolate. Jan from Phoenix recently emailed me that she bakes a batch of these just about every week. She is delighted that I've reduced the sugar by 75 percent and the fat by one-half, compared to the traditional recipe. But, most of all, she simply loves the cookies.

INGREDIENTS:

1 cup all-purpose flour

½ teaspoon baking soda

¼ cup margarine, softened

2 tablespoons prune purée★

⅔ cup Splenda Granular

3 tablespoons brown sugar

1 large egg white

1 ½ teaspoons vanilla

6 tablespoons mini chocolate chips

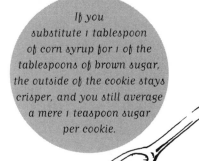

If you substitute 1 tablespoon of corn syrup for 1 of the tablespoons of brown sugar, the outside of the cookie stays crisper, and you still average a mere 1 teaspoon sugar per cookie.

STEPS:

1. Preheat oven to 375°F. Spray cookie sheet with nonstick cooking spray.

2. Combine flour and baking soda together in a small bowl. Set aside.

3. In a medium mixing bowl, with an electric mixer, beat margarine, prune purée, Splenda, and brown sugar until creamy. Add egg white and vanilla. Beat well. Stir in the flour mixture. Stir in chocolate chips.

4. Drop dough by level tablespoons onto cookie sheet. Press down on dough with the bottom of a glass or spatula to flatten.

5. Bake cookies for 4 minutes or until they "puff." Open oven and tap cookie sheet firmly against baking rack or the inside of the oven door to force cookies to drop and spread slightly.

6. Place cookies back in oven and bake 5 more minutes, or until lightly browned. Remove from pan and cool on rack. Cookies will remain crisp for several hours, then soften.

★You may replace the prune purée with margarine, but your calories per cookie will increase by 5, and fat grams by 1. You reduce the carbohydrate content by 1 gram.

PER SERVING (1 COOKIE)

Calories 80	Fat 3.5 grams (1 saturated)
Carbohydrate 11 grams	Fiber .5 grams
Protein 1 gram	Sodium 60 milligrams

Diabetic exchange = 1 Carbohydrate, ½ Fat
(2 cookies = 1 ½ Carbohydrate, 1 Fat)
WW point comparison = 2 points

Sugar Blend Chocolate Chip Cookies

Serves Thirty

I almost called these "Better for You Chocolate Chip Cookies" because although they still have all the indulgent ingredients (real butter, sugar, chocolate chips, and nuts), I have made them better for you. The butter has been reduced by using prune puree, the sugar by using Splenda Sugar Blend, the chips by using minis, and the nuts just by using fewer. Bottom line, though, these cookies look and taste just as good as any "real" chocolate chip cookie, and nothing's better than that.

INGREDIENTS

⅓ cup butter

⅓ Splenda Sugar Blend for Baking

3 tablespoons brown sugar

2 tablespoons prune puree

1 ½ teaspoons vanilla

1 large egg

1 cup all-purpose flour

½ cup whole-wheat pastry flour

¾ teaspoon baking soda

⅓ cup mini chocolate chips

⅓ cup chopped pecans or walnuts

STEPS:

1. Preheat oven to 375°F. Spray cookie sheet with nonstick cooking spray.

2. In a large bowl, with an electric mixer, cream butter, Splenda Sugar Blend, brown sugar, and prune puree until very light. Beat in vanilla and large egg.

3. In a small bowl, combine all-purpose flour, pastry flour, and baking soda. Mix to combine.

4. Add flour mixture to creamed mixture and beat to blend. Stir in chips and nuts.

5. Drop dough by level tablespoons onto baking sheet 2 inches apart. Flatten slightly with spatula.

6. Bake for 7-9 minutes or until set. Cool on pan until firm. Remove to wire racks to finish cooling.

PER SERVING

Calories 80	Fat 4 grams (1.5 saturated)
Carbohydrate 10 grams	Fiber 1 gram
Protein 1 gram	Sodium 85 milligrams

Diabetic exchange = ½ Carbohydrate, 1 Fat

WW point comparison = 2 points

Chopped dried cranberries or cherries can be used in place of the nuts; the calories won't change, but you will have 1 gram more carbohydrate and ½ gram less fat per cookie.

Old-Fashioned Peanut Butter Cookies

Serves Twenty-Six

Some of my most enjoyable cooking classes have been with children. My goal in selecting recipes is to choose foods kids love, in order to teach them the importance of good nutrition. These cookies provide a healthy alternative to junk food, and kids love 'em.

INGREDIENTS:

1 ½ cups all-purpose flour

1 teaspoon baking soda

½ teaspoon baking powder

½ cup + 2 tablespoons peanut butter

¼ cup margarine

2 tablespoons nonfat cream cheese

¾ cup Splenda Granular

3 tablespoons brown sugar

1 large egg

3 tablespoons 1% milk

2 teaspoons vanilla

STEPS:

1. Preheat oven to 375°F. Spray cookie sheet with nonstick cooking spray.
2. Combine flour, baking soda, and baking powder together in a bowl. Set aside.
3. In a medium mixing bowl, with an electric mixer, beat peanut butter, margarine, cream cheese, Splenda, and brown sugar until creamy. Add egg, milk, and vanilla. Beat well. Stir in flour mixture.
4. Roll dough, by level tablespoons, into balls. Place onto cookie sheet and flatten with a fork forming a crisscross on top of each cookie.
5. Bake for 9–10 minutes. Remove from pan and cool on rack.

Just add a glass of milk for a perfect balanced after-school snack. Not only fun to eat— it will be full of protein, "healthy" fat and some carbs for energy.

PER SERVING (1 COOKIE)

Calories 90	Fat 5 grams (1 saturated)
Carbohydrate 8 grams	Fiber .5 grams
Protein 3 grams	Sodium 45 milligrams

Diabetic exchange = ½ Carbohydrate, 1 Fat

WW point comparison = 2 points

Chocolate Chocolate Chip Cookies

Serves Twenty-Four

Chocolate and more chocolate—my kids think these are the best. Soft and oh-so-full of chocolate, these cookies benefit from the added milk, which helps them to spread nicely with only a touch of sugar.

INGREDIENTS:

1 cup all-purpose flour

3 tablespoons Dutch-process cocoa powder (like Hershey's European)

½ teaspoon baking soda

⅓ cup margarine

2 tablespoons prune purée

½ cup Splenda Granular

3 tablespoons brown sugar

1 egg

1 teaspoon vanilla

2 tablespoons 1% milk

⅓ cup mini chocolate chips

STEPS:

1. Preheat oven to 375°F. Spray cookie sheet with nonstick cooking spray.

2. Combine flour, cocoa, and baking soda together in a small bowl. Set aside.

3. In a medium mixing bowl, with an electric mixer, beat margarine, prune purée, Splenda, and brown sugar until creamy. Add egg and vanilla. Beat well. Stir in the flour mixture, alternating with milk. Stir in chocolate chips.

4. Drop dough, by level tablespoons, onto cookie sheet. Press down on dough with the bottom of a glass to flatten.

5. Bake cookies for 8-10 minutes. Remove from pan and cool on rack.

Good news— chocolate is good for you! Studies show that the type of saturated fat in chocolate (stearic acid) does not raise cholesterol and that chocolate also contains healthful antioxidants. Therefore, moderate amounts of chocolate, especially dark chocolate, are now considered health food—who would've guessed?

PER SERVING (1 COOKIE)

Calories 60	Fat 3 grams (1 saturated)
Carbohydrate 8 grams	Fiber 1 gram
Protein 1 gram	Sodium 30 milligrams

Diabetic exchange = ½ Carbohydrate, ½ Fat
WW point comparison = 1 point

Great Oatmeal Cookies

Serves Twenty-Two

Here's another classic cookie-jar recipe. Many low-fat oatmeal cookie recipes replace some or all of the fat with applesauce, but I found that doing so, along with the significant reduction in sugar, gives you a very gummy cookie. My cookie uses butter for flavor, oil for tenderness, and prune purée for color and texture. The result is a low-fat, low-sugar cookie that is worthy of the cookie jar.

INGREDIENTS:

¾ **cup all-purpose flour**

1 ½ **cups old-fashioned oats (not instant)**

½ **teaspoon baking soda**

1 **teaspoon cinnamon**

2 **tablespoons butter, softened**

2 **tablespoons canola oil**

2 **tablespoons prune purée**

⅔ **cup Splenda Granular**

3 **tablespoons brown sugar**

1 **large egg**

1 **teaspoon vanilla**

¼ **cup dried cranberries, finely chopped**

½ **teaspoon grated orange zest**

STEPS:

1. Preheat oven to 350°F. Spray cookie sheet with nonstick cooking spray.

2. Combine flour, oats, baking soda, and cinnamon together in a bowl. Set aside.

3. In a medium mixing bowl, with an electric mixer, beat butter, oil, prune purée, Splenda, and brown sugar until creamy. Add egg and vanilla. Beat well. Stir in cranberries and zest and then flour mixture.

4. Drop dough, by level tablespoons, onto cookie sheet. Press down on dough with the bottom of a glass to flatten. Bake cookies for 4 minutes or until they "puff." Open oven and tap cookie sheet firmly against baking rack or the inside of the oven door to force cookies to drop and spread slightly. Place cookies back in oven and bake 5–7 more minutes, or until lightly browned.

5. Remove from pan and cool on rack. Cookies will remain crisp for several hours, then soften.

To make old-fashioned oatmeal raisin cookies, substitute raisins for the dried cranberries, eliminate the orange zest, and increase the vanilla and cinnamon by ½ teaspoon each.

PER SERVING (1 COOKIE)

Calories 75	Fat 3 grams (1 saturated)
Carbohydrate 11 grams	Fiber 1 gram
Protein 2 grams	Sodium 35 milligrams

Diabetic exchange = 1 Carbohydrate, ½ Fat (2 cookies = 1 ½ Carbohydrate, 1 Fat)

WW point comparison = 2 points

Lacy Orange Oatmeal Cookies

Serves Fourteen

I love the wonderful combination of orange and pecans in these delicate cookies. Made like an Irish lace cookie with very little flour, the method and "dough" may appear odd, but I guarantee they are delicious. These are not a sturdy, cookie-jar cookie, and even have a tendency to crumble, but the lack of flour that creates this cookie also gives the oats and nuts a chance to shine.

INGREDIENTS:

3 tablespoons margarine or butter

2 tablespoons corn syrup

1 tablespoon 1% milk

½ cup Splenda Granular

1 teaspoon vanilla

2 egg whites

¾ cup old-fashioned oats

¼ cup finely chopped pecans

2 tablespoons all-purpose flour

½ teaspoon baking soda

1 teaspoon orange zest

STEPS:

1. Preheat oven to 375°F. Lightly spray cookie sheet with nonstick cooking spray.

2. In a medium saucepan, melt margarine. Stir in corn syrup, milk, Splenda, and vanilla. Remove from heat and thoroughly whisk in egg whites.

3. In a medium bowl, mix together remaining ingredients. Stir oat mixture into saucepan and let set 3 minutes.

4. Drop wet batter by tablespoonfuls onto cookie sheets, flattening middles slightly. Bake 12-14 minutes. Cool slightly before removing.

PER SERVING (1 COOKIE)

Calories 60	Fat 3.5 grams (.5 saturated)
Carbohydrate 6 grams	Fiber 1 gram
Protein 1 gram	Sodium 70 milligrams

Diabetic exchange = ½ Carbohydrate, 1 Fat
WW point comparison = 1 point

Sugar Blend Snickerdoodles

Serves Twenty-Four

My son James loves Snickerdoodle cookies, known for their sugar-cinnamon topping. To make sure they kept their trademark crunchy exterior and soft interior, I used Splenda Sugar Blend for Baking for my reduced-fat recipe, and I was very pleased with the result—a Snickerdoodle worthy of the name with only half the usual fat and sugar. James was also delighted.

INGREDIENTS:

1 ¾ cups all-purpose flour

½ teaspoon baking soda

½ teaspoon cream of tartar

⅓ cup margarine, at room temperature

½ cup Splenda Sugar Blend for Baking

1 tablespoon corn syrup

1 teaspoon vanilla

1 large egg

2 tablespoons sugar

2 teaspoons cinnamon

STEPS:

1. Preheat oven to 375°F. Lightly spray cookie sheet with nonstick cooking spray.

2. In a large bowl, combine flour, baking soda, and cream of tartar. Whisk to combine.

3. In a medium bowl, with an electric mixer, beat margarine and Splenda together until well blended.

4. Add the corn syrup, vanilla, and egg, and beat until light and creamy. Gradually add the flour mixture to the creamed mixture, beating until just combined. Cover and chill for 10 minutes.

5. In a small bowl, combine the sugar and the cinnamon.

6. With moist hands, roll dough into 24 1-inch balls. Roll the balls in the sugar/cinnamon mixture and place on prepared cookie sheet. Flatten cookies with the bottom of a drinking glass.

7. Bake for 5 minutes. Cookies will be slightly soft. Remove to a wire rack to cool.

PER SERVING (1 COOKIE)

Calories 75	Fat 2.5 grams (1 saturated)
Carbohydrate 12 grams	Fiber 0 grams
Protein 1 gram	Sodium 55 milligrams

Diabetic exchange = 1 Carbohydrate
WW point comparison = 2 points

Soft Sour Cream Sugar Cookies

Serves Twenty

Making soft tender "sugar" cookies with so little sugar is amazing. This recipe can also be used as a base recipe for any sugar cookie variation. You may choose one of your own, or use one of the two I've provided. I particularly enjoy the citrus flavor. To make this recipe as a rolled cookie, add 1 additional tablespoon flour and chill dough before rolling out (⅛-inch thick) and cutting into desired shapes.

INGREDIENTS:

1 ½ cups all-purpose flour

½ teaspoon baking soda

½ teaspoon baking powder

⅓ cup margarine

¾ cup Splenda Granular

2 tablespoons corn syrup

¼ cup sour cream

1 teaspoon vanilla

¼ teaspoon almond extract

1 egg yolk

To make Sour Cream Citrus Rounds, add the extra tablespoon of flour and zest of your choice and form dough into a log 2 ½ inches in diameter and 5 inches long. Chill for 30 minutes and then slice into ¼-inch slices. Bake at 375°F for 7-8 minutes.

STEPS:

1. Preheat oven to 375°F. Lightly spray baking sheet with nonstick cooking spray.

2. In a small bowl, sift together flour, baking soda, and baking powder. Set aside.

3. In a medium bowl, with an electric mixer, beat together margarine, Splenda, and corn syrup until creamy. Add sour cream, vanilla, almond extract, and egg yolk. Beat 2-3 minutes until light and fluffy.

4. Stir in flour mixture.

5. Drop by tablespoonfuls onto baking sheet. Press down on dough with bottom of glass or spatula to flatten. Bake 3 minutes; tap pan against baking rack to flatten cookies; bake 4-5 more minutes.

CITRUS VARIATION: Add 1 teaspoon lemon, lime, or orange zest to batter.

PER SERVING (1 COOKIE)

Calories 70	Fat 3 grams (1 saturated)
Carbohydrate 10 grams	Fiber 0 grams
Protein 1 gram	Sodium 70 milligrams

Diabetic exchange = ½ Fat, ½ Carbohydrate
WW point comparison = 2 points

Sliced Lemon Coconut Wafers

Serves Twenty

This is called a slice-and-bake cookie because the dough is formed into logs, chilled, and then sliced into cookies before baking. Flavored with fresh lemon zest and toasted coconut, they bake up nice and crisp. Try this lovely treat with a hot cup of tea.

INGREDIENTS:

2 cups all-purpose flour

1 teaspoon baking powder

⅛ teaspoon salt

½ cup margarine, softened

¼ cup Splenda Sugar Blend for Baking

1 large egg

1 tablespoon each lemon juice and water

1 teaspoon vanilla

½ cup shredded coconut, toasted

1 tablespoon lemon zest

STEPS:

1. In a medium bowl, mix together flour, baking powder, and salt. Set aside.

2. In a large bowl, with an electric mixer, cream margarine and Splenda Sugar Blend together until light and creamy. Add egg, water, lemon juice, and vanilla. Beat until thoroughly blended. Add flour mixture and beat just until blended.

3. Stir in coconut and lemon zest. Divide dough in half and form 2 logs, each about 2 inches in diameter and 5 inches long.

4. Wrap in Saran Wrap or waxed paper and chill in refrigerator until firm.

5. To bake, preheat oven to 375°F.

6. Slice cookies into ¼ inch slices and place onto ungreased cookie sheet. Bake for 8–10 minutes or until bottoms are lightly browned.

7. Remove and cool on rack. Store in an airtight container.

PER SERVING (2 COOKIES)

Calories 105	Fat 5 grams (1.5 saturated)
Carbohydrate 10 grams	Fiber .5 gram
Protein 2 grams	Sodium 65 milligrams

Diabetic exchange = 1 Carbohydrate, 1 Fat
WW point comparison = 2 points

Coconut Crispy Macaroons

Serves Twelve

These confection-like cookies use crispy rice cereal in place of some of the coconut in a traditional macaroon. The result is a terrific combination of crispy and chewy.

INGREDIENTS:

2 egg whites

Pinch cream of tartar

¾ cup Splenda Granular

1 teaspoon vanilla

1 ¾ cups crispy rice cereal

1 cup unsweetened coconut

STEPS:

1. Preheat oven to 275°F. Spray baking sheets with nonstick cooking spray.

2. In a large bowl, beat egg whites and cream of tartar until soft peaks form. Gradually add Splenda and beat until stiff.

3. Fold in vanilla, cereal, and coconut. Drop by tablespoonfuls onto pans.

4. Bake 18-20 minutes or until lightly browned and firm to touch.

Lining baking sheets with parchment or using silicone baking mats (like Silplat) works especially well with macaroons.

PER SERVING (2 COOKIES)

Calories 65	Fat 4 grams (4 saturated)
Carbohydrate 6 grams	Fiber 1 gram
Protein 1 gram	Sodium 55 milligrams

Diabetic exchange = ½ Carbohydrate, 1 Fat

WW point comparison = 1 point

Chocolate Chip Meringue Cookies

Serves Twelve

These easy-to-make chocolatey meringues are slightly chewy yet light as air. When you use Splenda Sugar Blend for Baking, there's enough sugar (for structure) so that the "simple" meringue method (simply beating egg whites and sugar together) works beautifully.

INGREDIENTS:

3 egg whites

¼ teaspoon cream of tarter

½ cup Splenda Sugar Blend for Baking

1 tablespoon cornstarch

6 tablespoons mini chocolate chips

STEPS:

1. Preheat oven to 225°F.

2. Spray cookie sheets and silicone liners or parchment (if using) with cooking spray. Set aside.

3. In a large mixing bowl, with an electric mixer on high speed, beat egg whites until foamy. Beat in cream of tartar and then continue to beat whites while adding Splenda Sugar Blend, 1 tablespoon at a time, until all is incorporated. Continue to beat until very stiff peaks form. Turn off mixer.

4. Sift in cornstarch and stir in chocolate chips.

5. Using a tablespoon, drop batter onto cookie sheets. Bake for 45 minutes or until meringues feel firm.

6. Store in airtight container.

For the holidays, substitute a couple of tablespoons of crushed peppermint for a couple tablespoons of the chocolate chips to create a Peppermint Chocolate Chip Meringue Cookie. But don't add cocoa powder to this recipe because the meringues won't dry.

PER SERVING (2 COOKIES)

Calories 65

Carbohydrate 12 grams

Protein 1 gram

Fat 1.5 grams (.5 saturated)

Fiber 0 grams

Sodium 20 milligrams

Diabetic exchange = 1 Carbohydrate

WW point comparison = 1 point

Italian Meringue Cookies

Serves Nine

There are two standard methods for making meringue cookies: the "simple or common method" and the "Italian method." The "simple" method of beating egg whites and sugar until stiff requires more real sugar for structure, but you can further reduce the sugar by using the "Italian" method in which you beat boiling sugar syrup into stiffened egg whites. Here, I substituted Splenda for most of the sugar in the recipe with great success.

INGREDIENTS:

¾ cup Splenda Granular

3 tablespoons sugar

⅔ cup water

3 egg whites

¼ teaspoon cream of tartar

½ teaspoon vanilla

½ teaspoon orange, lemon, peppermint, or other flavored extracts (optional)

According to Julia Child, perfectly baked meringues will not change shape or change color. The meringue mixture should simply dry out. It is during baking that meringues need adequate sugar for structure or they will collapse and turn brown.

STEPS:

1. Preheat oven to 275°F. Line baking sheet with parchment paper (or foil).

2. Combine Splenda sugar and water and swirl pan by its handle, but do not stir while syrup comes to a boil. Cover pan, reduce heat, and let simmer.

3. In a large bowl, beat egg whites until foamy. Beat in cream of tartar and increase speed until egg whites form stiff peaks.

4. Remove cover from sugar syrup and insert candy thermometer. Boil syrup until it reaches 235°F. Immediately remove from stove and gradually add boiling syrup into egg whites while beating vigorously.

5. Beat in vanilla and any optional flavorings until mixture is very stiff (5-6 minutes).

6. Drop by tablespoonfuls or pipe through a pastry bag onto baking sheets. Bake 1 hour, turn off oven, and allow meringues to cool in oven until they can be easily removed from parchment paper.

PER SERVING (2 COOKIES)

Calories 30	Fat 0 grams (0 saturated)
Carbohydrate 6 grams	Fiber 0 grams
Protein 2 grams	Sodium 20 milligrams

Diabetic exchange = ½ Carbohydrate
WW point comparison = 1 point (up to 5 cookies for 1 point!)

Molasses Cutouts

Serves Twenty-Four

These cookies are a hit with kids! Not only do they love making and rolling out the dough, but they gobble them up and ask for more. This recipe is great for holiday cutouts like gingerbread men or as an accent to ice cream by cutting them out with a 2 ½-inch decorative biscuit cutter.

INGREDIENTS:

2 cups all-purpose flour

2 teaspoons baking soda

1 teaspoon cinnamon

¾ teaspoon ginger

½ teaspoon cloves

¼ cup prune puree or 1 small jar baby food prunes

¼ cup shortening

1 cup Splenda Granular

3 tablespoons molasses

1 large egg

STEPS:

1. Preheat oven to 350°F. Lightly spray baking sheet with nonstick cooking spray.

2. In a small bowl, sift together flour, baking soda, cinnamon, ginger, and cloves. Set aside.

3. In a medium bowl with an electric mixer, beat together prunes, shortening, Splenda, molasses, and egg until creamy. Beat 2-3 minutes until light and fluffy.

4. Stir in flour mixture.

5. Divide the dough in half and wrap in plastic. Refrigerate until firm, at least 1 hour. (The dough can be refrigerated for up to 2 days.)

6. Remove 1 disk of dough from the refrigerator and cut in half. Return the unused portion to the refrigerator. Lightly flour a work surface. Roll the dough to ⅛-inch thickness and cut dough into desired shapes.

7. Place on baking sheet. Bake 6-8 minutes.

GINGER COOKIE VARIATION: For each cookie, roll 1 tablespoon dough into a ball and place on baking sheet. Flatten with bottom of glass. Dust lightly with granulated sugar if desired prior to baking.

PER SERVING (1 COOKIE)

Calories 70	Fat 2.5 grams (1 saturated)
Carbohydrate 11 grams	Fiber 1 gram
Protein 1 gram	Sodium 135 milligrams

Diabetic exchange = 1 Carbohydrate
WW point comparison = 1 point

Zebra Bars

Serves Fifteen

These moist, dark chocolate bars swirled with white sweetened cream cheese are hard to resist.

INGREDIENTS:

1 ounce semisweet chocolate

2 tablespoons margarine

¼ cup prune puree or 1 small jar baby food prunes

3 tablespoons brown sugar

⅔ cup Splenda Granular

¼ cup cocoa powder

1 large egg + 2 egg whites

1 ½ teaspoons vanilla

1 tablespoon hot tap water

¾ cup all-purpose flour

½ teaspoon baking powder

¼ teaspoon baking soda

½ cup tub-style light cream cheese

2 tablespoons egg white (reserved)

2 tablespoons Splenda Granular

1 tablespoon powdered sugar

½ teaspoon vanilla

STEPS:

1. Preheat oven to 325°F. Spray a 7 x 11- or 9 x 9-inch baking pan with nonstick cooking spray.

2. Melt chocolate and margarine together in medium bowl by microwaving on high for 30-60 seconds. Whisk in next 7 ingredients (prunes through hot water), reserving 2 tablespoons of egg white. Blend until smooth.

3. Sift in flour, baking powder, and baking soda. Mix just until flour is incorporated and pour batter into prepared baking pan.

4. In a small bowl, beat together last 5 ingredients (cream cheese through vanilla). Drop by teaspoonfuls onto top of chocolate batter. Pull knife through batter to create swirl pattern.

5. Bake 20-22 minutes, just until center feels firm to touch.

PER SERVING (1 BAR)

Calories 90	Fat 4 grams (2 saturated)
Carbohydrate 12 grams	Fiber 1 gram
Protein 3 grams	Sodium 105 milligrams

Diabetic exchange = 1 Carbohydrate, ½ Fat
WW point comparison = 2 points

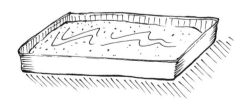

Chocolate Brownies

Serves Twelve

Before you look at the ingredients, let me warn you that I, too, would be skeptical of a brownie recipe that calls for black beans. Even though I had heard of this technique, I never before had any desire to make brownies with beans. However, attempts to use traditional low-fat brownie formulas with Splenda Sugar Blend for Baking didn't work, I finally thought, why not? Surprise—the pureed beans were just the ticket to keeping these cakey brownies dark, moist, and fudgey and all without any trace of bean flavor. And that's no beans...

INGREDIENTS:

¾ **cup black beans, drained**

3 **tablespoons butter, melted**

2 **large eggs**

1 **teaspoon vanilla**

½ **cup Splenda Sugar Blend for Baking**

6 **tablespoons Dutch-process cocoa powder**

¼ **cup all-purpose flour**

¼ **teaspoon baking powder**

3 **tablespoons chopped walnuts (optional)**

STEPS:

1. Preheat the oven to 325°F. Spray an 8 x 8-inch baking pan with nonstick cooking spray.

2. In a small bowl, combine cocoa powder, flour, and baking powder. Set aside.

3. Place beans and melted butter in a food processor and puree until beans are completely smooth (like a thick paste). Scrape bean mixture out of processor and into a medium-sized bowl.

4. With a wooden spoon, beat in eggs, vanilla, and Splenda Sugar Blend until well mixed. Add cocoa mixture and stir just until incorporated. Stir in nuts, if desired.

5. Spoon batter into prepared pan. Bake for 13-15 minutes or until center just springs back when touched (do not overbake).

6. Cool in pan on wire rack

Black beans are a great source of complex carbohydrates and fiber. And because they replaced some of the all-purpose flour in this recipe, they actually lowered the overall carbohydrates.

PER SERVING

Calories 100

Carbohydrate 14 grams

Protein 3 grams

Fat 4 grams (2 saturated)

Fiber 2 grams

Sodium 95 milligrams

Diabetic exchange = 1 Carbohydrate, 1 Fat

WW point comparison = 2 points

Frosted Pumpkin Bars

Serves Twenty-Four

Looking for a new holiday cookie recipe that is healthier than the rest? Here you go—these festive, cake-like pumpkin bars are sweet, moist, and very delicious. The finishing touch is the rich-tasting cream cheese frosting. All this and half your daily dose of vitamin A—it's enough to make you want to celebrate.

INGREDIENTS:

COOKIE BARS

2 cups all-purpose flour

1 teaspoon baking powder

½ teaspoon baking soda

1 ½ teaspoons cinnamon

½ teaspoon nutmeg

¼ teaspoon mace

6 tablespoons margarine, softened

1 2 ½-ounce jar baby food prunes

1 15-ounce can pumpkin purée

⅔ cup Splenda Granular

2 tablespoons molasses

1 ½ teaspoons vanilla

1 egg

¼ cup raisins, finely chopped

FROSTING

4 ounces tub-style light cream cheese

6 ounces nonfat cream cheese

¼ cup Splenda Granular

2 tablespoons orange juice

STEPS:

1. Preheat oven to 350°F. Spray a 9 x 13-inch pan with nonstick cooking spray.

2. Mix together flour, baking powder, baking soda, and spices.

3. In a large bowl, with an electric mixer, cream the margarine and prunes together. Add pumpkin purée, Splenda, molasses, vanilla, and egg. Beat well. Stir in flour mixture. Stir in raisins.

4. Spoon into prepared pan and smooth. Bake for 20 minutes, or until cake springs back when lightly touched in the center. Cool on rack.

5. In a small bowl, with an electric mixer, beat all frosting ingredients until smooth and fluffy. Spread frosting onto cool bars.

6. Refrigerate.

PER SERVING (1 BAR)

Calories 75	Fat 3.5 grams (1 saturated)
Carbohydrate 8 grams	Fiber .5 grams
Protein 3 grams	Sodium 120 milligrams

Diabetic exchange = ½ Carbohydrate, 1 Fat
WW point comparison = 2 points

In order to reduce the impact of an ingredient (whether the flavor or the nutritional consequence), you can eliminate it, substitute something else for it, or use less, like I did here. Because finely chopping the raisins disperses them better, you don't need as many, which helps to keep the sugar content low in this seasonal favorite.

High-Protein Peanut Butter Oat Bars

Serves Twenty

*I sent a pan of these to school with my third-grade
son. He brought back the empty pan and a stack of
thank-you notes. Not too bad for a "healthy" cookie.*

INGREDIENTS:

6 tablespoons chunky peanut butter

3 tablespoons margarine, softened

2 tablespoons honey

¾ cup Splenda Granular

2 eggs

1 ½ teaspoons vanilla

2 cups old-fashioned oats

½ cup nonfat milk powder

½ cup all-purpose flour

¼ teaspoon salt

½ teaspoon baking powder

¼ teaspoon baking soda

1 ounce semisweet chocolate

STEPS:

1. Preheat oven to 350°F. Spray a 9 x 13-inch
   pan with nonstick cooking spray.

2. In large bowl, beat together peanut butter,
   margarine, and honey. Add Splenda, eggs, and
   vanilla. Beat until fluffy (2–3 minutes). Stir in
   remaining ingredients except chocolate.

3. Press mixture into baking pan and bake for
   12–14 minutes. Remove from oven.

4. In a small bowl, melt chocolate in microwave
   for 30–60 seconds. Stir and drizzle with a fork
   over pan. Cool, cut, and serve bars.

*In the United
States, 50 percent
of all peanuts produced
are turned into peanut
butter, that very
American staple.*

PER SERVING (1 BAR)

Calories 95	Fat 5 grams (1 saturated)
Carbohydrate 10 grams	Fiber 1 grams
Protein 5 grams	Sodium 110 milligrams

Diabetic exchange = ½ Carbohydrate,
1 Medium-Fat Meat
WW point comparison = 2 points

Apricot Oat Bars

Serves Fifteen

These compact bar cookies are filled with the goodness of oats and the delectable taste of apricot jam. Because these cookies travel well, they would make a nice addition to your next picnic or potluck.

INGREDIENTS:

½ **cup all-purpose flour**

½ **cup graham-cracker crumbs**

1 **cup old-fashioned oats (not instant)**

½ **cup Splenda Granular**

⅓ **cup margarine**

¾ **cup low-sugar apricot preserves**

1 **tablespoon brown sugar**

Try any of your favorite low-sugar jams or preserves in these bars but remember that "all fruit" or "no sugar added" does not necessarily mean low sugar. Check the nutrition label: Smucker's Low-Sugar Apricot Preserves contain only 6 grams of sugar per tablespoon as opposed to the usual 12-14.

STEPS:

1. Preheat oven to 350°F. Spray an 8-inch square baking pan with nonstick cooking spray.

2. Place flour, graham cracker crumbs, oats, Splenda, and margarine in a food processor. Pulse several times until the mixture resembles coarse crumbs.

3. Press ⅔, or about 2 cups, of the mixture into the prepared baking pan.

4. Bake for 15 minutes. Remove from oven and spread preserves over hot crust.

5. Add 1 tablespoon of brown sugar to remaining oat mixture, and spread oat layer over jam. Press down lightly on oats layer.

6. Bake for 20-25 minutes, or until lightly browned. Cool in pan on wire rack.

PER SERVING (1 BAR)

Calories 115	Fat 4 grams (1 saturated)
Carbohydrate 17 grams	Fiber 1 gram
Protein 2 grams	Sodium 60 milligrams

Diabetic exchange = 1 Carbohydrate, 1 Fat
WW point comparison = 2 points

Old-Fashioned Lemon Squares

Serves Sixteen

Just like the traditional favorite: creamy, sweet, and tart lemon topping blankets a buttery crust. Be sure to use fresh lemon juice and zest for the best result. If you would like to create a lime square, use lime juice and zest and add 2 tablespoons Splenda Granular to the filling.

INGREDIENTS:

CRUST

1 cup all-purpose flour

⅓ cup Splenda Granular

¼ teaspoon salt

¼ teaspoon baking powder

4 tablespoons cold margarine or butter

2 tablespoons buttermilk

TOPPING

2 large eggs + 1 egg white

3 tablespoons all-purpose flour

½ cup Splenda Sugar Blend for Baking

⅔ cup lemon juice

⅓ cup buttermilk

1 tablespoon lemon zest

2 teaspoons powdered sugar (optional)

STEPS:

1. Preheat oven to 375°F. Spray an 8-inch square pan with nonstick cooking spray.

2. CRUST: In a medium bowl, mix together flour, Splenda, salt and baking powder. Cut in margarine or butter.until mixture resembles coarse crumbs. Sprinkle buttermilk over mix and blend. Press onto the bottom of the prepared pan. Chill for 15 minutes and then bake for 15–20 minutes or until lightly browned.

3. TOPPING: In a large bowl, beat the eggs and egg whites with flour and Splenda Sugar blend. Beat in the lemon juice, and zest. Pour over hot crust.

4. Turn oven down to 350°F and bake bars an additional 18–20 minutes or until top is set. Cool completely.

5. Just prior to serving, dust with powdered sugar if desired.

A pastry chef created these new lemon bars for me, using the original recipe from Fantastic Food with Splenda. She doubled the lemon juice, added buttermilk to both the crust and the filling, and used the Splenda Sugar Blend to create a terrific new take on an old favorite.

PER SERVING (1 BAR)

Calories 100	Fat 4 grams (1 saturated)
Carbohydrate 15 grams	Fiber 0 gram
Protein 2 grams	Sodium 75 milligrams

Diabetic exchange = 1 Carbohydrate, 1 Fat
WW point comparison = 2 points

Creamy Lemon Cheesecake Bars

Serves Twelve

I've seen some terrific low-fat lemon bar recipes. They may be low in fat, but the sugar—wow! There is sugar in the crust, more sugar in the filling, and, of course, they are topped with even more sugar. My lush lemon cheesecake bars are a wonderful alternative with less than half the calories, one-third the fat, and one-quarter the sugar content. Be sure not to overbake or the creamy filling may crack.

INGREDIENTS:

CRUST

½ cup all-purpose flour

½ cup graham-cracker crumbs

2 tablespoons brown sugar

3 tablespoons Splenda Granular

4 tablespoons cold margarine

FILLING

¾ cup low-fat cottage cheese

½ cup tub-style light cream cheese

¾ cup Splenda Granular

1 tablespoons all-purpose flour

½ teaspoon baking powder

½ teaspoon vanilla

1 tablespoon lemon rind

3 tablespoons lemon juice

1 large egg

1 large egg white

STEPS:

1. Preheat oven to 350°F. Spray an 8-inch square baking pan with nonstick cooking spray.

2. In a medium bowl, mix flour, graham cracker crumbs, brown sugar, and Splenda.

3. CRUST: Cut in margarine until mixture resembles fine crumbs. Press into prepared pan and bake for 15 minutes.

4. FILLING: Place cottage cheese in a food processor and puree until very smooth. Add the remaining ingredients, except egg and egg white and blend until smooth. Add egg and then egg white, pulsing just briefly to incorporate.

5. Pour filling over hot crust. Return to oven and bake for 18–20 minutes, or until cheese mixture appears just set.

PER SERVING (1 BAR)

Calories 135	Fat 6 grams (2 saturated)
Carbohydrate 14 grams	Fiber 0 grams
Protein 4 grams	Sodium 180 milligrams

Diabetic exchange = 1 Carbohydrate, 1 Fat
WW point comparison = 3 points

Traditional lemon bars use as much as 1 ½ cups of sugar for the same size recipe, which gives you 24 grams of sugar in every bar.

Raspberry Shortbread Triangles

Serves Nine

These pretty cookies remind me of an afternoon tea. They are quite attractive and rather tasty. Because the shortbread really stands out, I use butter in the crust for optimal flavor.

INGREDIENTS:

CRUST

1 cup all-purpose flour

6 tablespoons Splenda Granular

½ teaspoon lemon rind

¼ cup butter

2 tablespoons light cream cheese or buttermilk

TOPPING

½ cup raspberry low-sugar preserves

½ cup fresh or frozen (partially thawed) raspberries

¼ cup Splenda Granular

1 large egg white

1 teaspoon butter

⅛ teaspoon almond extract

⅓ cup sliced almonds

STEPS:

1. Preheat oven to 350°F. Spray an 8-inch square pan with nonstick cooking spray.

2. CRUST: In a medium bowl, mix together flour, Splenda, and lemon rind. Cut in butter. Mix in cream cheese or drizzle in buttermilk until you have fine crumbs.

3. Press onto the bottom of the prepared pan. Bake for 15 minutes.

4. TOPPING: In a medium bowl, with an electric mixer, beat preserves and remaining ingredients except almonds. Pour over hot, baked crust. Return to oven for 15 minutes longer.

5. Open oven and sprinkle almonds evenly over top. Continue to bake 10 minutes longer.

6. Cool on rack 15 minutes. Divide into 9 squares by cutting 3 x 3; then cut each square in half to form 18 triangles.

PER SERVING (2 COOKIES)

Calories 150	Fat 7 grams (4 saturated)
Carbohydrate 19 grams	Fiber 1 gram
Protein 3 grams	Sodium 65 milligrams

Diabetic exchange = 1 Carbohydrate, 1 ½ Fat

WW point comparison = 3 points

Chocolate Almond Biscotti

Serves Eighteen

In Italian, biscotti means "twice baked." Baking these cookies twice makes them crunchy and perfect for dipping. Serve biscotti with a cup of regular coffee or tea or choose one of the wonderful flavored versions from the "Tempting Hot Beverages and Homemade Dry Mixes" chapter.

INGREDIENTS:

¼ cup whole almonds

1 ¾ cups all-purpose flour

¼ cup cocoa powder

1 teaspoon baking powder

¼ teaspoon baking soda

⅛ teaspoon salt

2 tablespoons butter

3 tablespoons brown sugar

¾ cup Splenda Granular

2 eggs + 1 egg white

1 teaspoon almond extract

1 teaspoon vanilla extract

Dough may crack along the bottom edge of the biscotti due to expansion without sugar, which gives these biscotti a unique mushroom shape when sliced.

PER SERVING (2 COOKIES)

Calories 90

Carbohydrate 12 grams

Protein 1 gram

Fat 3 grams (0 saturated)

Fiber 1 gram

Sodium 70 milligrams

Diabetic exchange = 1 Carbohydrate

WW point comparison = 2 points

STEPS:

1. Preheat oven to 350°F. Lightly spray baking sheet with nonstick cooking spray.

2. Spread the almonds in another baking pan and place in oven. Bake for 5 minutes or until slightly browned. Remove and coarsely chop. Set aside.

3. In a medium bowl, sift together flour, cocoa powder, baking powder, baking soda, and salt. Stir in almonds.

4. In a medium bowl, cream butter and brown sugar with an electric mixer. Add Splenda, eggs, egg white, and almond and vanilla extracts. Beat until smooth. Fold in flour mixture with a spoon or spatula.

5. Use hands to form dough into 2 "logs" —each 8 inches long with 2-inch diameter. Place logs onto greased cookie sheet and flatten top slightly.

6. Bake for 30 minutes or until a toothpick inserted into the center comes out clean. Remove from oven; let cool 5-10 minutes. Reduce oven to 300°F. Slice ¼-inch slices on diagonal down each log.

7. Place cookies back on baking sheet and bake for 20 minutes longer until firm. Cookies will become even harder as they cool.

Orange Ginger Pecan Biscotti

Serves Thirty

Baking these fragrant cookies has become an annual holiday tradition for me. I love the compliments when I send them to friends and family. Package these with the Homemade Spice Chai Mix (page 72) for a lovely hostess gift.

Ingredients:

¼ **cup pecan halves**

2 **cups all-purpose flour**

¾ **teaspoon ground ginger**

½ **teaspoon ground nutmeg**

1 **teaspoon baking powder**

¼ **teaspoon baking soda**

1 ½ **tablespoons finely chopped crystallized ginger**

2 **whole eggs + 1 egg white**

1 **tablespoon oil**

2 **tablespoons orange juice concentrate**

¾ **cup Splenda Granular**

1 **tablespoon orange zest**

The traditional dunking cookie known as biscotti was enjoyed in Italy as early as the fourteenth century.

Steps:

1. Preheat oven to 350°F. Lightly spray cookie sheet with nonstick cooking spray.

2. Spread the pecans in a baking pan and place in oven. Bake for 5 minutes or until slightly browned. Remove and finely chop. Set aside.

3. In a medium bowl, sift together flour, ginger, nutmeg, baking powder, baking soda, and ginger. Stir in pecans.

4. In a medium bowl, whisk together remaining ingredients. Beat until smooth. Fold in flour mixture with a spoon or spatula. Use hands to form dough into 2 "logs"—each 8 inches long 2-inches in diameter. Place logs onto greased cookie sheet and flatten top slightly.

5. Bake for 30 minutes or until a toothpick inserted into the center comes out clean. Remove from oven and let cool 5-10 minutes. Reduce oven to 300°F. Slice ¼-inch slices on the diagonal down each log.

6. Place cookies back on baking sheet and bake for 20 minutes longer until firm. (Cookies will become firmer as they cool.)

Per Serving (1 Cookie)

Calories 50

Carbohydrate 9 grams

Protein 2 grams

Fat 1.5 grams (1 saturated)

Fiber 0 grams

Sodium 35 milligrams

Diabetic exchange = ½ Carbohydrate

WW point comparison = 1 point

Classic Pies

Single-Crust Pie Pastry

Graham-Cracker Pie Crust

Double Chocolate Crumb Crust

Vanilla Crumb Crust

Pumpkin Pie

Apple Pie in a Bag

Sour Cream Apple Pie

Strawberry Rhubarb Pie

Peach Custard Pie

Old-Fashioned Custard Pie

Key Lime Pie

Peanut Butter Pie

Triple Vanilla Cream Pie

Banana Cream Pie

Coconut Cream Pie

Chocolate Mint Cream Pie

Strawberry Dream Pie

Lemon Meringue Pie

Lemon Chiffon Pie

Pumpkin Chiffon Pie

Chocolate Chiffon Pie

The fact is, nothing is more classically American than a good old-fashioned fruit pie. The Pilgrims actually get credit for creating the first dessert pies (and no, they weren't pumpkin but fruit pies), but it was the early settlers who quickly adopted them and were soon found eating them at almost every meal. Before you knew it, pies were as American as—well, apple pie!

Far from the pioneer days, most pies today are bought rather than made, and they're so full of sugar, fat, and calories we can barely afford to eat a piece at one meal, let alone every meal. It's truly a shame because there isn't anything more welcoming, more impressive, or better-smelling than a home-baked pie.

To help you welcome those you love, this chapter offers easy-to-make crusts and comforting home-style pies like classic Strawberry Rhubarb and Peach Custard Pies that retain all their old-fashioned style albeit with new-found goodness. Sure to win you rave reviews are also the silky smooth cream pies like Coconut Cream and Chocolate Mint Cream Pie complete with sweet crumb crusts. Then there are the silky smooth cream pies like Coconut Cream and Chocolate Mint Cream Pie to help you get rave reviews with their sweet crumb crusts.

You will also find healthy updates for holiday classics such as Pumpkin Chiffon, Old-Fashioned Custard, and, of course, the old standby Apple Pie. And saving perhaps best for last (if you're a lemon-lover like me), there's a superb, sweet Lemon Meringue Pie, with an amazing 75 percent reduction in sugar. Anyway you slice it, these pies are set to please.

Single-Crust Pie Pastry

Serves Eight

In order to have a great pie, you have to start with a great pie crust. This tasty version has half the fat of some homemade crusts and only one-quarter the saturated fat. After many trials, I verified that solid fats are the best choice for a tender crust. Additionally, the small amount of sugar helps to reduce gluten formation, also resulting in a more tender crust. If you are short on time, or simply prefer to use a pre-made crust, many are available. Be sure to check labels to ensure the nutritional content is comparable to this one and you'll be fine.

INGREDIENTS:

1 cup all-purpose flour

1 tablespoon cornstarch

2 teaspoons sugar

¼ teaspoon salt (scant)

2 tablespoons shortening

2 tablespoons margarine (or butter, which adds 1 gram of saturated fat)

2 tablespoons ice water

2 tablespoons cold 1% milk

STEPS:

1. Stir together the flour, cornstarch, sugar, and salt in a medium mixing bowl. Cut in the margarine and the shortening, using either a pastry blender or fingers, until the margarine and shortening are evenly distributed in small crumbs.

2. Mix the milk and the water together and pour onto the flour mixture. Toss the pastry with a fork until it just starts to come together. Using your hands, form the pastry into a ball by gathering up all the flour mixture. (You may add a few more drops of milk or water, if necessary, to pull all the flour together.)

3. Pat the ball into a flat disk and place between two sheets of wax paper. Refrigerate for 30 minutes or longer. Roll dough from center to edge to form an 11-inch circle.

4. Remove paper and gently ease the pastry into a 9-inch pie pan. Press down on pastry to smooth. Patch as needed; turn excess under edges and crimp or flute, as desired.

Continues on next page...

PER SERVING

Calories 110	Fat 6 grams (1.5 saturated)
Carbohydrate 13	Fiber 0 grams
Protein 2 grams	Sodium 70 milligrams

Diabetic exchange = 1 Carbohydrate, 1 Fat
WW point comparison = 2 ½ points

5. To partially bake empty shell: Preheat oven to 425°F. Line entire shell, including edges, with aluminum foil, shiny side down, and fill foil with pie weights, rice, or dried beans. Place in bottom third of oven and bake for 10 minutes. Remove the foil and weights, prick the crust with a fork, and return to oven. Bake 10 minutes longer. If air pockets form, open oven and press down on crust with a spoon to flatten. Fill and bake according to recipe directions.

6. To fully bake empty shell: Preheat oven to 425°F. Line bottom and sides of shell with aluminum foil, shiny side down, and fill foil with pie weights, rice, or dried beans. Place in bottom third of oven and bake for 10 minutes. Remove the foil and weights, prick the crust with a fork, return to oven, and bake for 12–15 minutes more or until lightly browned. If air pockets form, open oven and press down on crust with a spoon to flatten.

The single gram of sugar in this pie pastry helps to keep the crust tender; do not substitute Splenda.

Graham-Cracker Pie Crust

Serves Eight

This pie crust is versatile and easy—and everyone loves a graham-cracker crust. I've lowered the fat by cutting back on butter and using some egg white to help bind the crust. When purchasing a pre-made graham-cracker crust, be sure to look for the low-fat version.

INGREDIENTS:

1 cup graham-cracker crumbs
  (about 16 squares)
2 tablespoons Splenda Granular
1 tablespoon margarine or butter, melted
1 tablespoon canola oil
2 tablespoons egg white

STEPS:

1. Preheat oven to 350°F. Lightly coat a 9-inch pie pan with nonstick cooking spray.

2. Combine crumbs in a small bowl or food processor (pulse to make crumbs from crackers).

3. Add Splenda, margarine, and oil, and stir or pulse. Add egg white and stir well, or pulse again.

4. Pour crumb mixture into pie plate. With your fingers, the back of a spoon, or with a sheet of plastic wrap, press down on the crumbs until they coat the bottom and sides of the pie plate.

5. Bake 8–10 minutes. Remove and cool.

Butter, margarine, or oil? This recipe calls for stick margarine (90 calories, 10 grams of fat, and trans fat and saturated fat combined, equal 3.5 grams per tablespoon) and canola oil (120 calories, 13.5 grams of fat, 1 saturated per tablespoon) to create a healthy and reduced-fat pie crust. You can substitute butter, with its great flavor, for some or all of the fat. Butter has 100 calories and 11 grams of fat, with 7 of them saturated, per tablespoon.

PER SERVING

Calories 90	Fat 4.5 grams (.5 saturated)
Carbohydrate 12 grams	Fiber 0 grams
Protein 1 gram	Sodium 105 milligrams

Diabetic exchange = 1 Carbohydrate, 1 Fat
WW point comparison = 2 points

Double Chocolate Crumb Crust

Serves Eight

This is a really good crust. A definite hit with all chocoholics. On my first attempt, I simply used chocolate graham crackers instead of cookie crumbs to lower the calories and the sugar content, but I was dismayed at the loss of the deep chocolate flavor. The solution—a bit of cocoa powder to give back the rich chocolate taste, and Splenda to sweeten it up. Chocolate grahams never had it so good.

INGREDIENTS:

1 cup chocolate graham-cracker crumbs (about 14 squares)

1 tablespoon Dutch-process cocoa powder (like Hershey's European)

¼ cup Splenda Granular

1 tablespoon margarine or butter, melted

1 tablespoon canola oil

1 large egg white (about 3 tablespoons)

STEPS:

1. Preheat oven to 350°F. Lightly coat a 9-inch pie pan with nonstick cooking spray.

2. Combine crumbs in a small bowl or food processor (pulse to make crumbs from crackers).

3. Add cocoa powder, Splenda, margarine, and oil, and stir or pulse. Add egg white and stir well, or pulse again.

4. Pour crumb mixture into pie plate. With your fingers, the back of a spoon, or with a sheet of plastic wrap, press down on the crumbs until they coat the bottom and sides of the pie plate.

5. Bake 8-10 minutes.

If you are really watching your carbohydrates, be sure to look closely before substituting a pre-made chocolate crumb crust. I have yet to see one on the market that does not have considerably more sugar, carbs, and calories.

PER SERVING

Calories 90
Carbohydrate 12 grams
Protein 2 grams

Fat 4.5 grams (.5 saturated)
Fiber 0 grams
Sodium 95 milligrams

Diabetic exchange = 1 Carbohydrate, 1 Fat
WW point comparison = 2 points

Vanilla Crumb Crust

Serves Eight

Would you believe there are actually fewer calories and grams of carbohydrate in this cookie crust than an ordinary pastry crust? I use this for the Coconut and Triple Vanilla Cream Pies, and it's wonderful. It would also be delicious filled with your favorite chocolate filling.

INGREDIENTS:

**1 generous cup crushed vanilla wafers
(about 28 wafers)**

1 tablespoon Splenda Granular

2 teaspoons margarine or butter, melted

1 tablespoon egg white

STEPS:

1. Preheat oven to 350°F. Lightly coat a 9-inch pie pan with nonstick cooking spray.

2. Combine crumbs in a small bowl or food processor (pulse to make crumbs from wafers). Add Splenda and margarine, and stir or pulse. Add egg white and stir well, or pulse again.

3. Pour crumb mixture into pie plate. With your fingers, the back of a spoon, or with a sheet of plastic wrap, press down on the crumbs until they coat the bottom and sides of the pie plate.

4. Bake 8–10 minutes.

Quick tip: Put your hand in a baggie before pressing on the crumbs. The crumbs don't stick to plastic, so it's easy to get them to stick to the pan rather than your hand.

PER SERVING

Calories 85

Carbohydrate 10 grams

Protein 1 gram

Fat 4.5 grams (1 saturated)

Fiber 0 grams

Sodium 60 milligrams

Diabetic exchange = ½ Carbohydrate, 1 Fat

WW point comparison = 2 points

Pumpkin Pie

Serves Eight

It just wouldn't be Thanksgiving without pumpkin pie. This lightened-up version is the perfect ending to a heavy holiday meal. If you prefer your pie to have a lighter rather than custard-like texture, simply beat the egg whites and fold them in last. The Pumpkin Custard Cups on page 252 feature a variation of this same delicious filling prepared in individual soufflé or custard cups to make a delicious, creamy custard that eliminates the crust and its calories altogether.

INGREDIENTS:

1 Single-Crust Pie Pastry, page 325, or prepared single pie crust★

1 large egg white beaten with 2 teaspoons water

FILLING

1 large egg

2 egg whites (or additional large egg)

1 15-ounce can pumpkin purée (not pie filling)

¾ cup Splenda Granular

1 tablespoon molasses

2 teaspoons cornstarch

1 ½ teaspoons cinnamon

½ teaspoon ginger

¼ teaspoon allspice (optional)

¼ teaspoon ground cloves

1 teaspoon vanilla

1 12-ounce can evaporated skim milk

★When choosing a frozen pie crust, select one that is "deep dish."

PER SERVING

Calories 200	Fat 7 grams (1.5 saturated)
Carbohydrate 26 grams	Fiber 3 grams
Protein 8 grams	Sodium 160 milligrams

Diabetic exchange = 1 Carbohydrate, 1 Fat,
½ Low-Fat Milk, ½ Vegetable
WW point comparison = 4 points

STEPS:

1. Preheat oven to 425°F.

2. Prepare a partially baked crust according to directions. Remove from oven and immediately brush bottom and sides of the crust with beaten egg white and water mixture. Set aside to dry.

3. In a large bowl, whisk egg and egg whites. Add pumpkin, Splenda, molasses, cornstarch, spices, and vanilla. Mix well. Whisk in milk.

4. Pour the filling into pre-baked crust.

5. Bake at 425°F for 10 minutes. Then reduce the heat to 350°F and bake 30-35 minutes longer, or until a knife inserted near the center comes out clean. Cool pie on wire rack.

A common problem with pumpkin pies is soggy crust. A low-fat shell only exacerbates the problem. The solution is partially baking and then sealing the crust to keep it crisp. Follow the same instructions if you choose to start with an uncooked convenience pie crust.

Apple Pie in a Bag

Serves Eight

When I was growing up, we visited "apple country" every fall. The area produced a cookbook, and one of our most treasured recipes: a one-crust apple pie with a crumb topping that you actually cooked in a paper grocery bag. The bag recirculates the steam and imparts a wonderful texture to the apples. I've made the pie many times with no ill effects. I mention this because the USDA now states that this cooking method may not be safe due to chemicals and dyes in the paper. My solution—use a cooking bag like the ones used to roast meat—although I must admit I miss ripping open that paper bag and finding a glorious, cooked apple pie inside.

INGREDIENTS:

1 Single-Crust Pie Pastry, page 325, or prepared single pie crust★

6 medium baking apples (about 2 ½ pounds)

1 tablespoon lemon juice

6 tablespoons Splenda Granular

1 tablespoon all-purpose flour

½ teaspoon cinnamon

TOPPING

½ cup Splenda Granular

6 tablespoons all-purpose flour

½ teaspoon cinnamon

3 tablespoons margarine

1 Brown-and-Serve cooking bag

1 tablespoon all-purpose flour

STEPS:

1. Preheat oven to 400°F.

2. Prepare and set aside one 9-inch unbaked pie pastry shell.

3. Pare, core, and quarter apples. Halve each quarter crosswise to make chunks. Place in a large bowl and sprinkle with lemon juice.

4. Add 6 tablespoons Splenda, flour, and cinnamon and toss to coat well. Spoon coated apples into shell.

5. TOPPING: Combine ½ cup Splenda, flour, and cinnamon in a small bowl. Cut in margarine until mixture resembles coarse crumbs.

6. Sprinkle over the apples, covering entire top of pie. Place 1 tablespoon of flour into Brown-and-Serve bag and shake. Slide pie into the cooking bag and seal.

7. Place on cookie sheet and place in oven. Bake for 50 minutes or until apples are bubbly and top is browned.

8. Carefully open bag and remove pie.

★When choosing a frozen pie crust, select one that is "deep dish."

PER SERVING

Calories 210	Fat 9 grams (2.5 saturated)
Carbohydrate 30 grams	Fiber 2 grams
Protein 2 grams	Sodium 140 milligrams

Diabetic exchange = 1 Fruit, 1 Carbohydrate, 2 Fat
WW point comparison = 5 points

Bakeries often sweeten no-sugar-added pies with concentrated apple juice which is the same as using sugar. Always check labels carefully—or better yet—make your own pie.

Sour Cream Apple Pie

Serves Eight

My goal was to create a truly old-fashioned, home-style recipe for apple pie, and this recipe hit the mark. This pie has a creamy texture, a cinnamon flavor, and a wonderful aroma that is sure to make any guest feel right at home. Prebaking the crust prevents the custard from making the crust soggy.

INGREDIENTS:

1 Single-Crust Pie Pastry, page 325, or
  1 prepared single piecrust
1 large egg white beaten with
  2 teaspoons water
2 large eggs
1 cup light sour cream
¾ cup Splenda Granular
2 tablespoons all-purpose flour
2 teaspoons vanilla
¼ teaspoon salt
2 ½ cups peeled, thinly sliced baking apples

STREUSEL TOPPING

4 tablespoons all-purpose flour
3 tablespoons butter
⅓ cup Splenda Granular
1 teaspoon cinnamon

★ When choosing a frozen pie crust,
  select one that is "deep dish."

STEPS:

1. Preheat oven to 425°F. Prepare a partially baked crust according to directions. Remove from oven and immediately brush bottom and sides of the crust with beaten egg white and water mixture. Set aside to dry.

2. In a large bowl, lightly beat together eggs, sour cream, Splenda, flour, vanilla, and salt. Stir in apples and pour into the prebaked pie shell. Bake for 15 minutes. Reduce heat to 350°F and bake for 20 minutes more, covering edges of pie crust with foil as needed to prevent overbrowning.

3. While pie is baking, combine the topping ingredients. Remove pie from oven and sprinkle on topping. Return pie to oven and bake an additional 20 minutes.

4. Cool completely before serving.

PER SERVING

Calories 190	Fat 11 grams (5 saturated)
Carbohydrate 20 grams	Fiber 1 gram
Protein 4 grams	Sodium 150 milligrams

Diabetic exchange = 1 Fruit, ½ Carbohydrate, 2 Fat
WW point comparison = 4 points

Strawberry Rhubarb Pie

Serves Eight

Contrary to what it may seem, a deep-dish pie is technically not a pie extra deep with filling, but a fruit pie with only a top crust. And in fact, it should baked it in a shallow dish to allow for enough crust in relation to the fruit. By eliminating the bottom crust, I have been able to ensure that there's a generous amount of the sweet and tangy filling that makes this pie special. I also spread the filling and the crust across a large 10-inch pie plate for more crust in each bite.

INGREDIENTS:

**3 cups 1-inch pieces fresh rhubarb
(about 1 ¼ pounds rhubarb stalks)**

3 cups hulled and halved fresh strawberries

¾ cup Splenda Granular

2 tablespoons cornstarch

½ teaspoon orange zest

**1 Single-Crust Pie Pastry, page 325,
or 1 sheet refridgerated pie dough**

1 tablespoon milk

1 teaspoon granulated sugar

STEPS:

1. Preheat oven to 375°F. Set aside 10-inch pie plate.

2. In a large bowl, toss rhubarb and strawberries with Splenda and cornstarch. Place berries into pie plate and sprinkle with orange zest.

3. Roll out pie dough on lightly floured surface or between two sheets of wax paper into an 11-inch round. Place pie crust on top of fruit and crimp edges onto edges of pie pan. Lightly brush surface of dough with milk and sprinkle with sugar.

4. Before placing pie in oven, cut several vents into crust. Bake for 40-45 minutes or until fruit juices are bubbling.

Fresh rhubarb is actually a vegetable, not a fruit, and you can find it most easily from early winter until early summer. It is a rich source of vitamin C and insoluble fiber.

PER SERVING

Calories 160

Carbohydrate 22 grams

Protein 2 grams

Fat 7 grams (1 saturated)

Fiber 3 grams

Sodium 120 milligrams

Diabetic exchange = 1 Carbohydrate, ½ Fruit, 1 Fat

WW point comparison = 3 points

Peach Custard Pie

Serves Eight

This pie is a sweet burst of summer. Fresh peaches are set into an open crust and covered with a creamy custard. There is just enough custard to hold the peaches together, letting the fresh peach taste shine through.

INGREDIENTS:

1 Single-Crust Pie Pastry, page 325, or prepared pie crust

1 egg white beaten with 2 teaspoons water

1 large egg

1 tablespoon melted butter or margarine

1 tablespoon all-purpose flour

1 tablespoon cornstarch

¼ teaspoon almond extract

¼ cup nonfat half-and-half

½ cup + 2 tablespoons Splenda Granular

2 pounds fresh peaches, peeled and sliced (8 medium peaches)

1 tablespoon all-purpose flour

1 teaspoon sugar (optional)

STEPS:

1. Preheat oven to 425°F.

2. Prepare a partially baked pie crust according to directions. Remove from oven and immediately brush bottom and sides of the crust with beaten egg white and water. Set aside.

3. In a small mixing bowl, whisk together the large egg and next 6 ingredients to make the custard. Set aside.

4. Place the peach slices in a large bowl, and toss with 2 tablespoons Splenda and 1 tablespoon flour. Place peaches into crust. You may arrange them by making circles, starting from the outside of the crust and working your way in, or you can just spoon them in randomly.

5. Pour the custard mixture over the peaches.

6. Bake at 425°F for 10 minutes. Turn oven down to 350°F and continue to bake 40 minutes longer, or until the custard appears firmly set when the pan is shaken.

7. Sprinkle 1 teaspoon of sugar for "sparkle" if desired. Let cool on a rack.

PER SERVING

Calories 190	Fat 9 grams (2.5 saturated)
Carbohydrate 25 grams	Fiber 2 grams
Protein 3 grams	Sodium 135 milligrams

Diabetic exchange = 1 Carbohydrate, ½ Fruit, 2 Fat
WW point comparison = 4 points

Compare this recipe to a piece of classic Peach Custard Pie, which has 398 calories, 21 grams of fat (13 saturated), 49 carbohydrate, and 26 grams of sugar.

Old-Fashioned Custard Pie

Serves Eight

When I say "old-fashioned," I really mean it. Fanny Farmer published a recipe for Custard Pie in 1918 that doesn't vary much from recipes of today. Back then, eggs and milk were common ingredients found on farms, which made this pie a household staple. Today, with so many choices, custard pie often takes a back seat, but when it comes to pies that will never fade away, this is one of them.

INGREDIENTS:

1 Single-Crust Pie Pastry, page 325 or prepared single pie crust★

4 large eggs

¾ cup Splenda Granular

⅛ teaspoon salt

2 cups 1% milk

½ cup nonfat half-and-half

1 ½ teaspoons vanilla

½ teaspoon nutmeg

★When choosing a frozen pie crust, select one that is "deep-dish."

PER SERVING

Calories 190	Fat 7 grams (2.5 saturated)
Carbohydrate 27 grams	Fiber 2 grams
Protein 7 grams	Sodium 200 milligrams

Diabetic exchange = 1 ½ Carbohydrate, 1 Vegetable, 1 Fat
WW point comparison = 4 points

STEPS:

1. Preheat oven to 425°F. Line pie crust with foil and fill with beans or pie weights and bake for 10 minutes.

2. Remove beans or weights, prick crust with a fork, and bake additional 10 minutes or until lightly browned. Remove from oven. Reduce heat to 325°F.

3. Meanwhile, in a large bowl, beat eggs until light. Beat in Splenda, salt, vanilla, and nutmeg. Set aside.

4. In a small saucepan, bring milks to a low simmer. Whisk a small amount of hot milk into eggs. Whisk remaining milk into egg mixture.

5. Pour hot custard mixture into hot crust and place on baking sheet. Place in oven and bake for 30 minutes or until sharp knife inserted into center comes out clean. Cool on rack and then refrigerate.

New research shows that eggs, once shunned because of the cholesterol found in the yolks, have lots of health benefits. Besides being nutritious, they may help reduce age-related macular degeneration and even reduce the risk for heart disease. In fact, the American Heart Association now says that an egg a day is fine for most people.

Key Lime Pie

Serves Eight

*The highly aromatic key lime is the key to this famous
Florida pie. These limes can be found in many markets
during the summer months. If you can't find fresh limes,
bottled key lime juice works in these recipes, too.*

INGREDIENTS:

**Prepare 1 Graham-Cracker Pie Crust,
page 327**

FILLING

1 envelope unflavored gelatin

⅔ cup key lime juice, divided

1 cup 1% milk

1 large egg + 2 egg yolks, lightly beaten

1 tablespoon lime zest

¾ cup Splenda Granular

4 ounces nonfat cream cheese

4 ounces tub-style light cream cheese

STEPS:

1. In a medium saucepan, dissolve the gelatin in ⅓ cup of the key lime juice for 3 minutes. Add milk, egg, egg yolks, remaining ⅓ cup key lime juice, lime zest, and Splenda. Cook for 10 minutes or until mixture thickens. Remove from heat. Cool slightly.

2. Place the cream cheeses in a large bowl and beat on medium speed with an electric mixer until creamy. Beat in lime mixture until smooth. Refrigerate mixture until thoroughly cooled, stirring every 10 minutes.

3. Pour mixture into cooled pie shell and chill at least 2 hours or overnight. Serve cold.

KEY LIME MOUSSE CUPS: Beat 1 large egg white and fold into cooked cooled custard. Pour key lime filling into 6 custard cups (130 calories, 6 grams fat, 9 grams each of carbohydrate and protein).

PER SERVING

Calories 160

Carbohydrate 16 grams

Protein 8 grams

Fat 6 grams (2.5 saturated)

Fiber .5 gram

Sodium 260 milligrams

Diabetic exchange = 1 Carbohydrate, 1 Fat
WW point comparison = 3 points

Key lime pie is the official pie of Florida and can be found in just about every restaurant in the Florida Keys. There are many versions, but those featuring graham-cracker crusts are by far the most common. Light whipped topping is what I recommend for a garnish.

Peanut Butter Pie

Serves Ten

Although a child could make this easy no-bake pie, it's definitely not just for kids. A Double Chocolate Crumb Crust is filled with a subtle, rich, and creamy peanut butter filling and topped with drizzled chocolate. This pie looks and tastes as decadent as it sounds.

INGREDIENTS:

Prepare 1 Double Chocolate Crumb Crust, page 328

½ cup low-fat peanut butter

4 ounces tub-style light cream cheese

4 ounces fat-free cream cheese

½ cup Splenda Granular

¼ cup 1% milk

½ teaspoon vanilla

1 ¾ cups light whipped topping, thawed

1 tablespoon Chocolate Fudge Sauce, page 430, or 2 teaspoons Hershey's light chocolate syrup

STEPS:

1. In a large mixing bowl, using an electric mixer, cream the peanut butter and the cream cheeses. Add the Splenda, milk, and vanilla. Beat until smooth. Fold in whipped topping and spoon into crust.

2. Warm the fudge sauce and drizzle back and forth across the top of the pie in a decorative fashion. You don't need to warm chocolate syrup.

3. Refrigerate for at least 1 hour before serving.

Studies show that the monounsaturated fats in peanut butter are good for your health. If you prefer even more peanut flavor, add 2 tablespoons more reduced-fat peanut butter. This increases calories by 20, and fat, carbohydrate, and protein by 1 gram each.

PER SERVING

Calories 210

Carbohydrate 20 grams

Protein 7 grams

Fat 11 grams (4 saturated)

Fiber 1 gram

Diabetic exchange = 1 Carbohydrate, 1 Medium-Fat Meat, 1 Fat

WW point comparison = 5 points

Triple Vanilla Cream Pie

Serves Eight

You get not one, not two, but three doses of vanilla in one creamy pie. This easy-to-make cream pie really fills the bill if you enjoy vanilla. After imagining how good vanilla pudding would taste in the Vanilla Wafer Crust, I couldn't resist putting the two together. Add a vanilla-scented cream topping and you've got one delectable pie.

INGREDIENTS:

1 Vanilla Crumb Crust, page 329

1 recipe Vanilla Pudding (pie variation) page 245

1 ½ cups light whipped topping, thawed

½ teaspoon vanilla extract

STEPS:

1. Prepare crust according to recipe and set aside.

2. Prepare pudding using the pie variation.

3. Pour hot filling into pie crust. Cover surface with plastic wrap. Cool completely on rack; then refrigerate until completely chilled.

4. In a medium bowl, combine whipped topping and vanilla extract. Spread over pie. Refrigerate.

PER SERVING

Calories 180　　　　　Fat 8 grams (3 saturated)
Carbohydrate 22 grams　Fiber 0 grams
Protein 4 grams　　　　Sodium 90 milligrams

Diabetic exchange = 1 ½ Carbohydrate, 1 Fat, ½ Lean Meat
WW point comparison = 4 points

Banana Cream Pie

Serves Eight

While watching The Food Network, I saw a very famous chef (okay, Mr."Bam") fixing his favorite Banana Cream Pie. Cream, butter, sugar, more sugar and bananas—served with not one, but two sauces—chocolate and caramel. Decadent? Definitely, but I wondered—just what one piece of that cost (nutritionally speaking). Take a deep breath—990 calories, 110 grams of carbohydrate (with 93 from sugar), a whole day's worth of fat and two days of saturated fat—bam! (PS: Thinking it must have been a huge portion? Nope, it was a 9-inch pie and served 10.)

INGREDIENTS:

1 Vanilla Crumb Crust, page 329

FILLING

1 ½ teaspoons unflavored gelatin

1 ¾ cups 1% milk

¾ cup nonfat half-and-half

¾ cup Splenda Granular

2 tablespoons cornstarch

1 egg + 1 egg white, lightly beaten

2 teaspoons vanilla

1 teaspoon brandy extract (may omit, but very good)

1 large banana, thinly sliced

1 cup light whipped topping

STEPS:

1. Prepare recipe according to recipe. Set aside.

2. In a small saucepan, sprinkle the gelatin over ¼ cup of the milk; let stand 3 minutes until softened. Set aside.

3. In a medium saucepan, whisk together 1 ½ cups milk, half-and-half, Splenda, cornstarch, egg, and egg white until smooth. Cook over medium heat, stirring constantly, being sure to include edges of pot, until pudding comes to a low boil. Then cook 1 minute more. Remove from the heat and stir in the dissolved gelatin, vanilla, and brandy extract. Set aside.

4. Spread ⅓ of the cream filling into the cooled pie shell. Top evenly with the sliced bananas; then spread the remaining cream filling evenly on top. Let cool to room temperature; refrigerate until firm, about 2 hours.

5. Serve each slice with 2 tablespoons whipped topping, or, for a pretty touch, pipe whipped topping all along the sides of the pie using a piping bag fitted with a large star tip.

Want to kick this up a notch? You may drizzle it with the Deep Dark Chocolate Sauce (page 429) and/or throw on a few chocolate shavings, like they do in Emeril's restaurant, for only a few extra calories.

PER SERVING

Calories 180	Fat 7 grams (2.5 saturated)
Carbohydrate 24 grams	Fiber 1 gram
Protein 5 grams	Sodium 135 milligrams

Diabetic exchange = ½ Low-Fat Milk, 1 Carbohydrate, 1 Fat
WW point comparison = 4 points

Coconut Cream Pie

Serves Eight

I love this dessert! I rarely eat more than a bite or two of cream pie because I know how very rich it is. A slice of traditional coconut cream pie can clock in at close to 500 calories. It took more than a trick or two to keep the luscious richness of the original, though using far less sugar and fat. I knew I had accomplished my goal when my neighbor, who has experience as a professional recipe developer, couldn't believe that this pie was not only low in fat but had only 2 tablespoons of sugar in the entire recipe.

INGREDIENTS:

1 Vanilla Crumb Crust, recipe page 329

FILLING

¾ cup Splenda Granular

¼ cup cornstarch

1 ½ cups 1% milk

1 cup nonfat half-and-half

1 large egg + 1 large egg yolk, lightly beaten

2 teaspoons coconut extract

½ teaspoon vanilla

2 tablespoons coconut

TOPPING

1 tablespoon cornstarch

2 tablespoons sugar

1/3 cup water

4 large egg whites (or 6 pasteurized eggs whites)

¼ teaspoon cream of tartar

½ cup Splenda Granular

3 tablespoons coconut

STEPS:

1. FILLING: In a medium saucepan, combine the Splenda and cornstarch. Stir in the milk and half-and-half; whisk until cornstarch completely dissolves. Add beaten eggs and whisk. Bring mixture to a low simmer over medium heat, stirring constantly. As the mixture starts to thicken, remove from heat briefly, and stir thoroughly, to discourage lumps. Return to heat, simmer, and stir for 1-2 minutes. Pudding should be thick and smooth.

2. Stir in extracts and coconut and remove from heat. Pour into the prepared crust and cover with plastic wrap while preparing topping.

3. Preheat oven to 400°F.

4. TOPPING: Place cornstarch and sugar in a small saucepan. Add water and stir to form a smooth, thin paste. Place over medium heat and bring to a boil. Stir and boil for 15 seconds. Cover the thick translucent paste with a lid.

PER SERVING

Calories 210	Fat 8 grams (4 saturated)
Carbohydrate 28 grams	Fiber 0 grams
Protein 6 grams	Sodium 150 milligrams

Diabetic exchange = 2 Carbohydrate, 1 Lean Meat, 1 Fat
WW point comparison = 5 points

5. In a medium (grease-free) bowl, beat egg whites until foamy. Beat in cream of tartar. Gradually beat in Splenda. Beat until stiff but not dry. Lower speed and beat in the cornstarch paste, 1 tablespoon at a time. Increase speed and beat 30 seconds.

6. Remove plastic wrap from pie and cover with meringue topping. Be sure to cover the pie all the way to the edges of the crust. Sprinkle the 3 remaining tablespoons of coconut on top.

7. Bake 10 minutes or until coconut toasts and meringue lightly browns. Remove and cool on rack. When completely cool, place in the refrigerator. The exterior of the meringue can toughen slightly after a day.

To make a meringue, you need to stabilize the egg whites. The cornstarch/sugar paste makes this possible with only a fraction of the sugar normally used in traditional meringue recipes.

Chocolate Mint Cream Pie

Serves Eight

One day when I was running into the grocery store for a few more testing ingredients, I happened to notice a local Girl Scout troop selling cookies. I wondered if there was anybody who didn't love those Thin Mint cookies. Just then, inspiration struck—the result was Chocolate Mint Cream Pie. Another Thin Mint fan, a lovely reader and Weight Watcher, told me she chose this pie for a gathering of her friends, and her only suggestion—you better make two!

INGREDIENTS:

1 Double Chocolate Crumb Crust, page 328

FILLING

¾ cup Splenda Granular

3 tablespoons cornstarch

2 tablespoons Dutch-process cocoa powder

½ cup nonfat half-and-half

1 ½ cups 1% milk

1 large egg, beaten

¹/₃ cup semisweet chocolate chips

1 teaspoon vanilla

TOPPING

1 ½ cups light whipped topping, thawed

2 tablespoons Splenda Granular

¼ teaspoon mint extract (scant)

STEPS:

1. FILLING: In a medium saucepan, combine the Splenda, cornstarch, and cocoa powder. Stir in the milk and half-and-half; whisk until cornstarch completely dissolves. Add the beaten egg and whisk. Bring mixture to a low simmer over medium heat, stirring constantly.

2. As the mixture starts to thicken, remove from heat briefly and stir thoroughly, including sides of the pot, to discourage lumps.

3. Add chocolate, return to heat, simmer and stir for 1–2 minutes. Pudding should be thick and smooth.

4. Add vanilla, stir, and remove from heat. Pour hot filling into pie-crust. Cover surface with plastic wrap. Cool completely on rack, then refrigerate until completely chilled.

5. TOPPING: In a medium bowl, fold Splenda and mint extract into whipped topping. Spread over pie. Refrigerate.

CHOCOLATE PEPPERMINT PIE VARIATION:
Substitute peppermint extract for mint.

PER SERVING

Calories 200	Fat 8 grams (4 saturated)
Carbohydrate 27 grams	Fiber 1 gram
Protein 5 grams	Sodium 150 milligrams

Diabetic exchange = 2 Carbohydrate, 1 Lean Meat, 1 Fat
WW point comparison = 4 points

Strawberry Dream Pie

Serves Seven

If you love your berries dished up with whipped cream, you'll love this easy, no bake pie.

INGREDIENTS:

1 Vanilla Crumb Crust, recipe page 329

FILLING

2 cups sliced strawberries

⅔ cup Splenda Granular

1 tablespoon lemon juice

1 envelope unflavored gelatin

¼ cup light cranberry juice

1 ½ cups light whipped topping

STEPS:

1. Mash the strawberries in a small bowl and stir in Splenda and lemon juice. Set aside for about 15 minutes, until the sugar dissolves and the mixture is very juicy.

2. Pour cranberry juice over gelatin. Let set 3 minutes. Heat to dissolve gelatin and cool slightly. Stir gelatin into strawberry mixture. Let cool completely. Fold in light whipped topping. Pour into the pie shell and chill until firm, for at least 1 hour.

3. Garnish with additional whip cream and a ring of whole strawberries.

It only took a few simple changes to slash most of the sugar and two-thirds of the fat from this easy-to-make luscious strawberry pie.

PER SERVING

Calories 170	Fat 9 grams (2 saturated)
Carbohydrate 21 grams	Fiber 2 grams
Protein 2 grams	Sodium 90 milligrams

Diabetic exchange = 1 Fruit, ½ Carbohydrate, 2 Fat
WW point comparison = 4 points

Lemon Meringue Pie

Serves Eight

My parents have a lemon tree so my mom bakes lots of lemon meringue pies. In an effort to cut back the sugar, she substituted the same amount of Splenda Sugar Blend for Baking and told me it was great. Uh-oh. Mom failed to note that she should have used only half as much "Blend" (see page 13). I worked hard with this recipe and in order to reduce the sugar without sacrificing the taste, I use both Splenda Sugar for Baking (for its real sugar qualities) and Splenda Granular (for its great sweetening power with minimal calories and carbs). The result is a lemon pie with only 25 percent of the original sugar that's good enough to pass on even to Mom.

INGREDIENTS:

1 pre-baked Single-Crust Pie Pastry, page 325, or prepared single pie crust

FILLING

¼ cup Splenda Sugar Blend for Baking

¾ cup Splenda Granular

½ cup lemon juice

1/3 cup cornstarch

1 ½ cups water

1 tablespoon lemon zest

Pinch salt

3 large egg yolks (may use additional yolk if desired)

1 tablespoon butter

TOPPING

1/3 cup water

1 tablespoon cornstarch

2 tablespoons Splenda Sugar Blend for Baking

4 large egg whites

¼ cup Splenda Granular

STEPS:

1. FILLING: Whisk Splenda Sugar Blend, Splenda Granular, lemon juice, and cornstarch together in a medium saucepan until smooth. Whisk in water, zest, salt, and egg yolks until there are no pieces of egg yolk visible. Place pan over medium heat and cook, stirring until mixture reaches a full boil. Simmer 1 minute, while stirring. Remove from heat and whisk in butter. Pour into prepared pie crust and cover with plastic wrap.

2. TOPPING: Immediately whisk together water, cornstarch, and Splenda Sugar Blend in a small saucepan. Place on medium heat and cook, while whisking, until mixture comes to a boil. Boil for 15 seconds until a thick, smooth, translucent paste forms. Cover. In a medium (grease-free) bowl, beat egg whites until foamy. Beat in cream of tartar. Beat in Splenda Granular until soft peaks form. Beat in cornstarch gel, 1 tablespoon at a time. Remove plastic wrap from pie and cover with meringue topping. Be sure to cover all the way to the edges of the crust. Bake for 10 minutes until meringue lightly browns. Cool on rack; then refrigerate.

PER SERVING

Calories 220	Fat 10 grams (4 saturated)
Carbohydrate 29 grams	Fiber 0 grams
Protein 4 grams	Sodium 145 milligrams

Diabetic exchange = 2 Carbohydrate, 2 Fat

WW point comparison = 5 points

Lemon Chiffon Pie

Serves Eight

Luscious and yet so light, this creamy no-bake pie is a nice change from traditional lemon meringue. You actually do make meringue, but rather than placing it on top of the filling, you fold it in. I have chosen to place this pie in a graham-cracker crust, but you can use a pre-baked pastry crust if you prefer.

INGREDIENTS:

1 Graham-Cracker Pie Crust, page 327

¹/₃ cup water

1 envelope unflavored gelatin

1 large egg + 2 large egg yolks, beaten (reserve whites to use below)

¾ cup + 3 tablespoons Splenda Granular

½ cup lemon juice

2 teaspoons grated lemon rind

2 large egg whites (or 3 pasteurized egg whites)

¼ teaspoon cream of tartar

1 cup light whipped topping, thawed

STEPS:

1. Place water in a small heavy saucepan and sprinkle gelatin on top. Let set for 3 minutes to soften gelatin.

2. Whisk in beaten eggs, ¾ cup Splenda, lemon juice, and lemon rind.

3. Stirring constantly with a wooden spoon or heatproof rubber spatula, cook over medium heat until the mixture thickens enough to coat spoon or spatula. Pour the mixture into a large bowl and refrigerate for 45 minutes–1 hour, until mixture mounds when dropped from a spoon, but is not set.

4. In a large bowl, beat egg whites and cream of tartar until foamy. Continue to beat; gradually add remaining Splenda and beat until stiff but not dry.

5. Using a large rubber spatula or spoon, gently fold egg whites into cooled lemon mixture. Fold in whipped topping. Spoon filling into crust and refrigerate for at least 3 hours.

PER SERVING

Calories 140	Fat 6 grams (2 saturated)
Carbohydrate 18 grams	Fiber 0 grams
Protein 6 grams	Sodium 145 milligrams

Diabetic exchange = 1 Carbohydrate, 1 Medium-Fat Meat
WW point comparison = 3 points

A traditional lemon chiffon recipe has twice the fat, but that is nothing compared to the sugar. Are you ready for this? It has 59 grams of carbohydrate, 53 of them from sugar.

Pumpkin Chiffon Pie

Serves Eight

I really wanted to create a nice, tall, light, no-bake pumpkin pie, so my testers and I were up to our elbows in pumpkin for days while creating this one. The funny thing is that after all of the testing, we unanimously agreed that the chiffon pie created from my original pumpkin pie ingredients took the prize. This pie is a delightful finish to a heavy holiday meal.

INGREDIENTS:

1 9-inch Graham-Cracker Pie Crust, page 327, or prepared graham cracker crust★

FILLING
¼ cup cold water

1 envelope unflavored gelatin

1 15-ounce can pumpkin

2 eggs, separated

1 can (12-ounce) low-fat evaporated milk

¾ cup Splenda Granular

1 tablespoon molasses

1 ½ teaspoons cinnamon

½ ground ginger

¼ teaspoon ground cloves

2 tablespoons sugar

★ When choosing a pre-made graham-cracker crust, choose one that is "deep dish."

STEPS:

1. Make pie crust and set aside to cool.

2. In a small bowl, sprinkle gelatin over cold water.

3. In a medium saucepan, combine pumpkin, egg yolks, milk, Splenda, molasses, cinnamon, ginger, and cloves. Stir to combine. Add gelatin mixture. Bring to a simmer over medium heat.

4. Remove from heat, transfer to a large bowl, and cool to room temperature. Move to refrigerator for ½ hour.

5. Place egg whites in a medium bowl. Beat until frothy. Add sugar and continue to beat until stiff but not dry.

6. Fold egg whites into cooled pumpkin mixture and spoon into pie crust, mounding towards center.

7. Cover and refrigerate for at least 4 hours.

Pumpkin is a definite fall favorite. In this book, you will also find Spicy Pumpkin Muffins, Pumpkin Scones, Pumpkin Pecan Bread, Frosted Pumpkin Bars, a Pumpkin Mousse with Gingersnaps, Pumpkin Cheesecake, Pumpkin Custard Cups, a festive Cream Cheese-Filled Pumpkin Roll, and, of course, traditional Pumpkin Pie.

PER SERVING

Calories 190	Fat 7 grams (2.5 saturated)
Carbohydrate 27 grams	Fiber 2 grams
Protein 7 grams	Sodium 200 milligrams

Diabetic exchange = 1 ½ Carbohydrate, 1 Vegetable, 1 Fat
WW point comparison = 4 points

Chocolate Chiffon Pie

Serves Eight

Deep, dark chocolate filling in a deep, dark chocolate crust. Need I say more?

INGREDIENTS:

1 Double Chocolate Crumb Crust, page 328

FILLING

1 envelope unflavored gelatin

¾ cup cold water

6 tablespoons cocoa powder

1 teaspoon cornstarch

½ cup Splenda Granular

3 egg yolks, lightly beaten

1 teaspoon vanilla

3 egg whites

2 tablespoons granulated sugar

¾ cup light whipped topping

STEPS:

1. Soften gelatin in ¼ cup cold water. Set aside.

2. Place ½ cup water in small saucepan. Thoroughly whisk in cocoa, cornstarch, Splenda, and egg yolks. Place over medium heat and cook, while stirring, until thickened and smooth. Whisk in softened gelatin and vanilla. Remove from heat.

3. Pour into a large bowl and let cool, stirring occasionally, until mixture mounds when dropped by spoon.

4. In a medium bowl, beat egg whites until frothy. Add sugar and beat until stiff but not dry. Fold into chocolate mixture. Gently fold in whipped topping and spoon into prepared crust.

MOCHA CHIFFON PIE VARIATION: Use ½ cup strong coffee in place of ½ cup water.

PER SERVING

Calories 160	Fat 6 grams (2 saturated)
Carbohydrate 21 grams	Fiber 2 grams
Protein 6 grams	Sodium 125 milligrams

Diabetic exchange = 1 Carbohydrate, 1 Fat
WW point comparison = 3 points

Crisps, Cobblers, Strudels, and Tarts

Apple Crisp

Kim's Mixed Berry Crisp

Blueberry Peach Crisp with
    Almond Topping

Strawberry Rhubarb Brown
    Sugar Crumble

Blackberry Cobbler

Apple Strudel

Sweet Cheese Strudel

Quick Raspberry Cream
    Cheese Strudel

Fresh Fruit Tart

Phyllo Apple Packets

Microwave Cinnamon Baked Apple

Wonderful crisps, cobblers, strudels, and tarts are all created when delicious fruit fillings are topped, wrapped, or placed on top of tender pastry doughs or sweetened crumbs. If you've ever wondered, the difference between a cobbler and a crisp is that a crisp is topped with a crumb or streusel topping, while a cobbler is topped with sweet biscuit or rolled-out pie dough. Strudels also use a dough, only it's rolled very thin and then folded to create crispy layers around the sweetened fruit that's rolled inside. And as for tarts, they are made like pies, only in fluted tart pans, with the fruit filling atop the sweetened pie dough or rich pastry.

The other two items that the traditional versions of all of these recipes have in common are butter and sugar—and lots of 'em.

What my fruit and pastry desserts have in common is that they all allow the beauty of the fruit to take center stage and not be overshadowed by sugar and fat. For example, Apple Strudel is easy and healthy when you replace high-fat pastry dough with phyllo dough, and Blueberry Peach Crisp has just the right amount of crisp topping created by using wholesome oats and almonds. Furthermore, Light Bisquick used with low-sugar raspberry jam and fresh raspberries creates a Quick Raspberry Cream Cheese Strudel indistinguishable from the original, while the beautiful Fresh Fruit Tart is a winner when made with low-sugar pastry cream and lots of fresh berries. Good for you fruit that tastes this good—now that really is wonderful.

Apple Crisp

Serves Six

In the autumn, when apples are plentiful and the weather turns cooler, my thoughts turn to apple crisp. With hot tender apples and crispy oat topping, apple crisp is one of life's great comfort foods. Many crisp recipes are low in fat but loaded with sugar, but this one is simply full of apples.

INGREDIENTS:

FILLING

2 pounds firm baking apples (about 5 medium) peeled, cored, cut into ¼-inch slices

2 tablespoons orange juice

¼ cup Splenda Granular

1 tablespoon all-purpose flour

½ teaspoon cinnamon

TOPPING

½ cup all-purpose flour

6 tablespoons old-fashioned oats

½ cup Splenda Granular

1 teaspoon cinnamon

4 tablespoons light butter

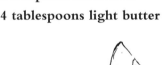

STEPS:

1. Preheat oven to 350°F. Lightly coat an 8 x 8-inch glass baking dish with nonstick cooking spray.
2. FILLING: In a large bowl, toss the apples with the orange juice.
3. Mix Splenda, flour, and cinnamon together in a small bowl. Sprinkle over the apples and toss.
4. Place apples in the prepared pan.
5. TOPPING: In a medium bowl, mix together the flour, oats, Splenda, and cinnamon. Cut in butter with a pastry blender, fork, or fingers until mixture resembles fine crumbs. Sprinkle topping over apples.
6. Bake for 40-45 minutes, or until apples are tender and crisp is bubbling. Delicious when served warm.

How do you make butter "light"? By whipping in water. Light butter has half the calories and fat of regular butter because it is half water. This makes it a poor choice for cookies and cakes that require a more solid fat, but a good choice here, by giving you twice the butter to cut in without adding any more fat or calories.

PER SERVING

Calories 175	Fat 4.5 grams (2 saturated)
Carbohydrate 33 grams	Fiber 4 grams
Protein 2 grams	Sodium 20 milligrams

Diabetic exchange = 1 Carbohydrate, 1 Fruit, 1 Fat
WW point comparison = 3 points

Kim's Mixed Berry Crisp

Serves Eight

Kim, a lifetime member of Weight Watchers, not only sent me a thank-you note for writing my dessert cookbook, but she also sent me her favorite recipe, which I love and would like to share with you. Thanks, Kim.

INGREDIENTS:

2 16-ounce bags frozen mixed berries, thawed slightly

¾ cup Splenda Granular

1 ½ tablespoons cornstarch

TOPPING

¾ cup old-fashioned oats

¾ cup Splenda Granular

¾ teaspoon cinnamon

1 tablespoon margarine

1 egg white

STEPS:

1. Preheat oven to 350°F. Spray a 9 x 13-inch pan with nonstick cooking spray, set aside.

2. In a large bowl, toss berries with Splenda and cornstarch. Pour into pan.

3. In a small bowl, cut margarine into oats, Splenda, and cinnamon. Gently stir in egg white and sprinkle over berries.

4. Bake for 30 minutes or until bubbling.

When it comes to fiber in fruit, you can't beat berries. Fresh raspberries, blackberries and boysenberries all contain an amazing 8 grams of fiber in every cup. Strawberries and blueberries have less but are no slouches at 4 grams. Add to that berries' low-calorie content— from 50 calories in a cup of sliced strawberries to 80 for a cup of fresh blueberries—and you clearly have a winner for those watching their weight.

PER SERVING

Calories 135	Fat 2.5 grams (0 saturated)
Carbohydrate 28 grams	Fiber 6 grams
Protein 2 grams	Sodium 15 milligrams

Diabetic exchange = 1 Fruit, ½ Carbohydrate, ½ Fat
WW point comparison = 2 points

Blueberry Peach Crisp with Almond Topping

Serves Eight

Nothing spells summer like fresh peaches and juicy blueberries. This crisp combines these two fabulous summer fruits with a crunchy almond-scented topping. Enjoy it with either a dollop of light whipped topping or a scoop of your favorite vanilla ice cream.

INGREDIENTS:

3 ½ cups fresh peaches, peeled, sliced

2 cups fresh or frozen blueberries

1 tablespoon all-purpose flour

2 teaspoons lemon juice

¼ cup Splenda Granular

TOPPING

¼ cup old-fashioned oats

¼ cup all-purpose flour

¼ cup sliced almonds

½ cup Splenda Granular

4 tablespoons light butter

STEPS:

1. Preheat oven to 375°F.

2. Coat 7 x 11-inch baking dish with nonstick cooking spray. Combine peaches, blueberries, flour, lemon juice, and Splenda in baking dish. Set aside.

3. In small bowl, combine oats, flour, almonds, and Splenda. Cut in butter and crumble on top of fruit mixture.

4. Place in baking dish and bake 30-40 minutes.

PER SERVING (¹/₂ CUP)

Calories 130	Fat 5 grams (2 saturated)
Carbohydrate 22 grams	Fiber 3 grams
Protein 2 grams	Sodium 20 milligrams

Diabetic exchange = 1 Fruit, ½ Carbohydrate, ½ Fat
WW point comparison = 2 points

Strawberry Rhubarb Brown Sugar Crumble

Serves Eight

The British name for a crisp that contains oats in the crunchy topping is a "crumble." This lovely crumble get its crunch from oats and bits of brown sugar. If you have Splenda Brown Sugar Blend, you may substitute it for the brown sugar and omit the ⅓ Splenda Granular in the topping.

INGREDIENTS:

4 cups 1-inch pieces fresh rhubarb
  (about 1 ½ pounds rhubarb stalks)

2 cups hulled and halved fresh strawberries

1 cup Splenda Granular

¼ cup water

1 tablespoon cornstarch

½ teaspoon orange zest

⅓ cup all-purpose flour

⅓ cup old-fashioned rolled oats

⅓ cup brown sugar

¼ teaspoon ground ginger

Pinch nutmeg (optional)

2 tablespoons light butter, cold

STEPS:

1. Preheat oven to 375°F. Set aside a 2-quart shallow baking dish.

2. In a large bowl, toss rhubarb and strawberries with ⅔ cup Splenda, water, cornstarch, and orange zest. Pour into baking dish.

3. In a small bowl, combine remaining ingredients except butter.

4. Cut butter into flour and oat mixture and sprinkle on top of fruit.

5. Bake for 40 minutes or until bubbling.

Rhubarb is prized for its unique tart taste and beautiful crimson color. When purchasing it, look for fresh, crisp stalks. Smaller and thinner stalks tend to be less fibrous, but large ones are also fine. If they have a bit of string to them, simply pull off (like celery): no peeling is required. Rhubarb can be refreshed by trimming the bottoms and standing it in cold water for 1 hour.

PER SERVING

Calories 145	Fat 2.5 (1 saturated)
Carbohydrate 29 grams	Fiber 3.5 grams
Protein 2 grams	Sodium 25 milligrams

Diabetic exchange = 1 Carbohydrate, ½ Fruit, ½ Fat
WW point comparison = 2 points

Blackberry Cobbler

Serves Five

There are many versions of cobblers. At one time, it was common to find cobblers made with pie dough, but a sweet, richer type of dough is now the norm. In some recipes, you'll find the dough covers only part of the fruit, and in others, like this one, it covers all of it. But any way you make them, cobblers are a fantastic way to eat your fruit.

INGREDIENTS:

3 cups blackberries (if frozen, defrost only slightly)

¼ cup Splenda Granular

1 tablespoon cornstarch

1 teaspoon lemon juice

TOPPING

¼ cup 1% milk

2 teaspoon lemon juice

1 ½ tablespoons butter or margarine (melted)

1 cup + 2 tablespoons all-purpose flour

2 tablespoons Splenda Granular

¾ teaspoon baking powder

¼ teaspoon baking soda

1 egg white beaten with 2 teaspoons water

2 teaspoons sugar (optional)

STEPS:

1. Preheat oven to 375°F. Lightly coat an 8 x 8-inch glass baking dish or a 9-inch glass pie plate with nonstick cooking spray.

2. In a large bowl, toss the berries lightly with the Splenda, cornstarch, and 1 teaspoon lemon juice. Place in baking dish.

3. TOPPING: In a small bowl, combine the milk, 2 teaspoons lemon juice, and the butter. Set aside.

4. In another bowl, whisk together the flour, 2 tablespoons Splenda, baking powder, and baking soda. Add the milk mixture and mix with a spoon just until dough comes together. Gently knead 3 to 4 times until it is soft and uniform. Dust the top and bottom of the dough with a touch of flour and place on a hard surface. Roll or pat the dough gently until it is the size of the top of the baking dish. Brush with egg-white mixture and sprinkle with sugar, if desired. Using a knife, make 3 vents by cutting small slits in dough.

5. Bake for 40-50 minutes or until berries are bubbly and crust is brown. Let cool 15 minutes before serving.

Substitute any fruit for the blackberries, or blend fruits together. Mixed berries, peaches and blueberries or cherries and apples are some winning combinations.

PER SERVING

Calories 170	Fat 4.5 grams (1 saturated)
Carbohydrate 29 grams)	Fiber 5 grams
Protein 3 grams	Sodium 190 milligrams

Diabetic exchange = 1 Carbohydrate, ½ Fruit, 1 Fat
WW point comparison = 3 points

Apple Strudel

Serves Eight

This is one of the desserts I delivered to the Rosie O'Donnell Show after her producers expressed interest in my dessert book, and I knew this strudel would not disappoint. The show soon ended, and the producers moved on—but they took my book with them—using it as their very first book club selection for their new show on The Food Network. I guess the strudel worked.

INGREDIENTS:

4 cups finely sliced, peeled apples (about 1 ½–1 ¾ pounds fresh)

⅓ cup Splenda Granular

¼ cup raisins, finely chopped

¼ cup pecans, finely chopped

1 ½ teaspoons cinnamon

1 tablespoon plain bread crumbs

6 sheets phyllo dough (12 x 16 inches)

Nonstick cooking spray

½ tablespoon butter, melted

1 tablespoon powdered sugar

Phyllo dough is a great low-fat replacement for pastry. Phyllo (or filo) dough can be found in the freezer section in grocery stores. Be sure to thaw the dough thoroughly before using and keep the sheets you're not working with covered with a damp cloth or plastic wrap to keep them from drying out.

PER SERVING

Calories 160   Fat 6 grams (1 saturated)
Carbohydrate 26 grams   Fiber 3 grams
Protein 2 grams   Sodium 75 milligrams

Diabetic exchange = 1 Fruit, ½ Carbohydrate, 1 Fat
WW point comparison = 3 points

STEPS:

1. Preheat oven to 350°F. Spray a baking sheet with nonstick cooking spray.

2. In a large bowl, combine apples and next 5 ingredients (Splenda through bread crumbs). Set aside.

3. Spread a large piece of plastic wrap or wax paper onto a large surface. Carefully lay 1 piece of the phyllo dough onto the work surface, with the long side closest to you. Lightly spray the entire sheet lightly with cooking spray. Lay another sheet of dough on top of the first. Spray again. Repeat until all 6 sheets are stacked. Spoon the apple mixture in a long strip across the center of the dough, leaving 3 inches on all sides. Starting with the long side of the dough that is closest to you, lift the empty dough up over the apples. Fold side ends and far side of dough up and over the apples to enclose. Carefully use the paper to help you turn the strudel, seam side down, onto the prepared baking sheet.

4. Brush with melted butter.

5. Bake 40–45 minutes or until the pastry is golden brown.

6. Cool slightly and sift powdered sugar over entire strudel. Best when served warm.

Sweet Cheese Strudel

Serves Six

*Sweet cheese strudels are a popular European tradition.
This is nice on its own or dressed up with either Boysenberry
Syrup (page 431) or Sweet Cherry Topping (page 428).*

INGREDIENTS:

CHEESE FILLING

½ cup tub-style light cream cheese

⅓ cup Splenda Granular

2 tablespoons + 1 teaspoon cornstarch

1 egg yolk

1 ½ teaspoons vanilla extract

½ teaspoon grated lemon or orange zest

1 cup part-skim ricotta cheese, preferably
without added gums or stabilizers

STRUDEL

6 sheets phyllo dough (14 x 18 inches, thaw
if frozen)

Nonstick cooking spray

½ tablespoon butter, melted

Confectioner's sugar for dusting

*Phyllo
sheets vary
slightly in size, so
don't be concerned
if yours is larger
or smaller.*

PER SERVING

Calories 130
Carbohydrate 12 grams
Protein 6 grams

Fat 6 grams (2 saturated)
Fiber 0 grams
Sodium 190 milligrams

Diabetic exchange = 1 Carbohydrate,
1 Lean Meat, ½ Fat
WW point comparison = 2 points

STEPS:

1. Preheat oven to 350°F. Lightly spray baking
   sheet with nonstick cooking spray

2. In a small bowl, combine cream cheese,
   Splenda, cornstarch, egg yolk, vanilla, and zest;
   mix until well combined. With a rubber spatula,
   gently fold in ricotta cheese just until combined.

3. Spread a large piece of plastic wrap or wax
   paper onto a large surface. Carefully lay 1 piece
   of the phyllo dough onto the baking sheet, with
   the long side closest to you. Spray the entire
   sheet lightly with cooking spray. Lay another
   sheet of dough on top of the first. Spray again.
   Repeat until all 6 sheets are stacked. Gently
   spoon the cheese filling in a long, 12 x 2-inch
   mound along one long edge of the phyllo
   layers, leaving a 2-inch border between the
   mound and the short edges of the phyllo. Fold
   up the long edge and loosely roll up the strudel.
   (Do not roll too tightly; the filling will expand
   during baking.) Set the strudel seam side down
   on the baking sheet. Fold and tuck the open
   ends securely but not tightly beneath the roll.

4. Brush the strudel with the melted butter.
   With a sharp paring knife, make four short
   (1-inch) diagonal slashes along the top of the
   strudel to allow steam to escape.

5. Bake for 35–40 minutes until golden brown.

6. Cool completely on a wire rack. Before
   serving, dust with confectioner's sugar.

Quick Raspberry Cream Cheese Strudel

Serves Eight

A pastry chef friend of mine developed this easy-to-make yet beautiful raspberry-filled strudel. Using only a handful of ingredients and a little more than 30 minutes, you can create this impressive table topper for your next brunch or family breakfast.

INGREDIENTS:

3 ounces light cream cheese

3 tablespoons margarine

2 cups Reduced-Fat Bisquick

4 tablespoons Splenda Granular

⅓ cup 1% milk

½ cup Smucker's Light Raspberry Preserves

½ pint fresh raspberries

1 egg white (for wash)

1 teaspoon sugar

Pastries such as this make a great addition to a healthful, well-rounded breakfast that might include scrambled eggs or egg substitute, lean breakfast meat such as Canadian bacon or reduced-fat sausage, and additional fresh berries, with fresh coffee, tea, or milk.

STEPS:

1. Preheat oven to 425°F.

2. In a large bowl, cut cream cheese and margarine into Bisquick until crumbly with pastry blender or fork. Blend in 2 tablespoons Splenda and milk. Bring dough together into a ball and turn onto lightly floured surface. Knead dough about 10 times just until soft dough forms. Roll dough out into a 16 x 8-inch rectangle.

3. Carefully move dough onto cookie sheet. Spread preserves down the center of dough (about 4 inches wide). Top preserves with raspberries and sprinkle them with remaining 2 tablespoons Splenda. To make criss-cross, cut bare dough (at 45-degree angle), every 1 ½ inches, from outside edge to just short of filling, down entire side. Fold dough strips across filling, alternating side to side.

4. Brush strudel with egg white and sprinkle with sugar.

5. Bake for 15 minutes until golden brown.

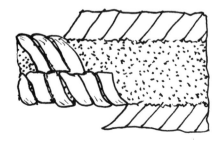

PER SERVING

Calories 185	Fat 6 grams (2 saturated)
Carbohydrate 28 grams	Fiber 4 grams
Protein 4 grams	Sodium 115 milligrams

Diabetic exchange = 1 ½ Carbohydrate, ½ Fruit, 1 Fat
WW point comparison = 4 points

Fresh Fruit Tart

Serves Eight

Just like the beautiful tarts in the bakery case, this is as nice to look at as it is to eat. Here I use my Single-Crust Pie Pastry, fill it with Pastry Cream, and top it with an assortment of fresh berries. But you have other options. First, you may choose any assortment of fresh fruit you prefer. For example, fresh sliced peaches are terrific when in season, and sliced kiwi adds a wonderful splash of color. For the filling, pastry cream is a bakery standard, but Lemon Curd (page 433) is also delicious. And last, you can substitute pre-prepared pie dough for my Single-Crust Pie Pastry when you are pressed for time.

INGREDIENTS:

1 recipe Single-Crust Pie Pastry, page 325

1 tablespoon Splenda Granular

1 recipe Pastry Cream, page 264

1 ½ cups thick strawberry slices

1 cup fresh blueberries (½ pint)

½ cup fresh raspberries

¼ cup low-sugar raspberry or strawberry jam

Another pretty and easy way to finish off the tart is to omit the jam and simply dust the fresh fruit with 2 teaspoons of powdered sugar just before serving (saves 10 calories and 2 grams of carbohydrate).

STEPS:

1. Preheat oven to 425°F. Set aside a 9-inch tart pan.

2. Make Single-Crust Pie Pastry according to directions, adding 1 tablespoon of Splenda to flour mixture.

3. Roll out dough out into a 10-inch circle. Gently lift dough and place in tart pan. Press onto bottom and into sides, trimming excess.

4. Fully bake shell as directed in recipe (be sure to use dried beans or pie weights to eliminate air pockets). Set shell aside (can be done 1 day ahead).

5. Prepare Pastry Cream according to recipe. Pour directly into prepared crust. Spread filling to create an even layer. Let cool to room temperature.

6. Working from the outside in, arrange the fruit in decorative single layers to cover the custard. In a small microwaveable bowl, heat jam for 30 seconds in microwave or until melted.

7. Using a small pastry brush, carefully brush fruit with melted jam for a pretty shine.

8. Place tart in refrigerator and serve the same day for best appearance.

PER SERVING

Calories 160	Fat 7 grams (2 saturated)
Carbohydrate 22 grams	Fiber 2 grams
Protein 4 grams	Sodium 95 milligrams

Diabetic exchange = 1 Carbohydrate, ½ Fruit, 1 Fat
WW point comparison = 3 points

Phyllo Apple Packets

Serves Six

These delicious apple pastries are fancy enough for your next dinner party. Developed by pastry chef Laura Johanson, an apprentice of mine from the Culinary Institute of America, these all-purpose apple packets can be prepared in advance and placed in the oven to bake while you eat. They make an impressive hot dessert. Dust them lightly with powdered sugar for a beautiful presentation.

INGREDIENTS:

APPLE FILLING

2 tablespoons butter

2 baking apples, diced (about ¾ pound)

½ cup Splenda Granular

2 teaspoons cinnamon

4 tablespoons lemon juice

¼ teaspoon salt

6 tablespoons unsweetened applesauce

6 sheets phyllo dough (12 x 16 inches)

STEPS:

1. Preheat oven to 350°F. Lightly spray baking sheet with nonstick cooking spray.

2. In a medium frying pan, melt butter on medium-high heat and toss in diced apples.

3. In a small mixing bowl, combine Splenda, cinnamon, lemon juice, and salt. Pour mixture over cooking apples. Cook apples just until fork tender.

4. Spread a large piece of wax paper onto work surface. Carefully lay one piece of phyllo dough onto surface with short side closest to you. Lightly spray with cooking spray and fold in half lengthwise. Spray again and fold in half away from you. Cut off excess phyllo to create a 6 x 6-inch square.

5. Place 1 tablespoon applesauce into center of square. Top with 2 tablespoons of cooked apple mixture. Fold each corner to the middle, covering the apple filling while spraying lightly with cooking spray to hold edges together. Repeat 5 times.

6. With a spatula, carefully place packets on baking sheet.

7. Bake for 25–30 minutes until golden brown.

PER SERVING (1 PACKETS)

Calories 150	Fat 7 grams (2.5 saturated)
Carbohydrate 20 grams	Fiber 2 grams
Protein 1 gram	Sodium 115 milligrams

Diabetic exchange = 1 Fruit, ½ Carbohydrate, 1 Fat
WW point comparison = 3 points

Microwave Cinnamon Baked Apple

Serves One

This is so simple but so good. We all know an apple a day keeps the doctor away, but most of us just don't consider a fresh apple a real dessert. This quick and easy recipe turns an ordinary apple into a taste treat even your doctor would endorse.

INGREDIENTS:

1 medium cooking apple

2 teaspoons Splenda granular (or 1 packet)

¼ teaspoon cinnamon

2 tablespoons light vanilla yogurt (or light ice cream)

STEPS:

1. Wash and dry apple. Core apple and use a peeler to strip away the peel on the top third of the apple (this is easy to do by peeling in a circle, starting from the top).

2. Place the apple in a small microwaveable dish.

3. Sprinkle Splenda and cinnamon over top and into core of apple.

4. Cover the dish tightly with plastic wrap and microwave for about 7 minutes on high or until apple is soft.

5. Remove from microwave, remove wrap, and spoon the collected "syrup" back onto top of apple.

6. Spoon cold yogurt into the hole of the apple.

Contrary to popular belief, fat doesn't make you feel full, but foods high in water and fiber content do. Apples are high in both water and fiber, yet they are low in calories, making them a great choice for those who are watching their waistlines.

PER SERVING

Calories 100	Fat .5 grams (0 saturated)
Carbohydrate 24 grams	Fiber 3 grams
Protein 1 gram	Sodium 20 milligrams

Diabetic exchange = 1 ½ Fruit

WW point comparison = 1 point

Cakes for All Occasions

Unbelievable Chocolate Cake

All-Purpose Light White Cake

Basic Yellow Cake

White Yogurt Cake

Fresh Banana Cake

Chocolate Carrot Cake

California Carrot Cake with
      Cream Cheese Frosting

Applesauce Snack Cake

Grandma's Gingerbread

Fruit Cocktail Snack Cake

Two-Bite Cupcakes

Orange Sunshine Cupcakes

Chocolate Cupcakes

Fran's Sour Cream Spice Cupcakes

Pineapple Upside Down Cake

Lemon Coconut Layer Cake

Citrus Chiffon Cake

Lemon Souffle Cakes

Creamy Chocolate Souffle Cakes

Sour Cream Pound Loaf Cake

Strawberry Short Cake

Chocolate Almond Torte

Cream Cheese-Filled Pumpkin Roll

Chocolate Cream-Filled Chocolate Roll

We all know that birthdays and cakes go hand in hand, but the truth is, cakes make any day or every occasion just a little more festive. Whether it's something as simple as a cake for Sunday dinner or a batch of after-school cupcakes, cakes make people smile.

That's part of the reason I love baking cakes, but what I don't love is the amount of sugar it takes to make one. I remember the first carrot cake recipe I ever made called for 2 cups of granulated sugar in the cake and an entire box, more than 4 cups, of powdered sugar for the frosting. Wow. I've come a long way since then. One of the first recipes I tackled with Splenda was none other than carrot cake with cream cheese frosting. And it's just as good—so good that a gal on a live television show blurted out that it was better than her mother's. That made *me* smile.

You will find my California Carrot Cake with Cream Cheese Frosting on page 371. Beyond carrot cake, you'll find a large assortment of cakes for all occasions.

From quick and easy one-bowl cakes like Fresh Banana and Unbelievable Chocolate Cake, to cakes for entertaining like Citrus Chiffon Cake and Creamy Chocolate Souffle Cakes, there's something for every occasion.

For picnics, look no further than a tote-worthy Chocolate Carrot Cake or a batch of Orange Sunshine Cupcakes. To tempt the kids, try Applesauce Snack Cake and Two-Bite Cupcakes (and don't forget the glass of milk).

And for holiday festivities, I suggest Grandma's Gingerbread or a picture-perfect Cream Cheese-Filled Pumpkin Roll. Hooray for cake!

Unbelievable Chocolate Cake

Serves Nine

A chocolate cake that takes only one bowl, a whisk, and 10 minutes to make and contains one ¼ cup of sugar is, well, pretty unbelievable! I've also received three great ideas from readers who doubled this recipe: 1) Bake in a 9 x 13 inch pan for 28-30 minutes for a sheet cake; 2) Bake in two 9-inch rounds for a layer cake; 3) Split the rounds in half and fill with the Whipped Cream Cheese Topping and Frosting (page 437) for a torte. I enjoy this cake dusted with powdered sugar and served with sliced strawberries.

INGREDIENTS:

¼ cup canola oil

1 large egg

1 teaspoon vanilla

¼ cup brown sugar, packed (use fresh brown sugar, with no hard lumps)

1 cup Splenda Granular

1 cup low-fat buttermilk

1 ¼ cups cake flour

1 teaspoon baking soda

1 teaspoon baking powder

¼ cup Dutch-process cocoa powder (like Hershey's European)

¼ cup hot water

2 teaspoons powdered sugar

Easy Chocolate Cream Frosting, page 438 (optional)

STEPS:

1. Preheat oven to 350°F. Spray an 8 x 8-inch★ baking pan with nonstick cooking spray.

2. In a large bowl, whisk together the oil and the egg for 1 minute until the mixture is thick and frothy. Add the vanilla, brown sugar, and Splenda, and beat with a whisk for 2 more minutes until the mixture is thick and smooth and the sugars have been thoroughly beaten into the mixture. Add 1 cup buttermilk and mix.

3. Using a sifter or a metal sieve, sift the flour, baking powder, baking soda, and cocoa powder into the liquid mixture. Whisk vigorously for 1-2 minutes until the batter is nice and smooth. Pour the hot water into the batter and whisk one more time until the batter is again nice and smooth. The batter will be thin.

4. Pour the batter into the prepared cake pan and tap the pan on the counter to level the surface and to help remove any air bubbles.

5. Bake for 18-20 minutes or just until the center springs back when touched and a cake tester or toothpick comes out clean. Do not overcook. Remove the cake from the oven and cool.

6. Before serving, sift powdered sugar over cake.

★ Be careful not to substitute a 9-inch square pan; if you need to substitute, use a 9-inch round pan.

PER SERVING

Calories 160	Fat 7 grams (1 saturated)
Carbohydrate 22 grams	Fiber 1 gram
Protein 3 grams	Sodium 200 milligrams

Diabetic exchange = 1 ½ Carbohydrate, 1 Fat
WW point comparison = 4 points

All-Purpose Light White Cake

Serves Twelve

Old-fashioned white layer cakes never go out of style. You can dress 'em up by layering them with fillings and frostings or dress them down by simply serving wedges with fresh fruit and a light dusting of powdered sugar. This cake, adapted from well-known baking expert Sarah Phillips, fills the bill for a healthy yet delicious all-purpose basic white cake.

INGREDIENTS:

2 cups cake flour

¼ cup nonfat dry milk powder

2 teaspoons baking powder

½ teaspoon baking soda

⅓ cup margarine or butter

½ cup Splenda Sugar Blend for Baking

1 large egg

1 teaspoon vanilla extract

¼ teaspoon almond extract

1 cup + 2 tablespoons 1% milk

When you cream a solid fat with sugar, the sharp edges of the sugar crystals cut against the fat and help the fat trap air, building lightness and volume. This cake uses the creaming method to take advantage of the sugar in Splenda Sugar Blend for Baking to create a nice, tall cake.

STEPS:

1. Preheat oven to 350°F. Spray an 8-inch round cake pan with nonstick cooking spray. Set aside.

2. In a medium bowl, whisk together flour, nonfat milk powder, baking powder, and baking soda. Set aside.

3. In another medium bowl, cream margarine and Splenda Sugar Blend with an electric mixer for 3-4 minutes or until creamy. Add egg and extracts and beat until light and fluffy.

4. With mixer on very low speed, briefly beat in ⅓ of flour mixture and then ½ of that milk. Repeat once more and finish off with last of flour mixture.

5. Gently spread batter into prepared pan. Bake for 25-30 minutes or until center of cake springs back when lightly touched. Cool pan on wire rack for 10 minutes. Loosen cake from pan and let cool.

PER SERVING

Calories 150	Fat 5 grams (2.5 saturated)
Carbohydrate 23 grams	Fiber 0 grams
Protein 4 grams	Sodium 200 milligrams

Diabetic exchange = 1 ½ Carbohydrate, 1 Fat
WW point comparison = 3 points

Basic Yellow Cake

Serves Eight

While developing the recipe for Pineapple Upside Down Cake (page 379), I discovered that even without the pineapple topping, the cake base was a winner. Simply dusted with powdered sugar, this cake is delicious. Use its wonderful light texture and golden appearance as a creative backdrop for your favorite toppings, textures, and flavors.

INGREDIENTS:

¼ **cup butter, softened**

⅔ **cup Splenda Granular**

1 large egg

1 teaspoon vanilla extract

1 ¼ cups all-purpose flour

1 ½ teaspoons baking powder

½ teaspoon baking soda

⅓ **cup 1% milk**

⅓ **cup pineapple juice**

STEPS:

1. Preheat oven to 350°F. Coat an 8-inch round cake pan with nonstick cooking spray.

2. In a medium bowl, using an electric mixer, cream butter and Splenda. Beat in egg and vanilla.

3. In a small bowl, sift together dry ingredients.

4. Alternate mixing dry and liquid ingredients into creamed mixture in three steps.

5. Pour batter into prepared pan and bake 25–30 minutes or until top springs back when touched. Cool in pan on wire rack.

The pineapple juice does not lend much pineapple flavor, but gives the batter just a touch of natural sugar, which helps both in color and rise. Apple juice or orange juice can be substituted.

PER SERVING

Calories 140

Carbohydrate 18 grams

Protein 3 grams

Fat 6 grams (1.5 saturated)

Fiber 1 gram

Sodium 230 milligrams

Diabetic exchange = 1 Carbohydrate, 1 Fat

WW point comparison = 3 points

White Yogurt Cake

Serves Eight

When I first started teaching the principles of healthy cooking, not many chefs agreed that low-fat cooking could be synonymous with great food. A decade later, many highly respected chefs have adopted the idea that healthy cooking techniques can indeed produce good food. One of those chefs is the world-renowned Jaques Pepin, whose own healthy cookbook, Simple and Healthy Cooking, inspired me to produce this Yogurt Cake. It is a basic moist white cake.

INGREDIENTS:

1 cup + 2 tablespoons cake flour

1 ½ teaspoons baking powder

¼ teaspoon baking soda

3 large egg whites

3 tablespoons granulated sugar

3 tablespoons canola oil

⅔ cup Splenda Granular

1 teaspoon vanilla extract

¼ teaspoon almond extract

1 large egg

½ cup plain nonfat yogurt

⅓ cup unsweetened applesauce

STEPS:

1. Preheat oven to 350°F. Spray an 8-inch round cake pan with nonstick cooking spray.

2. Sift the flour with the baking powder and soda and set aside.

3. In a medium bowl, beat egg whites until frothy. Gradually add the 3 tablespoons of sugar; continue to beat until soft peaks form when the mixer is lifted from the whites. Set aside.

4. In a large bowl, cream the oil and the Splenda. Add the next 5 ingredients (vanilla through applesauce) and beat for 1-2 minutes. (It may not look totally creamy.)

5. Add the flour sifted with the baking powder and soda to the bowl. Beat until smooth. Gently fold in the beaten egg whites.

6. Spoon the batter into the prepared pan. Bake for 20 minutes or until center of the cake springs back when lightly touched. Cool in pan on rack.

Yogurt is a wonderful baking ingredient in everything from cakes and pies to muffins and biscuits. Its thickness helps batters hold their structure and its acid content helps both rise and tenderness. When you substitute yogurt in recipes, use a bit of baking soda (½ teaspoon per cup of yogurt).

PER SERVING

Calories 150	Fat 6 grams (.5 saturated)
Carbohydrate 16 grams	Fiber 0 grams
Protein 4 grams	Sodium 190 milligrams

Diabetic exchange = 1 Carbohydrate, 1 Fat

Fresh Banana Cake

Serves Eight

Every time I have some overripe bananas, I think of this cake. The recipe is easy and practically foolproof. I have made it many times (as have my friends and my friends' friends). I have also made it with and without sugar and am happy to report it is just as wonderful without it. Lastly, this cake's so moist that you'll find it hard to believe it's so low in fat.

INGREDIENTS:

3 small bananas, mashed (about 1 cup purée)

2 tablespoons canola oil

⅔ cup Splenda Granular

1 tablespoon molasses (or honey)

1 large egg

1 large egg white

½ cup nonfat plain yogurt

2 teaspoons vanilla

1 ½ cups cake flour

1 teaspoon baking powder

¾ teaspoon baking soda

2 teaspoons powdered sugar (optional)

STEPS:

1. Preheat oven to 350°F. Spray a 9-inch cake pan with nonstick cooking spray.

2. Place banana purée in a large mixing bowl. Whisk in next 7 ingredients (oil through vanilla).

3. Sift cake flour, baking powder, and baking soda into the bowl. Stir to blend in dry ingredients.

4. Spoon batter into prepared pan. Bake for 30 minutes or until a toothpick inserted into the center of the cake comes out clean. Cool in pan on wire rack.

5. Sift powdered sugar over cake just prior to serving if desired.

This is a great old-fashioned homestyle cake. When serving it to guests, I warm it up and then top each piece with a spoonful of light whipped topping and a few slices of fresh banana.

PER SERVING

Calories 130 Fat 3.5 grams (0 saturated)
Carbohydrate 21 grams Fiber 1 gram
Protein 3 grams Sodium 300 milligrams

Diabetic exchange = 1 ½ Carbohydrate, ½ Fat
WW point comparison = 3 points

Chocolate Carrot Cake

Serves Sixteen

A novel twist on two favorites, Chocolate Carrot Cake appeals to both the chocolate lover and the health nut. It combines the moist texture of traditional carrot cake with a delicious chocolate cake. Easy to make and tote, it's great for picnics and potlucks. If you like, top with dollops of Whipped Cream Cheese Frosting (page 437).

INGREDIENTS:

1 ⅔ cups all-purpose flour

⅓ cup cocoa powder

2 ½ teaspoons baking soda

1 teaspoon baking powder

1 teaspoon cinnamon

1 ½ cups Splenda Granular

¼ cup prune puree or 1 small jar baby food prunes

¼ cup canola oil

1 large egg

3 large egg whites

1 ½ teaspoons vanilla extract

⅔ cup regular or light orange juice

2 cups carrots, grated (about 3 medium)

¼ cup coconut, shredded

¼ cup pecan pieces

2 teaspoons powdered sugar (optional)

STEPS:

1. Preheat oven to 350°F. Coat a 9 x 13-inch cake pan with nonstick cooking spray.

2. In a medium bowl, sift together flour, cocoa, baking soda, baking powder, and cinnamon. Add Splenda and set aside.

3. In a large mixing bowl, whisk together prune puree, canola oil, egg, egg whites, vanilla extract, and orange juice.

4. Fold flour mixture into prune mixture ½ cup at a time. When all the flour is folded in, fold in carrots, and then pour batter into prepared pan.

5. Before baking, sprinkle coconut and pecans on top. Bake for 25–30 minutes. Cool in pan on wire rack. Dust with powdered sugar if desired before serving.

You may wonder why I specify either light or regular orange juice. When the carbohydrate savings of using light orange juice is less than 1 gram of carbohydrate per serving, it's fine to just make the choice based on what you have on hand.

PER SERVING

Calories 140	Fat 6 grams (1 saturated)
Carbohydrate 18 grams	Fiber 2 grams
Protein 3 grams	Sodium 230 milligrams

Diabetic exchange = 1 Carbohydrate, 1 Fat
WW point comparison = 3 points

California Carrot Cake with Cream Cheese Frosting

Serves Fifteen

I remember my mom making this popular cake when I was a child. I'm sure she thought it was nice that such a delicious treat was also good for us. What she didn't realize is that her famed carrot cake—made with lots of oil and sugar—was loaded with fat and calories. I am so happy I was able to make a Carrot Cake that retains the same moist, sweet quality of the original with so much less sugar. When topped with its delicious cream cheese frosting, this cake is guaranteed to please.

INGREDIENTS:

1 cup all-purpose flour

1 cup wheat flour

2 teaspoons baking soda

1 teaspoon baking powder

2 teaspoons cinnamon

½ teaspoon nutmeg

¼ teaspoon cloves

⅓ cup chopped nuts

¼ cup prune purée/baby food prunes

¼ cup canola oil

1 large egg

3 large egg whites

1 teaspoon vanilla

¾ cup low-fat buttermilk

1 ½ cups Splenda Granular

8 ounces crushed pineapple, packed in unsweetened juice

1 ½ cups carrots, peeled and shredded

Whipped Cream Cheese Frosting, page 437

STEPS:

1. Preheat oven to 350°F. Coat a 9 x 13-inch cake pan with nonstick cooking spray.

2. In a medium bowl, combine the flours, baking soda, baking powder, spices, and chopped nuts. Stir to blend.

3. In a large bowl, measure the prune purée, oil, vanilla, and eggs. Whisk together. Add the buttermilk and Splenda. Whisk. Stir in the pineapple (including juice) and carrots. Add the flour mixture. Stir to form batter.

4. Transfer the batter into prepared pan.

5. Bake for 25–30 minutes or until a toothpick inserted in the center of the cake comes out clean. Let the cake cool in the pan on wire rack.

6. Prepare frosting according to recipe. Frost cake and serve or refrigerate.

PER SERVING

Calories 200	Fat 9 grams (3 saturated)
Carbohydrate 24 grams	Fiber 2 grams
Protein 7 grams	Sodium 300 milligrams

Diabetic exchange = 1 Carbohydrate, ½ Fruit, 2 Fat
WW point comparison = 4 points

Most carrot cakes, low in fat or not, are very high in sugar. Because they can have as much as 75 grams of carbohydrate apiece (more than a meal's worth of carbs for many persons with diabetes), they are off limits to lots of folks. This carrot cake, even with its ample pieces, actually allows you to have your cake—and dinner, too! Enjoy.

Applesauce Snack Cake

Serves Nine

Not only is this Applesauce Snack Cake quick and easy to make, but my true critics—my kids—loved it. I call it a snack cake because it's the perfect kind of cake for an afternoon treat. The cinnamon-and-sugar topping means no icing is required, but a spoonful of light whipped topping never hurts.

INGREDIENTS:

¼ cup canola oil

¾ cup + 1 tablespoon Splenda Granular

2 tablespoons molasses

1 large egg

¾ cup unsweetened applesauce

1 teaspoon vanilla

1 ½ cups all-purpose flour

1 teaspoon baking powder

¾ teaspoon baking soda

2 teaspoons cinnamon

½ teaspoon allspice

2 teaspoons sugar

½ teaspoon cinnamon

STEPS:

1. Preheat oven to 350°F. Spray an 8 x 8-inch cake pan with nonstick cooking spray.

2. In a large mixing bowl, stir together the oil, ¾ cup Splenda, molasses, egg, applesauce, and vanilla. Sift in the flour, baking powder, baking soda, and spices, and stir until smooth. Spoon batter into prepared pan.

3. In a small bowl, combine the sugar, 1 tablespoon Splenda, and ½ teaspoon cinnamon for the topping. Sprinkle with a spoon evenly over the top of the cake.

4. Bake for 20 minutes or until the center of the cake springs back when lightly touched.

PER SERVING

Calories 170	Fat 7 grams (.5 saturated)
Carbohydrate 24 grams	Fiber 2 grams (7 sugar)
Protein 3 grams	Sodium 170 milligrams

Diabetic exchange = 1 ½ Carbohydrate, 1 Fat
WW point comparison = 4 points

Grandma's Gingerbread

Serves Nine

Sweet accents of ginger and cinnamon combine with molasses to give this gingerbread its traditional old-fashioned flavor. For those of you who like it served up with a lemon sauce, the Hot Lemon Sauce on page 424 should fill the bill.

INGREDIENTS:

1 cup all-purpose flour

½ cup whole-wheat flour

1 teaspoon ginger

1 teaspoon cinnamon

¼ teaspoon cloves

1 teaspoon baking soda

¼ cup molasses

3 tablespoons canola oil

¼ cup prune puree or 1 small jar baby food prunes

1 large egg

½ cup water

½ cup Splenda Granular

STEPS:

1. Preheat oven to 350°F. Coat an 8-inch square cake pan with nonstick cooking spray.

2. In a medium bowl, sift together flours, spices, and baking soda. Set aside.

3. In a large mixing bowl, whisk together remaining ingredients.

4. Fold dry ingredients into molasses mixture and then pour batter into prepared pan.

5. Bake for 18–20 minutes or until top springs back when touched.

6. Cool and serve with light whipped topping if desired.

Molasses has a distinct flavor that brings depth of flavor and richness of color to many spice-laden recipes. Look for unsulphured molasses for the finest quality and sweetest flavor.

PER SERVING

Calories 160	Fat 5 grams (.5 saturated)
Carbohydrate 26 grams	Fiber 2 grams
Protein 3 grams	Sodium 150 milligrams

Diabetic exchange = 1 ½ Carbohydrate, 1 Fat
WW point comparison = 3 points

Fruit Cocktail Snack Cake

Serves Nine

This is a very moist and tender, fruity and delicious snack cake. The key ingredient can be found in a can right in your cupboard, allowing you to make this cake on a moment's notice, much to the delight of your your family and friends. Add a dollop of whipped topping to dress it up for a light summer dessert.

INGREDIENTS:

1 large egg

1 cup Splenda Granular

1 15-ounce can fruit cocktail, in light syrup (minus 2 tablespoons juice)

1 teaspoon baking powder

1 teaspoon baking soda

½ teaspoon salt

1 ¼ cups all-purpose flour

1 teaspoon vanilla extract

STEPS:

1. Preheat oven to 325°F. Coat an 8-inch square cake pan with nonstick cooking spray.

2. In a large mixing bowl, beat egg, Splenda, and fruit cocktail with a hand mixer until smooth.

3. In a medium bowl, sift together dry ingredients.

4. Fold dry ingredients into fruit cocktail mixture with a whisk; then add vanilla extract.

5. Pour batter into prepared pan. Bake for 30-35 minutes or until top springs back when touched. Cool and serve.

PER SERVING

Calories 110

Carbohydrate 23 grams

Protein 3 grams

Fat 1 gram (0 saturated)

Fiber 1 gram

Sodium 200 milligrams

Diabetic exchange = 1 Carbohydrate, ½ Fruit

WW point comparison = 2 points

Two-Bite Cupcakes

Serves Thirty

While in the checkout line of a grocery famous for its "wholesome" offerings, some cute little cupcakes caught my eye. Labeled as "Two-Bite Cupcakes," they were just big enough for two small bites or one big gobble. I liked the fun healthy aspects of satisfying your sweet tooth with two bites. Then I read the label—the cupcakes contained 330 calories and 40 grams of sugar! My version uses two of my favorite recipes to create sweet little nothings that are fun to eat without sacrificing your waistline.

INGREDIENTS:

1 recipe All-Purpose Light White Cake, page 366

1 ½ recipes Whipped Cream Cheese Frosting, page 437

Steps:

1. Preheat oven to 350°F. Spray 30 small or mini-muffin tins with nonstick cooking spray. (You may bake in batches.)

2. Make cake batter. Spoon 1 ½ tablespoons of batter into each muffin tin, filling ⅔ full.

3. Bake for 8-10 minutes or until center of a cupcake springs back when touched.

4. Remove from oven and set on rack to cool for 10 minutes. Remove from muffin tin and finish cooling.

5. While cooling muffins, make Whipped Cream Cheese Frosting according to recipe using 1 ½ times each ingredient.

6. Top each cooled cupcake with 2 tablespoons frosting.

Serve these on a nice big tray like you would serve cookies and watch the smiles. Be forewarned, though, because eating just one probably isn't an option.

PER SERVING

Calories 100	Fat 4 grams (2.5 saturated)
Carbohydrate 11 grams	Fiber 0 grams
Protein 4 grams	Sodium 160 milligrams

Diabetic exchange = 1 Carbohydrate, 1 Fat
WW point comparison = 2 points

Orange Sunshine Cupcakes

Serves Eight

The trickiest part about this recipe was coming up with a healthy reduced-sugar frosting. Although I've seen many reduced-fat frosting recipes, I've never found one also low in sugar. Then I remembered an icing I made as a teenager. You make a flour paste and beat it into a base of granulated sugar and shortening. Here, I lowered the fat by using light cream cheese and heightened the flavor with orange extract. Voilà, frosting with 2 tablespoons, not 2 cups, of powdered sugar.

INGREDIENTS:

CUPCAKES

1 cup cake flour

1 teaspoon baking powder

½ teaspoon baking soda

2 tablespoons margarine

2 tablespoons canola oil

⅔ cup Splenda Granular

1 large egg

1 teaspoon vanilla

¼ cup 1% milk

⅓ cup regular or light orange juice

WHIPPED FROSTING

½ cup 1% milk

2 tablespoons all-purpose flour

2 tablespoons vegetable shortening

4-ounce tub-style light cream cheese

1 cup Splenda Granular

2 tablespoons powdered sugar

½ teaspoon orange extract

PER SERVING

Calories 170	Fat 9 grams (3 saturated)
Carbohydrate 17 grams	Fiber 0 grams
Protein 2 grams	Sodium 210 milligrams

Diabetic exchange = 1 Carbohydrate, 2 Fat
WW point comparison = 4 points

STEPS:

1. Preheat oven to 325°F. Spray 8 muffin cups with nonstick cooking spray.

2. CUPCAKES: Sift the cake flour with the baking powder and baking soda. Set aside.

3. In a large bowl, cream the margarine and oil with an electric mixer. Add Splenda, egg, and vanilla and beat well. By hand, stir in half of flour mixture to the creamed ingredients. Add the milk and mix until smooth. Stir in the remaining flour and finish with the orange juice.

4. Spoon into the prepared pans, filling ⅔ full. Bake for 15 minutes or until cupcakes spring back when lightly touched in the center. Remove from oven and cool.

5. FROSTING: Pour milk into a small pot and add flour. Stir until smooth with no lumps. Place over low heat and cook until a smooth, thick paste forms. Set aside to cool slightly. Place shortening and cream cheese in a small mixing bowl. Beat at high speed with an electric mixer until creamy. Beat in Splenda. Add flour paste and continue to beat until smooth and creamy. Add powdered sugar and extract.

6. Frost each cooled cupcake with 1 ½ tablespoons of frosting. You will use most but not all of the frosting.

Chocolate Cupcakes

Serves Twelve

These light and airy (yet very chocolatey) cupcakes, made with Splenda Sugar Blend for Baking, are one of the newest to my "cupcake collection." To finish them off, you can spread them with Easy Chocolate Cream Frosting (page 438), or simply dust them with powdered sugar. Either way, no one will ever guess that these have half the fat and sugar of regular chocolate cupcakes.

INGREDIENTS:

⅓ cup butter or margarine, softened

¾ cup Splenda Sugar Blend for Baking

2 large eggs

1 ½ cups cake flour

½ cup Dutch-process cocoa powder

¾ teaspoon baking soda

1 teaspoon baking powder

1 cup buttermilk

1 teaspoon vanilla

STEPS:

1. Preheat oven to 350°F. Place paper cupcake cups in a muffin pan.

2. Put butter and Splenda in a medium bowl, and use an electric mixer to cream until light and fluffy.

3. Add the eggs, one at a time, beating well after each addition.

4. In a medium bowl, combine cake flour, cocoa, baking soda, and baking powder. Whisk to combine.

5. Add ½ the flour mixture to the egg mixture; then add ½ the buttermilk and the vanilla. Mix at low speed and repeat, finishing with the last ½ cup of buttermilk.

6. Spoon batter into cups, filling ⅔ full. Bake for 18–20 minutes or until a toothpick inserted into the center comes out clean.

PER SERVING

Calories 160	Fat 5 grams (1.5 saturated)
Carbohydrate 25 grams	Fiber 1 gram
Protein 4 grams	Sodium 220 milligrams

Diabetic exchange = 1 ½ Carbohydrate, 1 Fat
WW point comparison = 3 points

Fran's Sour Cream Spice Cupcakes

Serves Twelve

A very kind reader and web friend, Fran has sent me several recipes. She uses only the best traditional cookbooks as resources, and then does a wonderful job of cutting both sugar and fat. This recipe was adapted from A World of Baking by Dolores Casella, and it's fantastic. Everyone who was lucky enough to taste these big bold-flavored cupcakes loved them. Thank you, Fran.

INGREDIENTS:

½ stick butter, at room temperature

2 cups Splenda Granular

3 large eggs

2 tablespoons molasses

1 3.5-ounce container baby food plums and apples (Gerber's)

¼ teaspoon salt

1 teaspoon baking soda

2 teaspoons cinnamon

1 teaspoon ginger

¼ teaspoon nutmeg

¼ teaspoon cloves

2 ¼ cups flour

1 cup low-fat sour cream

STEPS:

1. Preheat oven to 375°F. Spray a 12-cup muffin tin with cooking spray.

2. In a large bowl, with an electric mixer, beat the butter and Splenda for 1 minute. Add eggs, one at a time, beating well after each addition until creamy.

3. Add molasses, baby food, salt, soda, and spices.

4. Add the flour in three portions and the sour cream in two, starting and ending with the flour and beating after each addition.

5. Divide the batter evenly among 12 muffin cups.

6. Bake for 30 minutes or until a toothpick inserted into the middle comes out clean.

I love these plain, just out of the oven, and my boys enjoy them cooled, dusted with a touch of powdered sugar. But if you really want to elevate them from fantastic to fabulous, try topping them with the Whipped Cream Cheese Frosting on page 437.

PER SERVING

Calories 195	Fat 7 grams (4 saturated)
Carbohydrate 27 grams	Fiber 1 gram
Protein 5 grams	Sodium 190 milligrams

Diabetic exchange = 2 Carbohydrate, 1 Fat

WW point comparison = 4 points

Pineapple Upside Down Cake

Serves Eight

Truly a classic, pineapple upside down cakes have been enjoyed for many generations. Some recipes call for as much as ¾ cup brown sugar and ½ stick of butter for the topping alone. This new-and-improved version keeps the look and the taste of the original sweet pineapple topping, atop a moist tender cake, with only a fraction of the usual sugar and fat. Aloha!.

INGREDIENTS:

TOPPING

2 tablespoons butter

2 tablespoons brown sugar

¼ cup Splenda Granular

½ teaspoon cinnamon

6 pineapple rings

CAKE

¼ cup butter, softened

⅔ cup Splenda Granular

1 large egg

1 teaspoon vanilla extract

1 ¼ cups all-purpose flour

1 ½ teaspoons baking powder

½ teaspoon baking soda

⅓ cup 1% milk

⅓ cup pineapple juice

STEPS:

1. Preheat oven to 350°F. Coat an 8-inch round cake pan with nonstick cooking spray.

2. TOPPING: In oven, melt butter in prepared 8-inch pan. After butter is melted, evenly sprinkle with brown sugar, Splenda, and cinnamon. Arrange pineapple slices in pan. Set aside.

3. CAKE: In a medium bowl, with an electric mixer, cream butter and Splenda. Beat in egg and vanilla.

4. In a small bowl, sift together dry ingredients. In another small bowl or liquid measure, combine milk and pineapple juice.

5. Alternate mixing liquid and dry ingredients into creamed mixture.

6. Pour batter over pineapple rings and bake 25–30 minutes. Turn cake out of pan. Cool on a wire rack.

In 1925, Dole Pineapple had a pineapple recipe contest, and they received 2,500 recipes for Pineapple Upside Down Cake.

PER SERVING

Calories 185	Fat 8 grams (2 saturated)
Carbohydrate 24 grams	Fiber 1 gram
Protein 3 grams	Sodium 260 milligrams

Diabetic exchange = 2 Fat, 1 Carbohydrate, ½ Fruit
WW point comparison = 4 points

Lemon Coconut Layer Cake

Serves Eight

Here's a birthday cake for those (like me!) who love lemon desserts. You split a simple white layer cake, then fill and frost it with a sumptuous lemon cream frosting. You can prepare the lemon curd far in advance of the cake and frosting, which makes putting this together a snap. I found it held very well in the refrigerator for several days.

INGREDIENTS:

3 egg whites

2 tablespoons granulated sugar

3 tablespoons canola oil

1 teaspoon vanilla

½ cup low-fat buttermilk

⅔ cup Splenda Granular

1 large egg

1 cup + 2 tablespoons cake flour

2 teaspoons baking powder

¼ teaspoon baking soda

½ cup Lemon Curd, page 433

1 ¼ cups light whipped topping

⅓ cup shredded coconut

STEPS:

1. Preheat oven to 350°F. Spray an 8-inch cake pan with nonstick cooking spray or line pan bottom with wax paper.

2. In a medium bowl, beat egg whites until frothy. Gradually add sugar and continue to beat until soft peaks form when the mixer is lifted from the whites. Set aside.

3. On medium speed, mix oil, vanilla, buttermilk, Splenda, and egg in a large bowl.

4. Sift together the cake flour, baking powder, and baking soda into the bowl and blend until smooth. Gently fold in the beaten egg whites.

5. Spoon into prepared pan and smooth top.

6. Bake for 20 minutes or until the center springs back when lightly touched. Cool cake in pan on rack for 10 minutes. Loosen cake from pan by inverting briefly. Let cake layer cool completely.

7. Set cake on plate and slice in half horizontally to make two layers.

8. Mix the Lemon Curd and the whipped topping together in a bowl. Place ½ cup of frosting on the first layer of the cake. Place second layer on top and frost top and sides with the remaining frosting. Sprinkle coconut over the top of the cake.

9. Refrigerate until time to serve.

PER SERVING

Calories 175	Fat 8 grams (1.5 saturated)
Carbohydrate 22 grams	Fiber 0 grams
Protein 4 grams	Sodium 200 milligrams

Diabetic exchange = 1 ½ Carbohydrate, 1 ½ Fat
WW point comparison = 4 points

Citrus Chiffon Cake

Serves Fourteen

A chiffon cake is a terrific cake made from a cake-like batter and lightened with egg whites. It's technically in a class of cakes called foam cakes. Like its cousin the angel food cake, the light chiffon cake is moist and often served with fresh fruit or fruit sauces. It slices and freezes well, which adds to its versatility as a great cake for entertaining

INGREDIENTS:

2 ¼ cups cake flour

1 tablespoon baking powder

½ teaspoon salt

1 cup Splenda Granular

3 egg yolks

⅓ cup canola oil

¾ cup light orange juice

Zest of 1 orange

Zest of 1 lemon

8 egg whites

¼ cup granulated sugar

½ teaspoon cream of tartar

STEPS:

1. Preheat the oven to 325°F. Set aside one 10-inch ungreased tube pan with a removable bottom (an angel food cake pan).

2. Sift together the cake flour, baking powder, and salt. Stir in the Splenda. Set aside.

3. In a large bowl, beat the yolks, oil, orange juice, and zest with an electric mixer at high speed until smooth. Incorporate the flour mixture on low speed.

4. In a separate, large, grease-free bowl, whip the egg whites and cream of tartar until soft peaks form. Fold ¼ of the egg whites into the batter. Carefully fold in the remaining whites.

5. Spoon the batter into the pan and smooth.

6. Bake for 45–50 minutes or until the top springs back when lightly pressed. Let cool upside down on a wire rack at least 1 ½ hours.

This recipe originally appeared in Unbelievable Desserts with Splenda. Someone wrote and told me she liked it so much that she thought it would make a good wedding cake, but every time she tried baking it in a larger, flatter pan, it fell. I have now adjusted the recipe for more stability and lift by beating some sugar into the whites. Better still, by switching to light orange juice, I've made sure that the total carbohydrates only increase 2 grams for this better-than-ever Citrus Chiffon Cake.

PER SERVING

Calories 145

Carbohydrate 18 grams

Protein 4 grams

Fat 6 grams (5 saturated)

Fiber 0 grams

Sodium 140 milligrams

Diabetic exchange = 1 Carbohydrate, 1 Fat

WW point comparison = 3 points

Lemon Soufflé Cakes

Serves Four

These really should be called "mistake cakes." I was trying to develop a lemon pudding cake and what came out of the oven was a cake, but there was no pudding. I thought I had a loss until I tasted the cake. Yum. It was very tasty and had a moist but airy texture. So I tried the recipe again, using 6-ounce ramekins to produce individual cakes. They were a hit. You can get the ramekins ready ahead of time and pop them in the oven while you eat. Serve them with a touch of light whipped topping and blueberries for a spectacular finish.

Ingredients:

4 large egg whites

¾ cup + 3 tablespoons Splenda Granular

1 tablespoon granulated sugar

2 large egg yolks

1 tablespoon butter or margarine, softened

¾ cup low-fat buttermilk

¼ cup lemon juice

1 tablespoon lemon rind

¼ cup all-purpose flour

1 teaspoon cornstarch

¼ teaspoon baking powder

2 teaspoons granulated sugar

Per Serving

Calories 160	Fat 5 grams (2 saturated)
Carbohydrate 20 grams	Fiber 0 grams
Protein 7 grams	Sodium 130 milligrams

Diabetic exchange = 1 ½ Carbohydrate,
1 Medium-Fat Meat
WW point comparison = 4 points

Steps:

1. Preheat oven to 350°F. Spray four 6-ounce ramekins or soufflé cups with nonstick cooking spray and place them in a larger baking pan that is at least 2 inches deep; set aside.

2. In a deep bowl, beat egg whites with an electric mixer on high speed until foamy. Beat in the 3 tablespoons Splenda and 1 tablespoon of granulated sugar until soft peaks form when beaters are lifted from the whites.

3. In another bowl, combine eggs yolks, butter, and remaining Splenda and beat until thick and creamy. Stir in the next 6 ingredients (buttermilk through baking powder) and beat until smooth. Fold in one quarter of the egg whites; stir to incorporate. Gently fold in remaining egg whites.

4. Divide the batter into the ramekins (¾ full).

5. Sprinkle ½ teaspoon of granulated sugar on top of each cake.

6. Place baking dish on middle rack of the oven. Pour boiling water into the larger pan until the water reaches halfway up the ramekins. Bake for 25–30 minutes or until center feels firm to the touch. They are done as soon as the center sets.

Creamy Chocolate Souffle Cakes

Serves Six

Like the Lemon Souffle Cakes, these creamy and decadent cakes are a cross between a cake and a soufflé—only these are meant for chocolate lovers. Great for entertaining, the chocolate mixture can be made ahead of time and baked right before serving. Your guests will be pleasantly surprised to hear that these Souffle Cakes are low in fat and sugar (never tell them until they've enjoyed them).

INGREDIENTS:

¾ cup Splenda Granular (divided)

¾ cup water

3 ounces semisweet or bittersweet chocolate, chopped (or ½ cup chips)

½ cup Dutch-process cocoa

2 egg yolks

1 tablespoon cornstarch

⅛ teaspoon salt

4 egg whites

¼ teaspoon cream of tartar

1 tablespoon granulated sugar

The water bath helps keeps the batter very moist. Be sure to remove the cakes from the oven as soon as the centers set, for the creamiest cake. Taken out too soon, they will seem a bit undone, but left too long, they will solidify into a good-tasting, but firmer cake.

PER SERVING

Calories 150	Fat 7 grams
Carbohydrate 20 grams	Fiber 3 grams
Protein 6 grams	Sodium 115 milligrams

Diabetic exchange = 1 Carbohydrate,
1 Medium-Fat Meat
WW point comparison = 3 points

STEPS:

1. Preheat oven to 350°F.

2. Spray six 6-ounce ramekins with cooking spray, and place them in a larger baking pan that's at least 2 inches deep; set aside.

3. In a medium saucepan, boil ½ cup of water and ½ cup Splenda. Turn off heat and whisk in chocolate until melted. Stir in cocoa and egg yolks until combined.

4. Whisk together cornstarch and ¼ cup water. Mix cornstarch mixture into chocolate. Whisk until smooth; set aside.

5. In a deep bowl, use the high speed of an electric mixer to beat egg whites and cream of tartar until foamy. Add granulated sugar and ¼ cup Splenda until stiff but not dry peaks form when you lift the beaters from the whites.

6. Gently fold egg whites ¼ at a time into chocolate mixture.

7. Fill each ramekin with chocolate mixture. Place in baking dish and put in oven on center rack. Pour boiling water into the larger pan until the water reaches halfway up the ramekins.

8. Bake for 15 minutes until just firm to the touch and slightly cracked. Serve warm.

Sour Cream Loaf Pound Cake

Serves Twelve

The first "pound" cakes (dating all the way back to the 1700s) were dense cakes, made with 1 pound each of butter, sugar, and flour. You won't find many pound cake recipes today quite that heavy, but the sticks of butter and cups of sugar in most recipes can definitely spell "pound" when you step on the scale. Adapted from a popular Sour Cream Pound Cake recipe featured in Cooking Light, this grand loaf is moist and tender with a fine tight crumb.

INGREDIENTS:

⅔ cup Splenda Sugar Blend for Baking

6 tablespoons margarine or butter, softened

2 large eggs + 2 large egg whites

1 ½ teaspoons vanilla

¾ cup light sour cream

¾ teaspoon baking soda

2 ¼ cups cake flour

⅛ teaspoon salt

Like all basic pound cake recipes, this cake adapts well to other flavors. You may add a teaspoon of lemon and/or orange zest; substitute almond, butter, or rum extract for some or all of the vanilla extract; or add chopped nuts to the batter. For entertaining, place the loaf on a platter, cutting the first few slices and surrounding it with bowls of fresh berries, one or more of the toppings, and light whipped topping.

STEPS:

1. Preheat oven to 325°F. Coat a 9 x 5-inch loaf pan with nonstick cooking spray.

2. In a large bowl, with an electric mixer, beat Splenda Sugar and margarine until very light and creamy (about 5 minutes). Add eggs and then egg whites, one by one, beating each time until creamy. Add vanilla.

3. Place sour cream in a large measuring cup (at least 2-cup size) or bowl. Stir in baking soda. Set aside. Sift flour and salt together. By hand, stir ½ of flour mixture into creamed mixture. Stir in ½ of sour cream and then repeat, gently mixing each time just to incorporate flour and sour cream.

4. Pour batter into prepared pan and bake for 55-65 minutes or until a toothpick inserted into the center of the loaf comes out clean. Cool in pan, on wire rack, for 10 minutes before removing from pan. Once it cools, you may wrap tight and freeze.

CHOCOLATE SOUR CREAM LOAF POUND CAKE VARIATION: Reduce cake flour to 1 ½ cups and sift in ½ cup cocoa powder (preferably Dutch process) into flour mixture.

PER SERVING

Calories 185	Fat 7 grams (2 saturated)
Carbohydrate 25 grams	Fiber 0 grams
Protein 5 grams	Sodium 240 milligrams

Diabetic exchange = 1 ½ Carbohydrate, 1 Fat, ½ Lean Meat

WW point comparison = 4 points

Strawberry Shortcake

Serves Eight

Strawberry shortcake is always a special treat. What makes this particular cake even better is that it only takes a short time to prepare. Using a reduced-fat baking mix makes it quick and easy to produce the tender sweet biscuits that will hold all those luscious fresh berries.

INGREDIENTS:

4 cups sliced strawberries

¼ cup Splenda Granular

2 cups reduced-fat baking mix (like Bisquick Reduced-Fat)

⅓ cup Splenda Granular

1 teaspoon baking powder

½ teaspoon baking soda

⅔ cup low-fat buttermilk

1 ½ tablespoons margarine or butter, melted

1 egg, beaten

1 teaspoon sugar (optional)

1 ½ cups light whipped topping, thawed

Who said strawberries owned shortcakes? Try substituting fresh peaches or other berries to give an old favorite a new twist.

STEPS:

1. Preheat oven to 425°F. Spray a baking sheet with nonstick cooking spray.

2. In a medium bowl, toss strawberries with ¼ cup Splenda. Set aside.

3. In a large bowl, combine baking mix, ⅓ cup Splenda, baking powder, and baking soda.

4. Mix buttermilk and melted butter together and pour over dry ingredients. Stir with a spoon until dough comes together.

5. Remove dough from bowl and place on lightly floured surface. Knead dough 10 times; then pat or roll into even ½-inch thickness.

6. Using a 2 ½-inch round cutter or a glass, cut out shortcakes and transfer them to the prepared baking sheet. Gather scraps of dough together and cut out more cakes for a total of 8.

7. Brush with beaten egg and sprinkle a little sugar on each cake.

8. Bake for 12-15 minutes. Transfer to rack and let cool slightly.

9. To assemble shortcakes: Split each shortcake in half. Place the bottoms on dessert plates. Cover with ½ cup berries on each cake. Cover with top of each shortcake.

10. Top with 3 tablespoons light whipped topping and serve immediately.

PER SERVING

Calories 195	Fat 6 grams (3 saturated)
Carbohydrate 31 grams	Fiber 2 grams
Protein 3.5 grams	Sodium 420 milligrams

Diabetic exchange = 1 ½ Carbohydrate, ½ Fruit
WW point comparison = 4 points

Chocolate Almond Torte

Serves Eight

In Austria and Germany, the word"torte" refers to any round cake. Here, the term torte is often reserved for cakes with many layers, or cakes that use ground nuts or bread crumbs in place of some or most of the flour. This torte uses ground almonds and very little flour to create a very dense and moist chocolate cake. Serve it dusted with powdered sugar, or with Quick Raspberry Sauce (page 423) for an elegant dessert. I like to warm the cake before placing each slice on a plate pooled with the raspberry sauce and then top it with light whipped topping.

INGREDIENTS:

½ **cup almonds, toasted**

¼ **cup all-purpose flour**

½ **cup Splenda Granular**

2 **tablespoons cocoa powder**

¼ **teaspoon baking powder**

¾ **cup semisweet chocolate morsels**

3 **tablespoons hot water**

⅓ **cup prune purée**

½ **teaspoon almond extract**

5 **egg whites**

⅓ **cup Splenda Granular**

½ **teaspoon cream of tartar**

2 **teaspoons powdered sugar (optional)**

STEPS:

1. Preheat oven to 375°F. Spray bottom of an 8-inch round springform or cake pan with nonstick cooking spray.

2. Toast almonds by placing on a pie plate and baking for 5 minutes. Using a food processor, grind nuts until almost as fine as flour. Pulse in flour, ½ cup Splenda, cocoa powder, and baking powder. Set aside.

3. Melt chocolate in a small pan over hot water or place in a bowl and microwave for 1 ½ minutes. Stir until all chips are melted and then stir in hot water, prune purée, and almond extract. Mix flour mixture into the chocolate (it will be thick).

4. In a separate bowl, beat egg whites and cream of tartar until frothy. Gradually add ⅓ cup of Splenda and beat until soft peaks form. Fold ⅓ of egg whites into cool chocolate mixture to lighten mixture. Gently fold in remaining whites.

5. Spoon mixture into prepared pan and smooth.

6. Bake for 20–22 minutes until center is just set. Do not overbake. Let cool in pan on wire rack for at least 30 minutes.

PER SERVING

Calories 190	Fat 9 grams (2.5 saturated)
Carbohydrate 24	Fiber 3 grams
Protein 4 grams	Sodium 50 milligrams

Diabetic exchange = 1 ½ Carbohydrate, 2 Fat
WW point comparison = 4 points

Cream Cheese-Filled Pumpkin Roll

Serves Eight

Put this on your list for holiday desserts. It is decorative, delicious, and definitely lights up any Thanksgiving or Christmas dessert table. Luscious with a cream cheese filling and spiced just right, this one is sure to be a crowd-pleaser. (See page 389 for cake rolling tip).

INGREDIENTS:

CAKE

3 large eggs

1 cup Splenda Granular

⅔ cup canned pumpkin

1 teaspoon molasses

1 ½ teaspoons cinnamon

½ teaspoon ginger

½ teaspoon nutmeg

¾ cup + 1 tablespoon all-purpose flour

1 teaspoon baking powder

¼ teaspoon baking soda

FILLING

8 ounces light cream cheese

3 tablespoons Splenda Granular

½ cup light whipped topping

2 teaspoons powdered sugar

STEPS:

1. Preheat oven to 350°F. Coat a 10 x 12-inch jellyroll★ pan with nonstick cooking spray. Line bottom of pan with wax paper. Lightly spray with nonstick cooking spray. Set aside.

2. CAKE: In a medium mixing bowl, with an electric mixer on high speed, beat eggs for 5 minutes; beat in Splenda. Whisk pumpkin, molasses, and spices into eggs.

3. Sift flour, baking powder, and baking soda into pumpkin mixture.

4. Pour batter into prepared pan. Using spatula, completely level batter. Bake for 8 minutes until cake is springy to the touch and edges appear dry. (Do not overbake or cake will crack when it is rolled.) Lay smooth towel onto work surface. Sift powdered sugar onto towel. As soon as cake comes out of oven, turn cake onto towel, and loosely roll up, starting with short side. Cool.

5. FILLING: In a small mixing bowl, beat light cream cheese and Splenda with electric mixer until smooth. Beat in whipped topping.

6. Unroll cooled cake. Spread filling over cake, stopping 1 inch from the farthest short side. Starting from the short side closest to you, reroll cake. Cover with plastic wrap and refrigerate cake until ready to serve. Dust with powdered sugar before serving if desired.

★You may substitute a 9 x 13-inch cake pan if you must.

PER SERVING

Calories 170	Fat 7 grams (4 saturated)
Carbohydrate 18 grams	Fiber 1 gram
Protein 7 grams	Sodium 310 milligrams

Diabetic exchange = 1 Carbohydrate, 1 Fat, 1 Lean Meat
WW point comparison = 4 points

Chocolate Cream-Filled Chocolate Roll

Serves Eight

"Yule logs"—traditionally, rich and moist cake rolls filled with buttercream and adorned with rich chocolate frosting—are often served at the holidays. The traditional version is deceptively "light." In contrast, I have created this moist chocolate sponge cake filled and rolled with a rich chocolate mousse filling that is heavy only in taste.

INGREDIENTS:

CAKE

⅓ cup Dutch-process cocoa

⅓ cup water

3 eggs, separated

½ cup Splenda Granular

¼ cup prune puree or 1 2.5-ounce jar baby food prunes

½ teaspoon vanilla

½ cup cake flour

2 egg whites

½ teaspoon cream of tartar

2 tablespoons granulated sugar

2 teaspoons cocoa powder (for rolling)

FILLING

½ cup tub-style light cream cheese

2 cups light whipped topping

¼ cup Dutch-process cocoa powder

½ cup Splenda Granular

½ teaspoon vanilla extract

1 teaspoon powdered sugar (optional)

STEPS:

1. Preheat oven to 350°F. Coat a 10 x 12-inch jellyroll pan with nonstick cooking spray. Line the bottom of the pan with wax paper and lightly spray wax paper with nonstick cooking spray. Set aside.

2. CAKE: In a small bowl, dissolve cocoa in water. Beat yolks with Splenda until thick and fluffy (about 5 minutes). Add dissolved cocoa, prune puree, and vanilla to beaten yolks. Sift half the flour over egg mixture and fold it in gently with balloon whisk or rubber spatula. Repeat with remaining flour.

PER SERVING

Calories 200

Carbohydrate 24 grams

Protein 7 grams

Fat 7 grams (4.5 saturated)

Fiber 2 grams

Sodium 120 milligrams

Diabetic exchange = 1 ½ Carbohydrate, 1 Lean Meat, 1 Fat

WW point comparison = 4 points

3. Beat egg whites until foamy. Add cream of tartar, and beat until soft peaks form. Beat in granulated sugar until stiff peaks form. Fold egg whites into batter and pour batter into prepared pan. Use spatula to completely level batter.

4. Bake for 18-21 minutes until cake is springy to the touch. (Do not overbake or the cake will crack when it is rolled.) Lay smooth towel onto work surface. Sift cocoa powder onto towel. Allow cake to cool in pan 2-4 minutes. Turn cake onto towel, and loosely roll up from short side. Cool.

5. FILLING: In a medium bowl with an electric mixer, beat cream cheese until smooth. Beat in whipped topping, cocoa powder, Splenda, and vanilla until smooth and fluffy.

6. Unroll cooled cake. Spread filling over cake, stopping 1 inch from the farthest short side. Starting from the short side closest to you, roll cake up again. Cover with plastic wrap and refrigerate cake until ready to serve.

7. Dust with powdered sugar before serving if desired.

To help avoid cake rolls from cracking, use the correct size pan, spread the batter evenly, take the cake out of the oven as soon as it is done, and roll while it is still warm.

Cheesecake, Cheesecake, and More Cheesecake

Cheesecake Crumb Crust

Heavenly Cheesecake

Everyday Cheesecake

Chocolate Cheesecake

Mocha Chip Cheesecake

Cherry Ricotta Cheesecake

Margarita Cheesecake

Luscious Lemon Cheesecake

Lemon Chiffon Cheesecake

Strawberry Swirl Cheesecake

Pumpkin Streusel Cheesecake

Cheesecake Squares

Breakfast Cheesecake Cups

Fresh Banana Cheesecake Cups

Strawberry-Topped New York
        Cheesecake

No-Bake Cheesecakes:

Blueberry Cheesecake Parfaits

Black Forest Cheesecake Parfaits

Key Lime Cheesecake

Almond Orange Ricotta Cheesecake

Chocolate Peppermint Cheesecake

10-Minute No-Bake Strawberry
        Cheese Pie

Nothing is as rich and creamy and satisfying as a piece of cheesecake. It's no wonder that entire books—entire restaurants—have been fashioned after this indulgent dessert.

But cheesecake isn't really cake at all.

Cheesecakes are technically custards, albeit very rich custards. Baked cheesecakes, like custards, depend on eggs to help the ingredients "set." With cheesecakes, however, the main ingredient (most often cream cheese) firms up enough to be sliced like a cake— hence, the name. The problem with using cheese as a main ingredient in a cake is when you're watching your intake of fat and calories. The fact is, a single piece of cheesecake can easily have more than 50 grams of fat and 600 calories—whoa. The good news is that there are lots of ways to produce creamy, sweet cheesecakes with far less fat and a fraction—if any—of the sugar.

This section of the book is devoted to cheesecakes, cheesecakes, and even more cheesecakes. Cheesecakes for every day and cheescakes for special occasions. Cheesecakes for holidays and cheesecakes for parties. Cheesecakes with fruit and cheesecakes with chocolate! Cheesecakes in cups and cheesecake in glasses. Cheesecakes you bake and cheesecakes you don't. You will even find cheesecake for breakfast! What you won't find are cheesecakes that are difficult to make—because cheesecake is easy. And to make the perfect cheesecake every time, here are a few tips:

» You may bake cheesecakes in a regular cake pan instead of a springform pan if you don't need to present the cake whole. This means you don't have to wrap the pan when you use the water bath.

» Make sure your cheeses are at room temperature before beating. To prevent lumps, beat them until they are very smooth before adding any liquid ingredients.

» Puree cottage cheese (when specified) until it
is completely smooth. This means it should be
creamy and have no visible curds left

» Add eggs last and beat them in just until blended
to help avoid cracks in the finished cheesecake.

» The best way to wrap a pan for a water bath is to
use a single sheet of heavy-duty aluminum foil.
This way there are no seams to allow for water
seepage. Set pan on foil, pull up all sides, and
tightly secure at the top rim of the pan.

» For water baths, place the pan with the cheesecake
mixture into the baking pan—and into the
oven—before adding the hot water.

» Cheesecakes are "done" and should be removed
from the oven when the center is barely set.
Remember, the center should still move slightly
because cheesecakes continue to set for hours after
baking.

» Cheesecakes should be left in the oven to cool for
the first 30 minutes (with the door open) to avoid
abrupt temperature changes that can create cracks.

» Not all cracks can be avoided (especially in low-
fat, low-sugar cakes), but all can be camouflaged
with sweetened sour cream, fruit toppings, or light
whipped topping.

Cheesecake Crumb Crust

Serves Twelve

This crumb crust is very similar to the one I use for pies. Because cheesecakes do not require a crust on the sides, you can use fewer crumbs. Cheesecake fillings also tend to seep into the crust and help to bind it together, which eliminates the need for some of the fat and the egg white used in graham-cracker pie crusts. In order to keep the fillings from seeping too much and creating a soggy crust, I like to bake the crust separately before filling.

INGREDIENTS:

¾ cup graham-cracker crumbs (about 12 squares)

2 tablespoons Splenda Granular

1 tablespoon margarine or butter, melted

These two basic crusts can be found on many of the cheesecakes, but other low-fat cookies such as gingersnaps and vanilla wafers can be also be used, as found in the Pumpkin Streusel Cheesecake and Cherry Ricotta Cheesecakes. Have some fun by mixing and matching fillings and crusts to suit your taste.

STEPS:

1. Preheat oven to 350°F. Spray an 8- or 9-inch springform pan, as specified in cheesecake recipe, with nonstick cooking spray.

2. If starting with whole graham crackers, place them in a blender or food processor and pulse to make fine crumbs.

3. Place the crumbs in a bowl and add Splenda and melted butter or margarine. Stir to mix. Pour the crumb mixture into the bottom of the prepared pan. With your fingers, the back of a spoon, or a sheet of plastic wrap, press down on the crumbs to cover the bottom of the pan.

4. Bake for 5 minutes. Cool. (Be sure the crust is completely cool when using for unbaked cheesecakes.)

CHOCOLATE CRUMB CRUST VARIATION: Substitute chocolate graham crackers for the regular grahams. Add 2 teaspoons cocoa powder, along with the 1 additional tablespoon Splenda and butter or margarine, to the crumbs.

PER SERVING

Calories 40

Carbohydrate 6 grams

Protein 0 grams

Fat 1.5 grams (.5 saturated)

Fiber 0 grams

Sodium 55 milligrams

Diabetic exchange = ½ Carbohydrate

WW point comparison = 1 point

Heavenly Cheesecake

Serves Twelve

This was the cheesecake in my family that was made only for special occasions. So, I really wanted my makeover to work on this one—and it did! But, I needed another opinion. A good friend and her husband happened to be coming over for dinner so I served it for dessert. My friend exclaimed, "This is my cheesecake!" And she was sure this was her's. In fact, our original recipes were almost identical. The real surprise came when she found out that my lightened version had a third of the calories, less than half the carbohydrate, and one-fifth the fat of our original recipes. Now that's "heavenly."

INGREDIENTS:

1 8- or 9-inch baked Cheesecake Crumb Crust, page 393

1 cup low-fat cottage cheese

8 ounces tub-style light cream cheese

8 ounces nonfat cream cheese, room temperature

1 ¼ cups Splenda Granular

2 tablespoons all-purpose flour

2 tablespoons cornstarch

1 teaspoon vanilla extract

½ teaspoon almond extract

1 large egg

3 large egg whites

1 ¼ cups light sour cream

If you prefer your cheesecake a bit more dense, with the sour cream on top, you'll love Strawberry-Topped New York Style Cheesecake. (page 410)

PER SERVING

Calories 180	Fat 8 grams (5 saturated)
Carbohydrate 15 grams	Fiber 0 grams
Protein 11 grams	Sodium 350 milligrams

Diabetic exchange = 1 Carbohydrate, 1 ½ Lean Meat
WW point comparison = 4 points

STEPS:

1. Preheat oven to 350°F. Wrap any 8-inch (or 9-inch) springform pan filled with crust tightly in heavy-duty foil to make waterproof.

2. Place cottage cheese into a food processor or blender. Purée until completely smooth. Spoon into a large mixing bowl and add nonfat and light cream cheeses. Using an electric mixer, beat on medium speed until creamy. Add the Splenda, flour, cornstarch, and extracts, and beat on low until smooth. Add large egg and then egg whites, beating just briefly after each addition to incorporate. Stir in the sour cream with a large spoon. Pour into the prepared crust and smooth top.

3. Place the foil-wrapped pan in a large, deep baking pan, and pour boiling water into the larger pan until it reaches halfway up the outside of the cheesecake pan.

4. Bake for 60 minutes or until sides of cake appear firm and center jiggles slightly. (For a 9-inch pan, bake 50-55 minutes.) Turn off heat, open oven door, and let cheesecake cool in the oven for 30 minutes. Remove from water bath and finish cooling.

5. Refrigerate at least 6 hours before serving.

Everyday Cheesecake

Serves Twelve

People usually think of cheesecakes as only for special occasions. This cheesecake, however, is so healthy and simple to make that there's no reason not to enjoy it every day. I have streamlined the steps and bake it in a regular 8-inch cake pan, eliminating your hunt for the cheesecake pan.

INGREDIENTS:

CRUST

1 tablespoon butter, melted

½ cup graham-cracker crumbs

2 tablespoons Splenda Granular

FILLING

8 ounces lowfat cottage cheese

8 ounces nonfat cream cheese, room temperature

8 ounces tub-style light cream cheese, room temperature

1 cup Splenda Granular

2 tablespoons cornstarch

2 tablespoons all-purpose flour

Zest of 1 lemon

1 teaspoon vanilla extract

2 large eggs

2 large egg whites

1 cup sour cream

STEPS:

1. Preheat oven to 350°F. Coat an 8-inch round cake pan with nonstick cooking spray.

2. CRUST: Place melted butter in cake pan. Toss in graham-cracker crumbs and Splenda. Using your hand, mix and pat onto bottom of pan. Set crust in oven for 10 minutes. Cool completely.

3. Place pan in a 9 x 13-inch or larger baking pan with 2- to 3-inch sides.

4. FILLING: Puree cottage cheese in a food processor or blender until completely smooth. Spoon into a large mixing bowl and add cream cheeses. Beat on medium speed with an electric mixer until creamy. Add Splenda, cornstarch, flour, zest, and vanilla. Beat on low until smooth. Add eggs and then egg whites, beating briefly after each addition. Stir in sour cream with a large spoon.

5. Pour mixture into set crust. Place cheesecake into large, deep baking pan and add hot water to reach halfway up sides of cake pan. Bake in water bath for 50–55 minutes or until sides of cake appear firm and center is barely set. Remove from water bath and cool. Chill at least 6 hours before serving.

To dress this cake up for any occasion use your choice of sauce or topping from the Sweet Embellishments section of the book.

PER SERVING

Calories 160

Carbohydrate 13 grams

Protein 10 grams

Fat 7 grams (4.5 saturated)

Fiber 0 grams

Sodium 330 milligrams

Diabetic exchange = 1 ½ Lean Meat, 1 Carbohydrate

WW point comparison = 4 points

Chocolate Cheesecake

Serves Twelve

Cheesecake and chocolate—how much better can it get? This creamy cake is for all you chocolate lovers. You start with a chocolate crumb crust, fill it with rich chocolate filling, and top the cheesecake with chocolate shavings (if that strikes your fancy). So, who said eating healthy isn't fun?

INGREDIENTS:

1 9-inch Chocolate Cheesecake Crumb Crust, page 418

2 cups low-fat cottage cheese

8 ounces tub-style light cream cheese

8 ounces nonfat cream cheese, room temperature

½ cup semisweet chocolate chips, melted and cooled

1 ½ cups Splenda Granular

4 tablespoons brown sugar

¼ cup Dutch-process cocoa powder (like Hershey's European)

2 tablespoons all-purpose flour

1 tablespoon cornstarch

1 teaspoon vanilla extract

½ teaspoon almond extract

1 large egg

3 large egg whites

½ cup light sour cream

STEPS:

1. Preheat oven to 350°F. Wrap a 9-inch springform pan filled with crust tightly in heavy-duty foil to waterproof.

2. Place cottage cheese into a food processor or blender. Purée until completely smooth. Spoon into a large mixing bowl, and add nonfat and light cream cheeses. Beat on medium speed with an electric mixer until creamy. Add the cooled, melted chocolate, Splenda, brown sugar, cocoa powder, flour, cornstarch, and extracts. Beat on low speed until smooth. Add whole egg and then egg whites, beating briefly after each addition to incorporate. Stir in the sour cream with a large spoon.

3. Pour mixture into the prepared pan and smooth top.

4. Place the foil-wrapped pan in a large, deep baking pan and pour boiling water into larger pan until it reaches halfway up the outside of the cheesecake pan.

5. Bake for 55-60 minutes or until sides of cake appear firm and center jiggles slightly. Turn off heat, open oven door, and let cheesecake cool in the oven for 30 minutes. Remove from water bath and finish cooling.

6. Refrigerate at least 6 hours before serving.

PER SERVING

Calories 220	Fat 8 grams (5 saturated)
Carbohydrate 24 grams	Fiber 1 gram
Protein 13 grams	Sodium 380 grams

Diabetic exchange = 1 ½ Carbohydrate, 2 Very Lean Meat
WW point comparison = 5 points

Mocha Chip Cheesecake

Serves Twelve

Coffee and chocolate—another great combination. This smooth cheesecake filling is lightly flavored with coffee and studded with miniature chocolate chips. It makes a great addition to any dinner party.

INGREDIENTS:

1 9-inch Chocolate Cheesecake Crumb Crust, page 393

1 cup low-fat cottage cheese

8 ounces tub-style light cream cheese

8 ounces nonfat cream cheese, room temperature

1 ½ cups Splenda Granular

2 tablespoons all-purpose flour

1 tablespoon cornstarch

½ teaspoon vanilla extract

1 tablespoon + 1 teaspoon instant coffee powder

2 tablespoons hot water

2 large eggs

2 large egg whites

2 teaspoons all-purpose flour

⅔ cup mini chocolate chips

STEPS:

1. Preheat oven to 350°F. Wrap a 9-inch springform pan filled with crust tightly in heavy-duty foil to waterproof.

2. Place cottage cheese into a food processor or blender. Purée until completely smooth. Spoon into a large mixing bowl and add nonfat and light cream cheeses. With an electric mixer, beat on medium until creamy. Add the Splenda, flour, cornstarch, and vanilla. Beat on low until smooth.

3. Dissolve coffee in the hot water and add to batter.

4. Add whole eggs and then egg whites, beating briefly after each addition to incorporate.

5. Coat the chocolate chips with 2 teaspoons of flour and stir in.

6. Pour into the prepared pan and smooth top. Place the foil-wrapped pan in a large, deep baking dish, and pour boiling water into larger pan until it reaches halfway up the outside of the cheesecake pan.

7. Bake for 60 minutes or until sides of cake appear firm and center jiggles slightly. Turn off heat, open oven door, and let cheesecake cool in oven for 30 minutes. Remove from water bath and finish cooling.

8. Refrigerate at least 6 hours before serving.

PER SERVING

Calories 220	Fat 10 grams (6 saturated)
Carbohydrate 22 grams	Fiber 1 gram
Protein 11 grams	Sodium 350 milligrams

Diabetic exchange = 1 ½ Carbohydrate, 1 ½ Medium-Fat Meat

WW point comparison = 5 points

Cherry Ricotta Cheesecake

Serves Twelve

This is one of those recipes I made so many times that by the time I finished, I knew it by heart. Yet I had a vision of something special for this and just wouldn't stop short. So here it is—a vanilla wafer crust topped with a creamy ricotta cheesecake batter that is studded with sweet, dark, almond-scented cherries and topped with a vanilla wafer-almond topping. Unique and beautiful, this would be perfect for a special occasion, like Christmas or Valentine's Day.

INGREDIENTS:

CRUST

1 ¼ cups crushed vanilla wafers

2 tablespoons margarine or butter, melted

2 tablespoons sliced almonds

FILLING

1 cup slightly thawed sweet dark cherries, unsweetened

1 cup + 1 tablespoon Splenda Granular

½ teaspoon almond extract

1 15-ounce carton low-fat ricotta

8 ounces tub-style light cream cheese

¼ cup all-purpose flour

1 teaspoon vanilla

¾ teaspoon almond extract

2 large eggs

3 large egg whites

½ cup light sour cream

PER SERVING

Calories 205   Fat 11 grams (5 saturated)

Carbohydrate 16 grams   Fiber 1 gram

Protein 9 grams   Sodium 210 milligrams

Diabetic exchange = 1 Carbohydrate, 1 Lean Meat, 1 ½ Fat

WW point comparison = 5 points

Steps:

1. Preheat oven to 325°F. Spray a 9-inch springform or cake pan with cooking spray.

2. Crust: In a small bowl, combine wafers and margarine. Press 1 cup into pan, reserving ¼ cup in a small bowl for topping. Bake crust for 5 minutes. Add sliced almonds to small bowl. Set aside.

3. Filling: In a small bowl, toss cherries with ½ teaspoon almond extract and 1 tablespoon Splenda. Set aside.

4. In a large bowl, with an electric mixer, beat ricotta cheese for 2 minutes. Add cream cheese and remaining Splenda and continue to beat for an additional 2 minutes. Add flour and extracts and beat until smooth. Add eggs, one at a time, and then egg whites, beating briefly after each addition, just to incorporate. Stir in sour cream with a large spoon.

5. Evenly arrange cherries on top of vanilla crust. Carefully spoon cheesecake batter over cherries (moving any cherries back into position or pressing them back into batter as necessary). Bake for 50 minutes or until cheesecake is almost firm all the way to the center (there may be some slight cracking).

6. Open oven and sprinkle almond crumb mixture on top of cheesecake, covering any cracks. Bake 10 more minutes and remove from oven. Cool. Chill at least 6 hours before serving.

Ricotta cheese, along with nuts and fruit, are common ingredients for Italian-style cheesecakes. Besides its unique flavor and texture, ricotta adds protein and calcium to this nutritious treat.

Margarita Cheesecake

Serves Twelve

Next time you're sipping a frosty margarita, imagine that refreshingly cool flavor blended into a creamy, sweet cheesecake. The thumbs-up was given to this recipe by my neighbors, who thought it succeeded in doing just that. So, why not head south of the border with a slice of this very adult-flavored cheesecake? It's a great party pleaser.

INGREDIENTS:

CRUST

¾ cup graham-cracker crumbs

2 tablespoons butter, melted

2 tablespoons Splenda Granular

FILLING

8 ounces 1% cottage cheese

8 ounces tub-style light cream cheese, room temperature

8 ounces fat-free cream cheese, room temperature

1 cup light sour cream

1 cup Splenda Granular

2 large eggs

3 large egg whites

2 tablespoons tequila

2 tablespoons triple sec

2 tablespoons fresh lime juice

TOPPING

2 tablespoons graham-cracker crumbs

1 tablespoon Splenda Granular

Variation: If you miss the salty taste, try finely crush salted pretzels for your crust. Ole'.

STEPS:

1. Preheat oven to 350°F. Coat a 9-inch springform pan with nonstick cooking spray. Wrap pan tightly with heavy-duty aluminum foil to make waterproof.

2. CRUST: In a small bowl, mix together graham-cracker crumbs, melted butter, and Splenda. Pat into the bottom of a prepared 9-inch round pan.

3. FILLING: Bake crust in oven for 10 minutes. Cool completely. Place pan in a 9 x 13-inch or larger baking pan with 2- to 3-inch sides.

4. Place cottage cheese in a food processor or blender. Puree until completely smooth. Spoon into a large mixing bowl and add cream cheeses. Beat on medium speed with an electric mixer until creamy. Add sour cream and Splenda and beat until smooth. Beat in eggs and whites one at a time. Stir in tequila, triple sec, and lime juice. Pour cheesecake batter into prepared crust.

5. Pour hot water into larger baking pan to reach halfway up sides of cake pan. Bake in water bath for 50-55 minutes just until set in center.

6. Combine graham-cracker crumbs and Splenda and sprinkle on top. Remove from water bath. Chill at least 6 hours before serving.

PER SERVING

Calories 170	Fat 6 grams (3.5 saturated)
Carbohydrate 14 grams	Fiber 0 grams
Protein 9 grams	Sodium 340 milligrams

Diabetic exchange = 1 ½ Lean Meat, 1 Carbohydrate
WW point comparison = 4 points

Luscious Lemon Cheesecake

Serves Twelve

The name says it all. This cheesecake is truly luscious. I sent it to work with my husband, and the cake was quickly gobbled up. No one ever suspected it wasn't a "regular" cheesecake. Mission accomplished!

INGREDIENTS:

1 9-inch baked Cheesecake Crumb Crust, page 393

1 cup low-fat cottage cheese

8 ounces tub-style light cream cheese

8 ounces nonfat cream cheese, room temperature

1 cup Splenda Granular

2 tablespoons all-purpose flour

2 teaspoons cornstarch

2 teaspoons lemon juice

1 tablespoon lemon zest

1 8-ounce carton nonfat lemon yogurt (not light)

2 large eggs

2 large egg whites

Top this cake with sliced strawberries or raspberries, and then brush on 2 tablespoons of melted low-sugar jam for shine, or sift 2 teaspoons of powdered sugar over berries just before serving. So pretty!

STEPS:

1. Preheat oven to 350°F. Wrap a 9-inch springform pan filled with crust tightly in heavy-duty foil (to make waterproof).

2. Place cottage cheese into a food processor or blender. Purée until completely smooth. Spoon into a large mixing bowl and add nonfat and light cream cheeses. Beat on medium speed with an electric mixer until creamy. Add the Splenda, flour, and cornstarch, and beat on low until smooth. Blend in the lemon juice, zest, and yogurt.

3. Add whole eggs and then egg whites, beating briefly after each addition to incorporate. Pour into the prepared pan and smooth top.

4. Place the foil-wrapped pan in a large deep baking pan and pour boiling water into larger pan until it reaches halfway up the outside of the cheesecake pan.

5. Bake for 60-65 minutes or until sides of cake appear firm and center jiggles slightly. Turn off the heat, open oven door and let cheesecake cool down in the oven for 30 minutes. Remove from water bath and finish cooling on rack.

6. Refrigerate at least 6 hours before serving.

PER SERVING

Calories 160
Carbohydrate 15 grams
Protein 10 grams

Fat 6 grams (3.5 saturated)
Fiber 0 grams
Sodium 340 milligrams

Diabetic exchange = 1 Carbohydrate, 1 ½ Lean Meat
WW point comparison = 4 points

Lemon Chiffon Cheesecake

Serves Twelve

Light and also luscious, this recipe was inspired by one that I once ate at a famous cheesecake restaurant. I was impressed with how light and chiffonlike it was. After several trials, I came up with a baked cheesecake that I enjoyed just as much. This is one of my favorite endings to a delicious and elegant meal.

INGREDIENTS:

CRUST

¾ cup graham-cracker crumbs

2 tablespoons Splenda Granular

2 tablespoons butter, melted

FILLING

1 cup 1% cottage cheese

8 ounces tub-style light cream cheese, room temperature

8 ounces fat-free cream cheese, room temperature

1 ¼ cups Splenda Granular

1 tablespoon cornstarch

1 tablespoon all-purpose flour

2 large egg yolks

¼ cup lemon juice

1 tablespoon lemon zest

4 large egg whites

STEPS:

1. Preheat oven to 350°F. Coat a 9-inch springform pan with nonstick cooking spray. Wrap pan tightly with heavy-duty aluminum foil to make waterproof.

2. CRUST: In a small bowl, mix together graham cracker crumbs, Splenda, and melted butter. Pat into the bottom of a prepared 9-inch round cake pan.

3. Bake crust in oven for 10 minutes. Cool completely. Place pan in a 9 x 13-inch or larger baking pan with 2- to 3-inch sides.

4. FILLING: Place cottage cheese in a food processor or blender. Puree until completely smooth. Spoon into a large mixing bowl and add cream cheeses. Beat on medium speed with an electric mixer until creamy. Add Splenda, cornstarch, flour, egg yolks, lemon juice, and zest. In a large mixing bowl, whip egg whites. Fold beaten whites into cheese mixture. Pour cheesecake batter into prepared crust.

5. Pour hot water into larger baking pan to reach halfway up sides of cake pan. Bake in water bath for 50-55 minutes or until sides of cake appear firm and center is barely set. Remove from water bath and cool.

6. Chill at least 6 hours before serving.

PER SERVING

Calories 140	Fat 6 grams (3.5 saturated)
Carbohydrate 11 grams	Fiber 0 grams
Protein 10 grams	Sodium 340 milligrams

Diabetic exchange = 1 ½ Lean Meat, 1 Carbohydrate
WW point comparison = 3 points

Strawberry Swirl Cheesecake

Serves Twelve

This is one gorgeous cheesecake. It's covered with a marbled strawberry topping that bakes right into the cheesecake. Because you can make it with either fresh or frozen strawberries, it can be enjoyed year-round.

INGREDIENTS:

1 9-inch baked Cheesecake Crumb Crust, page 393

1 ¼ cups fresh or frozen unsweetened strawberries

2 tablespoons low-sugar strawberry jam

2 tablespoons Splenda Granular

2 teaspoons lemon juice

1 cup low-fat cottage cheese

8 ounces tub-style light cream cheese

8 ounces nonfat cream cheese, room temp

1 ¼ cups Splenda Granular

2 tablespoons all-purpose flour

2 tablespoons cornstarch

1 teaspoon vanilla extract

½ teaspoon almond extract

1 large egg

3 large egg whites

1 ¼ cups light sour cream

Try substituting raspberries and low-sugar raspberry jam. Boysenberries are stunning, but force the puree through a sieve to remove the seeds before "swirling."

Steps:

1. Preheat oven to 350°F. Wrap 9-inch springform pan filled with crust tightly in heavy-duty foil to waterproof.

2. Combine the strawberries, jam, Splenda, and lemon juice in a medium saucepan. Stir and cook until strawberries are soft and mushy. Use a fork to mash berries completely to form a thick strawberry purée (or you may want to use a food processor or blender). Set mixture aside to cool.

3. Purée cottage cheese in a food processor or blender until completely smooth. Spoon into a large mixing bowl and add both cream cheeses. Beat on medium speed with an electric mixer until creamy. Add Splenda, flour, cornstarch, and extracts. Beat on low until smooth. Add whole egg and then egg whites, beating briefly after each addition. Stir in the sour cream with a large spoon. Pour into the prepared pan and smooth top.

4. Carefully place spoonfuls of the strawberry purée on top of the batter. Swirl a thin knife back and forth through the purée and batter to create a marbleized effect.

5. Place foil-wrapped pan in a large, deep baking pan and place on oven rack. Pour boiling water into larger pan until it reaches halfway up the outside of the cheesecake pan.

6. Bake for 70-75 minutes or until sides of cake appear firm and center jiggles slightly. Turn off heat, open oven door, and let cheesecake cool in the oven for 30 minutes. Remove from water bath and finish cooling. Refrigerate at least 6 hours before serving.

PER SERVING

Calories 190	Fat 8 grams (5 saturated)
Carbohydrate 17 grams	Fiber 1 gram
Protein 11 grams	Sodium 350 milligrams

Diabetic exchange = 1 Carbohydrate, 1 ½ Lean Meat
WW point comparison = 4 points

Pumpkin Streusel Cheesecake
Serves Twelve

This is one of my favorite desserts for the holidays. It looks festive and tastes fabulous. In the past, I've made it many times using sugar, but I'm happy to say that this sugar-free version is just as good as the original.

INGREDIENTS:

CRUST

18 gingersnap cookies, ground into crumbs (may substitute graham-cracker crumbs)

¼ cup Splenda Granular

1 tablespoon light margarine or butter, melted

FILLING

1 cup low-fat cottage cheese

8 ounces tub-style light cream cheese

8 ounces nonfat cream cheese, room temperature

1 ¼ cups Splenda Granular

1 15-ounce can solid pack pumpkin

2 tablespoons cornstarch

1 tablespoon all-purpose flour

1 teaspoon cinnamon

½ teaspoon ground ginger

½ teaspoon allspice

1 teaspoon vanilla

2 large eggs

4 large egg whites

½ cup light sour cream

STREUSEL

¼ cup all-purpose flour

1 tablespoon brown sugar

1 tablespoon light butter, cold

PER SERVING

Calories 200

Carbohydrate 21 grams

Protein 11 grams

Fat 7 grams (4 saturated)

Fiber 2 grams

Sodium 370 milligrams

Diabetic exchange = 1 ½ Carbohydrate, 1 ½ Medium-Fat Meat

WW point comparison = 4 points

STEPS:

1. Preheat oven to 350°F. Spray a 9-inch springform pan with nonstick cooking spray.

2. CRUST: In a small bowl, combine the cookie crumbs with the Splenda. Add the butter and stir to mix. Reserve ⅓ cup of the crumbs and press rest of crumbs onto the bottom of prepared pan.

3. Bake for 5 minutes. Set aside.

4. FILLING: Place cottage cheese into a food processor or blender. Purée until completely smooth. Spoon into a large mixing bowl and add nonfat and light cream cheeses. With an electric mixer, beat on medium until creamy.

5. Add the Splenda, pumpkin, flour, cornstarch, spices, and vanilla. Beat on low speed until smooth. Add whole eggs and then egg whites, beating briefly after each addition to incorporate. Stir in the sour cream with a large spoon.

6. Pour into the prepared crust and smooth top.

7. Bake for 75 minutes or until the sides are firm and the center jiggles slightly.

8. STREUSEL: Add flour and brown sugar to the reserved cookie crumbs. Cut in butter until a loose crumb forms. After baking cheesecake, open oven and sprinkle crumbs over entire cake (covering any cracks). Place back in oven for an additional 15 minutes. Turn off heat, open door, and let cheesecake cool in oven for 30 minutes. Remove from oven and place on rack to cool.

9. Refrigerate at least 6 hours before serving. Best if made a day or two in advance.

A very kind reader told me how much she was enjoying my recipes while keeping her blood sugar under control. She also passed on a great suggestion for this recipe—strain the juice and pour it into ice cube trays to make Strawberry Lemonade Ice Cubes. Drop into iced tea, and as she says, "Wow!"

Cheesecake Squares

Serves Twenty-Four

Virginia, from Toronto, Canada, sent me her original cheesecake recipe. I've taken out the sugar, and you can't even tell the difference. These creamy, sweet squares, placed on a large platter topped with sour cream and garnished with slices of fresh strawberries, are perfect for entertaining family and friends. Virginia says they're always a hit!

INGREDIENTS:

CRUST

1 ¼ cups graham cracker crumbs

2 tablespoons margarine or butter, melted

½ teaspoon cinnamon

2 tablespoon Splenda Granular

FILLING

2 8-ounce packages light cream cheese, room temperature

1 8-ounce package fat-free cream cheese, room temperature

3 large eggs

2 tablespoons lemon juice

2 tablespoons lemon zest

2 teaspoons vanilla

1 cup Splenda Granular

TOPPING

2 cups reduced-fat sour cream

½ cup Splenda Granular

2 teaspoons vanilla

STEPS:

1. Preheat oven to 325°F.

2. CRUST: In a small bowl, combine graham cracker crumbs, margarine, cinnamon, and Splenda; stir.

3. Pour crumb mixture into 9 x 13-inch pan. With your fingers, the back of a spoon, or a sheet of plastic wrap, press down on the crumbs until they coat the bottom and sides of the pan. Refrigerate at least 30 minutes.

4. FILLING: Using an electric mixer, beat cream cheeses, eggs, lemon juice, lemon zest, vanilla, and Splenda. Pour into refrigerated crust.

5. Bake 20-25 minutes. Remove from oven. Cool 10 minutes. Increase oven temperature to 400°F.

PER SERVING

Calories 120

Carbohydrate 7 grams

Protein 5 grams

Fat 7 grams (4 saturated)

Fiber 0 grams

Sodium 160 milligrams

Diabetic exchange = 1 Lean Meat, 1 Fat, ½ Carbohydrate

WW point comparison = 3 points

6. TOPPING: In medium bowl, combine sour
   cream, Splenda, and vanilla. Spread on slightly
   cooled cheesecake. Bake additional 5–8
   minutes to set topping. Cool and chill at least
   4 hours before serving.
7. Cut cheesecake into 24 squares (6 x 4).

FRUIT GARNISH VARIATION: Serve cheesecake
   squares in decorative paper cupcake cups
   and top with slices of fresh kiwi, strawberry
   halves, or candied cherries cut into quarters.

I like to literally "throw" raspberry sauce across the tops of these squares. Combine 3 tablespoons low-sugar raspberry jam, 3 tablespoons water, and ¼ cup Splenda in a microwaveable bowl. Heat for 15–30 seconds on high. Stir until smooth. To create a decorative splatter, spoon out sauce with a fork and flick it off the tines of the fork onto the entire cheesecake or the individual squares.

Breakfast Cheesecake Cups

Serves Seven

When teaching a cooking series called "Low-Carb Done Right," I offered my students none other than cheesecake for breakfast—now, that got a smile. These creamy orange-scented cheesecake cups have as much protein as two eggs—with less fat and calories. What a sweet way to start your day.

INGREDIENTS:

2 cups 1% cottage cheese

8 ounces tub-style light cream cheese, room temperature

⅔ cup Splenda Granular

½ teaspoon almond extract

½ teaspoon orange zest

2 large eggs

2 large egg whites

STEPS:

1. Preheat oven to 350°F. Set seven 6-ounce custard cups in a large baking pan (with at least 2-inch sides).

2. In a food processor, puree cottage cheese until completely smooth. Add cream cheese, Splenda, almond extract, and orange zest; process until smooth.

3. Add eggs and egg whites, one at a time; process to incorporate.

4. Pour mixture into custard cups. Add hot water to pan until halfway up sides of custard cups.

5. Bake for 25–30 minutes or until set in center.

6. Chill for at least 4 hours. Serve.

A healthy balance of carbohydrate, fat, and protein will keep you satisfied longer and keep your blood sugar on an even keel. Pair this with a cup of fresh berries for extra nutrients and fiber.

PER SERVING (½ CUP)

Calories 130	Fat 8 grams (4 saturated)
Carbohydrate 6 grams	Fiber 0 grams
Protein 14 grams	Sodium 380 milligrams

Diabetic exchange = 2 Lean Meat, ½ Carbohydrate
WW point comparison = 3 points

Fresh Banana Cheesecake Cups

Serves Eighteen

Inspired by a popular cheesecake restaurant, these luscious banana cheesecakes sit atop a sweet vanilla crumb crust. Unlike the restaurant's, these are cleverly portioned into cupcake liners, making them a wonderful version for a crowd (or you can halve the recipe for just a handful of cheesecake lovers). Adorn with a squirt of whipped cream and a curl of dark chocolate and watch your guests swoon.

INGREDIENTS:

1 cup + 2 tablespoons vanilla wafer crumbs (about 30 vanilla wafers)

3 tablespoons margarine, melted

12 ounces tub-style light cream cheese

12 ounces tub-style nonfat cream cheese

⅔ cup Splenda Granular

2 tablespoons cornstarch

2 teaspoons vanilla

¾ cup mashed bananas (about 1 ½ bananas)

2 large eggs + 2 egg whites

⅓ cup nonfat half-and-half

Bananas are the most popular fruit in the world. High in fiber, B vitamins, and potassium, they reduce the risk of high blood pressure and stroke and are a great source of quick energy.

STEPS:

1. Preheat oven to 325°F.

2. Place foil cupcake liners (removing paper liner) into 18 cupcake tins.

3. Finely crush vanilla wafers with food processor or blender. Add margarine and pulse until thoroughly combined. Press 1 tablespoon into each foil liner.

4. Place cupcake tins in refrigerator.

5. In a large bowl, with an electric mixer, beat cream cheeses until creamy. Add Splenda, cornstarch, and vanilla, and beat until smooth. Beat in mashed bananas. Add eggs and then whites, beating briefly after each addition. Mix in half-and-half with a spoon.

6. Spoon batter over prepared crusts, filling each cup about ¾ full (about ⅓ cup batter each). Place in oven.

7. Bake for 20 minutes (light cracks may appear); then turn off oven, open the door, and let sit additional 10 minutes.

8. Cool and then refrigerate for at least 4 hours.

PER SERVING

Calories 130	Fat 7 grams (3 saturated)
Carbohydrate 10 grams	Fiber 0 grams
Protein 6 grams	Sodium 250 milligrams

Diabetic exchange = 1 Fat, ½ Lean Meat, ½ Carbohydrate, ½ Fruit
WW point comparison = 3 points

Strawberry-Topped New York Cheesecake

Serves Sixteen

The base of this cheesecake is right out of the Big Apple, where they like their cheesecakes creamy and dense, with a faint hint of lemon. I added a touch of California by topping it with sweetened sour cream and fresh strawberries. This all adds up to one delicious showstopper that weighs more than five pounds! If you are a true New Yorker and prefer your cake unadorned, you can simply leave off the toppings.

INGREDIENTS:

CRUST

1 cup graham-cracker crumbs

2 tablespoons butter, melted

2 tablespoons Splenda Granular

FILLING

16 ounces regular cream cheese (2 8-ounce packages)

16 ounces fat-free cream cheese (2 8-ounce packages)

1 ¼ cups Splenda Granular

1 tablespoon lemon juice

1 teaspoon vanilla

½ teaspoon lemon zest

4 eggs

⅓ cup light sour cream

TOPPING

1 ½ cups light sour cream

⅓ cup Splenda Granular

1 quart fresh strawberries, stemmed and halved

2 tablespoons low-sugar strawberry jam

STEPS:

1. Preheat oven to 325°F. Wrap a 9-inch springform pan in heavy-duty foil to waterproof.

2. CRUST: In a large mixing bowl, combine graham cracker crumbs, margarine, and Splenda. Press into a 9-inch springform pan. Bake crust for 5 minutes. Cool.

3. FILLING: Place cream cheese in large mixing bowl. Using an electric mixer, beat on medium speed until very creamy.

4. Beat in Splenda, lemon juice, vanilla, and zest. Add eggs one at a time into bowl and beat briefly after each addition. Stir in sour cream. Pour cream cheese mixture into crust and smooth top.

PER SERVING

Calories 250	Fat 16 grams (8 saturated)
Carbohydrate 15 grams	Fiber 1 gram
Protein 16 grams	Sodium 330 milligrams

Diabetic exchange = 1 ½ Lean Meat, 1 Carbohydrate, 2 Fat
WW point comparison = 6 points

5. Place cheesecake pan into a 9 x 13-inch or larger baking pan. Pour hot water into pan till it reaches halfway up the sides of the cheesecake pan. Bake for 45–50 minutes or until sides of cake appear firm but the center still jiggles slightly.

6. TOPPING: In a small bowl, mix sour cream and ⅓ cup Splenda. Spoon sour cream over cheesecake; turn off heat and open door.

7. Leave cheesecake in the oven for an additional 15 minutes. Remove from water bath and completely cool.

8. When well chilled (or just prior to serving), top cheesecake with fresh strawberries. Melt jam in microwave and brush across berries for shine.

Did you know that cheesecake is actually a custard, not a cake? Just like a custard, cheesecake depends on eggs, not flour, for its basic structure.

Blueberry Cheesecake Parfaits

Serves Six

This is a really fun dessert. The presentation is original, and your family and guests are sure to love it. Besides looking incredible, it's smooth and rich and creamy. You'll love it, too, because it's so simple to prepare, and yet looks and tastes very impressive. These are also fabulous for entertaining because they are already portioned and convenient since they can be made ahead of time.

INGREDIENTS:

½ cup graham-cracker crumbs

2 tablespoons Splenda Granular

1 ½ tablespoons light butter

4 ounces tub-style light cream cheese

4 ounces nonfat cream cheese, room temperature

½ cup light sour cream

¼ cup Splenda Granular

1 cup light whipped topping, thawed

1 ¼ cups fresh blueberries

The original recipe for these parfaits called for regular cream cheese and whipping cream, and, of course, sugar. They clocked in at a whopping 490 calories each!

STEPS:

1. Select 6 tall stemmed glasses. (An 8-ounce wineglass or champagne glass is ideal.)

2. In a small bowl, mix graham-cracker crumbs, 2 tablespoons Splenda, and butter. Set aside.

3. In a medium mixing bowl, beat cream cheeses with an electric mixer until creamy. Add sour cream and ¼ cup Splenda and stir until smooth. Fold in light whipped topping with a spoon or spatula.

4. In the bottom of each glass, place 1 tablespoon graham cracker mix. Press down with spoon. Place about 3 tablespoons of cream cheese mix on top of each. (You will use only ½ of the cheese mixture for the 6 glasses). Divide the berries among the glasses, placing them on top of the cream cheese layer. Add one more layer of cream cheese. Finish the parfait by topping each with 1 tablespoon of crumbs.

5. Enjoy immediately or place in the refrigerator until ready to be served.

PER SERVING

Calories 185	Fat 8 grams (6 saturated)
Carbohydrate 20 grams	Fiber 1 gram
Protein 7 grams	Sodium 280 milligrams

Diabetic exchange = 1 Carbohydrate, 1 Low-Fat Meat, 1 Fat
WW point comparison = 4 points

Black Forest Cheesecake Parfaits

Serves Six

Chocolate and cherries, yum. These cheesecake parfaits are a terrific variation of my popular Blueberry Cheesecake Parfaits. These cheesecakes are just as delicious to eat, they're also unique and impressive to serve. They are also fabulous for entertaining becasue they, too, are already portioned and can be made ahead of time.

INGREDIENTS:

1 ½ cups frozen black cherries, thawed

¼ cup + 4 tablespoons Splenda Granular

½ teaspoon almond extract

½ cup chocolate graham-cracker crumbs

1 ½ tablespoons cocoa powder

½ tablespoon butter, melted

4 ounces tub-style light cream cheese, room temperature

4 ounces fat-free cream cheese, room temperature

½ cup light sour cream

1 ½ cups light whipped topping

STEPS:

1. Select 6 tall, stemmed glasses (8-ounce wineglasses or champagne glasses are ideal).

2. In a small bowl, mix cherries, 2 tablespoons Splenda, and almond extract. Set aside.

3. In another small bowl, mix graham-cracker crumbs, 2 tablespoons Splenda, cocoa powder, and butter. Set aside.

4. In a medium mixing bowl, beat cream cheeses with an electric mixer until creamy. Add sour cream and remaining Splenda and stir until smooth. Fold in whipped topping with a spoon or spatula.

5. In the bottom of each glass, place 1 tablespoon graham-cracker mix. Press down with spoon. Place about 3 tablespoons of cream cheese mix on top of each. (You will use only half of the cheese mixture for the 6 glasses.) Divide the cherries among the glasses, placing them on top of the cream cheese layer. Add one more layer of cream cheese. Finish the parfait by topping each with 1 tablespoon of crumbs.

6. Enjoy immediately or place in the refrigerator until you are ready to serve.

PER SERVING

Calories 200	Fat 8 grams (2 saturated)
Carbohydrate 24 grams	Fiber 1 gram
Protein 7 grams	Sodium 290 milligrams

Diabetic exchange = 1 ½ Carbohydrate, 1 Lean Meat, 1 Fat
WW point comparison = 4 points

Key Lime Cheesecake

Serves Twelve

If you like key lime pie, this is the cheesecake for you. It has a lighter texture than most cheesecakes, and, of course, has the wonderful tartness of key limes. Key lime juice can be found next to the bottled lemon juice in most markets.

INGREDIENTS:

1 9-inch Cheesecake Crumb Crust, page 393

1 envelope unflavored gelatin
  (2 ½ teaspoons)

¾ cup key lime juice

2 large eggs, lightly beaten

1 cup Splenda Granular

8 ounces tub-style light cream cheese

8 ounces nonfat cream cheese, room temperature

4 large pasteurized egg whites
  (or 2 regular egg whites★)

¾ cup Splenda Granular

1 ½ cups light whipped topping

Note: See eggs on page 27 for information regarding the safety of raw eggs.

STEPS:

1. In a medium saucepan, dissolve the gelatin in the key lime juice for 3 minutes. Add 1 cup of Splenda and the 2 beaten eggs.

2. Place on stove and turn heat to medium while stirring, and cook for 10 minutes or until mixture thickens. Remove from heat. Cool slightly.

3. Place the cream cheese in a large bowl, and beat on medium speed with an electric mixer until creamy. Slowly add the lime mixture and beat on low until smooth. Refrigerate mixture until thoroughly cooled, stirring every 10 minutes.

4. In a separate bowl, beat the egg whites until foamy or until soft peaks begin to form; this can take 5 minutes or more with pasteurized egg whites. Slowly add the ¾ cup Splenda until incorporated.

5. Fold egg white mixture into the chilled lime-cheese mix. Pour onto prepared crust.

6. Refrigerate until set, about 2 hours.

7. Spread whipped topping over cake.

PER SERVING

Calories 160	Fat 7.5 grams (4 saturated)
Carbohydrate 16 grams	Fiber 0 grams
Protein 7 grams	Sodium 270 milligrams

Diabetic exchange = 1 Carbohydrate, 1 Lean Meat, 1 Fat

The original recipe for this yummy and sweet yet tart cheesecake had 40 grams of sugar per piece.

Almond Orange Ricotta Cheesecake

Serves Eight

This no-bake cheesecake is lovely. Scented with orange and sitting pretty on an almond shortbread crust, it is truly perfect for summer. Unlike many ricotta cheesecakes, this is smooth and creamy rather than dry and dense.

INGREDIENTS:

CRUST

⅓ cup all-purpose flour

3 tablespoons finely chopped almonds (about ¼ cup whole)

2 tablespoons Splenda Granular

2 ½ tablespoons margarine or butter

FILLING

1 envelope unflavored gelatin (or 2 ½ teaspoons)

¼ cup cold water

2 cups part-skim ricotta cheese

⅔ cup Splenda Granular

1 tablespoon vanilla extract

2 teaspoons orange extract

1 teaspoon lemon zest

8 ounces low-fat evaporated or skim milk

TOPPING

2 tablespoons sliced almonds

1 teaspoon granulated sugar (optional)

STEPS:

1. Coat an 8-inch round cake pan with nonstick cooking spray.

2. CRUST: In a small bowl, mix flour, almonds, and Splenda. Cut in margarine with a fork or fingers until mixture resembles coarse crumbs. Pat crust into prepared pan.

3. FILLING: In another small bowl, sprinkle gelatin over water. Set aside.

4. Puree the ricotta in a food processor and add Splenda with extracts and zest.

5. In a small saucepan, simmer evaporated milk until bubbles appear on rim of pot; pull off heat. Whisk in gelatin. Pour into food processor and blend with the ricotta mixture.

6. Pour cheesecake batter into prepared crust. Refrigerate until set (at least 4 hours).

7. TOPPING: Sprinkle almonds around outside rim of cake. Sprinkle sugar on top of almonds (to make them sparkle) if desired.

A twist of orange placed right in the middle of the cake is the perfect adornment.

PER SERVING

Calories 180	Fat 10 grams (4 saturated)
Carbohydrate 12 grams	Fiber 1 gram
Protein 11 grams	Sodium 160 milligrams

Diabetic exchange = 1 ½ Lean Meat, 1 Carbohydrate, 1 Fat
WW point comparison = 4 points

Chocolate Peppermint Cheesecake

Serves Ten (I usually cut 12 pieces, but splurge—it's Christmas!)

Here it is—your Christmas cheesecake. It's wonderful. Start with a chocolate crumb crust that is filled with a peppermint-flecked cream cheese mixture, and finish with crushed peppermint candies and chocolate on the top. No, you're not dreaming. This cheesecake is still low in sugar, fat, and calories. And, best of all—it's a cinch to make, leaving you free for all your other holiday chores.

INGREDIENTS:

1 Chocolate Cheesecake Crumb Crust, page 393

1 envelope unflavored gelatin

¼ cup cold water

8 ounces tub-style light cream cheese

8 ounces nonfat cream cheese, room temperature

½ cup Splenda Granular

⅓ cup 1% milk

12 sugar-free peppermint hard candies, finely crushed

½ teaspoon peppermint extract

1 ½ cups light whipped topping, thawed

6 sugar-free peppermint hard candies, crushed

1 1.5-ounce milk chocolate bar or semisweet chocolate bar

STEPS:

1. In a small saucepan, sprinkle the gelatin over water; let stand for 3 minutes. Place over low heat, stirring, until gelatin dissolves. Remove from heat.

2. In a large mixing bowl, beat the cream cheeses and Splenda with an electric mixer until creamy. Add the gelatin mixture and the milk. Beat on low speed until smooth.

3. Stir in the 12 crushed peppermints and the extract. Chill until the mixture mounds slightly when dropped from a spoon.

4. Fold in the whipped topping. Pour into the prepared crust and smooth top.

5. Refrigerate at least 3 hours.

6. Before serving, sprinkle top of the cake with remaining crushed peppermint candies. As a final decorative touch, use a vegetable peeler to shave chocolate curls directly onto the top of the cake—and wait for the oohs and aahs.

I found my sugar-free hard peppermints in the candy aisle of my local grocery.

PER SERVING

Calories 190	Fat 8 grams (5 saturated)
Carbohydrate 22 grams	Fiber 0 grams
Protein 8 grams	Sodium 320 milligrams

Diabetic exchange = 1 ½ Carbohydrate, 1 Lean Meat, 1 Fat
WW point comparison = 4 points

10-Minute No-Bake Strawberry Cheese Pie

Serves Eight

This is simple to make and pretty to serve. If you want to make it a day ahead, cover the cheese-filled pie and place it in the refrigerator. Within 1 to 2 hours of serving time, cover with the fresh berries and glaze.

INGREDIENTS:

1 low-fat store-bought graham-cracker crumb crust

½ cup low-fat cottage cheese

4 ounces light cream cheese

¼ cup Splenda Granular

2 tablespoons low-sugar strawberry jam, melted

½ cup light sour cream

1 ½ cups strawberry slices (8 ounces fresh berries)

2 tablespoons low-sugar strawberry jam

STEPS:

1. Place the cottage cheese in a food processor or blender and purée until entirely smooth.

2. Pour into a medium bowl and beat in cream cheese, Splenda, and jam with an electric mixer. Stir in sour cream and spoon mixture into crust.

3. Arrange strawberry slices in a decorative manner to cover top of pie.

4. Melt 2 tablespoons of jam (microwave 20–30 seconds on high) and strain by pouring it through a mesh strainer.

5. Brush strained jam over berries.

6. Refrigerate for 1–2 hours before serving.

This is a great grab-and-go pie. The first time I made it, I took it to my mother-in-law's for dinner. Since then, she has given it several times to friends who watch their diets. Don't forget to keep it cool during your travels.

PER SERVING

Calories 180	Fat 7 grams (3 saturated)
Carbohydrate 22 grams	Fiber 2 grams
Protein 7 grams	Sodium 260 milligrams

Diabetic exchange = ½ Carbohydrate, ½ Fruit, ½ Low-Fat Milk, 1 Fat

WW point comparison = 4 points

Sweet Embellishments

"Embellish" —to decorate, adorn, beautify, enhance, or make fancy.

Rich Custard Sauce

Bourbon Sauce

Quick Raspberry Sauce

Hot Lemon Sauce

Sun Sweet Orange Sauce

Blueberry Sauce and Coulis

Strawberry Sauce and Coulis

Sweet Cherry Topping

Dark Chocolate Sauce

Chocolate Fudge Sauce

Boysenberry Syrup

Apple Cider Butter Syrup

Lemon Curd

Orange Cream Cheese

Strawberry Cream Cheese

Lemon Zest Cheese Spread and
    Whipped Topping

Whipped Cream Cheese Topping
   and Frosting

Easy Chocolate Cream Frosting

Crunchy Cinnamon Pecans

Sweet and Spicy Cajun Nuts

Chocolate Cream Cheese Truffles

To make ordinary desserts and sweet treats extraordinary, embellish them—with wonderful toppings, sweet sauces, and creamy spreads. Through the versatility of Splenda, I have included a wonderful variety of delicious enhancers that can be used for the recipes in this book (or for your own favorites). These toppers are the secret to creating beautiful, wow'em dishes and desserts. Whether spooned, poured, drizzled, pooled, or plopped (also called dolloped), you'll find that they always add the perfect finishing touch.

While testing (and tasting) many of the recipes in the book, thoughts of how I might pair these with my "embellishments" popped into my head, and you will find these ideas noted in the recipes. In addition to those suggestions, here are just a few more thoughts to help you create a memorable look with a great taste experience:

» Create a spectacular red, white, and blue sundae bar with Strawberry and Blueberry Sauce, low-sugar vanilla ice cream and light whipped topping.

» Serve an elegant afternnoon treat with a cup of tea, and small spoonfuls of Hot Lemon Sauce atop Lemon Blueberry Bread.

» Dazzle your guests by drizzling Boysenberry Syrup on plates before topping them with slices of Sour Cream Loaf Pound Cake; add a few fresh boysenberries and a small dusting of powdered sugar to each plate.

» Triple your chocolate pleasure. Lay a piece of Chocolate Cream-Filled Chocolate Roll in a pool of Dark Chocolate Sauce, or spread Easy Chocolate Cream Frosting onto Chocolate Cupcakes and garnish with chocolate curls.

» Simple but elegant—put out a small bowl of Crunchy Cinnamon Pecans or a plate of Chocolate Cream Cheese Truffles with your coffee service.

Rich Custard Sauce

Serves Nine

I love fresh fruit, especially berries. But fresh fruit for dessert, well—it's still just fresh fruit. But if you place some berries in a nice glass and pour on a little Rich Custard Sauce, voilà—real dessert. So simple, so good! You can use this sauce to doll up unfrosted cakes like the Citrus Chiffon Cake or your favorite angel food cake.

INGREDIENTS:

2 tablespoons Splenda Granular

1 tablespoon cornstarch

2 egg yolks

1 cup 1% milk

¼ cup nonfat half-and-half

1 ½ teaspoons vanilla

For a delicious treat, add a touch of orange zest or 1 tablespoon of orange liqueur to this versatile sauce.

STEPS:

1. Place Splenda, cornstarch, and egg yolks in a small saucepan. Whisk together until eggs have lightened in color and Splenda and cornstarch are dissolved. Whisk in milk and half-and-half.

2. Place pan on stove and turn heat to medium. Heat, stirring constantly, until mixture comes to a low boil. Turn heat down and let simmer 1 minute. Custard should be thick enough to coat a spoon but not as thick as pudding.

3. Whisk in vanilla and immediately remove from heat.

4. Pour into a bowl and cover with plastic wrap.

5. Cool and refrigerate until ready to serve.

PER SERVING (2 TABLESPOONS)

Calories 35

Carbohydrate 3 grams

Protein 2 grams

Fat 1.5 grams (.5 saturated)

Fiber 0 grams

Sodium 15 milligrams

Diabetic exchange = ¼ Low-Fat Milk

WW point comparison = 1 point

Bourbon Sauce

Serves Eight

This sauce was created for the New Orleans Bread Pudding (page 258) but is a real keeper on its own. Spiked with real bourbon, you can also use it over French toast to "kick it up a notch"—your brunch guests will love you for it.

INGREDIENTS:

6 tablespoons fat-free half-and-half

6 tablespoons low-fat milk

¼ cup Splenda Granular

2 teaspoons cornstarch

2 tablespoons bourbon

½ teaspoon vanilla

1 ½ tablespoons butter, softened

STEPS:

1. In a small saucepan, whisk together half-and-half, milk, Splenda, and cornstarch until smooth.

2. Place over medium heat and cook, stirring, until mixture comes to a low boil and thickens.

3. Whisk in bourbon, vanilla, and butter and immediately remove from heat.

4. Serve sauce warm.

You may also substitute Whiskey, Dark Rum (or ½ teaspoon rum extract) to make Whiskey or Rum Sauce. For a nonalcoholic version, substitute orange juice for bourbon. It will impart a delicious, light orange accent.

PER SERVING (2 TABLESPOONS)

Calories 45	Fat 2.5 grams (1.5 saturated)
Carbohydrate 3 grams	Fiber 0 grams
Protein 1 gram	Sodium 30 milligrams

Diabetic exchange = ½ Fat
WW point comparison = 1 point

Quick Raspberry Sauce
Serves Eight

It doesn't get any quicker than this. No fancy ingredients are required for this easy sauce, whipped up in the microwave in just seconds. Drizzle Quick Raspberry Sauce over cakes or on cake plates for dramatic presentations, or simply use it on your favorite ice cream.

INGREDIENTS:

6 tablespoons low-sugar raspberry jam

6 tablespoons water

¼ cup Splenda Granular

STEPS:

1. Place all the ingredients in a small microwaveable bowl.
2. Heat for 30–45 seconds on high.
3. Stir until smooth. Use warm or cold.

This recipe can be made with any low-sugar jam. I like Smucker's. It's just fruit, with 50 percent less sugar and calories than ordinary jam. Watch out for reduced-sugar or "fruit-only" jams that use concentrated fruit juices to make up for the reduction in sugar. They can have as much or even more sugar than regular jams.

PER SERVING (1 ½ TABLESPOONS)

Calories 16   Fat 0 grams (0 saturated)
Carbohydrate 4 grams   Fiber 0 grams
Protein 0 grams   Sodium 0 milligrams

Diabetic exchange = 1 Free Food
WW point comparison = 0 points

Hot Lemon Sauce

Serves Eight

While I was testing this sauce, a couple of my assistants looked at me strangely because they wanted to know what it was for. But as soon as they tasted it, they, too, had lots of ideas on ways to use it. It tastes like hot lemon meringue pie filling, right off the spoon. After you make it once, you're sure to have more ideas of your own.

INGREDIENTS:

1 large egg yolk

¼ cup fresh lemon juice

1 tablespoon cornstarch

1 cup water

½ cup Splenda Granular

2 tablespoons granulated sugar

1 ½ tablespoons butter

This is delicious, either pooled under or spooned over a piece of Sour Cream Loaf Cake (page 384), drizzled onto Lemon Soufflé Cakes (page 382), served with Cheese Blintzes (page 91) and as an extraordinary hot topping for vanilla ice cream and, of course, any lemon cheesecake.

STEPS:

1. Place egg yolk in a small bowl and beat briefly; set aside.

2. In a small pot, whisk together lemon juice and cornstarch until smooth. Whisk in water, Splenda, and sugar.

3. Place pot on heat and turn to medium. Bring mixture to low simmer while whisking.

4. Take pot off heat and whisk a small amount of hot lemon sauce into egg yolk, while stirring (you don't want cooked egg yolk).

5. Add an additional spoon of hot sauce and then pour yolk mixture into pot. Place back on heat and bring to low boil. Boil for 1 minute or until thick and cleared.

6. Remove from heat and stir in butter until melted. Serve warm or cool and refrigerate for later use.

PER SERVING

Calories 45	Fat 2 grams (1 saturated)
Carbohydrate 7 grams	Fiber 0 grams
Protein 0 grams	Sodium 25 milligrams

Diabetic exchange = ½ Carbohydrate

WW point comparison = 1 point

Sun Sweet Orange Sauce

Serves Eight

After developing the orange sauce for my Ginger-Infused Flan, I decided (along with several tasters) that a makeover was in store for my original Sun Sweet Orange Sauce. This has a great bright orange flavor with just enough butter to give it some richness.

INGREDIENTS:

1 ½ cups light orange juice

2 tablespoons Splenda Granular

1 teaspoon orange zest

Pinch salt

1 tablespoon cornstarch mixed with 1 tablespoon water

1 ½ tablespoons butter

STEPS:

1. In a small saucepan, combine orange juice, Splenda, orange zest, and pinch salt, and place over medium heat. Simmer for 5 minutes or until juice concentrates to 1 cup.

2. Whisk in cornstarch mixture and bring to a low boil; cook 1 minute or until sauce thickens and clears. Stir in butter. Serve warm or cold.

Here's another fine sauce to accompany any plain cake or cheesecake. Another great flavor combination is orange and chocolate—with the Chocolate Sour Cream Loaf Cake, this would be my choice.

PER SERVING (2 TABLESPOONS)

Calories 35	Fat 2.5 grams (1.5 saturated)
Carbohydrate 4 grams	Fiber 0 grams
Protein 0 grams	Sodium 60 milligrams

Diabetic exchange = ½ Fat

WW point comparison = 1 point

Blueberry Sauce and Coulis

Serves Eight

This would make a lovely gift. Once made and bottled, it will hold for up to two weeks in the refrigerator. This sauce is a wonderful complement to lemon desserts as well as good old vanilla ice cream.

INGREDIENTS:

2 cups fresh or frozen blueberries (1 pint)

¼ cup Splenda Granular

⅓ cup cold water

2 teaspoons cornstarch

1 teaspoon lemon juice

1 tablespoon crème de cassis liqueur (optional)

STEPS:

1. Place the berries in a heavy non-aluminum saucepan. Add remaining ingredients (except liqueur) and stir until cornstarch dissolves.

2. Place over medium heat and bring to a boil. Turn down heat and simmer for 1 minute, stirring constantly.

3. Remove from heat and stir in liqueur if desired.

BLUEBERRY COULIS VARIATION: Strain the blueberry sauce through a fine strainer or sieve, pressing on the fruit to drain all the liquid. Throw away pulp. Serving size for coulis is 2 tablespoons.

Coulis, pronounced kool-ee, are smooth or puréed sauces of fruit or vegetables. Fruit coulis are very popular with pastry chefs because they can be made with almost any fruit and are a mainstay for plated dessert presentations.

PER SERVING (3 TABLESPOONS)

Calories 20	Fat 0 grams (0 saturated)
Carbohydrate 5 grams	Fiber 1 gram
Protein 0 gram	Sodium 0 milligrams

Diabetic exchange = 1 Free Food
WW point comparison = 0 points

Strawberry Sauce and Coulis

Serves Eight

This is one of the most versatile sauces I've ever come across. Unstrained, it makes a nice chunky sauce for ice cream or plain cakes. Strained, it's a smooth fruit sauce (coulis) that's an elegant accompaniment to desserts such as Heavenly Cheesecake and Strawberry Soufflé.

INGREDIENTS

2 cups strawberries, fresh or frozen

⅓ cup Splenda Granular

1 tablespoon lemon juice

½ cup water

2 teaspoons cornstarch

1 tablespoon orange liqueur (optional)

STEPS:

1. Place the berries in a heavy non-aluminum saucepan. Add remaining ingredients (except liqueur) and stir until cornstarch dissolves. Place over medium heat and bring to a boil. Turn down and simmer for 1 minute, stirring constantly.

2. Remove from heat and stir in liqueur if desired.

STRAWBERRY COULIS VARIATION: Strain the strawberry sauce through a fine strainer or sieve, pressing on the fruit to drain all the liquid. Throw away pulp.

For a dramatic and elegant presentation, drizzle, pool, or paint Strawberry Coulis onto plates before adding dessert. A squeeze bottle normally used for ketchup is a handy tool for drizzling sauces.

PER SERVING (2 TABLESPOONS)

Calories 15	Fat 0 grams (0 saturated)
Carbohydrate 3 grams	Fiber 0 grams
Protein 0 grams	Sodium 0 milligrams

Diabetic exchange = 1 Free Food
WW point comparison = 0 points

Sweet Cherry Topping

Serves Eight

Canned cherry-pie filling pales in comparison to this topping, which is bursting with plump cherries and fresh orange peel. You'll find that Sweet Cherry Topping is as good as any found in a gourmet food market, and it makes a perfect gift in a jar for Christmas—just the thing for someone who is watching the sugar in her diet.

INGREDIENTS:

16 ounces (about 3 cups) frozen dark cherries, slightly thawed

⅔ cup Splenda Granular

¾ cup water

1 tablespoon cornstarch

2 tablespoons orange liqueur or brandy

½ teaspoon vanilla

½ teaspoon almond extract

1–2 tablespoons orange peel (thin strips)

STEPS:

1. Place cherries in a medium saucepan. Add Splenda, water, and cornstarch, and stir.
2. On medium heat, cook slowly for 5 minutes or until cherries are warm. Turn heat up and bring to a low boil; cook, stirring just until mixture clears and sauce is thickened.
3. Stir in liqueur and cook 1 minute.
4. Remove from heat and stir in vanilla, almond extract, and orange peel. Cool slightly and spoon into container.

When you're in the freezer section, look for dark, sweet cherries with no sugar added (not sour red cherries), for the best results.

PER SERVING (¼ CUP)

Calories 50	Fat 0 grams (0 saturated)
Carbohydrate 9 grams	Fiber 1 gram
Protein 1 gram	Sodium 0 milligrams

Diabetic exchange = ½ Carbohydrate
WW point comparison = 1 point

Dark Chocolate Sauce

Serves Eight

Deep, dark, and delicious this oh-so-chocolatey sauce lends itself to many uses (even if it's only on a spoon). Regular chocolate sauce recipes use melted chocolate, half-and-half, sugar, and corn syrup. I use similar elements in this sauce, retaining just enough of the corn syrup and melted chocolate to ensure a rich smooth taste.

INGREDIENTS:

¼ **cup Dutch-process cocoa powder**

⅓ **cup Splenda Granular**

¼ **cup water**

⅓ **cup fat-free half-and-half**

1 tablespoon light corn syrup

1 ounce semisweet chocolate, chopped

1 teaspoon vanilla

STEPS:

1. Combine cocoa, Splenda, water, half-and-half, and corn syrup in a small saucepan.

2. Whisk over low heat until mixture is smooth and hot. (Do not boil.)

3. Remove from heat and whisk in chocolate and vanilla until chocolate melts and sauce is smooth again.

Americans consume an average of 12 pounds of chocolate per person per year for a total of more than 3 billion pounds annually. In fact, we eat almost half of the world's total production.

PER SERVING (2 TABLESPOONS)

Calories 45	Fat 2 grams (1 saturated)
Carbohydrate 8 grams	Fiber 1 gram
Protein 1 gram	Sodium 15 milligrams

Diabetic exchange = ½ Carbohydrate

WW point comparison = 1 point

Chocolate Fudge Sauce

Serves Eleven

This recipe made my day. I had tried other low-sugar fudge sauce recipes and was never quite satisfied because they were all missing the characteristic texture that sugar imparts. Then I saw a recipe that used maple syrup in place of sugar, and that idea piqued my interest. After trying the recipe (using Low-Calorie Log Cabin Syrup made with Splenda) and making a few modifications, I finally hit on a winner. Just like the best fudge sauces, this tightens up in the refrigerator. Heat gently in the microwave or on the stove before using.

INGREDIENTS:

2 ounces semisweet chocolate

2 tablespoons Dutch-process cocoa powder (like Hershey's European)

2 tablespoons sugar-free syrup (Log Cabin brand)

¼ cup Splenda Granular

⅓ cup water

½ teaspoon vanilla

STEPS:

1. Chop semisweet chocolate into small pieces.

2. Place in a medium-size microwaveable bowl. (You may also make this in a saucepan on the stove.)

3. Add remaining ingredients.

4. Heat in microwave on high for 45 seconds; chocolate will not be completely melted.

5. Remove and stir thoroughly until smooth. Add vanilla.

Compare this Chocolate Fudge Sauce to Hershey's Chocolate Fudge Topping, which has 70 calories per tablespoon and 10 grams of sugar.

PER SERVING (1 TABLESPOON)

Calories 30	Fat 1.5 grams (1 saturated)
Carbohydrate 4 grams	Fiber 0 grams
Protein 0 grams	Sodium 0 milligrams

Diabetic exchange = ½ Fat
WW point comparison = 1 point

Boysenberry Syrup

Serves Twelve

While developing the recipe for Buttermilk Boysenberry Sherbet, I happened to taste a spoonful of the boysenberry/sugar syrup mixture. It was wonderful and inspired me to develop this boysenberry syrup that can also be used on pancakes, cakes, and frozen desserts. The visual effect of this dark purple syrup drizzled over plain cheesecake is especially dramatic and will dazzle guests.

INGREDIENTS:

½ cup Splenda Granular

½ cup water

1 12-ounce bag (about 2 cups) frozen boysenberries, partially thawed

2 teaspoons cornstarch + 2 tablespoons cold water

STEPS:

1. In a medium saucepan, heat Splenda and water over medium heat. Bring to simmer and add boysenberries. Cook for 5 minutes.

2. Remove from heat and strain through a sieve, pressing down on berries with the back of a spoon to force pulp through sieve.

3. Return syrup to pan and add cornstarch mixture. Heat until mixture thickens and clears. Mixture will thicken further on cooling.

PER SERVING (2 TABLESPOONS)

Calories 25	Fat 0 grams (0 saturated)
Carbohydrate 6 grams	Fiber 1 gram
Protein 0 grams	Sodium 0 milligrams

Diabetic exchange = Free Food
WW point comparison = 0 points

Apple Cider Butter Syrup

Serves Four

Here is a delicious alternative that has only a fraction of the sugar of traditional syrup, proving that syrups don't have to be sweet, sticky concoctions that add undue sugar and calories to already high-calorie foods.

INGREDIENTS:

¾ **cup apple cider**

½ **cup Splenda Granular**

1 teaspoon cornstarch + 2 teaspoons cold water

1 tablespoon butter

STEPS:

1. In a small saucepan, simmer apple cider and Splenda over medium heat until it reduces by ⅓ (to about ½ cup).

2. Mix in cornstarch and water and bring to low boil; stir until syrup clears.

3. Whisk in butter.

Compare this to 2 tablespoons of maple syrup plus 1 pat of butter at 140 calories and 28 grams of carbohydrate.

PER SERVING (2 TABLESPOONS)

Calories 60   Fat 3 grams (2 saturated)

Carbohydrate 9 grams   Fiber 0 grams

Protein 0 grams   Sodium 25 milligrams

Diabetic exchange = ½ Fruit

WW point comparison = 1 point

Lemon Curd

Serves Fourteen

This is a filling or topping that can easily be converted to a sauce. It is often used in place of jam on biscuits and as a filling for cakes or tarts. I use it to make a luscious lemon cream frosting for the Lemon Coconut Layer Cake on page 380. If you want to make a thick lemon sauce, simply thin the curd with some hot water and stir until smooth.

INGREDIENTS:

⅔ cup lemon juice

2 tablespoons water

1 large egg, beaten

1 large egg yolk

2 tablespoons cornstarch

⅔ cup Splenda Granular

1 tablespoon granulated sugar

2 tablespoons light butter

STEPS:

1. In a medium non-aluminum saucepan, thoroughly whisk together the first 6 ingredients (lemon juice through Splenda).

2. Place pan on stove and turn heat to medium. Cook, whisking constantly, until mixture comes to a boil. Boil, whisking, for 1 minute. Mixture should be thick and clear.

3. Remove from the heat and stir in the butter. Cool.

Mix a couple of tablespoons of lemon curd into softened light cream cheese for a delicious spread you can use on muffins and biscuits.

PER SERVING (1 TABLESPOON)

Calories 25	Fat 1.5 grams (.5 saturated)
Carbohydrate 4 grams	Fiber 0 grams
Protein 0 grams	Sodium 0 grams

Diabetic exchange = ¼ carbohydrate
WW point comparison = 1 point

Orange Cream Cheese

Serves Eight

I served Orange Cream Cheese with my Pumpkin Pecan Bread (page 118), and all my tasters declared it a huge hit. This topping also complements fruit and bran muffins, biscuits, and mini-bagels.

INGREDIENTS:

4-ounce tub-style light cream cheese

1 tablespoon orange juice

2 teaspoons Splenda Granular

1 teaspoon grated orange zest

STEPS:

1. Place all the ingredients in a small bowl.

2. Beat until creamy. Orange Cream Cheese keeps well in the refrigerator for 1–2 weeks.

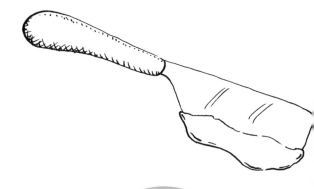

So much tastier than butter, this Orange Cream Cheese has only ⅓ the calories and a fraction of the saturated fat.

PER SERVING (1 TABLESPOONS)

Calories 30	Fat 2.5 grams (1 saturated)
Carbohydrate 1.5 grams	Fiber 0 grams
Protein 1 gram	Sodium 65 grams

Diabetic exchange = ½ Fat

WW point comparison = 1 point

Strawberry Cream Cheese

Serves Ten

You can buy strawberry-flavored cream cheese in the deli case, but this is the real McCoy, sweetened with fresh strawberries for a freshness that can't be beat. Put out a bowl the next time you serve bagels or breakfast breads and be prepared for compliments.

INGREDIENTS:

1 8-ounce package reduced-fat cream cheese

¼ cup Splenda Granular

½ teaspoon grated orange zest

½ cup sliced fresh strawberries, chopped (or ½ cup frozen unsweetened berries, thawed)

STEPS:

1. In a medium bowl, soften cream cheese with a wooden spoon.
2. Add Splenda, zest, and ½ of the berries; mix well, using a fork to mash berries.
3. Mix in the rest of the berries.
4. Cover and refrigerate until serving.

Bagels come in all flavors and sizes. Bagel-store bagels often contain 60 to 70 grams of carbohydrate and 300 to 400 calories. Better choices are whole-wheat English muffins, which have about 140 calories and 27 grams carbohydrate (or reduced-carb whole-grain bagels).

PER SERVING (2 TABLESPOONS)

Calories 55	Fat 5 grams
Carbohydrate 2 grams	Fiber 0 grams
Protein 1 gram	Sodium 75 milligrams

Diabetic exchange = 1 Fat
WW point comparison = 1 point

Lemon Zest Cheese Spread and Whipped Topping

Serves Six

Here is another nice spread for biscuits, scones, and breads. You may want to take this one step further and turn it into a luscious lemon-flavored whipped cream cheese topping for fruit or cakes, such as the Light White Cake on page 366.

INGREDIENTS:

½ cup low-fat cottage cheese

¼ cup light cream cheese

3 tablespoons Splenda Granular

Zest of 1 lemon

1-2 drops lemon extract (optional)

1 cup light whipped topping (for Whipped Topping)

STEPS:

1. In a food processor, blend the cottage cheese until completely smooth.

2. Add the cream cheese, Splenda, lemon zest, and lemon extract (if you're using it). Pulse lightly just until blended. (Overprocessing leaves the spread too soft.)

3. Move to a small bowl; cover and refrigerate until time to serve.

Simply fold in 1 cup of light whipped topping (like Light Cool Whip) to convert the spread into a topping; this makes 1 ½ cups (30 calories, 1 gram fat, and 2 carbohydrates per serving).

PER SERVING (2 TABLESPOONS)

Calories 45	Fat 2 grams (1.5 saturated)
Carbohydrate 2 grams	Fiber 1 gram
Protein 4 grams	Sodium 105 milligrams

Diabetic exchange = ½ Fat
WW point comparison = 1 point

Whipped Cream Cheese Topping and Frosting

Serves Eighteen

I first made this light whipped frosting to adorn my California Carrot Cake (page 371), only to find that the frosting was a star all by itself. Never a fan of heavy, cloying cream cheese frostings, I added a bit of light whipped topping to create a cream cheese frosting that's light, smooth, and fluffy but still retains that great cream cheese taste. After you try it, you'll surely find other uses for it (one of my readers told me she enjoyed it best straight out of the bowl).

INGREDIENTS:

8 ounces tub-style light cream cheese

4 ounces nonfat cream cheese

¼ cup Splenda Granular

1 cup light whipped topping

STEPS:

1. In a small mixing bowl, beat the cream cheeses with an electric mixer until smooth.
2. Add the Splenda and beat for 1 minute longer.
3. On slow speed, beat in the whipped topping, beating briefly, just until smooth.

PER SERVING (2 TABLESPOONS)

Calories 40	Fat 2 grams (1.5 saturated)
Carbohydrate 3 grams	Fiber 0 grams
Protein 2 grams	Sodium 80 milligrams

Diabetic exchange = 1 Fat

WW point comparison = 1 point

Easy Chocolate Cream Frosting

Serves Nine

This is a quick way to turn light whipped topping into a nice chocolate topping or frosting. The recipe makes enough to frost a 9-inch round or square cake or a dozen cupcakes.

INGREDIENTS:

1 ¾ cups light whipped topping, thawed

2 tablespoons Dutch-process cocoa powder (like Hershey's European)

¼ cup Splenda Granular

STEPS:

1. Place whipped topping in a medium bowl.

2. Gently fold in the cocoa powder and Splenda. Overmixing will break down cream topping.

3. Refrigerate until use. Spread or spoon onto cakes or muffins.

Because frostings either rely on lots of fat (like butter or melted chocolate) or powdered sugar for bulk, cutting the fat and the sugar is tricky. I have found light whipped topping makes a perfect base.

PER SERVING

Calories 35

Carbohydrate 4 grams

Protein 0 grams

Fat 1.5 grams (1.5 saturated)

Fiber 0 grams

Sodium 0 milligrams

Diabetic exchange = ½ Carbohydrate

Crunchy Cinnamon Pecans

Serves Eight

These pecans are great Christmas gifts. Your friends and family will never believe there's no sugar in these nuts. The heated egg white mixture provides the perfect foundation for the sweet cinnamon mixture that enrobes the pecans.

INGREDIENTS:

1 large egg white

½ cup Splenda Granular

2 cups pecans

1 tablespoon cinnamon

STEPS:

1. Preheat oven to 350°F. Lightly spray baking sheet with nonstick cooking spray.

2. Beat egg white and Splenda together in a double boiler over medium heat. Remove from heat.

3. Toss pecans in egg white mixture and add cinnamon. Spread coated pecans onto prepared sheet pan.

4. Bake for 15 minutes, mixing nuts after baking halfway. Cool and serve.

PER SERVING (1 OUNCE)

Calories 200
Carbohydrate 6 grams
Protein 3 grams

Fat 19 grams (2 saturated)
Fiber 2 grams
Sodium 5 milligrams

Diabetic exchange = 1 Fat
WW point comparison = 5 points

Sweet and Spicy Cajun Nuts
Serves Eight

You'll find these Cajun Nuts in my book Fantastic Food with Splenda. They're a variation under the Crunchy Cinnamon Pecans recipe. But I thought it was time they stood out on their own because these are the ones I make most often. Just like the Crunchy Cinnamon Pecans, they make nice treats when packaged up as a gift. Plus, these make great cocktail nibblers.

INGREDIENTS:

1 large egg white

½ cup Splenda Granular

2 cups pecan halves

1 tablespoon Cajun spice blend (or more if you like them very spicy)

STEPS:

1. Preheat oven to 350°F. Lightly spray baking sheet with nonstick cooking spray.

2. Beat egg white and Splenda together in a double boiler. Place over medium heat and heat until warm. Remove pan from heat.

3. Toss pecans in egg white mixture and add Cajun spice.

4. Spread coated pecans onto prepared sheet pan.

5. Bake for 15 minutes, mixing nuts after baking halfway. Cool and serve.

6. Store remaining nuts in airtight container.

Nuts are a great addition to healthy diets (and even weight-loss diets), as long as you eat them in moderation.

PER SERVING (1 OUNCE)

Calories 200	Fat 19 grams (2 saturated)
Carbohydrate 6 grams	Fiber 2 grams
Protein 3 grams	Sodium 5 milligrams

Diabetic exchange = 4 Fat
WW point comparison = 4 points

Chocolate Cream Cheese Truffles

Serves Twelve

Reduced-fat cream cheese makes these sweet truffles smooth and creamy, just like ones full of cream and butter. The slight hint of orange was a big plus for all my tasters, but you can omit it or use a few drops of any of the many candy oil flavorings found where candy and cake decorating supplies are sold.

INGREDIENTS:

1 ½ ounces bittersweet chocolate, chopped

4 ounces Neufchatel cheese, room temperature

⅛ teaspoon orange extract

⅔ cup Splenda Granular

4 tablespoons Dutch-process cocoa powder

3 tablespoons powdered sugar

STEPS:

1. In a small container, melt chocolate in microwave by heating for 1 minute on medium power and then stirring, or use double boiler. Set aside.

2. In small bowl, stir cream cheese with a wooden spoon until creamy. Add melted chocolate, orange extract, and Splenda. Stir. Sift in 2 tablespoons cocoa powder and powdered sugar and stir until creamy. (Mixture will be very stiff.) Cover and place in refrigerator to chill for at least 1 hour.

3. Shape mixture into 1-inch balls (about 1 tablespoon each) using hands (coating hands with a small amount of cocoa powder, if necessary). Then roll truffles in remaining 2 tablespoons of cocoa powder.

4. Store in airtight container in refrigerator.

Unlike many "sugar-free" candies, these contain no sugar alcohols. Sugar alcohols, like malitol, mannitol, and sorbitol, are commonly found in sugar-free chocolates and can cause gastrointestinal distress. These luscious candies can safely be served to everyone.

PER SERVING (1 TRUFFLE)

Calories 55	Fat 3 grams (2 saturated)
Carbohydrate 6 grams	Fiber 1 gram
Protein 2 grams	Sodium 40 milligrams

Diabetic exchange = ½ Fat, ½ Carbohydrate
WW point comparison = 1 point

Celebration Cocktails

Mojito

Pina Colada

Daiquri

Frozen Strawberry Daiquri

Margarita

Strawberry Margarita

Coconut Creamsicle

Lemon Drop Martini

Lemon Raspberry Slush

Ramos Gin Fizz

Lynchburg Lemonade

Fourth of July Lemonade

Marlene's Moose Milk

Frozen Coffee Cocktail

Black and White Russians

Irish Coffee

Mexican Coffee

Hot Buttered Rum

Sangria

Orange Liqueur

Coffee Liqueur

Cranberry Liqueur

Festive drinks are a wonderful way to celebrate special occasions. According to The Science of Healthy Drinking by Gene Ford, scientific studies have shown that moderate drinking of spirits such as vodka, gin, whiskey, bourbon, and tequila may also reduce your risk for coronary artery disease, atherosclerosis, gallstones, memory loss, and even the common cold. Even if you have diabetes, you can safely consume moderate amounts of alcohol with meals because straight alcohol is metabolized like fat—not carbohydrate (meaning it doesn't cause a spike in insulin or blood sugar).★

But wait, not so fast to the glass. The sugary, syrupy mixers that make that Daiquiri so sweet and the fat that makes that Pina Colada so creamy (and full of calories) are another story altogether. Suffice it to say, the "mixer" in mixed drinks can wreak havoc—not only to the diets of diabetics but, actually, to anyone's diet.

Fortunately, with the help of Splenda, there are ways to put some fun back in the festivities. With Fourth of July Lemonade for the Fourth, of course, to Hot Buttered Rum for the holidays, and Irish Coffee for your dinner guests, these libations will give you a whole new reason to celebrate.

They can also perk up your meals—think about pairing a refreshing Mojito with Grilled Scallops with Mango Relish, a perfect Margarita with Simple Southwest Salmon, or a Coconut Creamsicle with Caribbean Chicken, and you'll find lots more ways to enjoy these drinks.

And last, you will be absolutely amazed that you can make your own liqueurs with only a touch of the normal sugar—cheers!

★ Hypoglycemia may occur with excessive alcohol consumption without food. Be sure to check with your physician or health care provider for personalized guidelines.

Mojito

Serves One

The ever-popular Cuban mo-HEE-toe made with fresh muddled mint is a perfect summer (okay, anytime) sipper. If you have never had one, I think you will be surprised at just how refreshing this drink is when temperatures start to soar.

INGREDIENTS:

Fresh mint

1 ounce fresh lime juice (about ½ fresh lime)

4 teaspoons Splenda Granular (or 2 packets)

1 ½ ounces white rum

Splash of club soda

Slice of lime (optional)

STEPS:

1. In a tall Collins glass, using the back of a spoon, muddle 8-10 mint leaves with lime and Splenda.

2. Fill glass with crushed ice.

3. Add rum and top off with club soda.

4. Garnish with slice of lime and/or additional fresh mint.

"Muddling" is the technique of mashing or breaking up fruit or herbs with the back of a spoon or wooden muddler to help them release their oils and flavors.

PER SERVING

Calories 110

Carbohydrate 4 grams

Protein 0 grams

Fat 0 grams

Fiber 0 grams

Sodium 0 milligrams

Diabetic exchange = 2 Fat

WW point comparison = 2 points

Pina Colada

Serves One

This tropical favorite has been called "paradise in a glass." My version has only half the calories and a fraction of the sugar of the standard bar version—yet still has the same creamy, sweet, pineapple-coconut flavor everyone loves. That's what I call paradise.

INGREDIENTS:

2 ounces rum

2 ounces nonfat half-and-half

1 ounce unsweetened pineapple juice

1 tablespoon Splenda Granular (or 1 ½ packets)

½ teaspoon coconut extract

1 cup crushed ice

STEPS:

1. Pour all ingredients except ice into blender. Blend until smooth.

2. Add crushed ice and blend on high until smooth and frosty.

3. Pour into a large rocks glass or wine goblet. Add umbrella if desired.

Although you will find no fat in this recipe, you may note that the diabetic exchanges include fats. That is because alcohol metabolizes as a fat. Like fats, it does not require insulin and doesn't raise blood sugar. Check with your health care professional to see if alcohol is permissible in your diet.

PER SERVING

Calories 180	Fat 0 grams
Carbohydrate 12 grams	Fiber 0 grams
Protein 2 grams	Sodium 60 milligrams

Diabetic exchange = 1 Carbohydrate, 2 ½ Fat

WW point comparison = 4 points

Daiquiri

Serves One

This daiquiris is served "up" (with no ice) as they were originally served in the 1800s. If you prefer, you may strain the drink into an ice-filled rocks glass.

INGREDIENTS:

2 ounces white rum

1 ounce lime juice

2 teaspoons Splenda Granular (or 1 packet)

Lime twist

STEPS:

1. Pour all ingredients into a shaker ⅔ full of ice. Shake well.
2. Strain into chilled cocktail glass.
3. Garnish with lime twist.

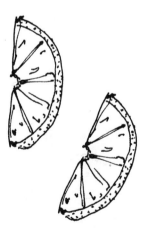

With drinks so simple, the trick is the technique. For the best drink, be sure you have clean, odorless ice and a perfectly chilled glass. Chill the glass by placing it in the freezer for a few minutes (except for fine crystal) or swirl crushed ice with a bit of water in the glass and then toss it out just prior to straining the drink into the glass.

PER SERVING

Calories 140

Carbohydrate 4 grams

Protein 0 grams

Fat 6 grams (0 saturated)

Fiber 0 grams

Sodium 0 milligrams

Diabetic exchange = 2 ½ Fat

WW point comparison = 3 points

Frozen Strawberry Daiquiri

Serves One

It's hard to believe this fruity and luscious drink isn't high in sugar, especially when it tastes just like the traditional bar version that can easily contain 40 grams of sugar or more. Addition of an umbrella is optional.

INGREDIENTS:

2 ounces light rum

½ ounce lime juice

3 large, whole, frozen strawberries

2 tablespoons Splenda Granular (or 3 packets)

½ cup crushed ice

STEPS:

1. Pour all ingredients except strawberries and ice into blender. Add strawberries and blend until smooth.

2. Add crushed ice and blend on high until smooth and thick.

3. Pour into a cocktail glass.

Frozen strawberries give this drink a much smoother texture than fresh ones do. Be sure to buy them unsweetened.

PER SERVING

Calories 155	Fat 0 grams
Carbohydrate 7 grams	Fiber 1 gram
Protein 0 grams	Sodium 0 milligrams

Diabetic exchange = ½ Carbohydrate, 2 ½ Fat
WW point comparison = 3 points

Margarita

Serves One

Sipping this drink of Mexico has definitely become an American pastime. To significantly lower the carbs (and get a better drink), skip the sugary mixers and make your margaritas the traditional way with freshly squeezed lime.

INGREDIENTS:

2 ounces tequila

½ ounce Grand Marnier

1 ounce lime juice

2 teaspoons Splenda Granular (or 1 packet)

Lime wedge (optional)

Coarse salt (optional)

STEPS:

1. Pour tequila, Grand Marnier, lime juice, and Splenda into a shaker ⅔ full of ice. Shake well.
2. Rim the edge of an ice-filled rocks glass with lime.
3. If desired, wet the rim of the glass with the lime wedge and dip rim into salt. Strain drink into glass.

A margarita made with a bottled mix or sweet-and-sour can have as much as 30 grams of sugar and only a small amount of lime juice.

PER SERVING

Calories 165	Fat 0 grams
Carbohydrate 7 grams	Fiber 0 grams
Protein 0 grams	Sodium 0 milligrams

Diabetic exchange = ½ Carbohydrate, 3 Fat

WW point comparison = 3 points

Strawberry Margarita

Serves One

Nothing says summer like a big cold Strawberry Margarita by the pool. As in the case of the frozen Strawbery Daiquiri, frozen berries work best to impart the right texture to this drink. If you prefer fresh berries, clean, stem, and freeze them first.

INGREDIENTS:

2 ounces gold tequila

½ ounce lime juice

1 ½ tablespoons Splenda Granular (or 2 packets)

⅛ teaspoon orange extract

3 large, whole, frozen strawberries

½ cup crushed ice

STEPS:

1. Pour all ingredients except strawberries and ice into blender.

2. Add strawberries and blend until smooth.

3. Add crushed ice and blend on high until cold and frosty.

4. Pour into a large margarita glass.

For easy entertaining, mix a big batch of the tequila, lime juice, Splenda, and extract together. For every 2 drinks, blend ⅔ cup mix, 6 strawberries, and 1 cup ice until smooth.

PER SERVING

Calories 155	Fat 0 grams
Carbohydrate 7 grams	Fiber 1 gram
Protein 0 grams	Sodium 0 milligrams

Diabetic exchange = ½ Carbohydrate, 2 ½ Fat
WW point comparison = 3 points

Coconut Creamsicle

Serves One

Coconut milk adds a tropical flair to this big and refreshing 12-ounce drink reminiscent of the frozen orange sherbet and vanilla ice cream for which this is named.

INGREDIENTS:

3 ounces light coconut milk

2 ounces vodka

1 tablespoon Splenda Granular
(or 1 ½ packets)

½ teaspoon vanilla extract

¼ teaspoon orange extract
(or ½ teaspoon orange zest)

1 large egg white

1 cup crushed ice

Orange twist

STEPS:

1. Pour all ingredients except orange twist into blender.
2. Blend on high until smooth and creamy.
3. Garnish with orange twist.

You save 9 grams of fat by using light rather than regular coconut milk in this drink. You can also substitute nonfat half-and-half and ½ teaspoon coconut extract for the light coconut milk.

PER SERVING

Calories 215
Carbohydrate 4 grams
Protein 4 grams

Fat 8 grams (6 saturated)
Fiber 0 grams
Sodium 65 milligrams

Diabetic exchange = ½ Carbohydrate,
½ Very Low-Fat Meat, 3½ Fat
WW point comparison = 5 points

Lemon Drop Martini

Serves One

Trendy drinks come and go, but this current hit is a definite keeper. With the great taste of the popular candy that lends this cocktail its name, you'll find that it's guaranteed to make you smile.

INGREDIENTS:

Lemon twist

½ teaspoon sugar

1 ½ ounces Citron vodka

½ ounce lemon juice

2 teaspoons Splenda Granular (or 1 packet)

STEPS:

1. Wet lemon twist with a couple drops of lemon juice. Run around rim of chilled cocktail glass.

2. Holding glass horizontally over a plate, sprinkle sugar around rim.

3. Pour vodka, lemon juice, and Splenda into a shaker ⅔ full of ice. Shake.

4. Strain into the sugar-rimmed glass. Add twist.

The pretty sugar-rimmed glass helps to give this drink its lemon-drop feel. One-half teaspoon of sugar and 2 grams of carbohydrate are all it takes—far less than the amount you save while creating the drink itself without sugar.

PER SERVING

Calories 110	Fat 0 grams
Carbohydrate 4 grams	Fiber 0 grams
Protein 0 grams	Sodium 0 milligrams

Diabetic exchange = 2 Fat

WW point comparison = 2 points

Lemon Raspberry Slush

Serves One

This cold and frosty "slush" full of fresh lemon and raspberries is definitely not for children, but can be a very fun way to get your vitamin C.

INGREDIENTS:

1 ½ ounces Citron vodka

1 ounce lemon juice

¼ cup fresh raspberries

2 tablespoons Splenda Granular (or 3 packets)

½ teaspoon lemon zest

1 cup crushed ice

Lemon twist

STEPS:

1. Put all ingredients except ice into blender.
2. Add raspberries and blend until smooth.
3. Add crushed ice and blend on high until smooth and frosty.
4. Pour into a large rocks glass. Garnish with lemon twist and a straw.

PER SERVING

Calories 130	Fat 0 grams
Carbohydrate 8 grams	Fiber 2 grams
Protein 0 grams	Sodium 0 milligrams

Diabetic exchange = ½ Carbohydrate, 2 Fat

WW point comparison = 2 points

Ramos Gin Fizz

Serves One

This classic Sunday brunch cocktail gives you a workout when you have to shake it a full 3 minutes. Maybe that's intended to burn off the calories of brunch food.

INGREDIENTS:

2 ounces gin

2 teaspoons lemon juice

1 teaspoon lime juice

1 tablespoon Splenda Granular

1 tablespoon nonfat half-and-half

1 large egg white★

1 dash (or ⅛ teaspoon) orange extract

2 ½ ounces club soda

STEPS:

1. Combine all ingredients except club soda in a shaker filled ¾ full of ice.

2. Shake for 3 minutes.

3. Strain into a chilled wine goblet.

4. Add club soda and stir briefly.

★ Foodborne illness from raw eggs is increasingly rare. It is a good precaution, however, to make sure the egg you choose is fresh and free of cracks. For extra safety, you might also choose a different kind of libation for someone who is elderly or in compromised health.

PER SERVING

Calories 165

Carbohydrate 5 grams

Protein 4 grams

Fat 0 grams

Fiber 0 grams

Sodium 75 milligrams

Diabetic exchange = ½ Carbohydrate, ½ Very Low-Fat Meat, 2 ½ Fat

WW point comparison = 3 points

Lynchberg Lemonade

Serves One

The T.G.I.F. restaurant chain serves up this sweet touch of Southern hospitality in a large goblet, with an even larger straw, of course. It also comes with more than 10 times the sugar.

INGREDIENTS:

1 ½ ounces Jack Daniel's bourbon

½ ounce vodka

1 ounce lemon juice

2 teaspoons Splenda Granular (or 1 packet)

⅛ teaspoon orange extract

3 ounces diet lemon-lime soda (Sprite or 7-Up)

Lemon slice

STEPS:

1. Fill a tall Collins glass with ice.
2. Pour all ingredients except soda into glass. Stir.
3. Add soda and stir lightly.
4. Garnish edge with lemon slice.

Be careful: this goes down real easy—even if you usually don't care for whiskey. Remember to have a glass of water for every drink, and be sure to keep the calories in mind.

PER SERVING

Calories 140	Fat 0 grams
Carbohydrate 3 grams	Fiber 0 grams
Protein 0 grams	Sodium 0 milligrams

Diabetic exchange = 2 ½ Fat
WW point comparison = 3 points

Fourth of July Lemonade

Serves Five

The Fourth of July (or any celebration for that matter) calls for "real" lemonade, the kind you make with freshly squeezed lemons. Why is this one especially perfect for the Fourth? Because it comes with a bang!

INGREDIENTS:

1 cup freshly squeezed lemon juice

1 cup vodka

2 cups water

⅓ cup Splenda Granular

1 tablespoon lemon zest

Steps:

1. Pour lemon juice into a large pitcher.

2. Add vodka, water, Splenda, and lemon zest. Stir.

3. Serve in Collins glass over ice.

PER SERVING

Calories 120   Fat 0 grams

Carbohydrate 6 grams   Fiber 0 grams

Protein 0 grams   Sodium 0 milligrams

Diabetic exchange = ½ Carbohydrate, 2 Fat

WW point comparison = 2 points

Marlene's Moose Milk

Serves Four

Although no one knows where the unusual name came from, this type of creamy drink with just a touch of pucker has long been the drink of choice for brunch in my family. The traditional recipe uses frozen lemonade and half-and-half, but I have re-created it with fresh lemon juice and nonfat half-and-half, for a luscious drink with far less sugar and fewer calories. Even my family approves.

INGREDIENTS:

½ **cup lemon juice**

2 **teaspoons lemon extract**

½ **cup Splenda Granular**

½ **cup nonfat half-and-half**

½ **cup vodka**

3 **cups crushed ice**

STEPS:

1. Pour all ingredients except ice into a blender. Blend until smooth.

2. Add ice and blend on high until smooth and frosty.

3. Pour into pitcher or individual wineglasses.

With two simple changes, I reduced the calories and sugars in this drink by half. One-half cup of granulated sugar has close to 400 calories and 100 grams of sugar; Splenda Granular has only 96 calories and 24 grams of carbohydrate. One-half cup of regular half-and-half has 160 calories and 14 grams of fat; ½ cup of nonfat half-and-half has only 70 calories and no fat.

PER SERVING

Calories 100	Fat 0 grams
Carbohydrate 9 grams	Fiber 0 grams
Protein 0 grams	Sodium 30 milligrams

Diabetic exchange = ½ Carbohydrate, 2 ½ Fat
WW point comparison = 2 points

Frozen Coffee Cocktail

Serves One

Frozen coffee drinks are all the rage, so I thought it would be fun to come up with a cool and creamy version of what I call a "dessert cocktail." Here, I take advantage of my sugar-free coffee liqueur. This treat is sure to give you an extra jolt!

INGREDIENTS:

 2 ounces coffee liqueur (see page 465)

1 ounce nonfat half-and-half

1 tablespoon Splenda (or 1 ½ packets)

1 tablespoon hot water

1 teaspoon instant coffee

1 cup crushed ice

STEPS:

1. Pour all ingredients into a blender. Blend on high until smooth.
2. Pour into a tall Collins glass.

Although you may be tempted to use regular coffee liqueur in this drink, do beware because it will add 20 additional grams of carbohydrate and 80 calories.

PER SERVING

Calories 120	Fat 0 grams
Carbohydrate 9 grams	Fiber 0 grams
Protein 0 grams	Sodium 30 milligrams

Diabetic exchange = ½ Carbohydrate, 2 ½ Fat

WW point comparison = 2 points

Black and White Russians

Serves One

This drink has been described as "espresso with a kick." Homemade sugar-free coffee liqueur is the trick to significantly cutting the sugar. For a White Russian, you simply add one ounce of nonfat half-and-half into your Black Russian, and that tacks on a mere 20 calories.

INGREDIENTS:

1 ounce vodka

1 ounce coffee liqueur (see page 465)

STEPS:

1. Fill rocks glass with ice.
2. Pour in vodka and coffee liqueur. Stir.

Like the great taste of coffee and chocolate? Make a Mocha Russian by adding 1 ounce of sugar-free chocolate-flavored syrup (like DaVinci or Torani brands) before stirring.

PER SERVING

Calories 110   Fat 0 grams
Carbohydrate 2 grams Fiber 0 grams
Protein 0 grams   Sodium 0 milligrams

Diabetic exchange = 2 ½ Fat
WW point comparison = 4 points

Irish Coffee

Serves One

Back in 1952, the owner of the Buena Vista Bar in San Francisco set out to perfect a coffee drink to replicate one that he had drunk in Ireland. It took him almost a year, but, boy, was it ever worth it. Real Irish whiskey and good freshly brewed coffee are essential for this belly-warming drink that has since made the Buena Vista in San Francisco world-renowned.

INGREDIENTS:

1 ½ ounces Irish whiskey

2 teaspoons Splenda Granular (or 1 packet)

5 ounces freshly brewed coffee

1 squirt light whipped cream
  (3 tablespoons)

STEPS:

1. Stir together the Irish whiskey and Splenda in an Irish coffee glass (glass coffee mug or wineglass).

2. Add coffee. Stir.

3. Top with whipped cream.

The Buena Vista Bar in San Francisco has come a long way since 1952. They now average serving a staggering 2,000 Irish coffees a day.

PER SERVING

Calories 125	Fat 2 grams
Carbohydrate 3 grams	Fiber 0 grams
Protein 0 gams	Sodium 0 milligrams

Diabetic exchange = 2 Fat
WW point comparison = 3 points

Mexican Coffee

Serves One

Here's a terrific way to top off your next dinner party. With this winning combination of coffee, chocolate, and whipped cream, who needs dessert? Ole!

INGREDIENTS:

1 ½ ounces coffee liqueur (page 465)

5 ounces hot black coffee

**1 squirt light whipped cream
(3 tablespoons)**

**Sprinkle of shaved semisweet chocolate
(1 tablespoon)**

STEPS:

1. Pour coffee liqueur into coffee mug.

2. Add coffee.

3. Top with 2 tablespoons whipped topping and shaved chocolate.

Serve coffee as part of your dessert menu by placing light whipped topping and shaved chocolate in glass bowls and homemade coffee and/or Orange Liqueur (page 464) in decorative carafes along with freshly brewed coffee.

PER SERVING

Calories 115	Fat 3 grams
Carbohydrate 7 grams	Fiber 0 grams
Protein 0 grams	Sodium 0 milligrams

Diabetic exchange = ½ Carbohydrate, 2 ½ Fat
WW point comparison = 2 points

Hot Buttered Rum

Serves Nine

When hosting guests for the holidays, cocktails are often part of the festivities, and nothing welcomes guests or wards off a cold weather chill like a steaming mug of Hot Buttered Rum. The buttery mix fragrant with tantalizing spices will keep for several months in the refrigerator.

INGREDIENTS:

1 cup Splenda Granular

1 teaspoon molasses

1 ½ teaspoons cinnamon

¾ teaspoon nutmeg

½ teaspoon cloves

3 tablespoons butter, cut in pieces

Dark rum

STEPS:

1. Place Splenda, molasses, and spices in a food processor and process until mixed. Drop butter into dry mix and pulse until blended.

2. Remove mix into a small container and store in refrigerator until ready for use.

3. For each drink, measure 1 tablespoon of mix into a mug. Add 5 ounces of boiling water and 1 ½ ounces of dark rum. Stir briskly.

For an open house, pair this with some seasonal goodies like Pumpkin Scones (page 111), Cranberry Orange Tea Bread (page 122), crunchy Orange Ginger Pecan Biscotti (page 321), and creamy Chocolate Peppermint Cheesecake (page 416).

PER SERVING

Calories 140

Carbohydrate 3 grams

Protein 0 grams

Fat 4 grams (2 saturated)

Fiber 0 grams

Sodium 40 milligrams

Diabetic exchange = 3 Fat

WW point comparison = 4 points

Sangria

Serves Eight

Sangria made its American debut when first served at the New York's World Fair in 1964. Like the Spanish tradition, red wine and fresh fruit blend together to make a beautiful display in this refreshing and easy-to-make libation. Place several pitchers on a buffet table and watch how fast it disappears!

INGREDIENTS:

1 bottle (750 milliliters) red wine (moderately priced Cabernet or Spanish Rioja)

4 ounces brandy

½ cup reduced-calorie orange juice (such as Tropicana Light 'n Healthy)

2 tablespoons lemon juice

2 tablespoons Splenda Granular (or 3 packets)

½ teaspoon orange extract

1 orange, sliced thinly

1 lemon, sliced thinly

2 cups sugar-free (diet) ginger ale

STEPS:

1. Pour wine and brandy into a large glass serving pitcher.

2. Add fruit juices, Splenda, and orange extract. Stir. Push fruit slices down into wine mixture. (Stop here if you're not serving the Sangria right away; the mixture will keep for several hours.)

3. Just prior to serving, add ginger ale. Stir briefly.

4. To serve, pour 6 ounces into an ice-filled Collins glass. (To serve buffet-style, add ice to pitcher before serving.)

The health benefits of red wine are undisputed; it can help reduce the risk for heart disease, stroke, and some types of cancer. The key, however, is to drink it in moderation. That's one glass a day for women and no more than two for men.

PER SERVING

Calories 100	Fat 0 grams
Carbohydrate 4 grams	Fiber 0 grams
Protein 0 grams	Sodium 15 milligrams

Diabetic exchange = 2 ½ Fat

WW point comparison = 2 points

Orange Liqueur

Serves Sixteen

Grand Marnier orange liqueur from France uses a rich cognac base with orange for its wonderful complex flavor. The result, though delicious, is both pricey and sugar-loaded. Here's how to make your own for a fraction of the cost with a fraction of the sugar.

INGREDIENTS:

2 cups cognac (moderately priced like a good V.S.)

1 medium orange

½ cup Splenda Granular

2 tablespoons granulated sugar

STEPS:

1. Pour the cognac into a 2-cup jar with lid.

2. Using a zester or vegetable peeler, slice several long pieces of orange peel (avoiding white pith) off the orange, and place in jar.

3. Peel and separate orange sections. Cut each section lengthwise and place into jar.

4. Add Splenda and sugar. Stir or cover, and shake.

5. Let set at room temperature for at least 2 weeks.

6. Strain orange liqueur into a bottle or jar, discarding fruit and peel. Cover. Keeps indefinitely.

Just like Grand Marnier, this concoction is delicious brushed onto a cake, drizzled over ice cream, added to coffee, and sipped out of a beautiful cordial glass.

PER SERVING (1 OUNCE)

Calories 75	Fat 0 grams
Carbohydrate 3 grams	Fiber 0 grams
Protein 0 grams	Sodium 0 milligrams

Diabetic exchange = 1 ½ Fat
WW point comparison = 1 point

Coffee Liqueur

Serves Forty-Six

This recipe is amazing. It tastes as good as Kahlua brand liqueur, only it costs less and has a fraction of the sugar and calories. This is also incredibly versatile. You can use it for drinks like Black Russians and Mexican Coffee. Or top ice cream with it (yummy when drizzled over reduced-sugar coffee ice cream). Or use Coffee Liqueur as a gift for someone who's watching sugar or counting carbs.

INGREDIENTS:

2 cups hot water

3 cups Splenda Granular

½ cup instant coffee

1 tablespoon good vanilla (or 1 vanilla bean★)

1 bottle (750 milliliters) vodka

★ If using vanilla bean, split lengthwise and place into container or bottle before adding coffee mixture.

STEPS:

1. Place hot water into a medium pitcher. Add Splenda and instant coffee and stir to dissolve.

2. Add vanilla and vodka. Stir.

3. Pour into a covered container or through a funnel into decorative bottles (makes approximately 1.5 liters).

4. Let set at least 2 weeks, especially if you use vanilla bean. Keeps indefinitely.

Coffee liqueur can have up to 14 grams of carbohydrate per ounce—the equivalent of 1 tablespoon of sugar in each 2-tablespoon serving. This liqueur has no added sugar.

PER SERVING (1 OUNCE)

Calories 45	Fat 0 grams
Carbohydrate 2 grams	Fiber 0 grams
Protein 0 grams	Sodium 0 milligrams

Diabetic exchange = 1 ½ Fat

WW point comparison = 1 point

Cranberry Liqueur

Serves Thirty-Two

Splenda works wonders for reducing the sugar in sugar-laden liqueurs. This one is unique and terrific for the holidays. For drinks, shake it up with ice for a Cranberry Martini or serve it over ice with sparkling soda for a light and refreshing drink. It's also beautiful when drizzled over cake or vanilla ice cream.

INGREDIENTS:

¼ cup granulated sugar

1 cup water

2 teaspoons cornstarch mixed with 2 tablespoons water

1 12-ounce bag fresh cranberries

3 pieces fresh orange peel

1 ¾ cups Splenda Granular

1 bottle (750 milliliters) vodka

STEPS:

1. In a medium pot, combine sugar, water, and cornstarch. Bring to a low boil and cook for 1 minute. Set aside.

2. Place cranberries in a food processor and pulse until finely chopped (1-2 minutes).

3. In a large pitcher, mix cranberries with water mixture. Add vodka and stir.

4. Pour mixture into a large jar. Place in a cool spot and shake every few days for 2-3 weeks.

5. Strain mixture through a fine mesh strainer or cheesecloth. Discard cranberries and peel and pour through a funnel into bottle(s). Keeps indefinitely.

Cranberry Splash: Fill one half of a tall glass with ice. Add 1 ounce Cranberry Liqueur. Top with diet lemon lime soda (like 7-Up). Stir. Garnish with fresh mint.

PER SERVING (1 OUNCE)

Calories 30	Fat 0 grams (0 saturated)
Carbohydrate 3 grams	Fiber 0 grams
Protein 0 grams	Sodium 0 milligrams

Diabetic exchange = 1 Fat

WW point comparison = 1 point

Notes

Index

a

agua frescas, 41
almond(s)
    chocolate biscotti, 320
    chocolate torte, 386
    coconut coffeecake, 126
    orange ricotta cheesecake, 415
    raspberry crumb cake, 126
    sour cream poppy seed loaf, 124
    strawberry soy smoothie, 52
    substituting with, 159
    topping, crisp, 353
antioxidants, 117
apple(s)
    baked, microwave cinnamon, 361
    butter, 215
    cinnamon puffed pancake, 86
    crisp, 351
    juice concentrate, 331
    oatmeal streusel muffins, 108
    onions and, 179
    packets, phyllo, 360
    pie, 331, 332
    strudel, 356
    Waldorf slaw, 139
apple cider
    butter syrup, 190, 432
    spiced tea, 68
applesauce
    about, 25, 303
    cinnamon, microwave, 217
    snack cake, 372
apricot
    oat bars, 316
    oat bran muffins, 95

Asian. *See also* sweet and sour; Thai
    barbecued pork tenderloins, 228
    Chinese chicken salad, 159
    Oriental cucumber salad, 147
    Oriental pesto, 237
    peanut slaw, 140
    pepper medley, 183
    shrimp satay sticks, 239
    soba noodle bowl, 240
asparagus with lemon tarragon vinaigrette, 186
avocado rotisserie chicken salad, 160

b

bacon dressing, hot, 157, 171
bagels, about, 118, 435
"baggie ice cream," 293
baking
    cakes, 383
    cheesecakes, 391–92
    cookies, 297
    fat substitutes for, 23–25, 303, 327, 351, 368
    mixes, 126
    sugar substitutes for, 11, 21–23, 299, 305,
        313, 326, 331
balsamic vinaigrette, sweet, 164
banana(s)
    about, 51, 120, 409
    bran muffins, 98
    bread, 120, 121
    cake, 369
    cheesecake cups, 409
    chocolate peanut butter high-protein
        smoothie, 55
    strawberry smoothie, 51

bar cookies
    biscotti, 320, 321
    chocolate brownie, 313
    lemon cheesecake, 318
    lemon squares, old-fashioned, 317
    peanut butter oat, high-protein, 315
    pumpkin, frosted, 314
    raspberry shortcake, 319
    zebra, 312
barbecue sauce
    dipping, quick smooth, 203
    sweet smoky, 204
    barbecued meat loaf muffins, 224
barbecued pork
    sandwiches, 226
    tenderloin, Asian, 228
bean(s)
    baked, 188, 191
    black, 145
    in brownies, 313
    salad, 144, 145
beef
    salad, 158
    spicy orange, 222
beef, ground
    barbecued meat loaf muffins, 223
    cocktail meatballs, 225
    sloppy joes, 221
    stuffed cabbage, 222
beet(s)
    orange-sauced, 182
    red onion salad, marinated, 152
bell pepper medley, Asian, 183
berry(ies). *See also specific types of berries*
    about, 172, 352
    blast smoothie, 49
    crisp, Kim's mixed, 352
    dessert, Sicilian, 269
    ice pops, 295
    lemon muffins, 106
    sorbet, 281
beverages. *See also* cocktails
    cold, 35–55
    holiday, 67–70, 456

    hot, 57–74
    mixes for, 71–74
    sugar in, 35, 37, 44
biscotti
    chocolate almond, 320
    orange ginger pecan, 321
black and white Russians, 459
black forest cheesecake parfaits, 413
blackberry(ies)
    about, 352
    cobbler, 355
blintzes, cheese, blueberry-topped, 91
blood sugar levels, 14. *See also* diabetes
blueberry(ies)
    about, 117, 352
    berry blast smoothie, 49
    buckle, 132
    cheese blintzes, 91
    cheesecake parfait, 412
    coulis, 426
    lemon bread, 117
    muffins, 99, 100
    peach crisp with almond topping, 353
    rice pudding with, 256
    sauce, 87, 91, 426
    scones, 110
    yogurt parfait, 265
Bob's Red Mill, 84, 165
Boston baked beans, 188
bourbon
    chicken, 230
    sauce, 258, 422
boysenberry(ies)
    about, 352
    buttermilk sherbert, 287
    syrup, 89, 91, 431
bran muffins, 97
    banana, 98
    oat apricot, 95
brandy orange coffee, 60
bread pudding, New Orleans, 258
bread, quick. *See also* coffeecake
    about, 115
    banana, 120, 121

chocolate, 123
cranberry orange tea, 122
holiday, 125, 128
Irish soda, 125
lemon blueberry, 117
pumpkin pecan, 118
sour cream almond poppy seed, 124
zucchini walnut, 119
breakfast. *See also* coffeecake; muffins; scones
    bars, 82
    cheesecake cups, 408
    cookies, 81
    dessert for, 81, 103, 123, 358, 408
    holiday dishes for, 89
    importance of, 75
brines, 229
British desserts, 258, 264, 354
broccoli salad, 142
brown sugar
    crumble, strawberry rhubarb, 354
    substitutes for, 246, 299, 354
brownies
    chocolate, 313
    zebra bars, 312
bulgur wheat, about, 155
buns, 226
butter
    about, 28, 327, 351
    apple cider syrup, 190, 432
buttermilk
    about, 25, 112, 263
    boysenberry sherbert, 287
    cornbread, 193
    pecan crumb cake, 127
butternut squash soufflé, 189
butterscotch pudding, 246

c

cabbage
    about, 139
    Grandma Claire's stuffed, 223
    shredding, 137 (*See also* slaw)
    sweet and sour, 187

café au lait ice cream, 288
café mocha, 59. *See also* mocha
    mix, 73
café orange, 60
Cajun
    sweet and spicy nuts, 440
    sweet and spicy rub, 205
cake(s). *See also* crumb cake; cupcakes; frosting
    about, 363, 366
    applesauce snack, 372
    banana, 369
    carrot, 370, 371
    chocolate, 365
    chocolate almond torte, 386
    chocolate carrot, 370
    chocolate cream-filled chocolate, 388–89
    chocolate mousse, 274–75
    chocolate soufflé, 383
    citrus chiffon, 381
    cream cheese-filled pumpkin, 387
    fruit cocktail snack, 374
    gingerbread, Grandma's, 373
    lemon coconut layer, 380
    lemon soufflé, 382
    pineapple upside down, 367, 379
    rolls, 387–89
    snack, 372, 374
    sour cream loaf pound, 384
    strawberry shortcake, 385
    white, 366, 368, 375
    yellow, basic, 367
California carrot cake, 371
canning, 208
carbohydrates
    diabetes and, 18
    recipe analysis of, 21
Caribbean chicken, 232
carrot(s)
    cake, 370, 371
    dill glazed, 180
    muffins, 101
    raisin salad, 143
    silly, 184
Casella, Dolores, 378

Catalina dressing, fat-free, 167
cereal. *See* bran muffins; oatmeal
chai tea, 65
    mix, 72
cheese
    blintzes, blueberry-topped, 91
    spread, lemon zest, 436
    strawberry pie, 417
    strudel, sweet, 357
cheesecake
    about, 391–92, 411
    almond orange ricotta, 415
    banana, 409
    black forest parfait, 413
    blueberry parfait, 412
    breakfast, 408
    cherry ricotta, 398–99
    chocolate, 396
    chocolate peppermint cheesecake, 416
    crusts, 393
    cups, 408, 409
    everyday, 395
    heavenly, 394
    key lime, 414
    lemon, 401, 402
    lemon bars, 318
    lemon ice cream, 290
    margarita, 400
    mocha chip, 397
    New York, 410–11
    parfaits, 412, 413
    pumpkin streusel, 404–5
    squares, 406–7
    strawberry cheese pie, 417
    strawberry swirl, 403
cheesy jalapeno cornbread, 194
cherry(ies)
    black forest cheesecake parfaits, 413
    chocolate muffins, 102
    ice pops, 294
    ricotta cheesecake, 398–99
    topping, sweet, 87, 91, 428
chicken
    bourbon, 230

Caribbean, 232
    lettuce wraps, 233
    pasta marinara dinner, 241
    salads, 159, 160
    satay sticks, 239
    soba noodle bowl, 240
    strips, zesty, 234
    sweet and sour, 231
chiffon
    cake, citrus, 381
    cheesecake, lemon, 402
    pies, 345–47
Child, Julia, 310
Chinese chicken salad, 159
chocolate
    about, 302, 429
    almond biscotti, 320
    almond torte, 386
    banana peanut butter protein shake, 55
    black forest cheesecake parfaits, 413
    brownies, 313
    cake, 365
    cake roll, 388–89
    carrot cake, 370
    cheesecake, 396
    cherry muffins, 102
    chiffon pie, 347
    chocolate chip cookies, 302
    cream, 388–89
    cream cheese truffles, 441
    crumb crust, 328, 393
    cupcakes, 377
    custard, 251
    frosting, 438
    frosty, 46
    fudge sauce, 430
    hot, 62–64, 71
    ice cream, 289
    loaf, 123
    mint dream pie, 342
    mousse cake, 274–75
    mousse, dark, 273
    peppermint cheesecake, 416
    pudding, double, 247

sauce, 429, 430
sorbet, 283
soufflé cake, 383
sour cream loaf pound cake, 384
zebra bars, 312
chocolate chip
    cookies, 299, 300, 302, 309
    meringue, 309
    muffins, 103, 109
Christmas, 89, 115, 128, 188, 387, 398
chutney
    about, 210
    cranberry, 209
    mint, 212
    peach, 210, 211
Cinnabon, 80
cinnamon
    applesauce, microwave, 217
    baked apple, microwave, 361
    bun oatmeal mix, quick, 79
    coffeecake, 130, 133
    french toast, sweet, 90
    pancakes, high-protein, 84
    pancakes, puffed apple, 86
    pecans, crunchy, 439
    rolls, quick, 80
    snickerdoodles, 305
    streusel, 133
citrus. *See also specific types of citrus fruit*
    chiffon cake, 381
    splash, 42
cobbler. *See also* crisp
    about, 349, 355
    blackberry, 355
cocktail meatballs, 225
cocktails. *See also* liqueur
    about, 443
    black and white Russians, 459
    coconut creamsicle, 451
    coffee, 458–61, 465
    cranberry liqueur, 466
    daiquiri, 447, 448
    Fourth of July lemonade, 456
    holiday, 456, 462

    hot buttered rum, 462
    Irish coffee, 460
    lemon drop martini, 452
    lemon raspberry slush, 453
    lemonade, 455, 456
    Lynchberg, 455
    margarita, 449, 450
    Marlene's moose milk, 457
    Mexican coffee, 461
    mojito, 445
    orange liqueur, 464
    pina colada, 446
    Ramos gin fizz, 454
    sangria, 463
cocoa powder, about, 26, 73, 102, 273.
       See also chocolate
coconut
    coffeecake, almond, 126
    cream pie, 340–41
    creamsicle cocktail, 451
    custard, 250
    lemon layer cake, 380
    lemon wafers, sliced, 307
    macaroons, crispy, 308
    peachy slender shake variation, 50
cod, 238
coffee. *See also* mocha
    café au lait ice cream, 288
    café orange, 60
    cocktails, 458–61, 465
    creamy iced, 44
    custard, 250
    french vanilla mix, 74
    granita, 284
    Irish, 460
    liqueur, 458, 459, 461, 465
    Mexican, 461
    tiramisu in a glass, 270–71
coffeecake. *See also* crumb cake
    about, 115
    blueberry buckle, 132
    cinnamon, 130, 133
    coconut almond, quick, 126
    gingerbread, 128

coffeecake, *continued*
  streusel, 133
coleslaw. *See* slaw
condiments
  about, 197
  holiday, 199, 206, 207, 209
cookies. *See also* bar cookies
  about, 297
  breakfast, 81
  chocolate chip, 299, 300, 302, 309
  chocolate chocolate chip, 302
  coconut macaroon, crispy, 308
  holiday, 309, 311
  Italian meringue, 310
  lacy orange oatmeal, 304
  lemon coconut wafer, sliced, 307
  meringue, 309, 310
  molasses cutout, 311
  oatmeal, 81, 303, 304
  oatmeal pancake, 83
  peanut butter, old-fashioned, 301
  snickerdoodle, 305
  sour cream citrus rounds, 306
  sugar, soft sour cream, 306
Cooking Light, 105, 129
cooking sprays, 28
Cookwise: The Hows and Whys of Successful Cooking
        (Corriher), 297
corn
  bean salad, Southwest, 145
  pudding, sweet Southwestern-style, 195
  zucchini relish, 208
corn syrup, 299
cornmeal
  blueberry corn muffins, 100
  buttermilk cornbread, 193
  cheesy jalapeno cornbread, 194
  waffles, crispy, 87
Corriher, Shirley O., 297
cottage cheese
  about, 26
  crepe filling, 92
  lemon pancakes, 85
coulis

blueberry, 426
strawberry, 427
cranberry(ies)
  about, 207
  chutney, 209
  in cookies, 300, 303
  jello salad, holiday, 154
  liqueur, 466
  orange muffins, 107
  orange tea bread, 122
  relish, 207
  sauce, two-way, 206
  splash cocktail, 466
cream
  chocolate, 388–89
  French, 277
  pastry, 259
  pies, 338–42
cream cheese. *See also* cheese; cheesecake
  about, 26
  chocolate filling, 388–89
  chocolate truffles, 441
  french toast with, 88, 89
  frosting, 314, 376, 437
  lemon, danish muffins with, 106
  orange, 101, 434
  pumpkin cake roll filled with, 387
  raspberry strudel, quick, 358
  strawberry, 435
  zebra bars, 312
cream puffs, 266–67
crepes
  flourless stuffed, 92
  orange, creamy, 278
crisp(s)
  about, 349
  apple, 351
  blueberry peach, with almond topping, 353
  Kim's mixed berry, 352
  strawberry rhubarb brown sugar
        crumble, 354
crumb cake
  buttermilk pecan, 127
  raspberry almond, 129

s'more, 131
crumb crust
    cheesecake, 393
    chocolate, 328, 393
    vanilla, 329
crumble, strawberry rhubarb brown sugar, 354
crust. *See* cheesecake; pie crust
cucumber
    agua de pepino, 41
    pickles, 213, 214
    salads, 146, 147
cupcakes
    chocolate, 377
    Fran's sour cream spice, 378
    orange sunshine, 376
    two-bite white, 375
curd, lemon, 433
custard
    about, 243, 391, 411
    chocolate, 251
    coconut, 250
    coffee, 250
    eggnog, 250
    flan, 253, 254
    French, 292
    frozen, 292
    pie, 334, 335
    pumpkin, 252, 330
    sauce, 421
    traditional, 249

d

daiquiris, 447, 448
dairy, switching to low-fat, 49, 146, 201.
    See also specific types of dairy
danish muffins, lemon cheese, 106
dessert
    about, 243, 261, 279, 297, 323, 349,
        363, 391
    for breakfast, 81, 103, 123, 358
    British, 258, 264, 354
    coffee, 461
    embellishments, about, 419
    frozen, 279

holiday, 309, 311, 387, 416
    protein-packed, 248, 249, 269, 270, 291, 315
    Sicilian berry, 269
diabetes
    about, 18–19
    exchanges for, 20, 446
    fiber and, 78
dill
    carrots, glazed, 180
    cucumber salad, creamy, 146
    mustard sauce, 238
dip
    mustard, sweet, 202, 234
    sour cream, 168
dressing
    about, 161
    bacon, hot, 157, 171
    balsamic vinaigrette, sweet, 164
    Catalina, fat-free, 167
    lemon tarragon vinaigrette, 186
    mustard sauce and dip, 202
    mustard vinaigrette, sweet, 165
    poppy seed, creamy, 169
    raspberry vinaigrette, 163
    sesame ginger, 170
    sour cream dip and, 168
    spinach salad, 157, 171
    strawberry yogurt fruit salad, 172
    thousand island, 166

e

eggnog
    old-fashioned, 69
    rich instant, for one, 70
eggs
    about, 26–27, 335
    beating whites, 129, 268
    raw, 454
    substitutes *v.* real, 70, 292
    traditional custard, 249
embellishments, about, 419. *See also* sauce (sweet)
Emeril, 339

f

Fantastic Food with Splenda (Koch), 11

fat
    about, 16–17
    baking substitutes for, 23–25, 303, 327, 351, 368
    creaming, 366
    recipe analysis of, 20

fiber
    about, 188, 361
    benefits of, 78, 95, 96, 97, 145, 188
    sources of, 78, 95, 96, 97, 144, 145, 188, 191, 352

filo dough. *See* phyllo dough

fish, baked, with Oriental pesto, 237

fish sauce, 176

flan, 253, 254

flavorings, about, 27

flour
    about, 27
    protein powder replacement for, 84
    whole-wheat *v.* all-purpose, 119

flourless stuffed crepes, 92

food coloring, 209, 216

Food Network, 276, 339, 356

fool, strawberry, 264

Fourth of July lemonade, 456

Fran's sour cream spiced cupcakes, 378

French
    cream with raspberry sauce, 277
    custard, 292

french toast
    baked, 89
    cinnamon, sweet, 90
    stuffed, 88

frosting
    chocolate cream, 438
    cream cheese, 314, 376, 437

frozen. *See also* ice pops; sorbet
    custard, creamy French vanilla, 292
    fruits, 51, 110, 122, 428, 448
    pie crust, 330, 331
    yogurt, 285, 286

fruit
    cheesecake squares, 407
    cocktail snack cake, 374
    frozen, 51, 110, 122, 428, 448
    punch, Hawaiian, 40
    salad, 172
    tart, 259, 359

g

garlic peanut sauce, 240

gelatin. *See also* cheesecake; mousse; pie
    desserts, 263
    salads, 153–54, 206

German potato, green bean, and mushroom salad, 192

gin fizz, Ramos, 454

ginger
    flan, 254
    honey green tea, 43
    molasses cutout cookies, 311
    orange pecan biscotti, 321
    orange scones, 112
    sesame dressing, 170
    tomato jam, 199

gingerbread
    cake, Grandma's, 373
    coffecake, 128
    molasses cutout cookies, 311

gingersnaps, 276

glycemic index, lowering, 78

Grand Marnier, 464

Grandma Claire's stuffed cabbage, 223

granita, coffee, 284

granola, 77, 265

Greek hearts of palm salad, 148

green beans
    German potato mushroom salad, 192
    sesame, 181

green tea, ginger and honey, 43

h

half-and-half, nonfat, 28, 61, 245, 286

ham steaks, maple-glazed, 227

Hawaiian fruit punch, 40
hearts of palm salad, Greek, 148
herbs
    choosing, 179
    preparing, 158
Hershey's, 102, 273, 430
hoisin sauce, 200, 228
holidays
    beverages for, 67–70
    breads for, 125, 128
    breakfast dishes for, 89
    cocktails for, 456, 462
    condiments for, 199, 206, 207, 209
    desserts for, 309, 311, 387, 416
    gifts for, 199
    salads for, 154
honey, green tea with ginger and, 43
horseradish sauce, sweet, 201
hot chocolate
    decadent, 63
    deep dark, 62
    Mexican, 64
    mix, 71
hot lemonade, 66

i

ice cream, 291–93. *See also* sorbet; yogurt
    baggie, 293
    buttermilk boysenberry sherbert, 287
    café au lait, 288
    chocolate, 289
    labels on, 291
    lemon cheesecake, 290
    vanilla, 291, 293
ice pops
    cherry, 294
    strawberry lime, 295
icing. *See* frosting
Indian chai tea, 65, 72
ingredients, about, 25–31
insulin levels, 14. *See also* diabetes
Irish coffee, 460
Irish soda bread, 125

Italian
    meringue cookies, 310
    pudding, creamy, 248
    tomato salad, sweet, 149

j

jalapeno cornbread, cheesy, 194
jam. *See also* chutney
    about, 316
    as cheesecake topping, 403, 407
    peach freezer, 215
    strawberry freezer, 215
    tomato ginger, 199
jellied cranberry sauce, 206
Jell-O, 153
Johanson, Laura, 360

k

Kahlua, 465
ketchup, 231
key lime
    cheesecake, 414
    mousse, 336
    pie, 336
Kim's mixed berry crisp, 352
Knudsen dairy, 146
Koch, Marlene, 11, 184
Krista's spiced tea, 67

l

lemon
    blueberry bread, 117
    cheese danish muffins, 106
    cheese spread, 436
    cheesecake, 290, 318, 401, 402
    chiffon pie, 345
    coconut layer cake, 380
    coconut wafers, sliced, 307
    cottage cheese pancakes, 85
    curd, 433
    drop martini, 452
    ice cream, cheesecake, 290

lemon, *continued*
    lime sorbet, 282
    meringue pie, 344
    mousse, 272
    raspberry scones, 114
    raspberry slush cocktail, 453
    sauce, hot, 91, 373, 424
    soufflé cake, 382
    squares, old-fashioned, 317
    tarragon vinaigrette, 186
    whipped topping, 436
lemonade
    cocktails, 455, 456
    hot, 66
    Lynchberg, 455
    sparkling, 37
    strawberry, 38, 405
lettuce wraps, chicken, 233
lime. *See also* key lime
    daquiri, 447
    lemon sorbet, 282
    strawberry ice pops, 295
limeade, sparkling, 39
liqueur
    coffee, 458, 459, 461, 465
    cranberry, 466
    orange, 464
liquid smoke, 187

m

macaroons, crispy coconut, 308
mandarin spinach salad, 156
mango sauce, 236
maple syrup
    baked beans, 191
    ham steaks, glazed, 227
    oat scones, 113
Marco Polo, 281
margarine, about, 28, 299, 327
margarita
    cheesecake, 400
    cocktails, 449, 450
marinades
    about, 161
    citrus, 175
    spicy Thai, 176
    teriyaki, 173, 174
Marlene's moose milk, 457
Marlene's pasta marinara dinner, 241
marmalade, 101, 112
martini, lemon drop, 452
mayonnaise, substitutes, 201, 202
meal replacement drinks, 53
meat loaf muffins, barbecued, 224
meatballs, cocktail, 225
Mediterranean banana bread, 121
melon, agua de, 41
meringue
    coconut cream pie, 340–41
    cookies, 309, 310
    lemon, 344
Mexican
    coffee, 461
    flan, 253
    hot chocolate, 64
microwave
    cinnamon applesauce, 217
    cinnamon baked apple, 361
milk
    about, 28
    powdered, 53, 54, 72–74, 109, 315
    steamed, 61
mint. *See also* peppermint
    chocolate cream pie, 342
    chutney, 212
mocha
    café, 59, 73
    chiffon pie variation, 347
    chip cheesecake, 397
    frosty, 45
    russian cocktail, 459
mojitos, 445
molasses, about, 373. *See also* gingerbread
moose milk, Marlene's, 457
mousse
    about, 261
    cake, 274–75

chocolate, 273, 274–75
key lime, 336
lemon, 272
pumpkin, gingersnap, 276
muddling, 445
muffins
    about, 93
    apple oatmeal streusel, 108
    banana bran, 98
    barbecued meat loaf, 224
    blueberry, 99
    blueberry corn, 100
    bran, best, 97
    buttermilk cornbread, 193
    carrot, 101
    cheesy jalapeno cornbread, 194
    chocolate, 102, 103
    chocolate chip, 109
    cranberry orange, 107
    danish, lemon cheese, 106
    oat bran apricot, 95
    oatmeal, 96, 108
    pumpkin, spicy, 104
    strawberry-filled cinnamon, 105
mushroom(s)
    marinated, 185
    salad, German potato, green bean and, 192
mustard
    dill sauce, 238
    sauce and dip, sweet, 202, 234
    vinaigrette, sweet, 165

n

New Orleans bread pudding, 258
New York cheesecake, strawberry-topped, 410–11
noodle bowl, soba, 240
nutritional analysis, 19–21
nuts, sweet and spicy Cajun, 440. *See also*
        specific types of nuts

o

oat(s)
    apricot bars, 316

bran apricot muffins, 95
crepes, flourless stuffed, 92
granola, 77
maple scones, 113
oatmeal
    about, 28
    apple streusel muffins, 108
    baked, 78
    breakfast bar, peanut butter and, 82
    cookie pancakes, 83
    cookies, 81, 303, 304
    mix, quick cinnamon bun, 79
    muffins, 96, 108
oils, about, 29, 121, 181, 321
onion(s)
    apples and, 179
    beet salad, marinated, 152
    grating, 156
orange(s)
    about, 29, 230, 370
    almond ricotta cheesecake, 415
    beef, spicy, 222
    beets, 182
    brandy coffee, 60
    cranberry chutney, 209
    cranberry muffins, 107
    cranberry relish, 206, 207
    cranberry tea bread, 122
    cream cheese, 101, 434
    creamsicle frappe, 48
    crepes, creamy, 278
    ginger pecan biscotti, 321
    ginger scones, 112
    glazes, 122, 180
    juice, 29, 230, 370
    liqueur, 464
    mandarin spinach salad, 156
    oatmeal cookies, lacy, 304
    pineapple layered gelatin mold, 153
    romaine salad, 151
    sauce, 182, 254, 425
    snow, 263
    sunshine cupcakes, 376
    sunshine smoothie, 47

Oriental
    cucumber salad, 147
    pesto, 237

p

pancakes
    apple cinnamon puffed, 86
    cinnamon, high-protein, 84
    frozen, 85
    lemon cottage cheese, 85
    oatmeal cookie, 83
parfait
    black forest cheesecake, 413
    blueberry cheesecake, 412
    Sicilian berry dessert, 269
    tiramisu, 270–71
    yogurt, 265
    zebra pudding, 247
pasta
    marinara dinner, Marlene's, 241
    soba noodle bowl, 240
pastry. *See also* pie crust
    cream, 259
    phyllo dough for, 356
peach
    blueberry crisp with almond topping, 353
    chutney, 210, 211
    custard pie, 334
    frozen yogurt, 285
    jam, 216
    vanilla slender shake, 50
peanut butter
    about, 315, 337
    chocolate banana shake, 55
    cookies, old-fashioned, 301
    oat bar cookies, high-protein, 315
    oat breakfast bar, 82
    pie, 337
peanut sauce
    garlic, 240
    Thai, 200, 239
peanut slaw, Asian, 140
pecan(s)
    buttermilk crumb cake, 127

    cinnamon, crunchy, 439
    orange ginger biscotti, 321
    pumpkin bread, 118
pectin, 216
Pepin, Jacques, 368
Pepperidge Farm, 226
peppermint
    chocolate cheesecake, 416
    chocolate chip meringue cookie, 309
    hot chocolate mix, 70
    pie variation, 342
pesto, Oriental, 237
Phillips, Sarah, 366
phyllo dough, 27, 356
    apple packets, 360
pickles, 213, 214
picnics, 140, 152
pie
    about, 323
    apple, in a bag, 331
    banana cream, 339
    chiffon, 345–47
    chocolate chiffon, 347
    chocolate mint cream, 342
    coconut cream, 340–41
    cream, 338–42
    custard, old-fashioned, 335
    fruit tart, 259, 359
    key lime, 336
    lemon chiffon, 345
    lemon meringue, 344
    lemon mousse, 272
    mocha chiffon, 347
    no-bake, 337, 343, 345, 346
    peach custard, 334
    peanut butter, 337
    pumpkin, 252, 330
    pumpkin chiffon, 346
    sour cream apple, 332
    strawberry cheese, 417
    strawberry dream, 343
    strawberry rhubarb, 333
    vanilla cream, triple, 245, 338

pie crust
    chocolate crumb, double, 328
    frozen, 330, 331
    graham cracker, 327
    pastry, single, 325–26
    vanilla crumb, 329
pina colada, 446
pineapple
    juice, about, 232, 367
    orange layered gelatin mold, 153
    upside down cake, 367, 379
poppy seed
    dressing, creamy, 169
    sour cream almond loaf, 124
popsicles. *See* ice pops
pork
    sandwiches, barbecued, 226
    tenderloin, Asian barbecued, 228
portion sizes, 19
    picnic, 140, 152
potato, green bean, and mushroom salad,
        German, 192
pound cake, 384
protein powder
    benefits of, 51
    as flour replacement, 84
    shakes using, 55
    smoothies using, 53, 54
protein-packed desserts, 248, 249, 269, 270, 291,
        315
protein-packed entrees, 219. *See also specific types
        of meat and fish*
prune puree. *See also* cookies
    about, 29
    using, 299, 300
pudding
    about, 243
    butterscotch, 246
    chocolate, double, 247
    corn, sweet Southwestern-style, 195
    Italian, creamy, 248
    New Orleans bread, 258
    rice, 256, 257
    tapioca, 255

    vanilla, 245, 266
pudding mix
    chocolate breakfast drink, 54
    french vanilla coffee mix, 74
pumpkin
    bars, frosted, 314
    cake roll, cream cheese-filled, 387
    chiffon pie, 346
    custard cups, 252, 330
    mousse with gingersnaps, 276
    muffins, spicy, 104
    pecan bread, 118
    pie, 252, 330
    scones, 111
    streusel cheesecake, 404–5
punch
    citrus splash, 42
    Hawaiian fruit, 40

q

quick bread. *See* bread

r

raisin carrot salad, 143
Ramos gin fizz, 454
raspberry(ies)
    about, 352
    almond crumb cake, 129
    cream cheese strudel, quick, 358
    crepe filling, 92
    lemon scones, 114
    lemon slush cocktail, 453
    sauce, 277, 423
    shortbread triangles, 319
    sorbet, 281
    vinaigrette, 163
relish. *See also* chutney; pickles
    cranberry, 207
    zucchini and corn, 208
rhubarb
    strawberry brown sugar crumble, 354
    strawberry pie, 333
rice pudding, 256, 257

rice wine vinegar, about, 30, 173
ricotta
    about, 92, 248, 269, 399
    almond orange cheesecake, 415
    cherry cheesecake, 398–99
romaine and orange salad, 151
Rosie O'Donnell Show, 356
rubs, sweet and spicy Cajun, 205
rum
    hot buttered, 462
    sauce, 422

☀

salad(s). *See also* dressing; slaw
    about, 135
    beet and red onion, marinated, 152
    broccoli, 142
    carrot and raisin, creamy, 143
    chicken, 159, 160
    Chinese chicken, 159
    cranberry jello, 154
    cucumber, 146, 147
    gelatin, 153–54, 206
    German potato, green bean, and mushroom,
        192
    Greek hearts of palm, 148
    holiday, 154
    Italian tomato, sweet, 149
    orange-pineapple layered gelatin mold, 153
    romaine and orange, 151
    seven-layer, old-fashioned, 141
    Southwest black bean and corn, 145
    spinach, 156, 157
    tabbouleh, sweet, 155
    Thai beef, 158
    three bean, 144
    zucchini, sweet and sour, 150
salmon
    about, 235
    grilled, with mustard dill sauce, 238
    Southwest, 235
sandwiches, barbecued pork, 226
sangria, 463
sauce (savory). *See also* relish

barbecue, 203, 204
chicken lettuce wraps, 233
cranberry, two-way, 206
fish, 176
garlic peanut, 240
hoisin, 200, 228
horseradish, sweet, 201
mango, 236
mustard dill, 238
mustard, sweet, 202
orange, beets with, 182
peanut, 200, 239, 240
pesto, Oriental, 237
spicy Thai marinade and dipping, 176
sweet and sour, 225
teriyaki, 173, 174
Thai peanut, 200, 239
Worcestershire, 221
sauce (sweet). *See also* frosting; syrup
    about, 419
    blueberry, 87, 91, 426
    bourbon, 258, 422
    cherry topping, 87, 91
    chocolate, 429, 430
    custard, 421
    lemon, hot, 91, 373, 424
    orange, 254, 425
    raspberry, 277, 423
    rum, 422
    strawberry, 427
    waffle, 87
    whiskey, 422
scallops, with mango sauce, 236
scones
    about, 93, 110
    blueberry, 110
    orange ginger, 112
    pumpkin, 111
    raspberry lemon, 114
seafood. *See* fish; scallops; shrimp
serving dishes, 141, 251, 284. *See also* parfait
sesame
    ginger dressing, 170
    green beans, 181

shakes
    chocolate banana peanut butter
        high-protein, 55
    chocolate breakfast drink, 54
    peachy vanilla slender, 50
sherbert, buttermilk boysenberry, 287
shortbread triangles, raspberry, 319
shortcake, strawberry, 385
shrimp
    satay sticks, 239
    soba noodle bowl, 240
Sicilian berry dessert, 269
Silly Carrots, 184
Simple and Healthy Cooking (Pepin), 368
slaw(s)
    about, 135
    Asian peanut, 140
    creamy, 138
    sweet and sour party, 137
    Waldorf, 139
sloppy joes, 221
Smith, Art, 276
smoothies
    berry blast, 49
    chocolate breakfast drink, 54
    orange creamsicle frappe, 48
    orange sunshine, 47
    peachy vanilla slender shake, 50
    strawberry almond soy, 52
    strawberry banana, 51
    vanilla breakfast drink, 53
s'more crumb cake, 131
snapper, 238
snickerdoodles, Sugar Blend, 305
soba noodle bowl, 240
sodium reduction, 175, 205, 214, 227
sorbet
    berry, 281
    chocolate, 283
    coffee granita, 284
    lemon-lime, 282
soufflé
    butternut squash, 189
    chocolate cake, 383

lemon cake, 382
ramekins, 251
strawberry, cold, 268
sour cream
    about, 30, 146
    almond poppy seed loaf, 124
    apple pie, 332
    chocolate chocolate chip muffins, 103
    dip and dressing, 168
    loaf pound cake, 384
    spice cupcakes, Fran's, 378
    sugar cookies, 306
Southwest
    black bean and corn salad, 145
    peach chutney, 211
    salmon, 235
    sweet corn pudding, 195
soy
    benefits of, 52
    protein powders, 84
spaghetti squash, 241
spice(d)
    cupcakes, Fran's sour cream, 378
    tea, 67, 68
spicy
    orange beef, 222
    pumpkin muffins, 104
    sweet Cajun nuts, 440
    sweet Cajun rub, 205
    teriyaki sauce, 174
    Thai marinade and dipping sauce, 176
spinach salad, 156, 157
    dressing, 171
Splenda
    about, 13–14
    Brown Sugar Blend, 245, 354
    carmelization and, 253
    finding, 30
    Granular, 21, 22–23, 30
    popularity of, 11
    Sugar Blend for Baking, 11, 22, 30, 300, 305,
        313
spreads. *See* cream cheese
squash

squash, *continued*
    soufflé, butternut, 189
    spaghetti, marinara, 241
    sweet potatoes *v.,* 190
St. Patrick's Day, 125
stabilizers, 165
Starbucks Chantico Drinking Chocolate, 63
Starbucks Frappuccino, 44
steaks, ham, maple-glazed, 227
steamers, hot vanilla, 61
Stewart, Martha, 66
strawberry(ies)
    agua de fresa, 41
    almond soy smoothie, 52
    banana smoothie, 51
    cheese pie, 417
    coulis, 427
    cream cheese, 435
    daquiri, 448
    dream pie, 343
    fool, 264
    frozen yogurt, 286
    jam, freezer, 216
    lemonade, 38, 405
    lime ice pops, 295
    margarita, 450
    muffins filled with, cinnamon, 105
    New York cheesecake topped with, 410–11
    poppy seed dressing for, 169
    rhubarb brown sugar crumble, 354
    rhubarb pie, 333
    sauce, 427
    shortcake, 385
    sorbet, 281
    soufflé, cold, 268
    swirl cheesecake, 403
    yogurt fruit salad dressing, 172
streusel
    about, 349
    coffeecake, cinnamon, 133
    muffins, apple oatmeal, 108
    pumpkin cheesecake, 404–5
    topping, sour cream apple pie, 332
strudel

    about, 349
    apple, 356
    raspberry cream cheese, quick, 358
    sweet cheese, 357
sugar
    about, 15–16
    alcohols, 441
    baking substitutes for, 11, 21–23, 299, 305, 313, 326, 331
    cookies, soft sour cream, 306
    creaming, 366
    diabetes and, 18
Sugar Blend. *See also* Splenda
    chocolate chip cookies, 300
    snickerdoodles, 305
sweet and sour. *See also* spicy
    chicken, 231
    party slaw, 137
    red cabbage, 187
    sauce, 225
    stuffed cabbage, 223
    zucchini salad, 150
sweet potatoes with apple cider syrup, 191
syrup. *See also* maple syrup
    apple cider butter, 190, 432
    boysenberry, 89, 91, 431
    carbohydrates in, 86

t

tabbouleh salad, 155
tapioca pudding, 255
tarragon lemon vinaigrette, 186
tart(s)
    about, 349
    fruit, 259, 359
tea
    chai, 65, 72
    green, 43
    spiced, 67, 68
tea breads. *See* bread
teriyaki sauce, 173, 174
Thai
    beef salad, 158

marinade and dipping sauce, spicy, 176

peanut sauce, 200, 239

Thanksgiving, 115, 122, 330, 387

thousand island dressing, 166

tiramisu in a glass, 270–71

tofu. *See also* soy

soba noodle bowl, 240

strawberry almond soy smoothie, 52

tomato(es)

about, 205, 231

ginger jam, 199

pasta marinara dinner, 241

salad, sweet Italian, 149

soup, silly carrots with, 184

topping. *See* sauce (sweet)

torte, chocolate almond, 386

truffles, chocolate cream cheese, 441

turkey breast, brined, 229

turkey, ground. *See* beef, ground

u

Unbelievable Desserts with Splenda (Koch), 11, 381

v

Valentine's Day, 398

vanilla

breakfast drink, triple, 53

coffee mix, 74

cream pie, triple, 338

crumb crust, 329

frozen custard, 292

hot steamer, 61

ice cream, 291, 293

peachy slender shake, 50

pie, 245, 338

pudding, 245, 266

vegetables

about, 177

pickled, 213

satay sticks with, 239

vinaigrettes, 163–65, 186

vinegar, 30, 164, 173

w

waffles

crispy cornmeal, 87

sauces for, 87

Waldorf slaw, 139

walnut zucchini bread, 119

watermelon agua fresca, 41

Weight Watchers point comparisons, 11, 20, 63

whipped topping

about, 30

chocolate cream, 438

cream puffs, 266–67

lemon zest, 436

whiskey sauce, 422. *See also* bourbon

white cake

all-purpose light, 366

two-bite, 375

yogurt, 368

white Russians, 459

wine, about, 463

Worcestershire sauce, 221

A World of Baking (Casella), 378

x

xanthan gum, 165

y

yellow cake, basic, 367

yogurt. *See also* smoothies

about, 31, 368

cake, white, 368

frozen, 285, 286

as low-fat substitute, 92

parfait, 265

strawberry fruit salad dressing, 172

z

zebra

bars, 312

pudding parfait, 247

zests. *See also specific citrus fruits*

about, 31

zests, *continued*
    coffee grinds and, 60
    in cookies, 304, 306, 307
    in dressings, 169, 172
    in granita, 284
    in spreads, 436
zucchini
    corn relish, 208
    walnut bread, 119

About the Author

Marlene Koch is a registered dietitian, professional cooking instructor, and nutrition educator who takes the most pride in creating delicious, yet healthful recipes. Marlene has taught on behalf of such professional organizations as the American Culinary Association (the national association of professional chefs) and the American Diabetic Association, as well as having been featured as a guest on many radio and network television programs. Her first book, *Unbelievable Desserts with Splenda*, was a book club selection on The Food Network and recipes from that book were featured on "The Today Show" and in *Cooking Light, Diabetic Cooking, Women's Fit* and *Fitness and Low-Carb Energy* magazines. Marlene, her sweet-loving husband, and two energetic sons reside in California. She can also be found on the web at www.marlenekoch.com

Illustrator Christopher Dollbaum holds a Master's in Fine Arts degree from the University of Washington in Seattle, where he currently resides. He is known for his work in ceramic sculpture as well as his fine drawings.